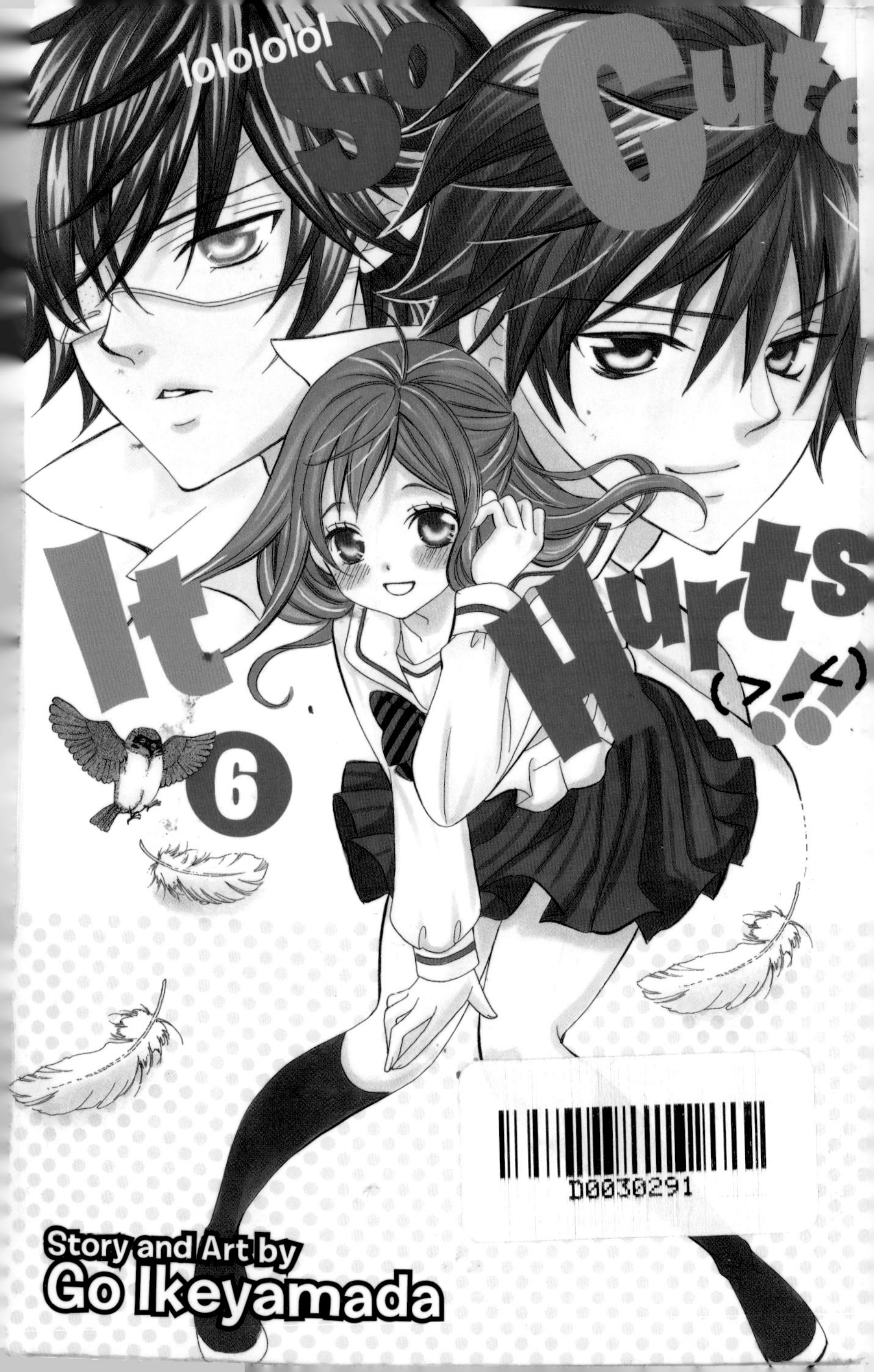
lolololol
So Cute
It Hurts!!
(>_<)
6
Story and Art by
Go Ikeyamada

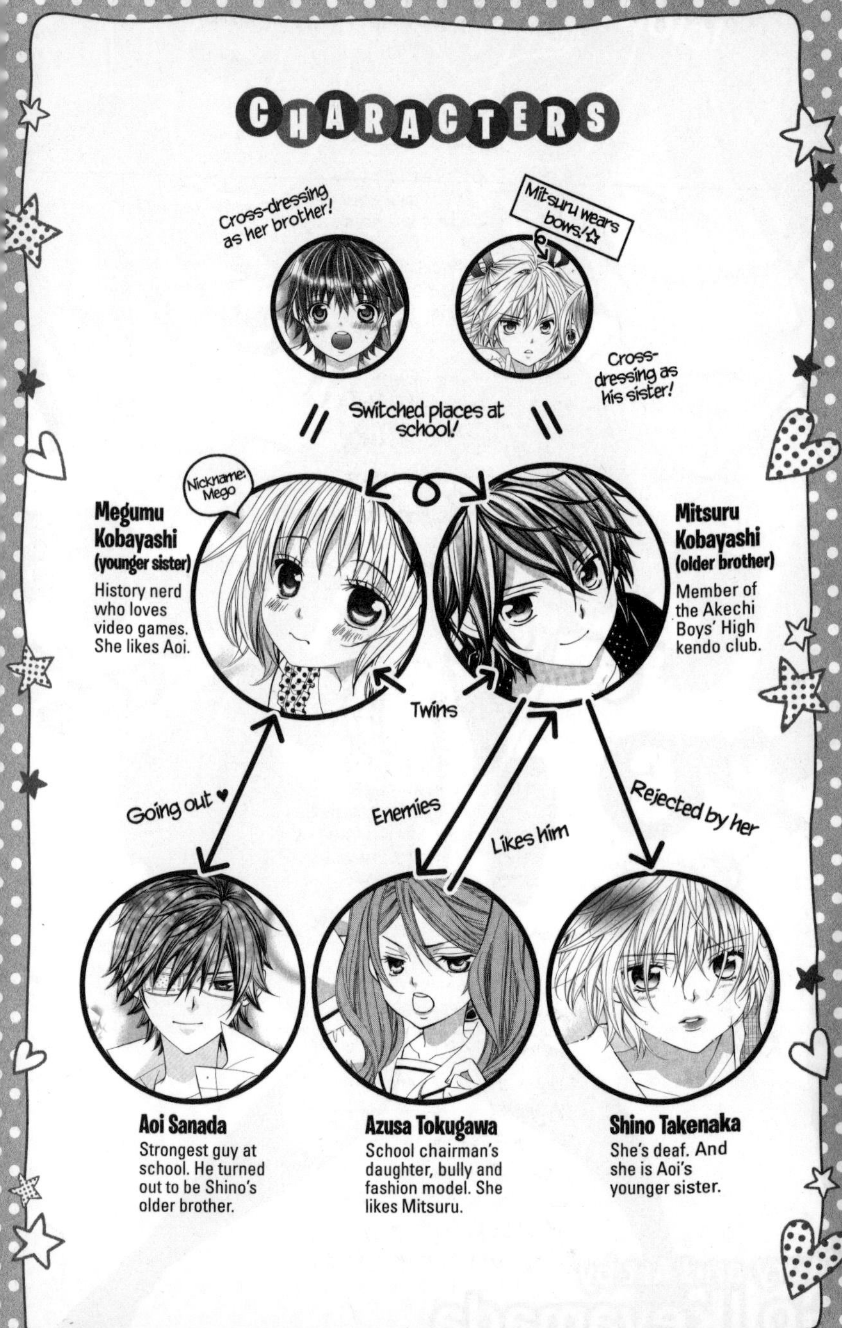
CHARACTERS
Cross-dressing as her brother!
Mitsuru wears bows!☆
Cross-dressing as his sister!
Switched places at school!
Nickname: Mego
Megumu Kobayashi (younger sister)
History nerd who loves video games. She likes Aoi.
Mitsuru Kobayashi (older brother)
Member of the Akechi Boys' High kendo club.
Twins
Going out ♥
Enemies
Likes him
Rejected by her
Aoi Sanada
Strongest guy at school. He turned out to be Shino's older brother.
Azusa Tokugawa
School chairman's daughter, bully and fashion model. She likes Mitsuru.
Shino Takenaka
She's deaf. And she is Aoi's younger sister.

STORY

★ Mitsuru and Megumu are twins. One day they switch places and go to each other's school for a week! That's when Megumu falls in love with Aoi and Mitsuru falls in love with Shino. Azusa and Aoi both discover the twins' ruse but keep quiet for reasons of their own. When the week is over, Megumu declares her love for Aoi, and they start dating. They need to stay two feet apart because of Aoi's extreme discomfort around women, but the more they date, the closer they can slowly get to each other.

★ Mitsuru finds out that Shino is in love with someone else, and after some soul-searching he decides to help her. With his support, Shino tells Ishida she loves him, and they start going out. Meanwhile, Azusa's feelings for Mitsuru get stronger.

★ Time passes, and the twins are now in their second year of high school. Aoi starts working part-time to help get acclimated to women because he wants to be able to be close to Megumu. Azusa forgets her cell phone, and Mitsuru brings it to her at a photo shoot. He's really impressed at how she stands up for herself when the other models harass her and nearly ruin her shoot!

CONTENTS

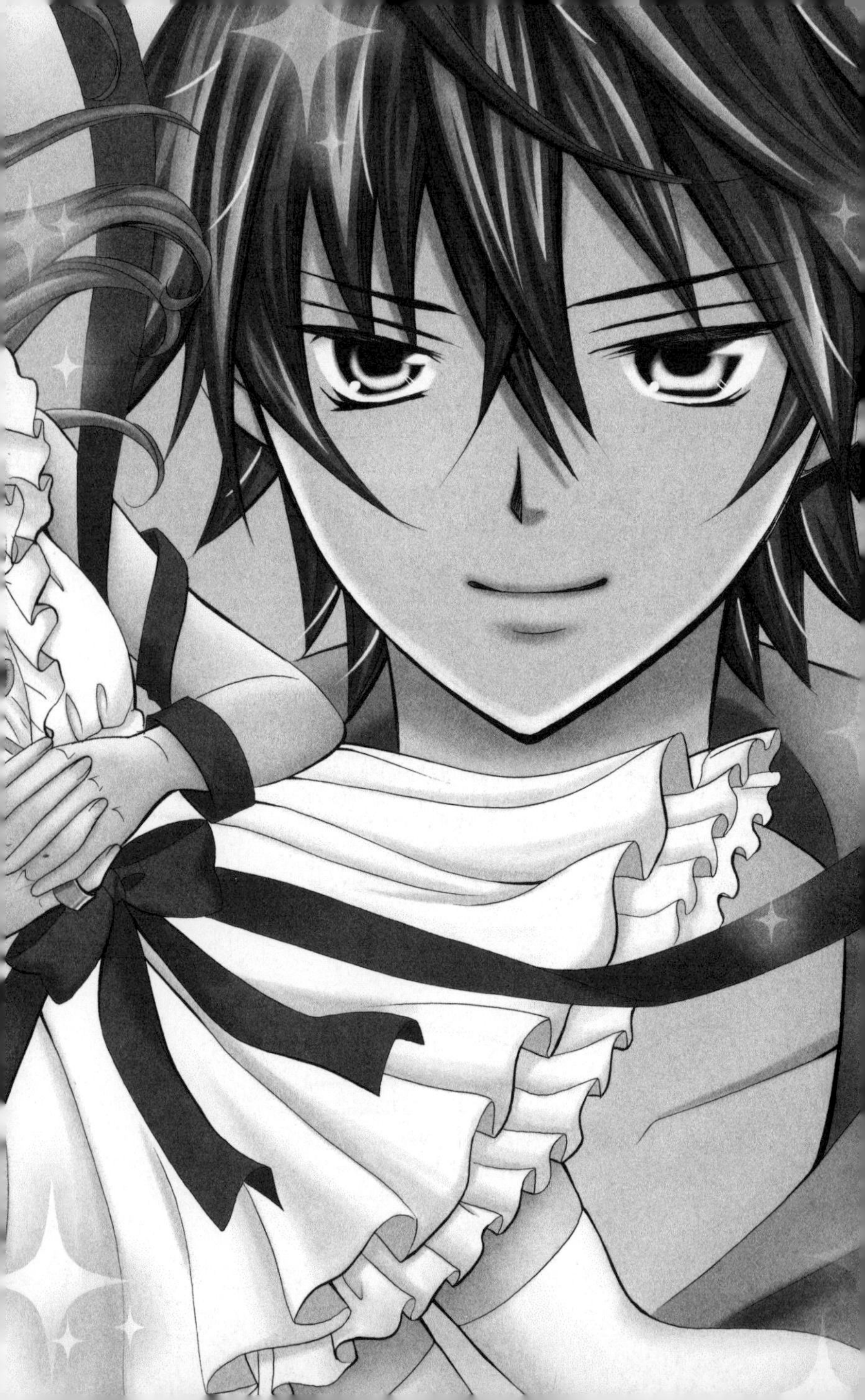

Chapter 26

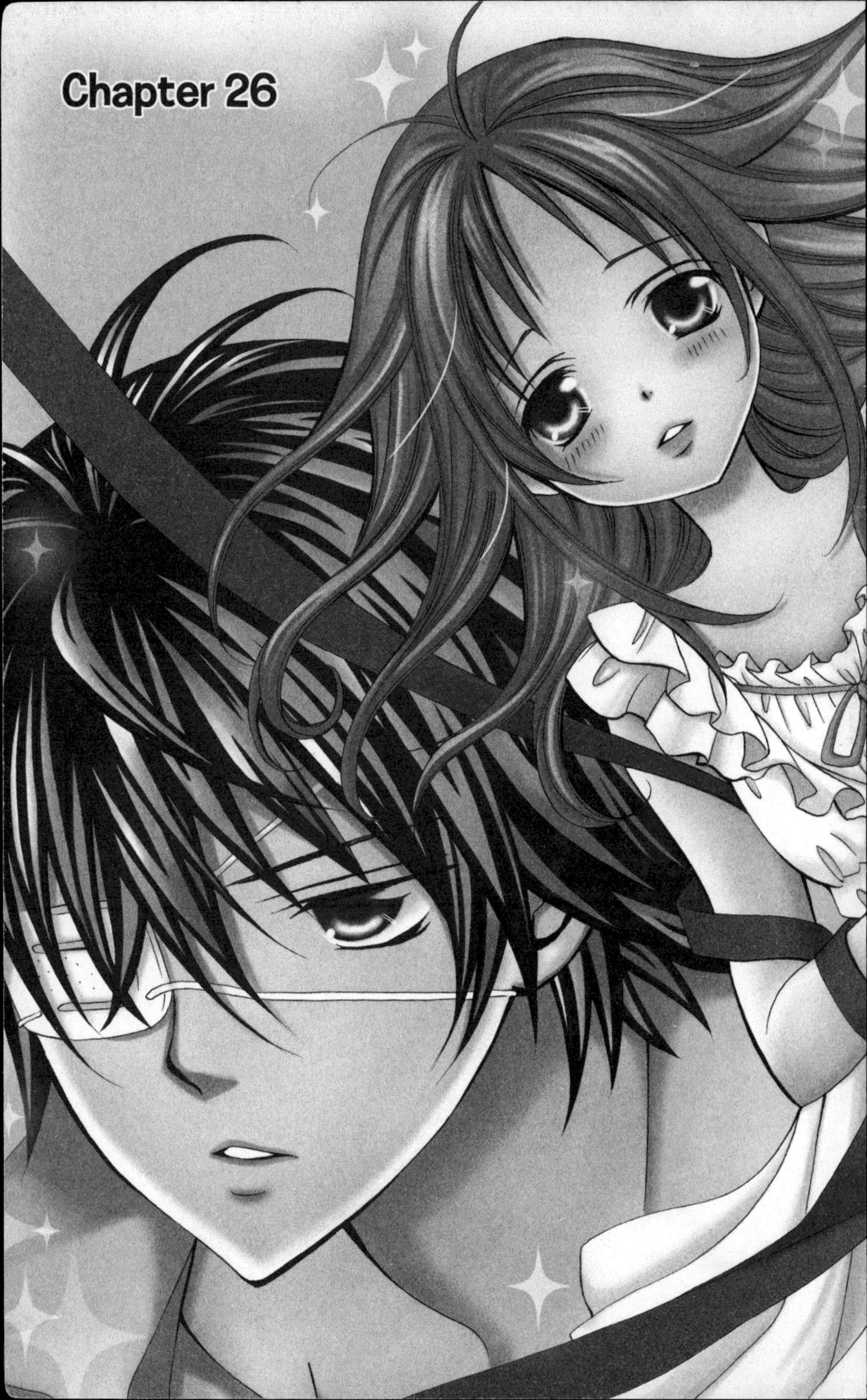

THE SECOND *SO CUTE!*
ANIME DVD IS OUT IN JAPAN! ♪ ♪
THE STORY IS A COMPLETELY NEW ONE! THE
SCREENWRITER, MY EDITOR AND I CAME UP
WITH THE STORY TOGETHER, AND I REALLY
ENJOYED WORKING ON IT! ♪ ♪ THE STORY
IS FULL OF LOVE, OF COURSE, AND LOTS OF
SCENES THAT'LL MAKE YOU LAUGH, SO I
HOPE YOU WATCH IT! ♡♡

THE SECOND SO CUTE! ANIME DVD!

〈CAST〉
AOI SANADA: MR. DAISUKE ONO
SEBASTIAN FROM *BLACK BUTLER*, MIDORIMA FROM *KUROKO'S
BASKETBALL*, SINBAD FROM *MAGI* AND OTHERS

MITSURU/MEGUMU KOBAYASHI: MS. AYUMI FUJIMURA
MISAKI AYUZAWA FROM *MAID-SAMA!*, HIKARU KAGEYAMA FROM *INAZUMA
ELEVEN GO!*, MIX FROM *AQUARION: EVOL* AND OTHERS

PLUS!
MOYUYU APPEARS IN THE ORIGINAL DRAMA CD YOU CAN BUY VIA
SHO-COMI'S MAIL-ORDER SITE! (SMILE)
YUKIMITSU MOGAMI (MOYUYU): MR. DAIKI YAMASHITA
SAKAMICHI ONODA, LEAD IN *YOWAMUSHI PEDAL*, AND OTHERS

PLEASE ENJOY THE *SO CUTE!* ANIME AND DRAMA CD
WITH THEIR FABULOUS CASTS! ♡♡♡♡

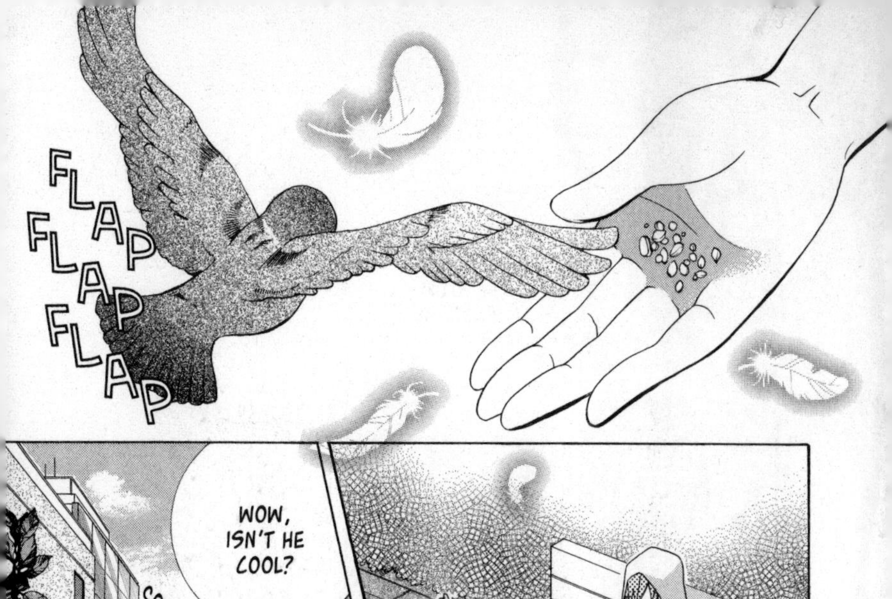
FLAP FLAP FLAP
WOW, ISN'T HE COOL?
SQUEE SQUEE
IS HE IN HIGH SCHOOL?
HE LOOKS LIKE A MODEL! ♡

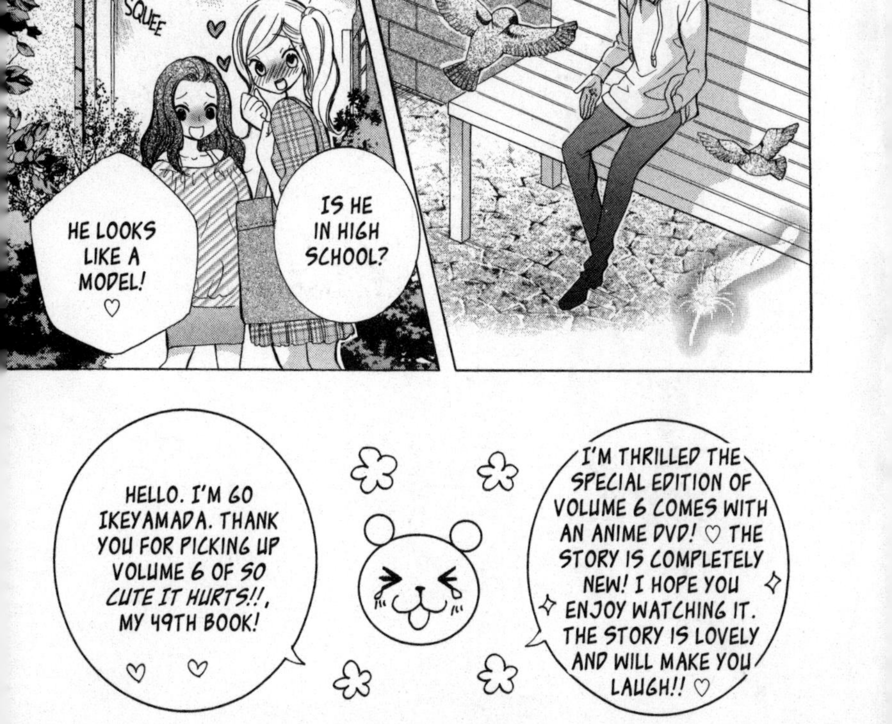
HELLO. I'M GO IKEYAMADA. THANK YOU FOR PICKING UP VOLUME 6 OF SO *CUTE IT HURTS!!*, MY 49TH BOOK! ♡ ♡
I'M THRILLED THE SPECIAL EDITION OF VOLUME 6 COMES WITH AN ANIME DVD! ♡ THE STORY IS COMPLETELY NEW! I HOPE YOU ENJOY WATCHING IT. THE STORY IS LOVELY AND WILL MAKE YOU LAUGH!! ♡

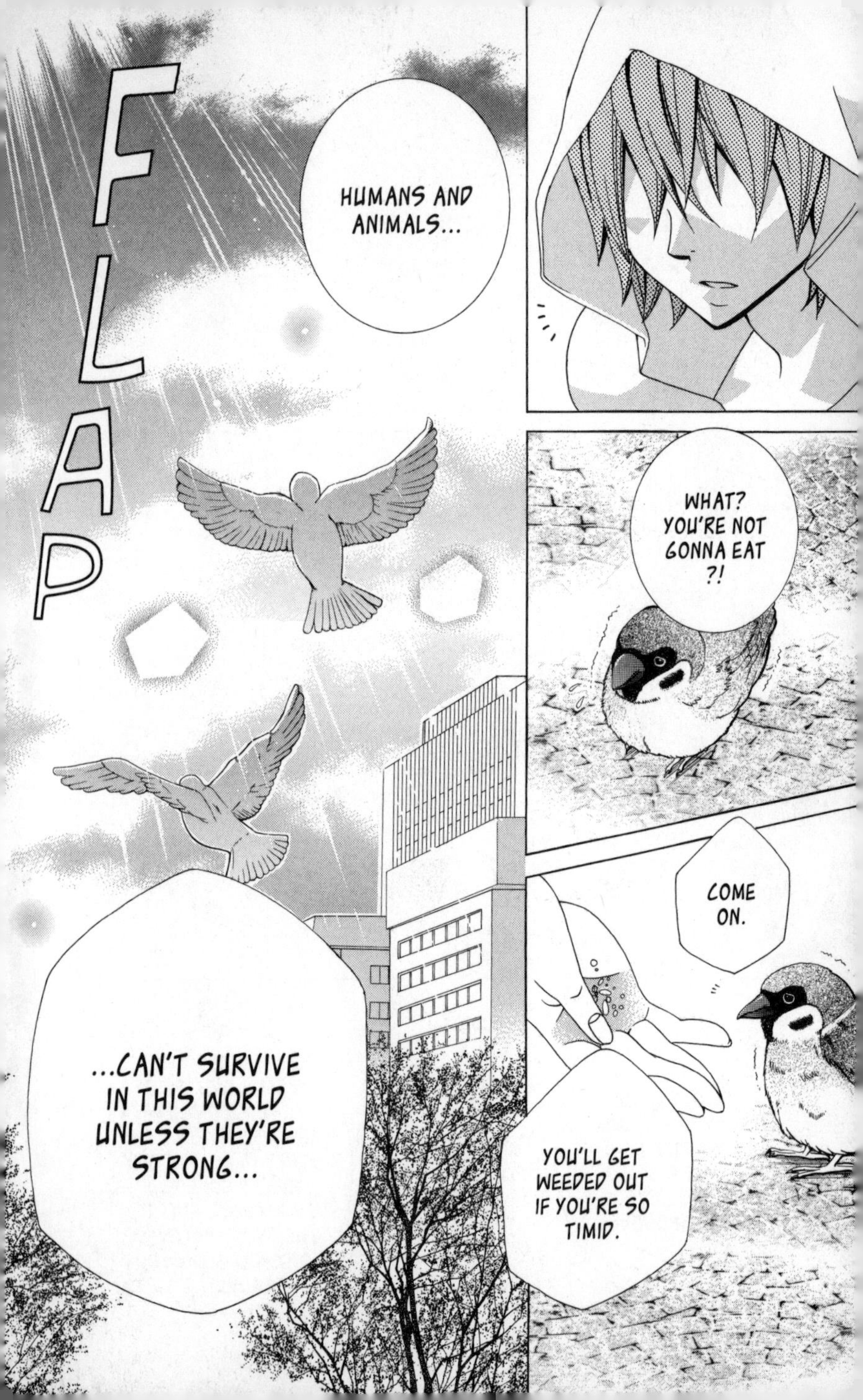
WHAT? YOU'RE NOT GONNA EAT ?!
COME ON.
YOU'LL GET WEEDED OUT IF YOU'RE SO TIMID.
FLAP
HUMANS AND ANIMALS...
...CAN'T SURVIVE IN THIS WORLD UNLESS THEY'RE STRONG...

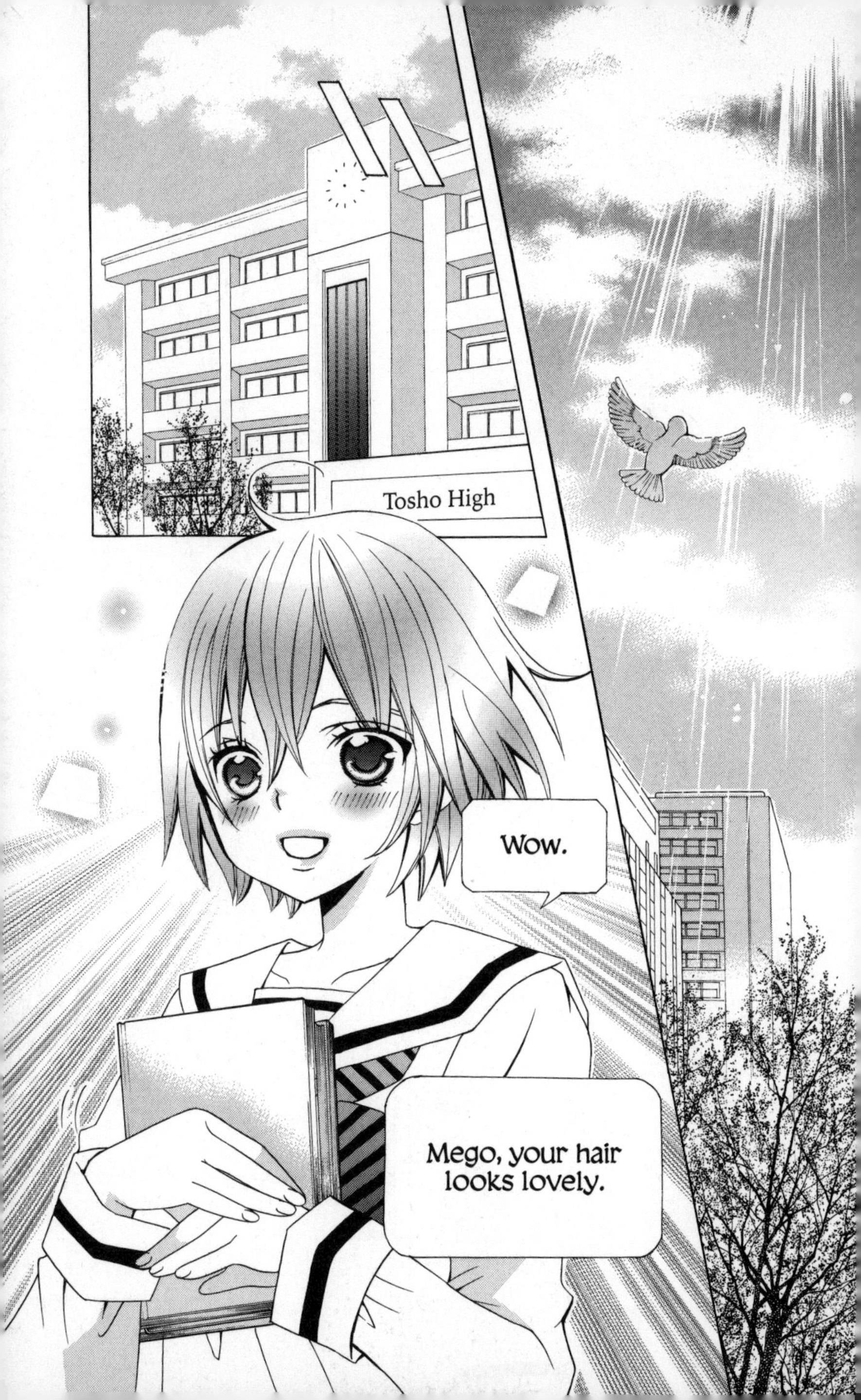
Tosho High
Wow.
Mego, your hair looks lovely.

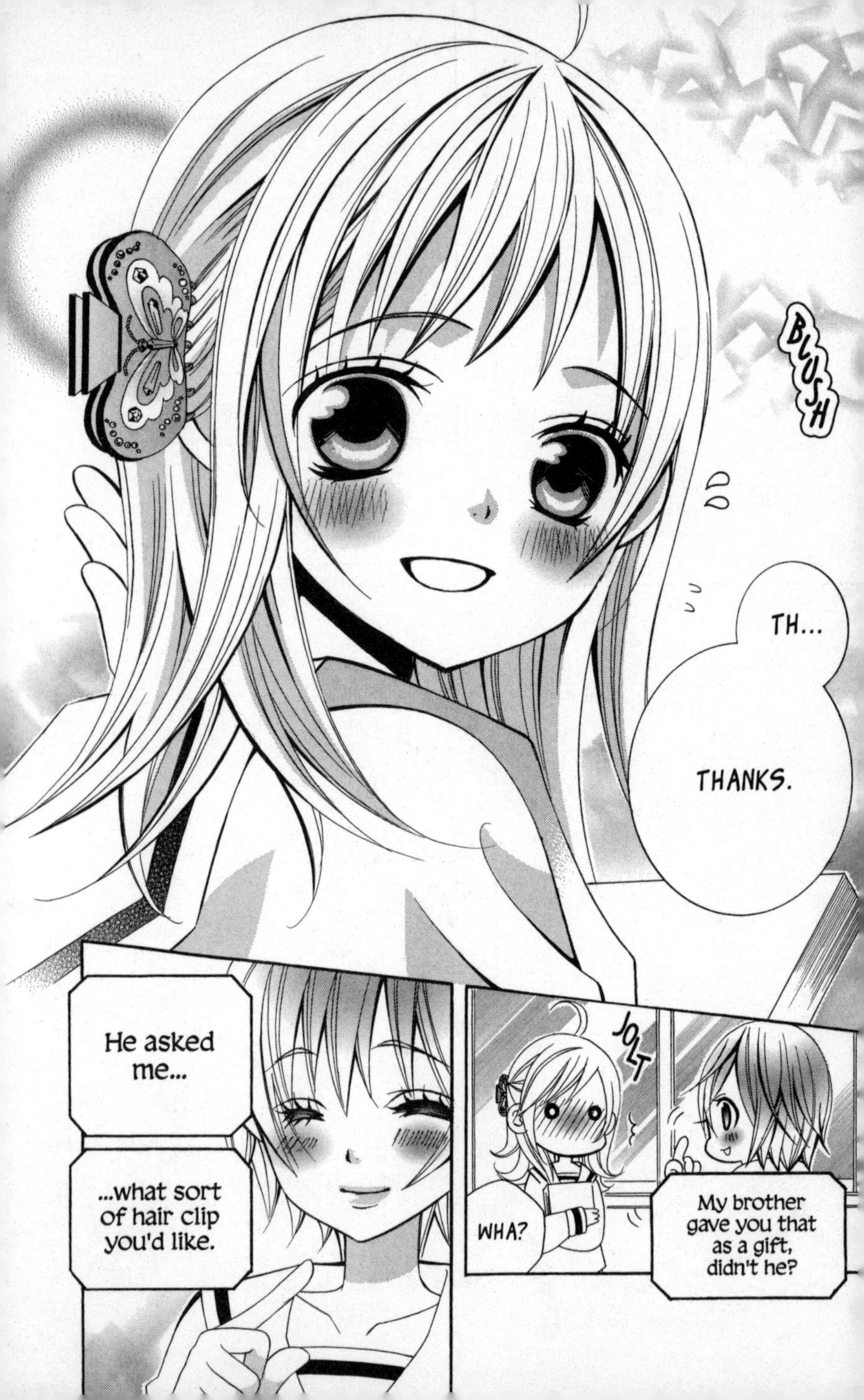
BLUSH
TH...
THANKS.
JOLT
My brother gave you that as a gift, didn't he?
WHA?
He asked me...
...what sort of hair clip you'd like.

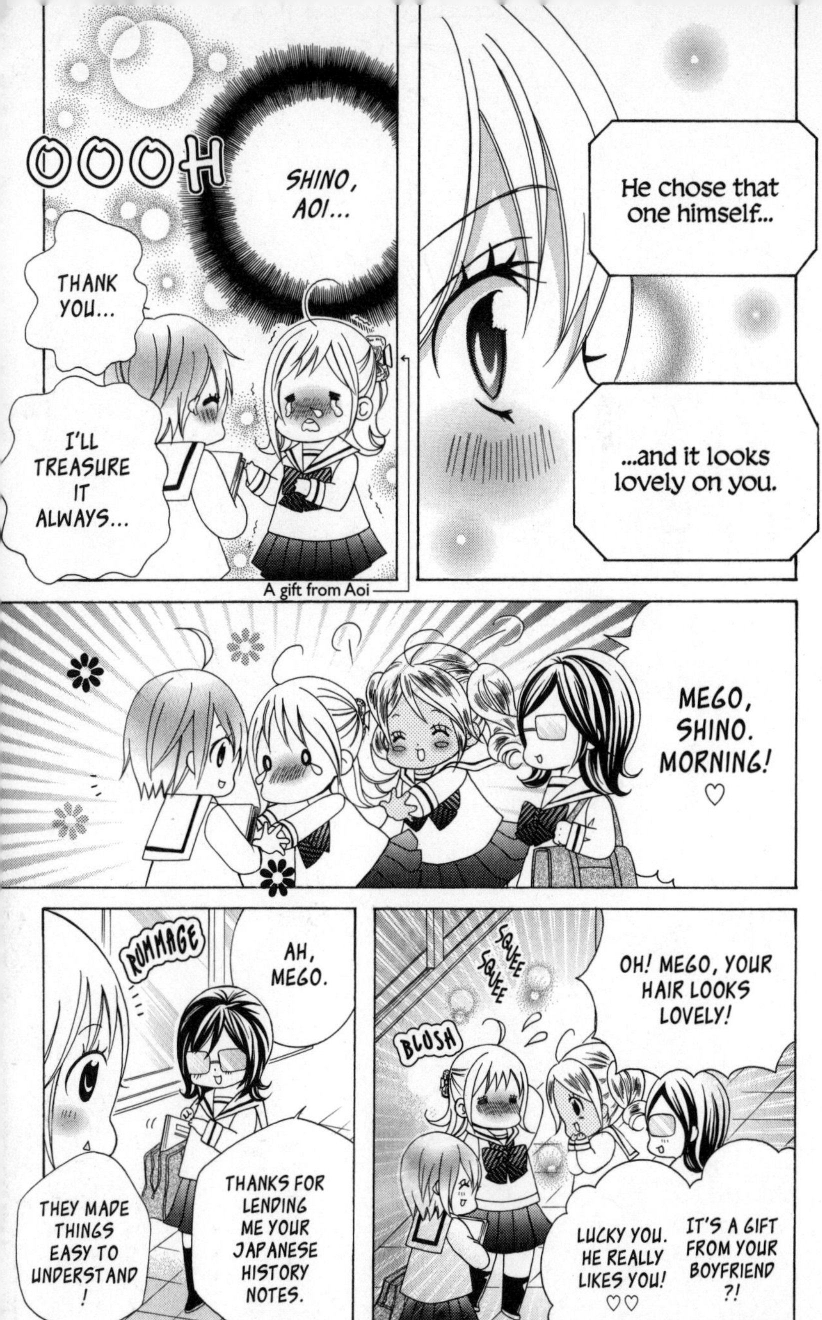
He chose that one himself...
...and it looks lovely on you.
OOOH
SHINO, AOI...
THANK YOU...
I'LL TREASURE IT ALWAYS...
A gift from Aoi
MEGO, SHINO. MORNING! ♡
SQUEE SQUEE
OH! MEGO, YOUR HAIR LOOKS LOVELY!
BLOSH
IT'S A GIFT FROM YOUR BOYFRIEND?!
LUCKY YOU. HE REALLY LIKES YOU! ♡♡
AH, MEGO.
RUMMAGE
THANKS FOR LENDING ME YOUR JAPANESE HISTORY NOTES.
THEY MADE THINGS EASY TO UNDERSTAND!

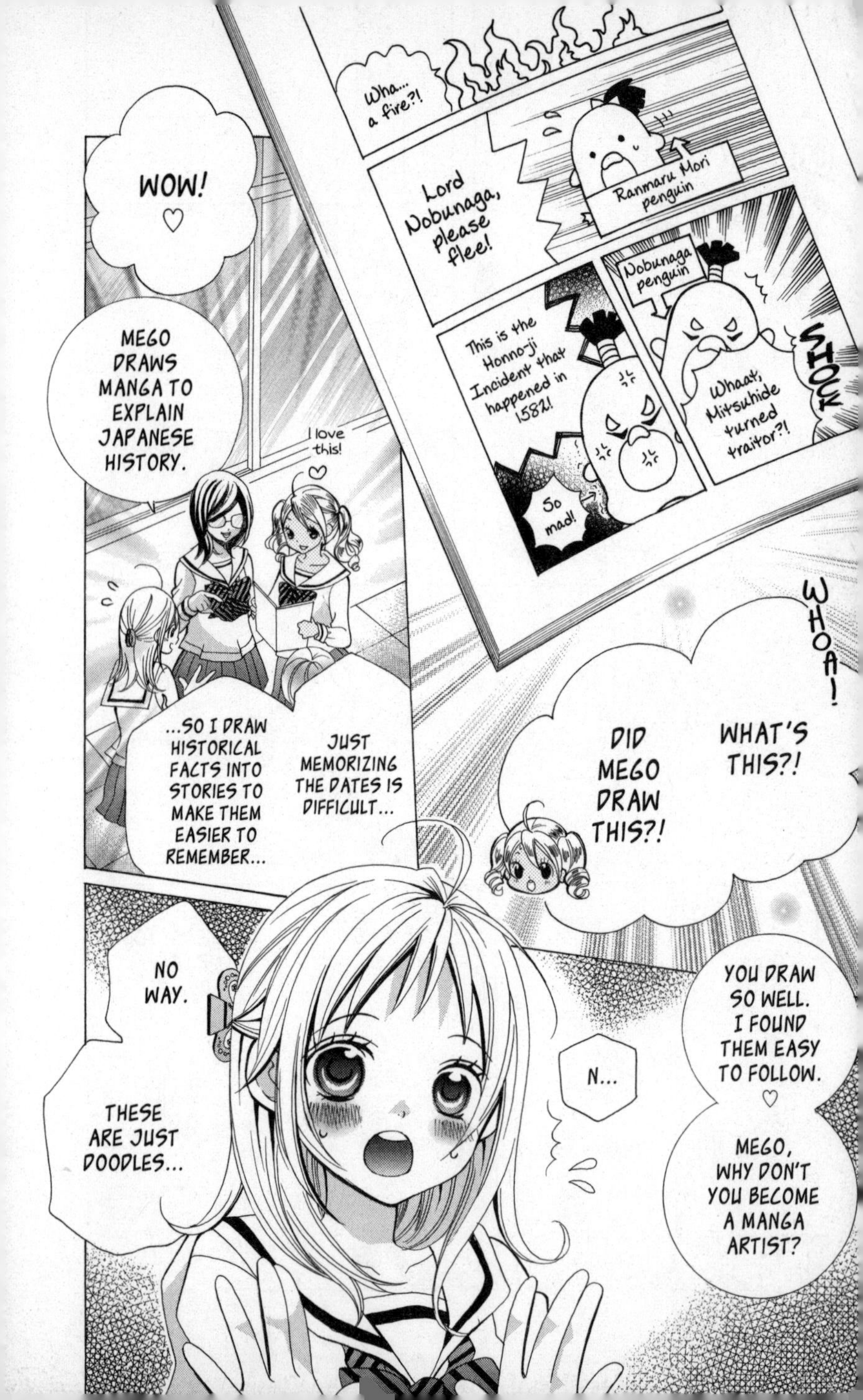
Wha... a fire?!
Lord Nobunaga, please flee!
Ranmaru Mori penguin
Nobunaga penguin
SHOCK
Whaat, Mitsuhide turned traitor?!
This is the Honno-ji Incident that happened in 1582!
So mad!
WHOA!
WHAT'S THIS?!
DID MEGO DRAW THIS?!
WOW! ♡
MEGO DRAWS MANGA TO EXPLAIN JAPANESE HISTORY.
I love this! ♡
JUST MEMORIZING THE DATES IS DIFFICULT...
...SO I DRAW HISTORICAL FACTS INTO STORIES TO MAKE THEM EASIER TO REMEMBER...
YOU DRAW SO WELL. I FOUND THEM EASY TO FOLLOW. ♡
MEGO, WHY DON'T YOU BECOME A MANGA ARTIST?
N...
NO WAY.
THESE ARE JUST DOODLES...

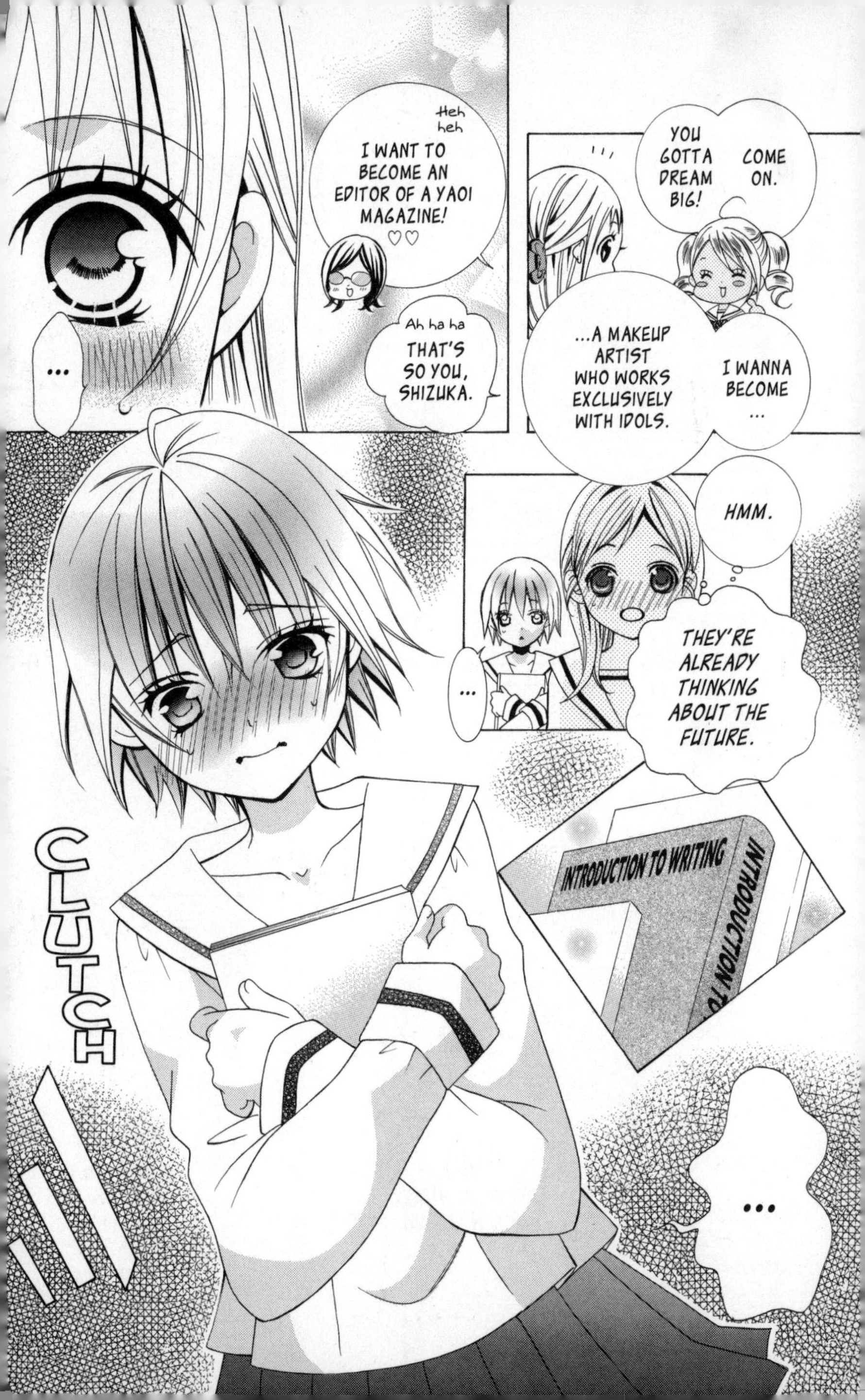
COME ON.
YOU GOTTA DREAM BIG!
I WANNA BECOME ...
...A MAKEUP ARTIST WHO WORKS EXCLUSIVELY WITH IDOLS.
Heh heh
I WANT TO BECOME AN EDITOR OF A YAOI MAGAZINE! ♡♡
Ah ha ha
THAT'S SO YOU, SHIZUKA.
...
HMM.
THEY'RE ALREADY THINKING ABOUT THE FUTURE.
...
INTRODUCTION TO WRITING
INTRODUCTION TO
CLUTCH
...

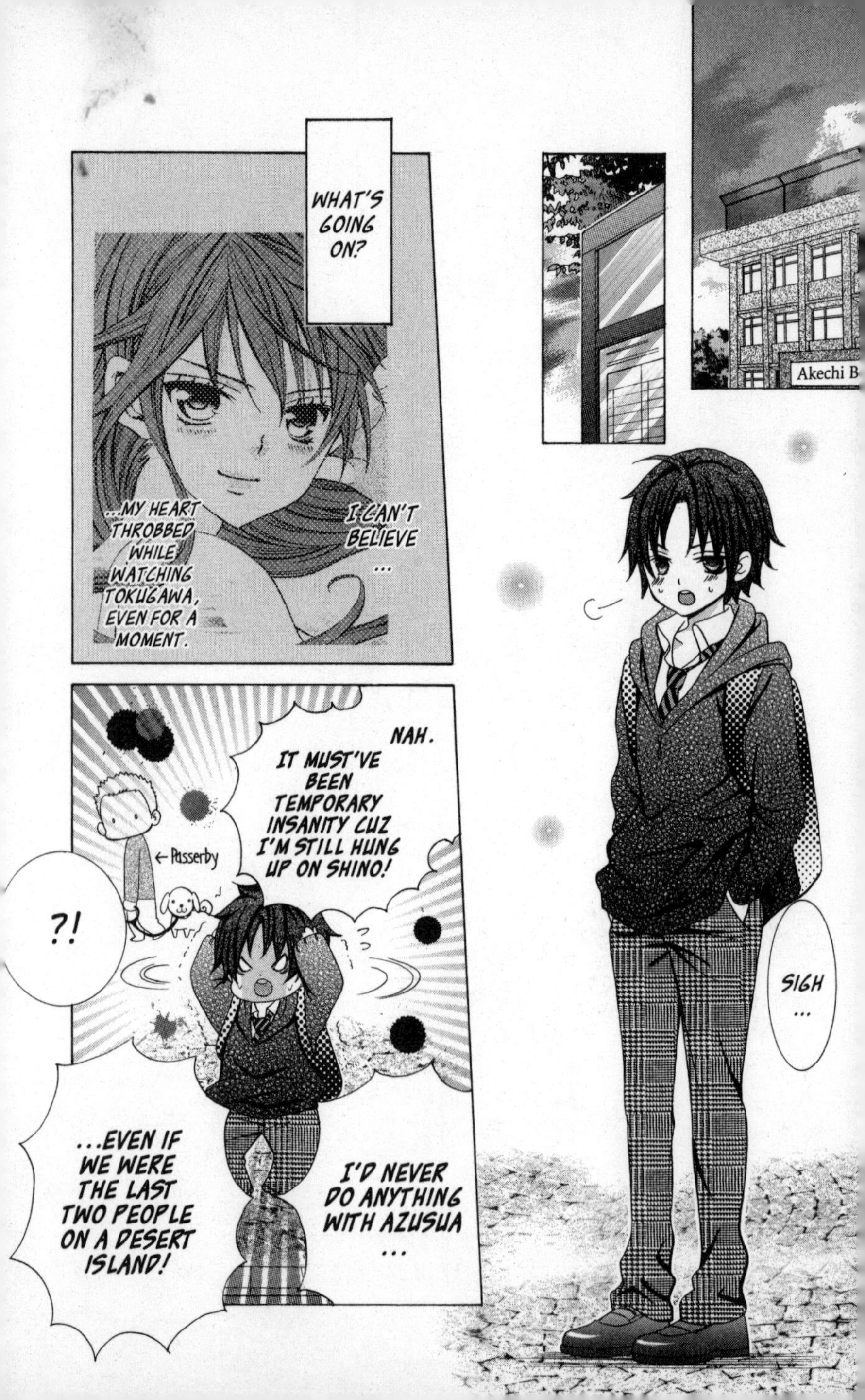

Akechi B
SIGH ...
WHAT'S GOING ON?
I CAN'T BELIEVE ...
...MY HEART THROBBED WHILE WATCHING TOKUGAWA, EVEN FOR A MOMENT.
NAH. IT MUST'VE BEEN TEMPORARY INSANITY CUZ I'M STILL HUNG UP ON SHINO!
← Passerby
?!
I'D NEVER DO ANYTHING WITH AZUSUA ...
...EVEN IF WE WERE THE LAST TWO PEOPLE ON A DESERT ISLAND!

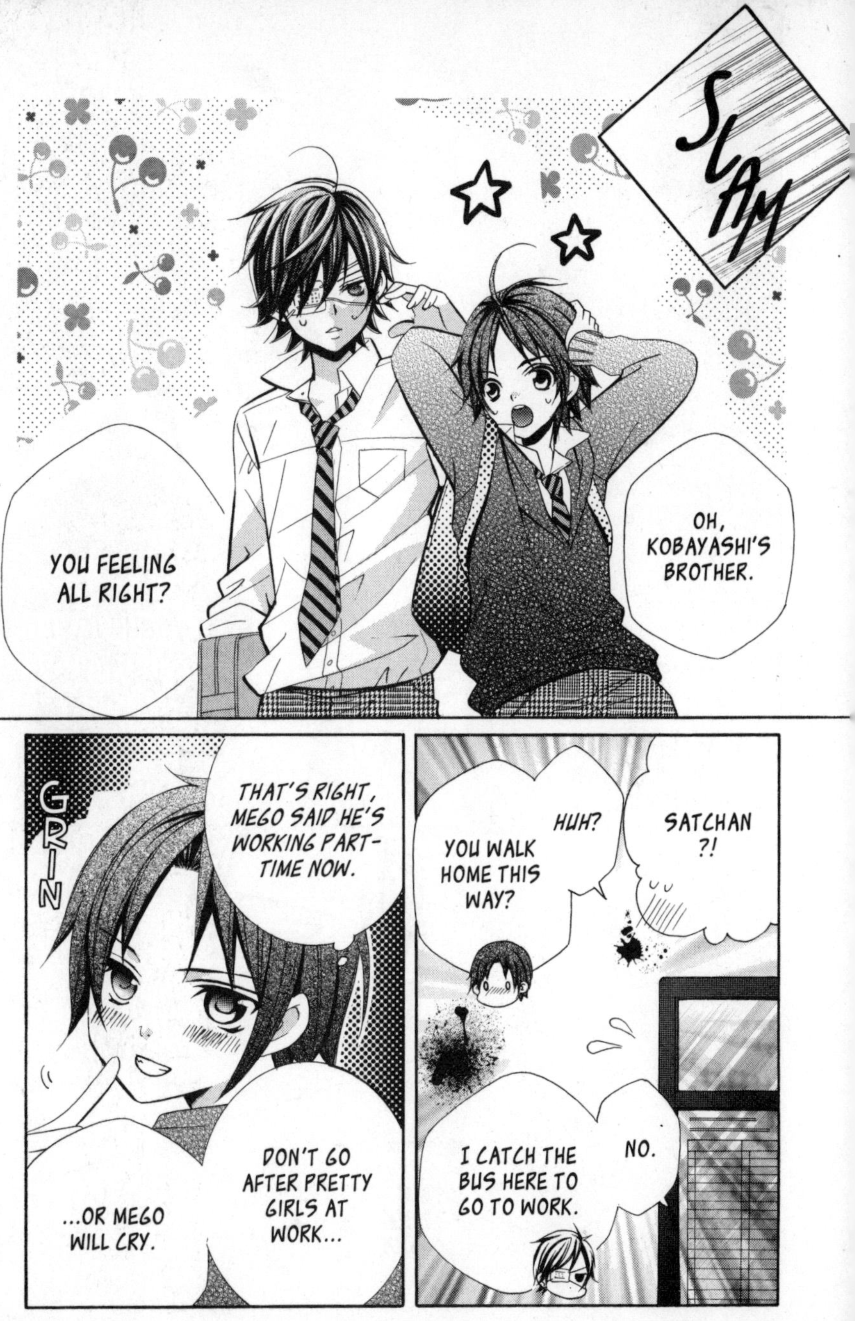
SLAM
OH, KOBAYASHI'S BROTHER.
YOU FEELING ALL RIGHT?
SATCHAN ?!
HUH?
YOU WALK HOME THIS WAY?
NO.
I CATCH THE BUS HERE TO GO TO WORK.
GRIN
THAT'S RIGHT, MEGO SAID HE'S WORKING PART-TIME NOW.
DON'T GO AFTER PRETTY GIRLS AT WORK...
...OR MEGO WILL CRY.

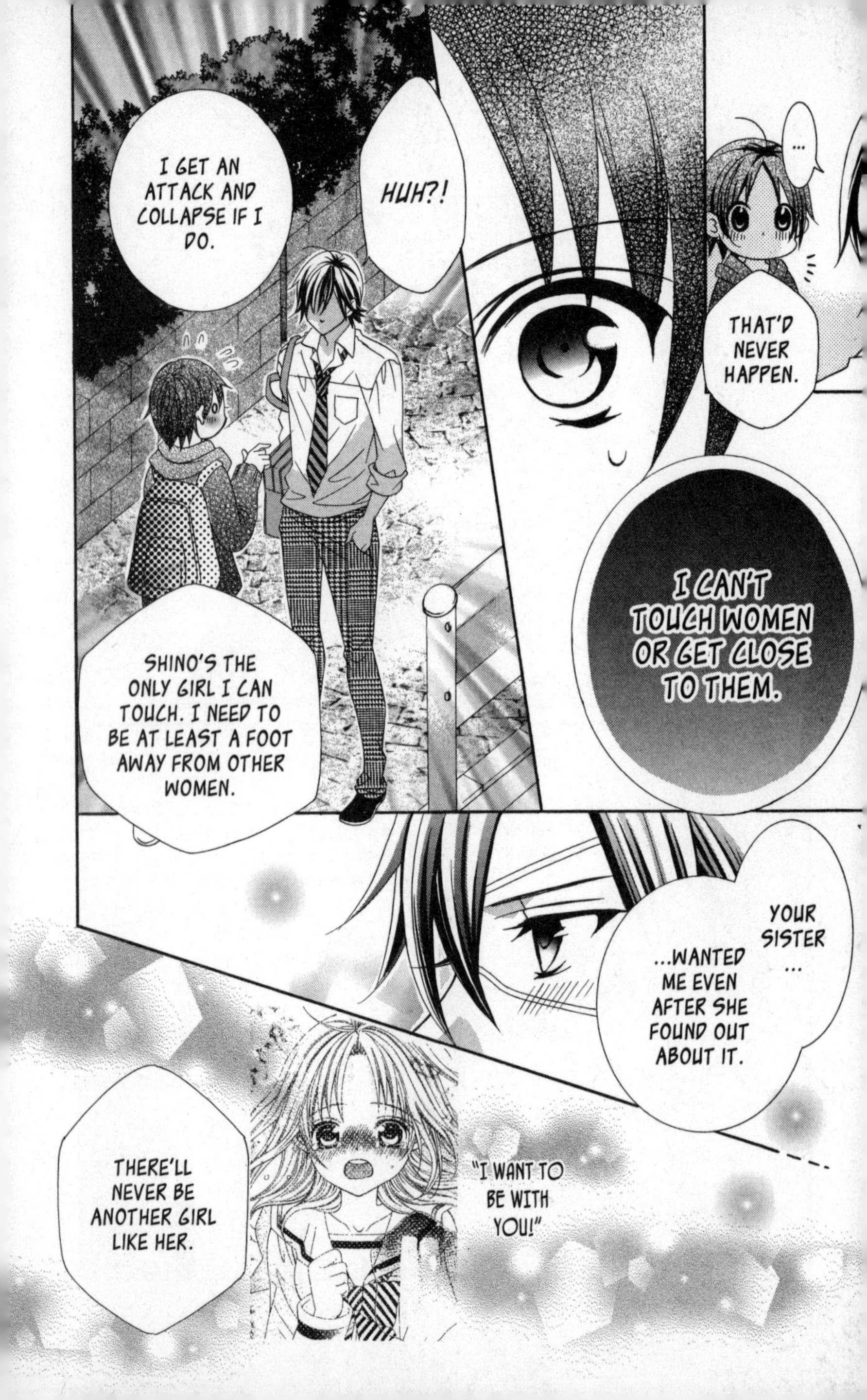
...
THAT'D NEVER HAPPEN.
I CAN'T TOUCH WOMEN OR GET CLOSE TO THEM.
HUH?!
I GET AN ATTACK AND COLLAPSE IF I DO.
SHINO'S THE ONLY GIRL I CAN TOUCH. I NEED TO BE AT LEAST A FOOT AWAY FROM OTHER WOMEN.
YOUR SISTER ...
...WANTED ME EVEN AFTER SHE FOUND OUT ABOUT IT.
"I WANT TO BE WITH YOU!"
THERE'LL NEVER BE ANOTHER GIRL LIKE HER.

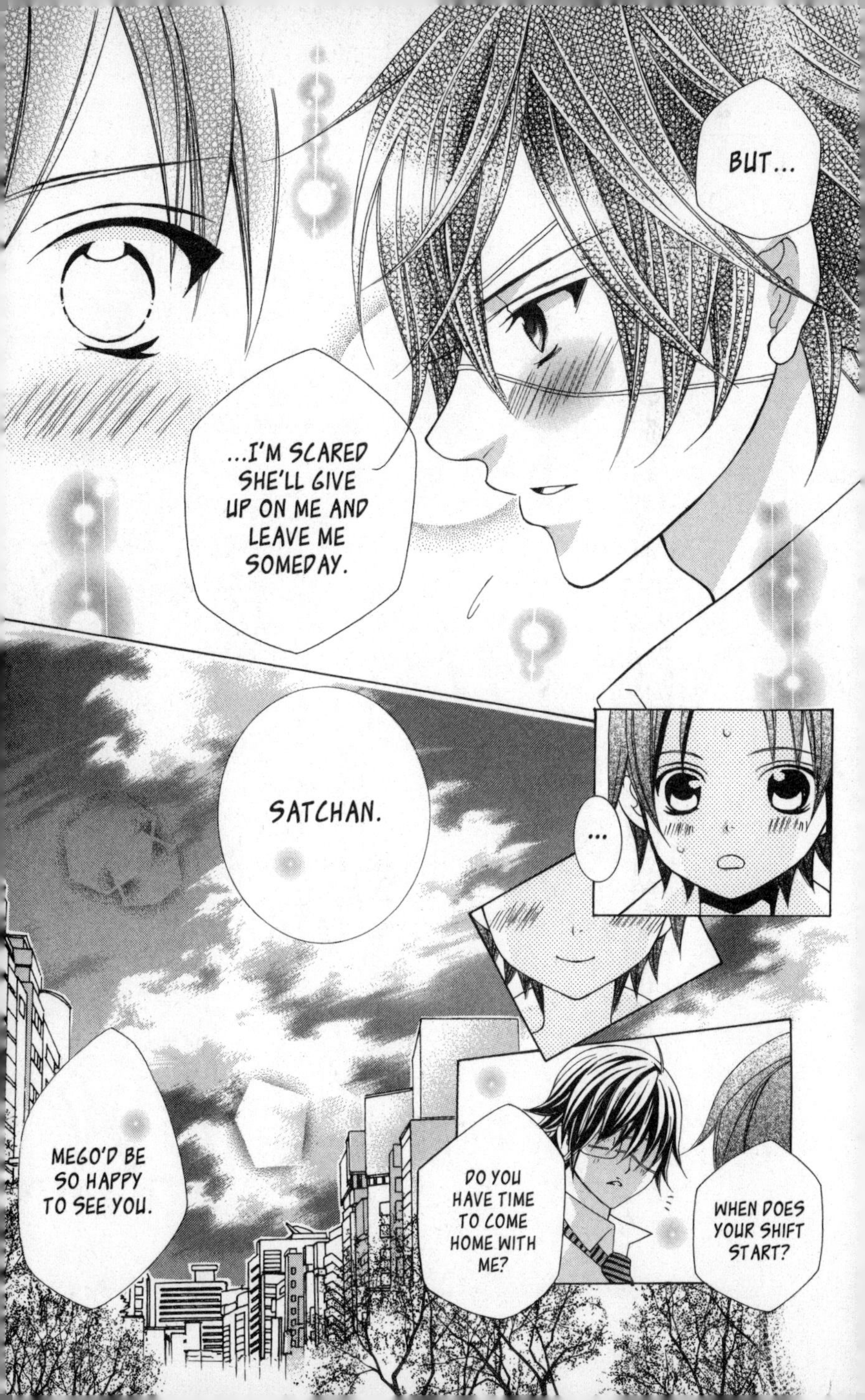
BUT...
...I'M SCARED SHE'LL GIVE UP ON ME AND LEAVE ME SOMEDAY.
...
SATCHAN.
WHEN DOES YOUR SHIFT START?
DO YOU HAVE TIME TO COME HOME WITH ME?
MEGO'D BE SO HAPPY TO SEE YOU.

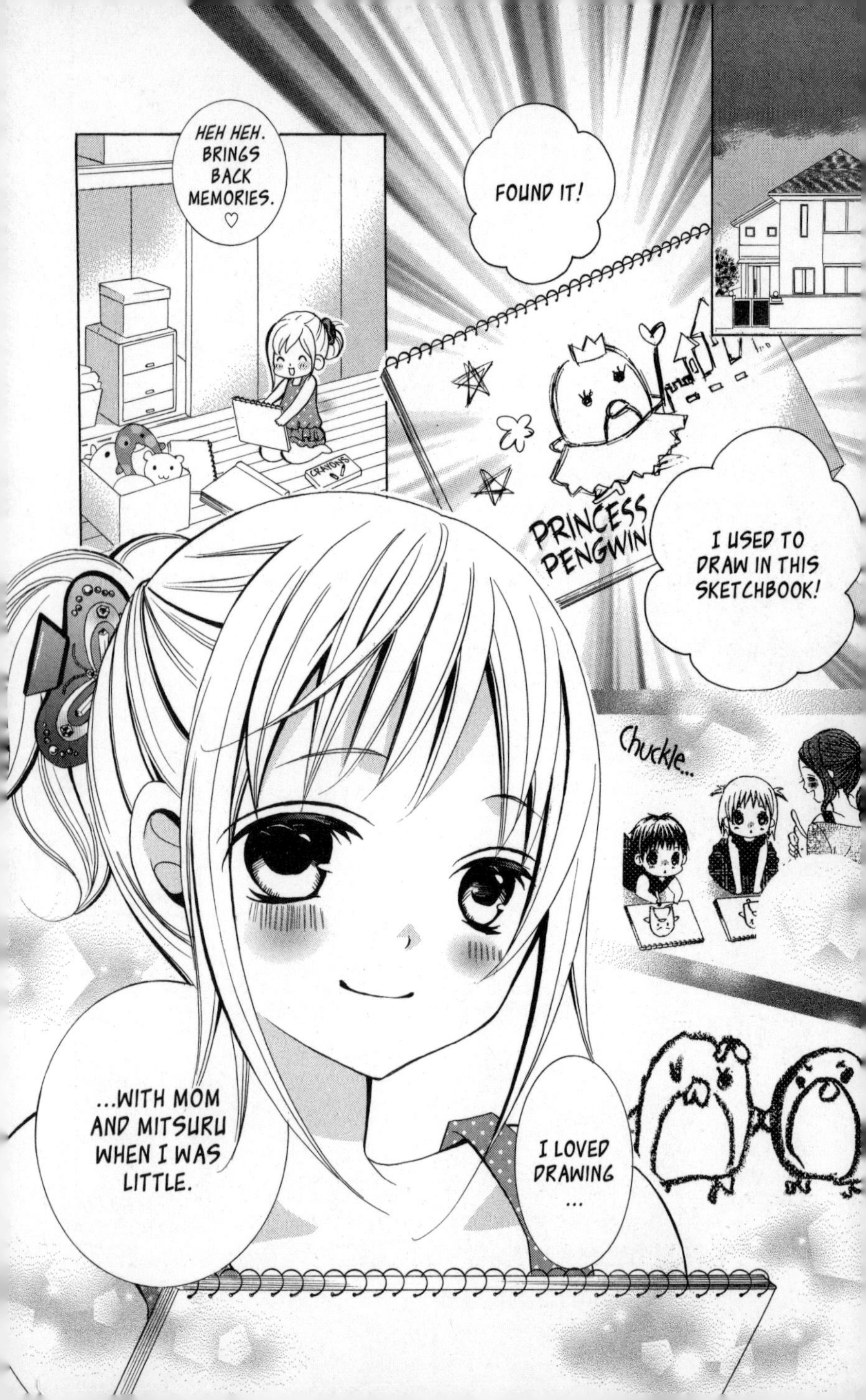
FOUND IT!
HEH HEH. BRINGS BACK MEMORIES. ♡
CRAYONS
PRINCESS PENGWIN
I USED TO DRAW IN THIS SKETCHBOOK!
Chuckle...
I LOVED DRAWING ...
...WITH MOM AND MITSURU WHEN I WAS LITTLE.

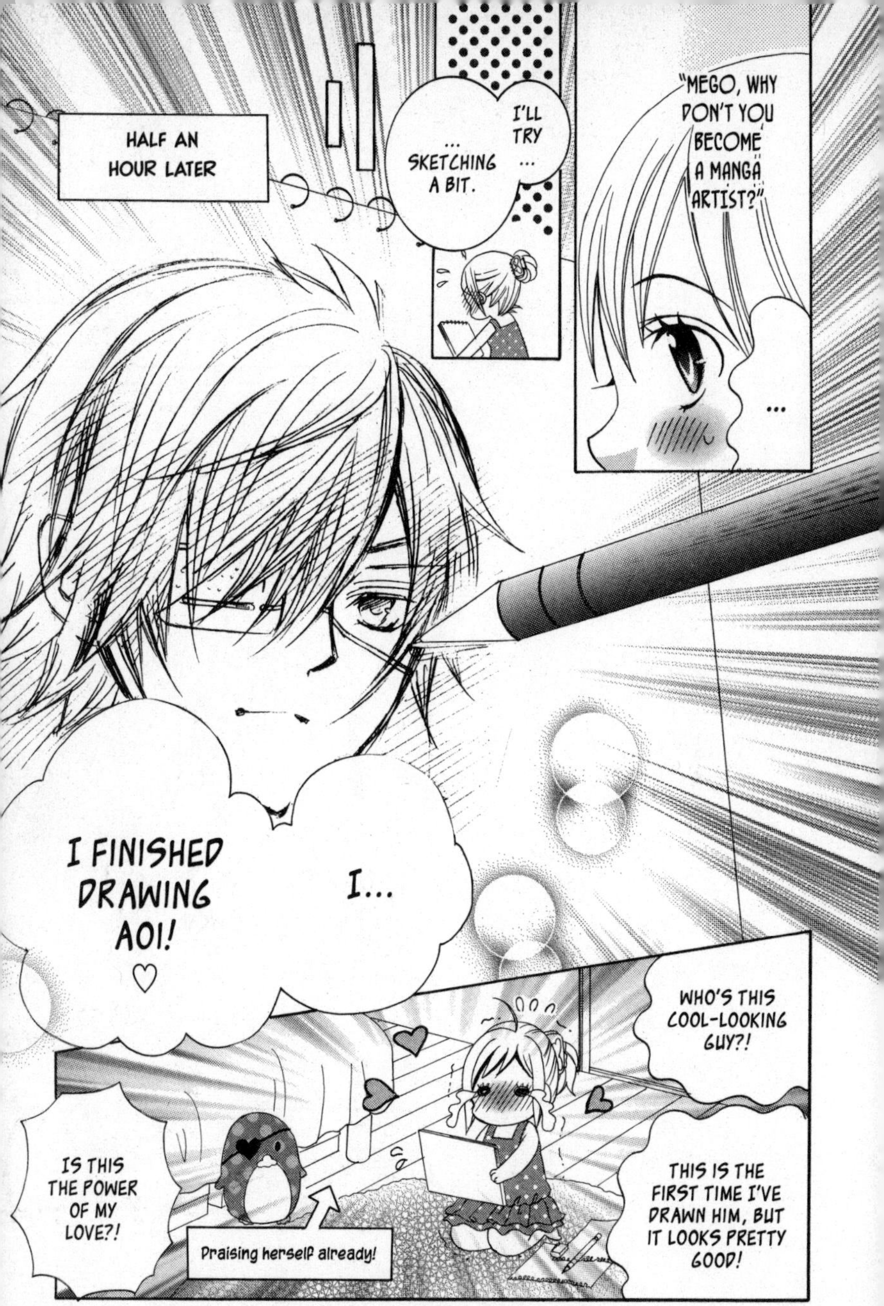
"MEGO, WHY DON'T YOU BECOME A MANGA ARTIST?"
...
I'LL TRY ... ... SKETCHING A BIT.
HALF AN HOUR LATER
I...
I FINISHED DRAWING AOI! ♡
WHO'S THIS COOL-LOOKING GUY?!
THIS IS THE FIRST TIME I'VE DRAWN HIM, BUT IT LOOKS PRETTY GOOD!
IS THIS THE POWER OF MY LOVE?!
Praising herself already!

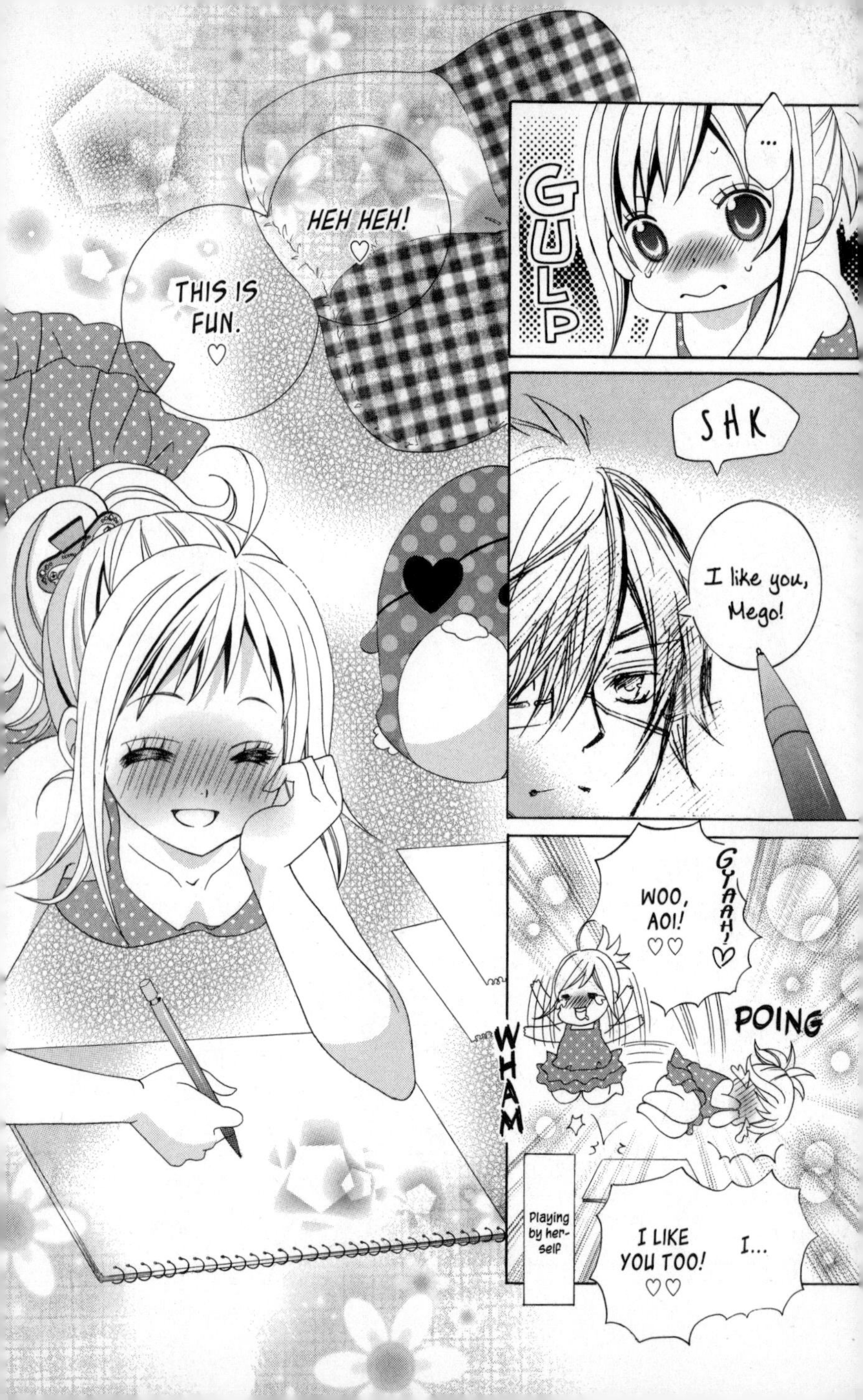
...
GULP
SHK
I like you, Mego!
GYAAAH! ♡
WOO, AOI! ♡♡
POING
WHAM
I... I LIKE YOU TOO! ♡♡
Playing by her-self
HEH HEH! ♡
THIS IS FUN. ♡

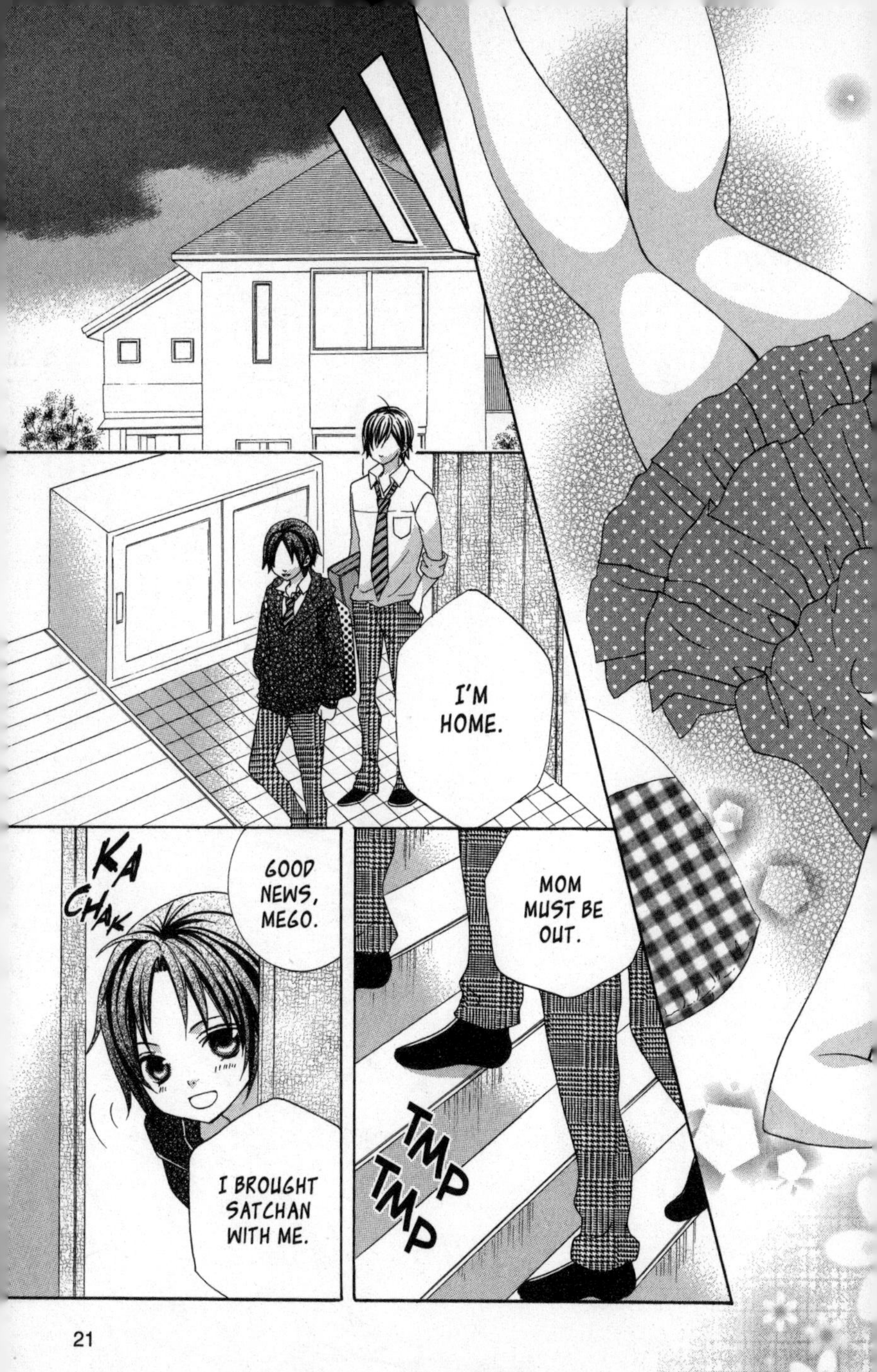
I'M HOME.
MOM MUST BE OUT.
TMP TMP
KA CHAK
GOOD NEWS, MEGO.
I BROUGHT SATCHAN WITH ME.

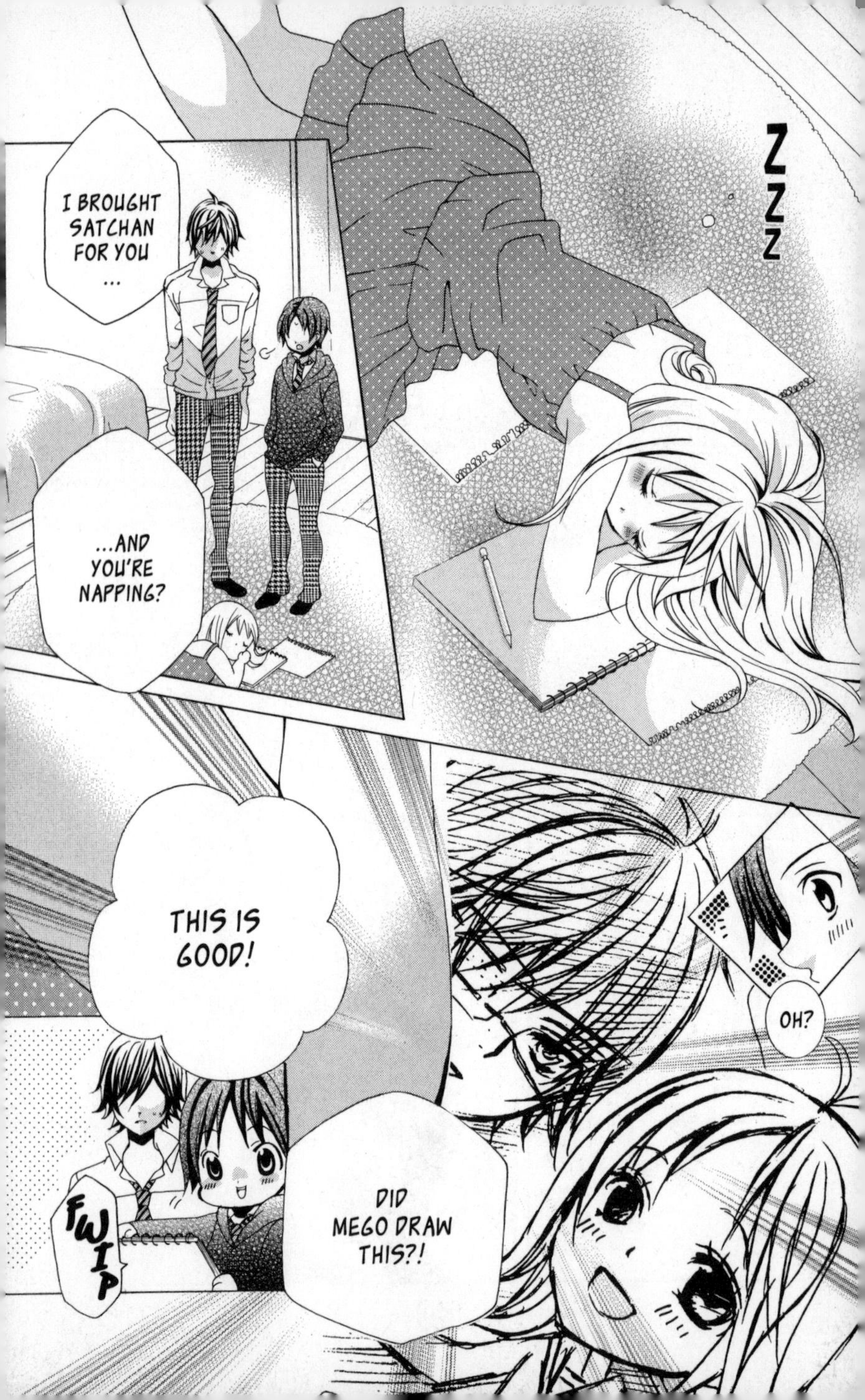
ZZZ
I BROUGHT SATCHAN FOR YOU ...
...AND YOU'RE NAPPING?
OH?
THIS IS GOOD!
FWIP
DID MEGO DRAW THIS?!

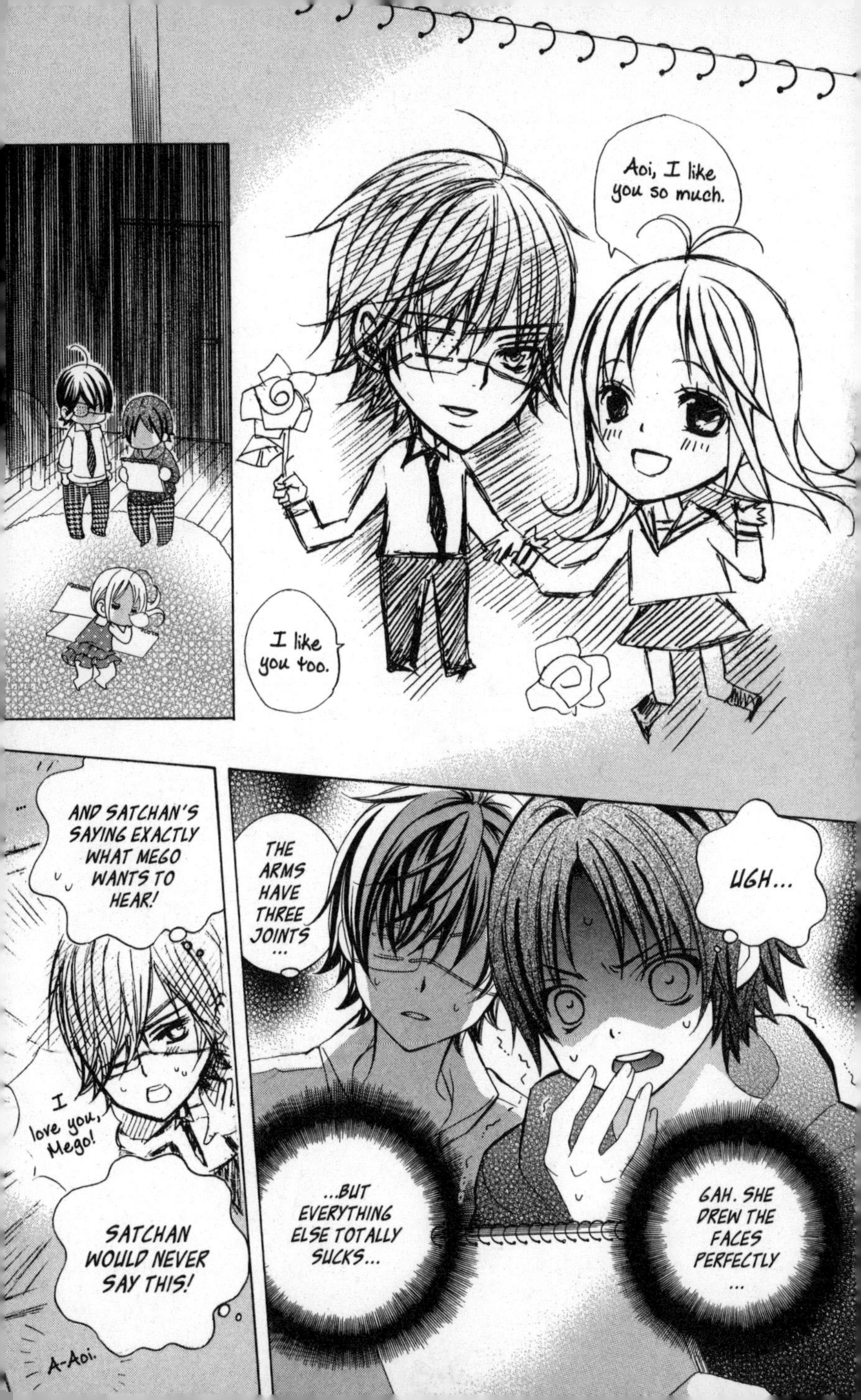
Aoi, I like you so much.
I like you too.
UGH...
THE ARMS HAVE THREE JOINTS...
GAH. SHE DREW THE FACES PERFECTLY...
...BUT EVERYTHING ELSE TOTALLY SUCKS...
AND SATCHAN'S SAYING EXACTLY WHAT MEGO WANTS TO HEAR!
I love you, Mego!
SATCHAN WOULD NEVER SAY THIS!
A-Aoi.

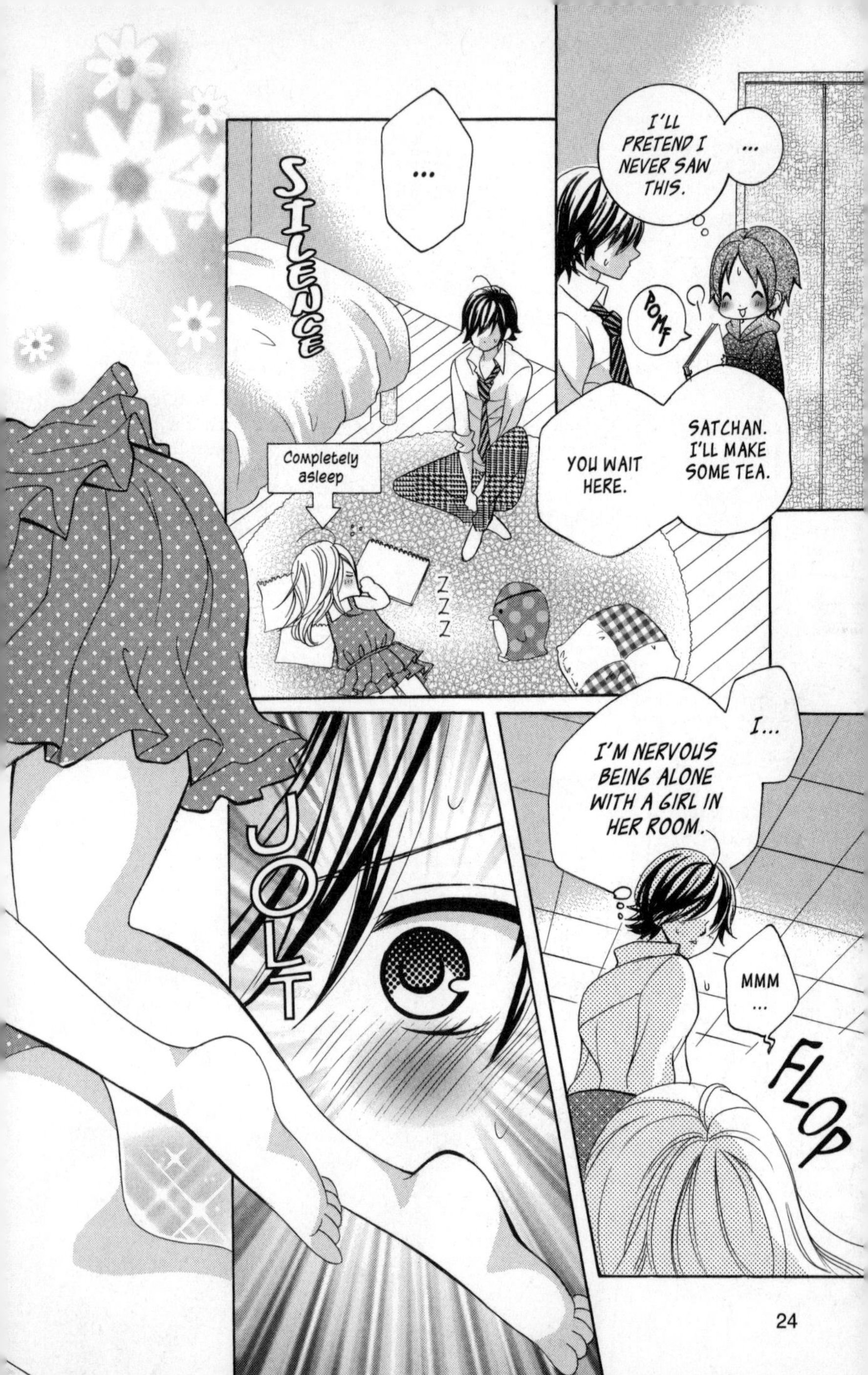

I'LL PRETEND I NEVER SAW THIS.
...
POMF
SATCHAN. I'LL MAKE SOME TEA. YOU WAIT HERE.
...
SILENCE
Completely asleep
ZZZ
I...
I'M NERVOUS BEING ALONE WITH A GIRL IN HER ROOM.
MMM...
FLOP
JOLT

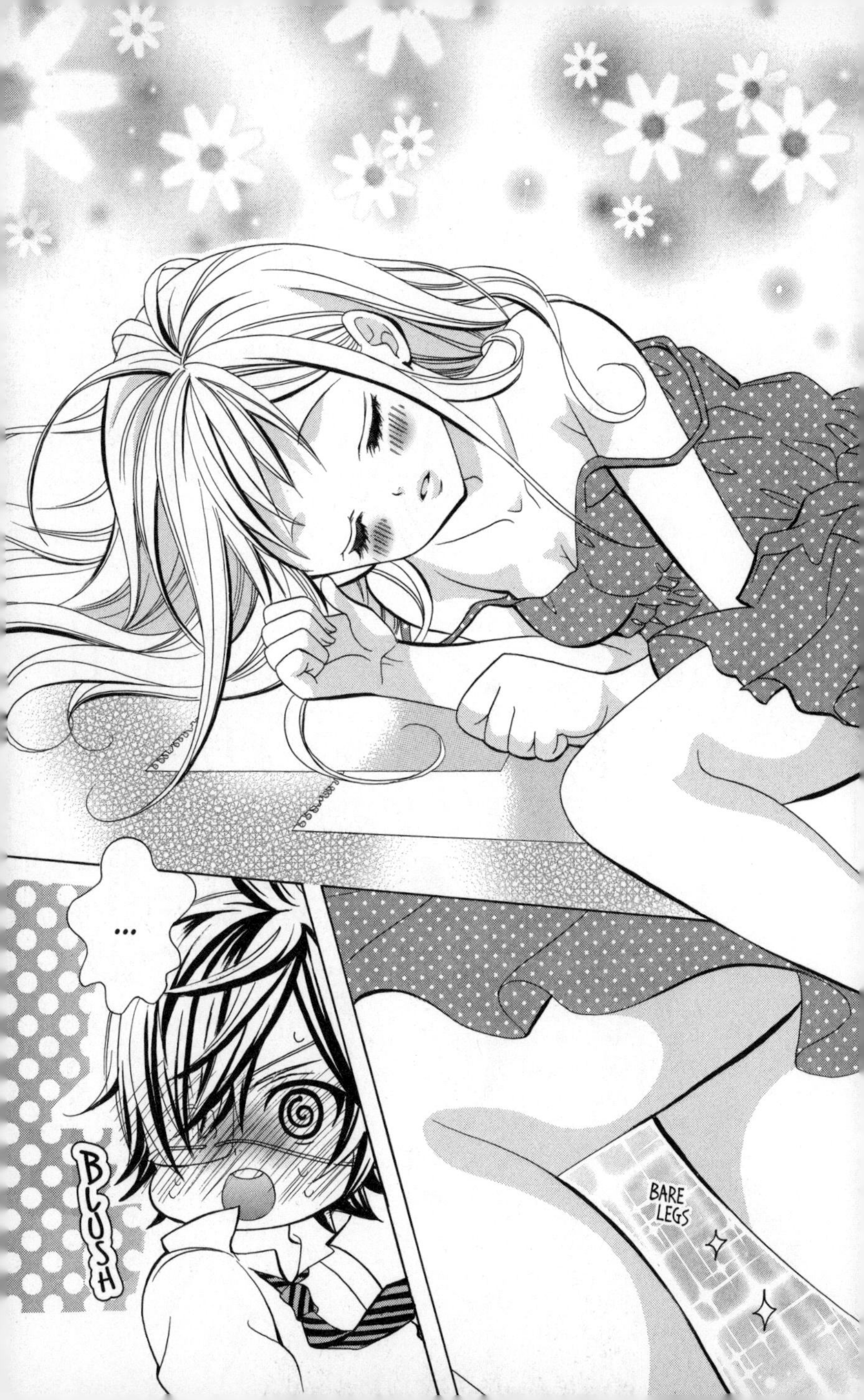
BARE LEGS
...
BLUSH

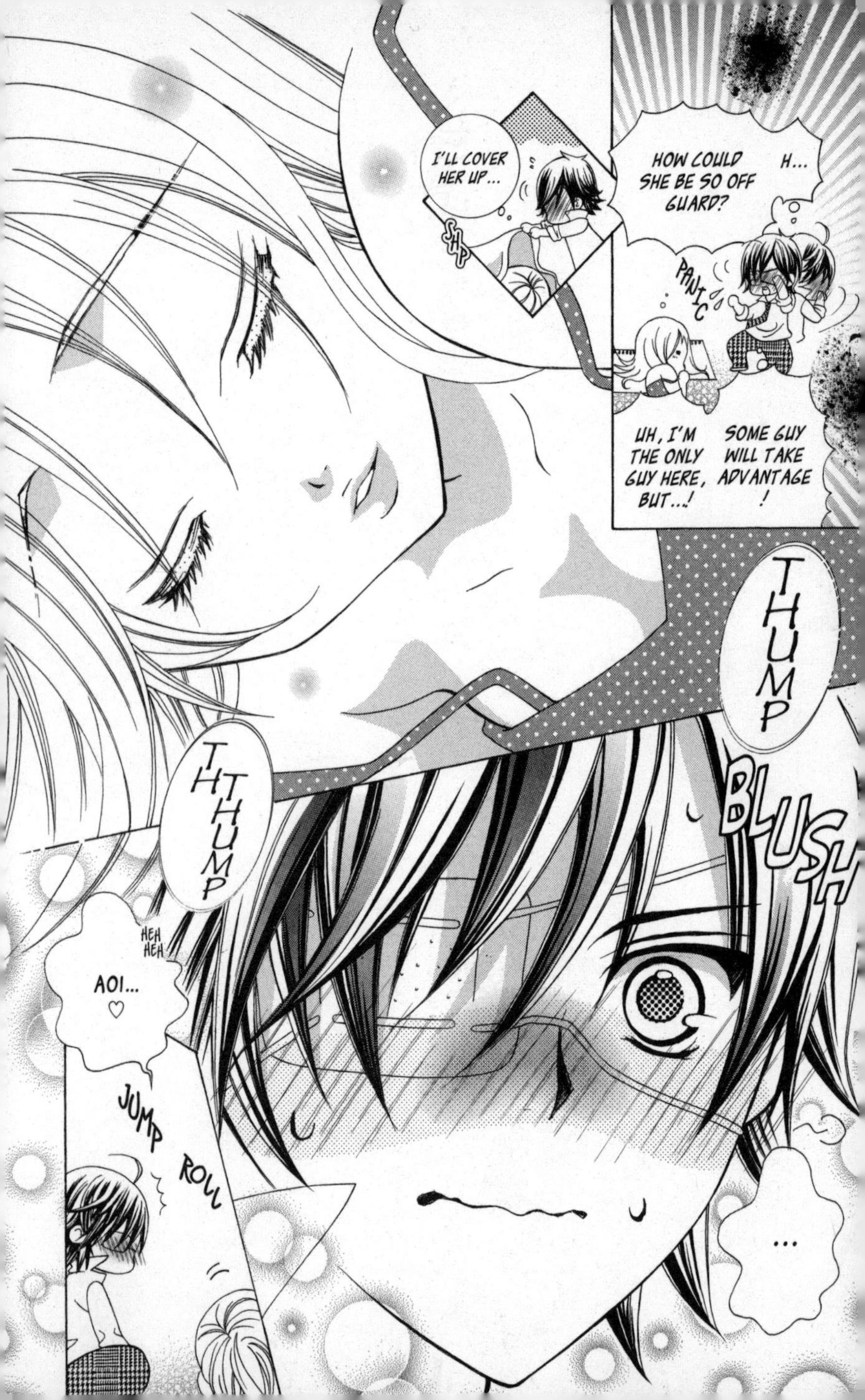
H...
HOW COULD SHE BE SO OFF GUARD?
PANIC
SOME GUY WILL TAKE ADVANTAGE!
UH, I'M THE ONLY GUY HERE, BUT...!
I'LL COVER HER UP...
SHP
THUMP
BLUSH
THTHUMP
...
HEH HEH
AOI... ♡
JUMP
ROLL

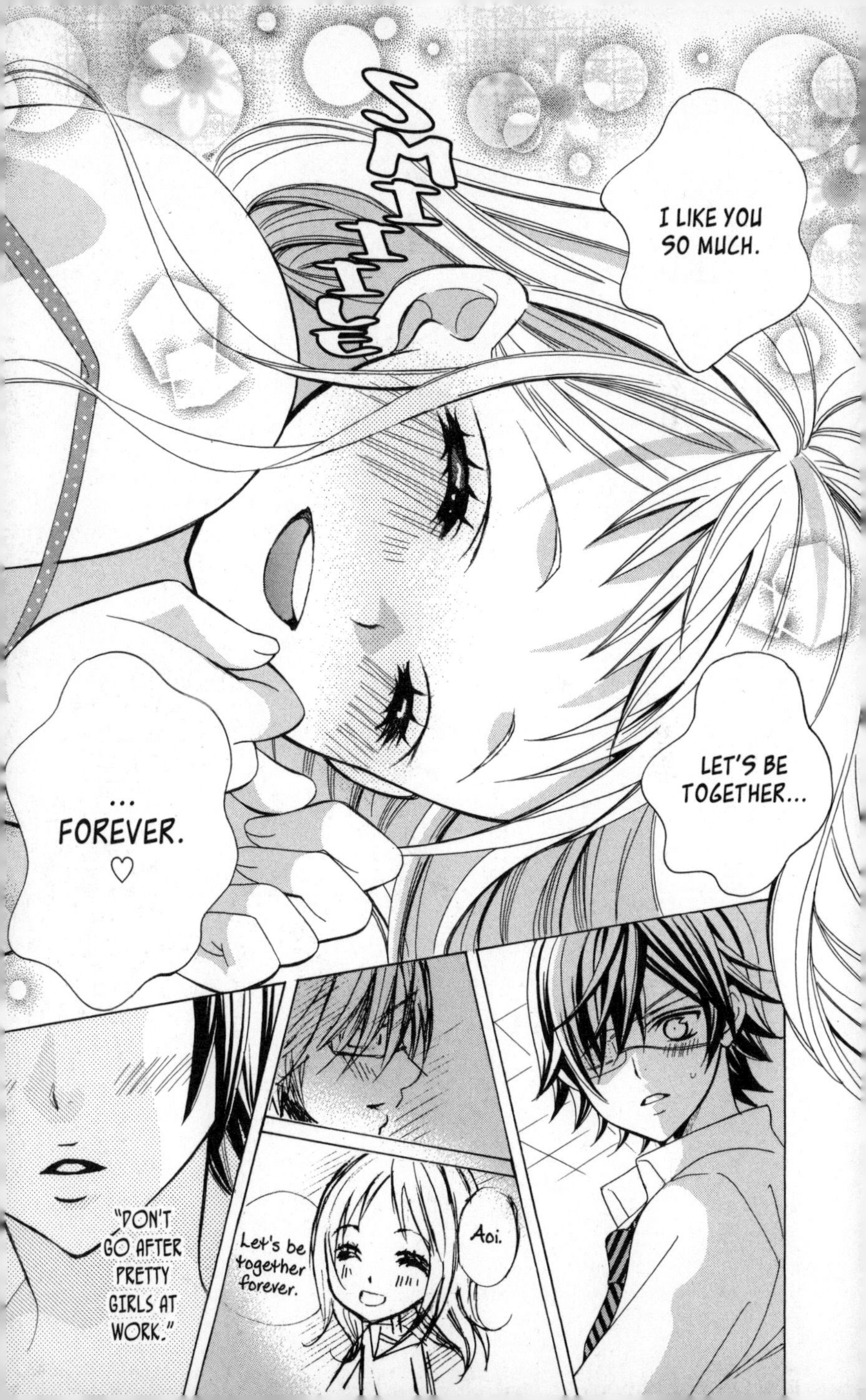
SMILE
I LIKE YOU SO MUCH.
LET'S BE TOGETHER...
... FOREVER. ♡
Aoi.
Let's be together forever.
"DON'T GO AFTER PRETTY GIRLS AT WORK."

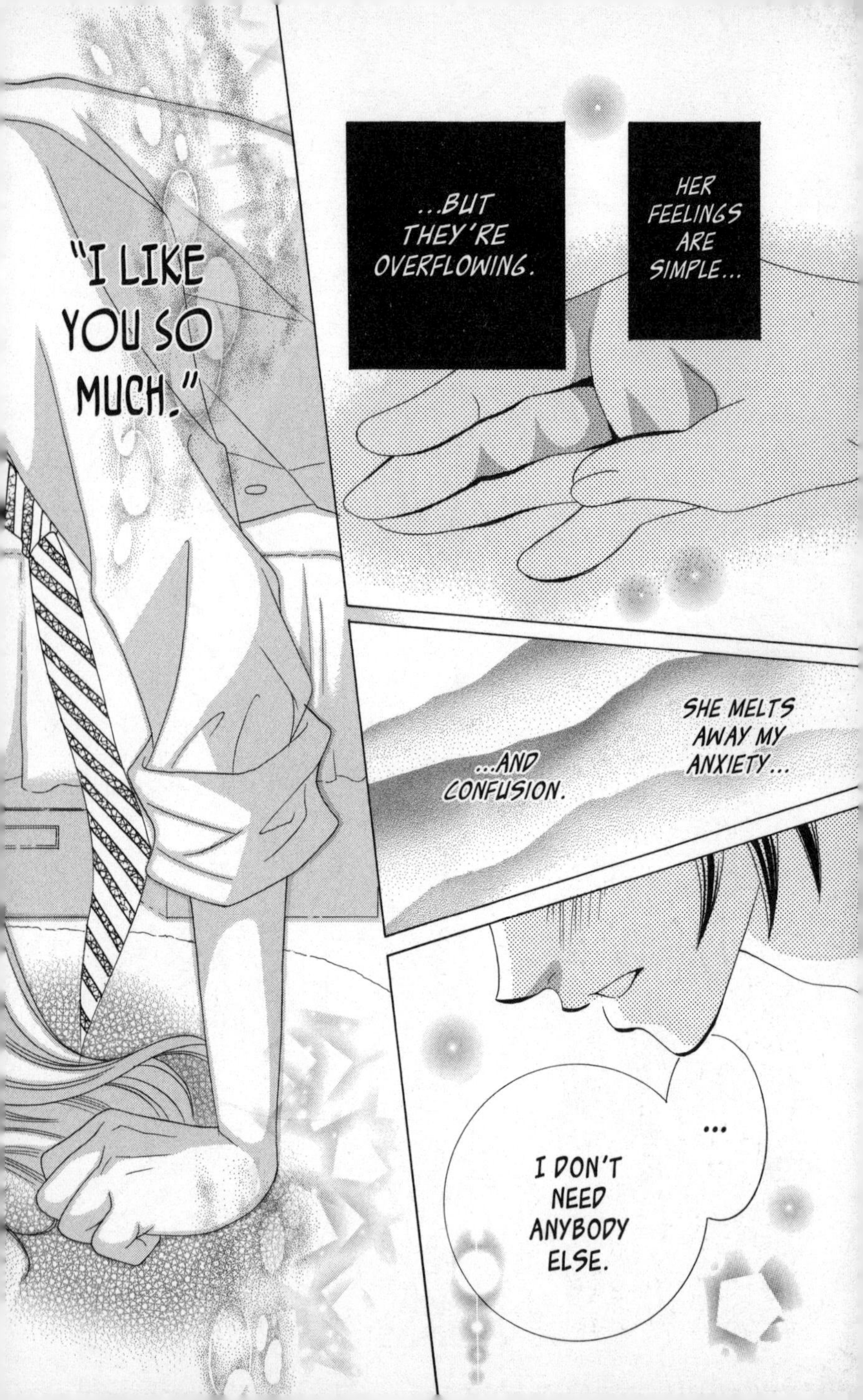
HER FEELINGS ARE SIMPLE...
...BUT THEY'RE OVERFLOWING.
SHE MELTS AWAY MY ANXIETY...
...AND CONFUSION.
...
I DON'T NEED ANYBODY ELSE.
"I LIKE YOU SO MUCH."

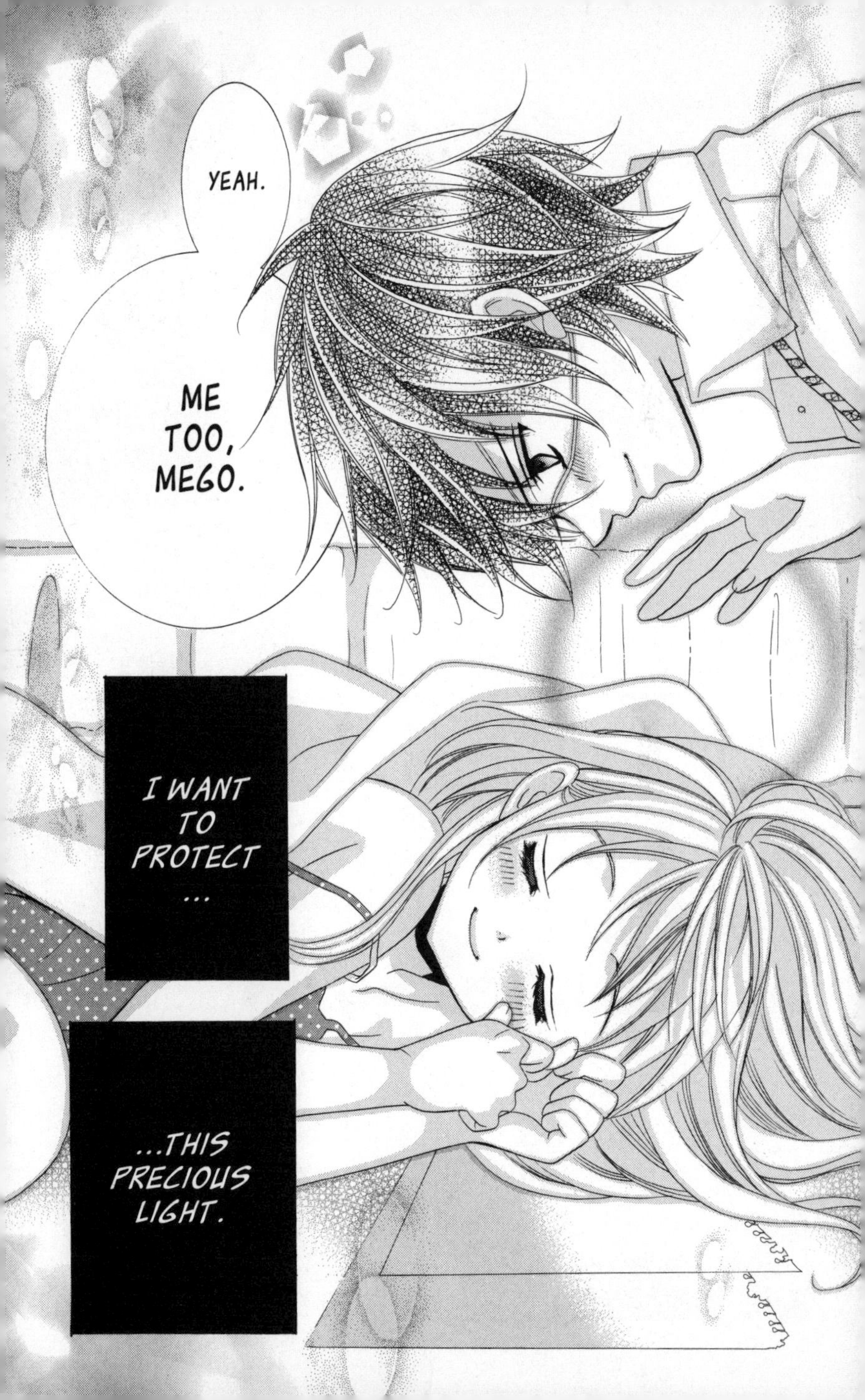
YEAH.
ME TOO, MEGO.
I WANT TO PROTECT...
...THIS PRECIOUS LIGHT.

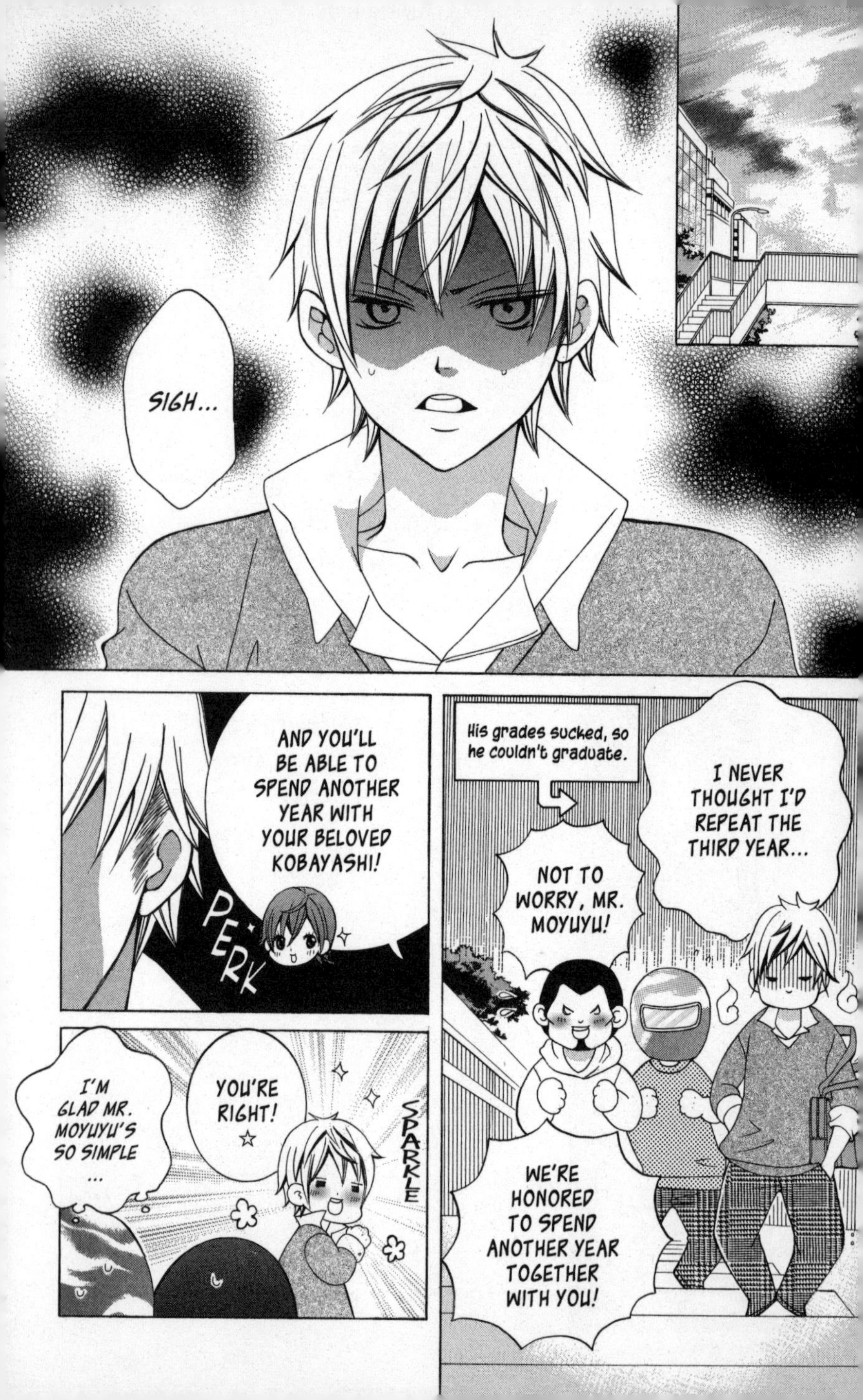
SIGH...
I NEVER THOUGHT I'D REPEAT THE THIRD YEAR...
His grades sucked, so he couldn't graduate.
NOT TO WORRY, MR. MOYUYU!
WE'RE HONORED TO SPEND ANOTHER YEAR TOGETHER WITH YOU!
AND YOU'LL BE ABLE TO SPEND ANOTHER YEAR WITH YOUR BELOVED KOBAYASHI!
PERK
YOU'RE RIGHT! ☆
SPARKLE
I'M GLAD MR. MOYUYU'S SO SIMPLE ...

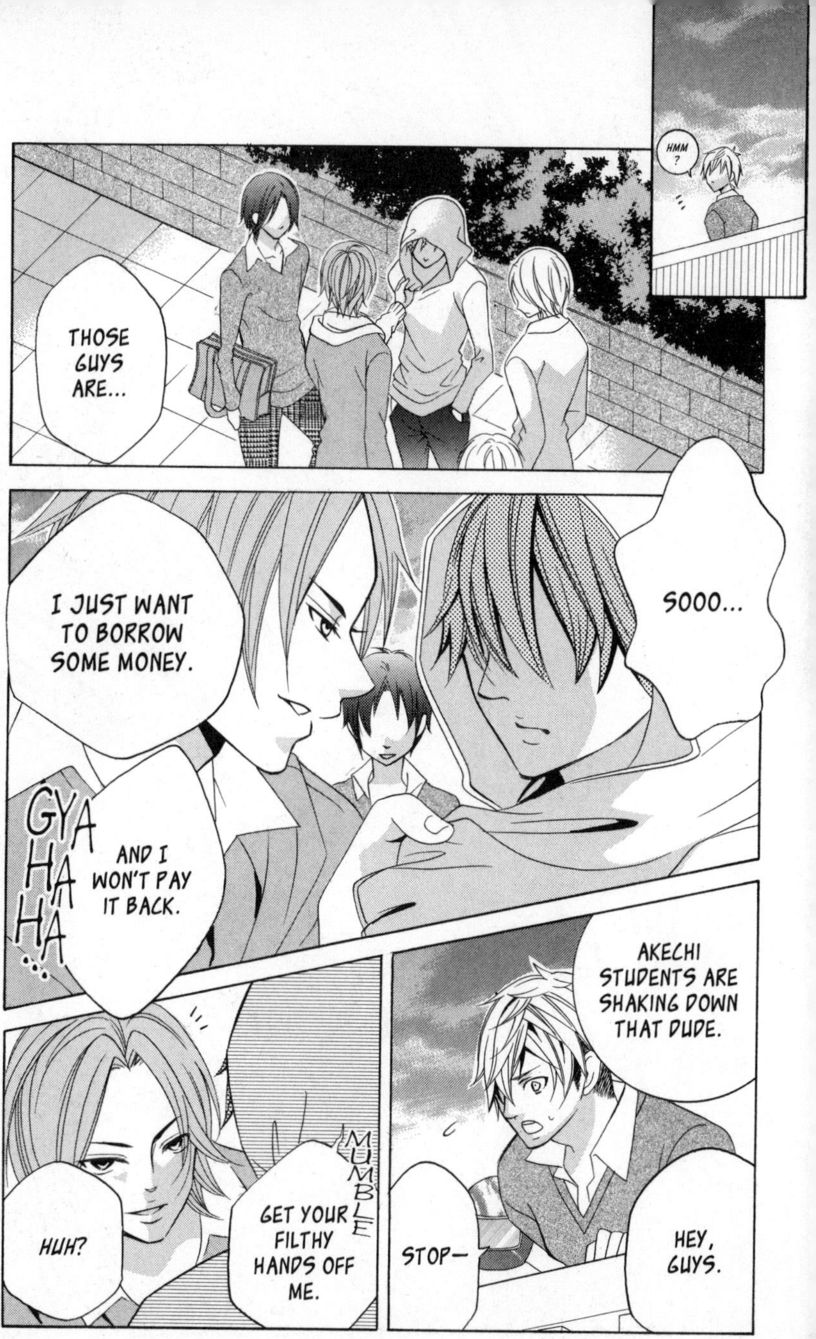
HMM?
THOSE GUYS ARE...
SOOO...
I JUST WANT TO BORROW SOME MONEY.
AND I WON'T PAY IT BACK.
GYAHAHAHA...
AKECHI STUDENTS ARE SHAKING DOWN THAT DUDE.
HEY, GUYS.
STOP—
MUMBLE
GET YOUR FILTHY HANDS OFF ME.
HUH?

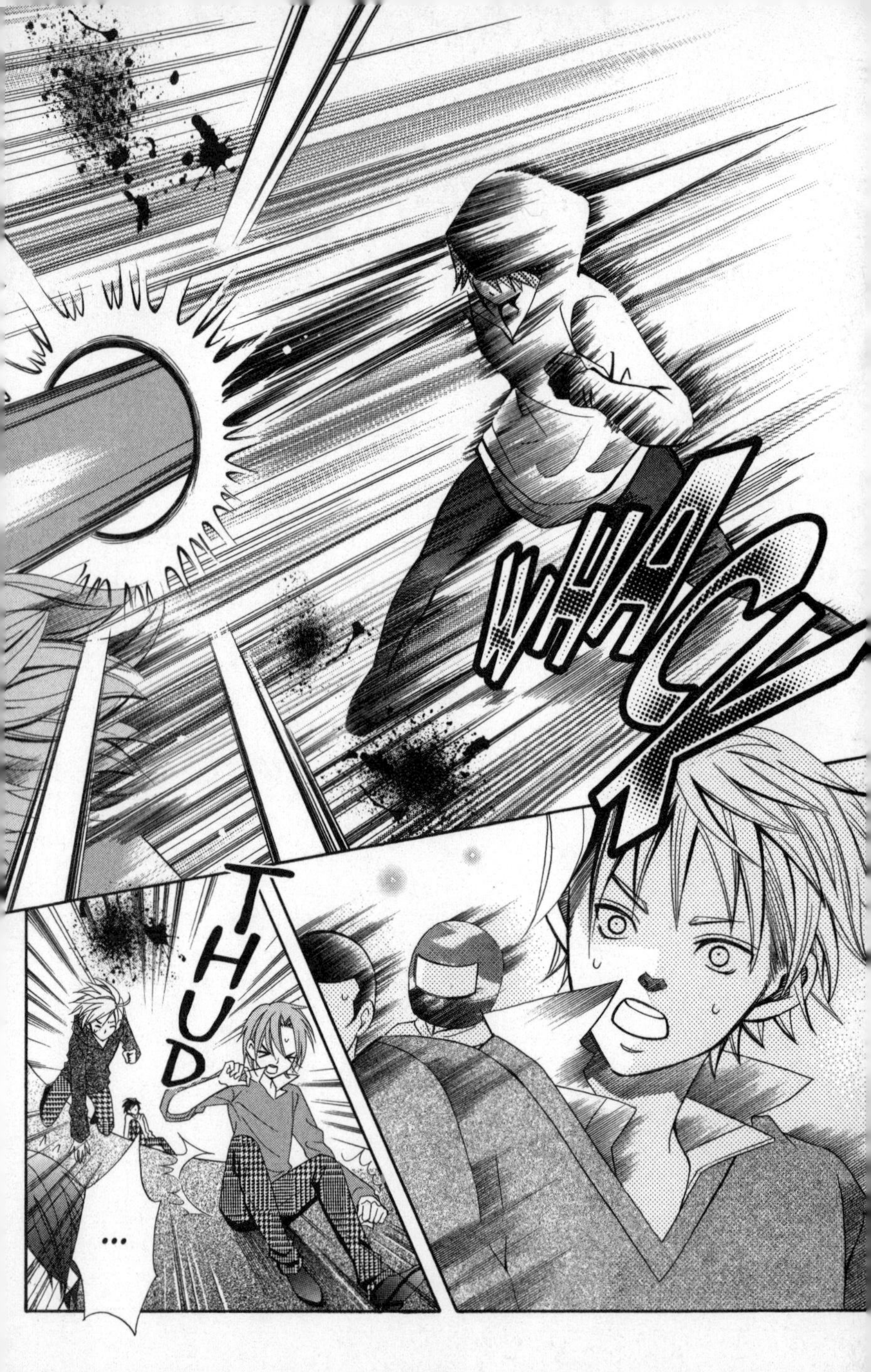
WHACK
THUD
...

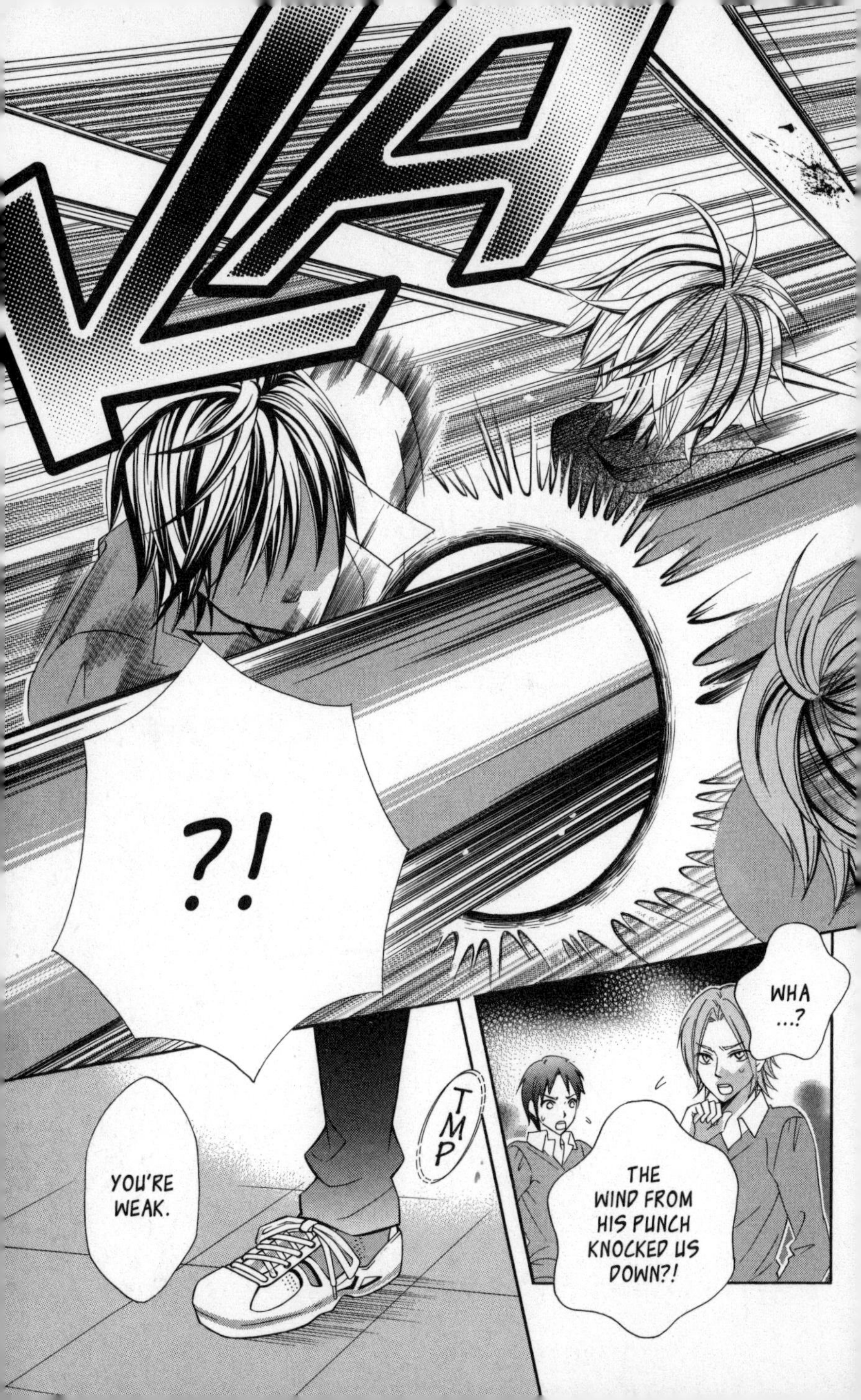
?!
WHA ...?
THE WIND FROM HIS PUNCH KNOCKED US DOWN?!
TMP
YOU'RE WEAK.

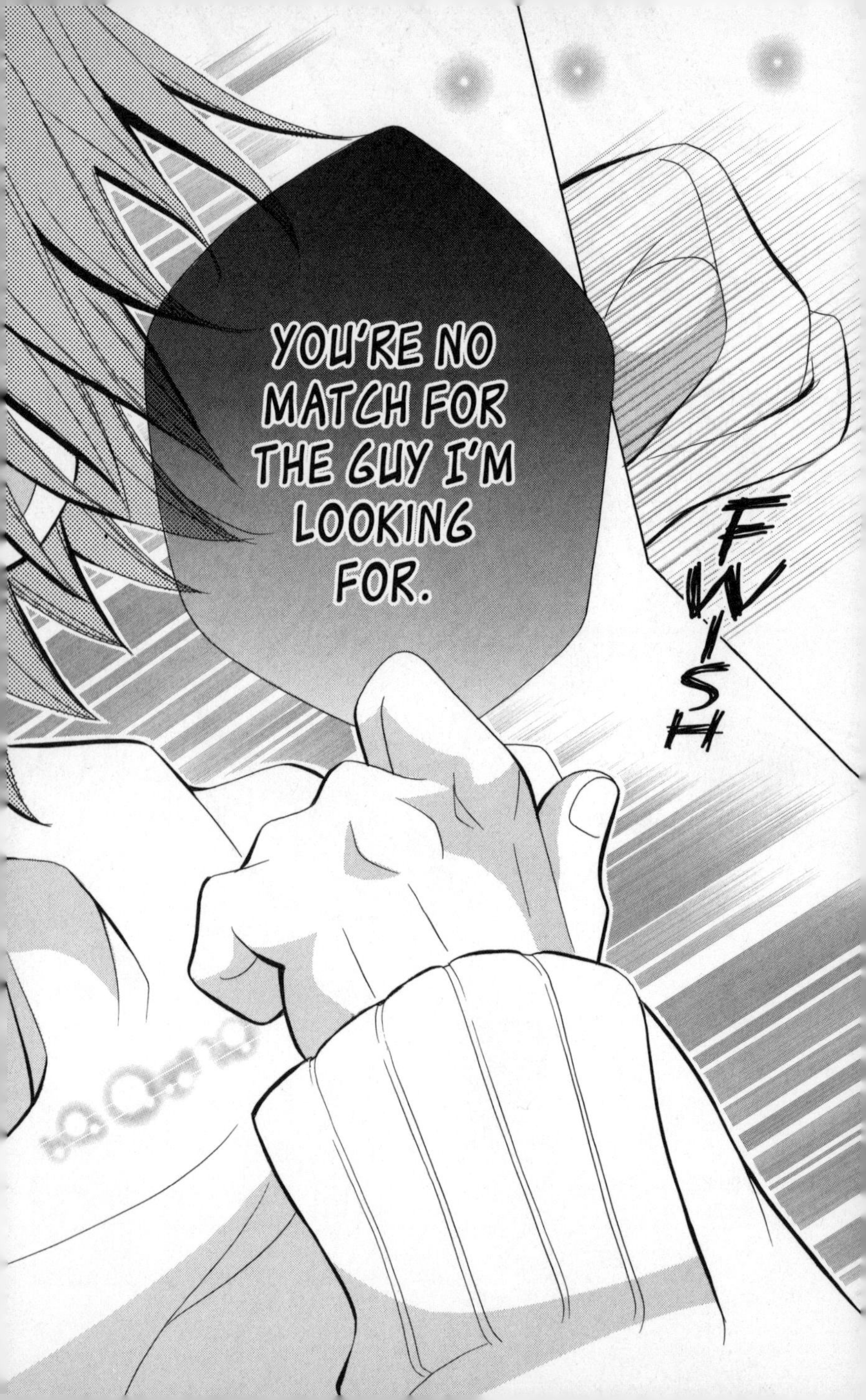
YOU'RE NO MATCH FOR THE GUY I'M LOOKING FOR.
FWISH

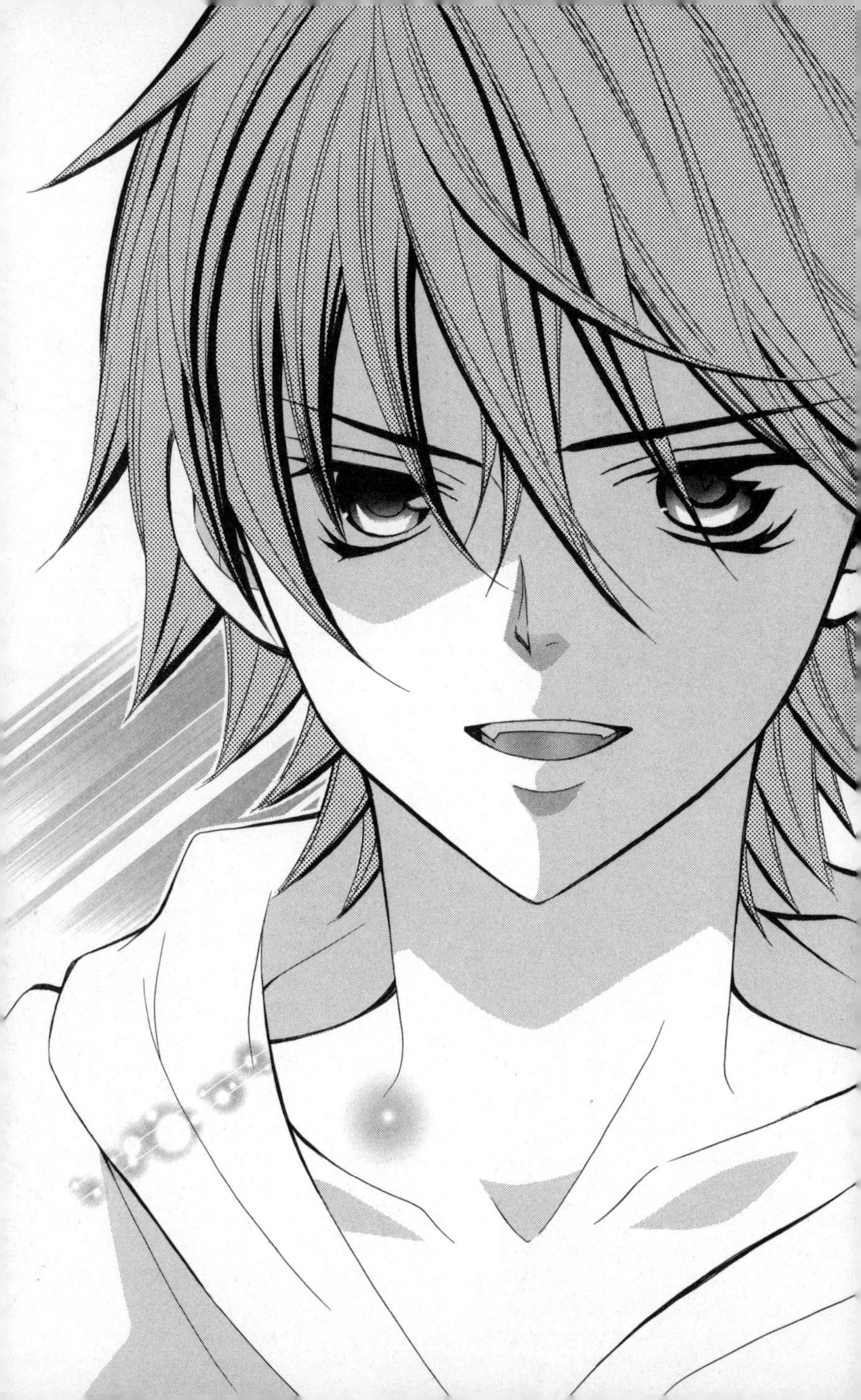

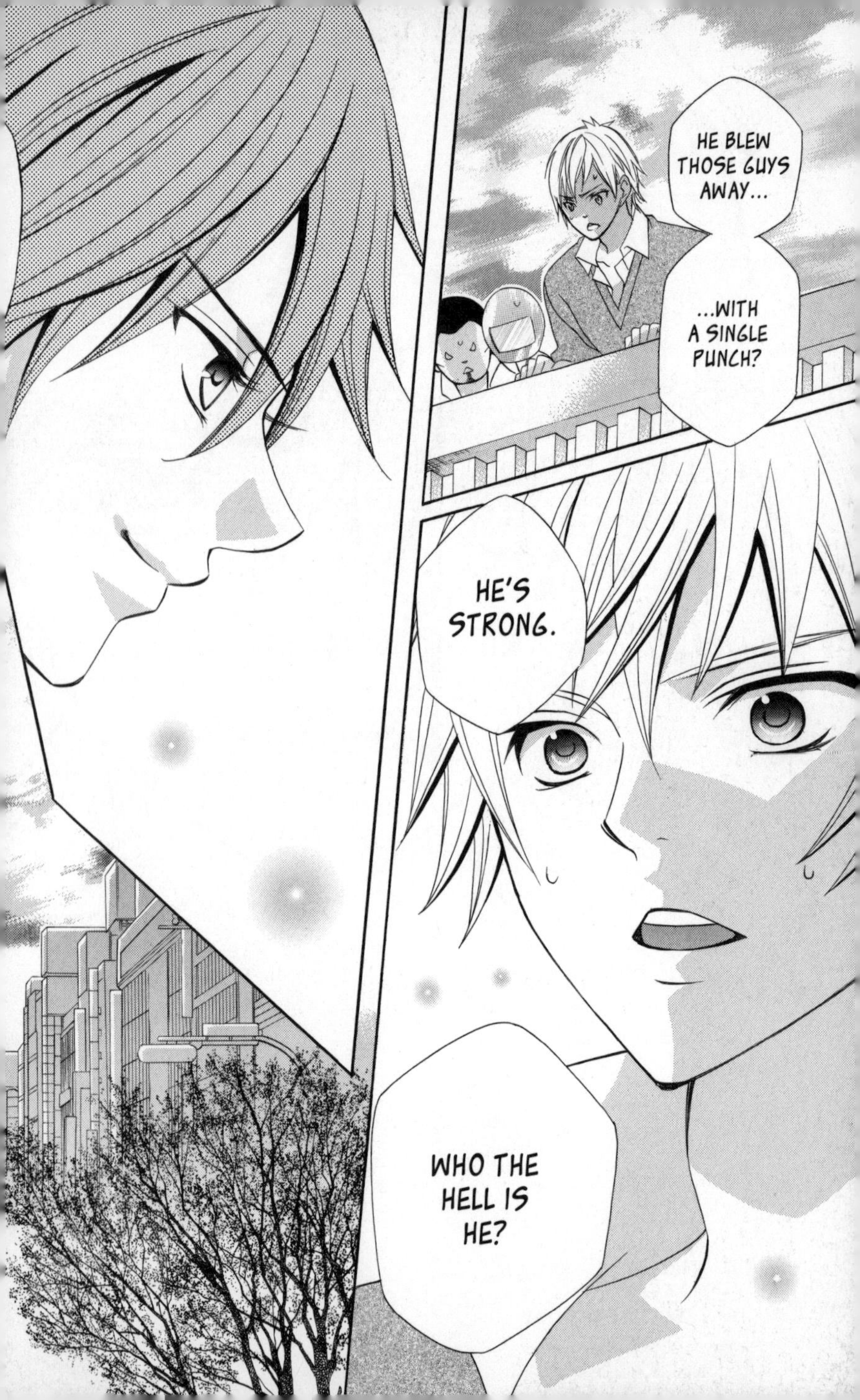
HE BLEW THOSE GUYS AWAY...
...WITH A SINGLE PUNCH?
HE'S STRONG.
WHO THE HELL IS HE?

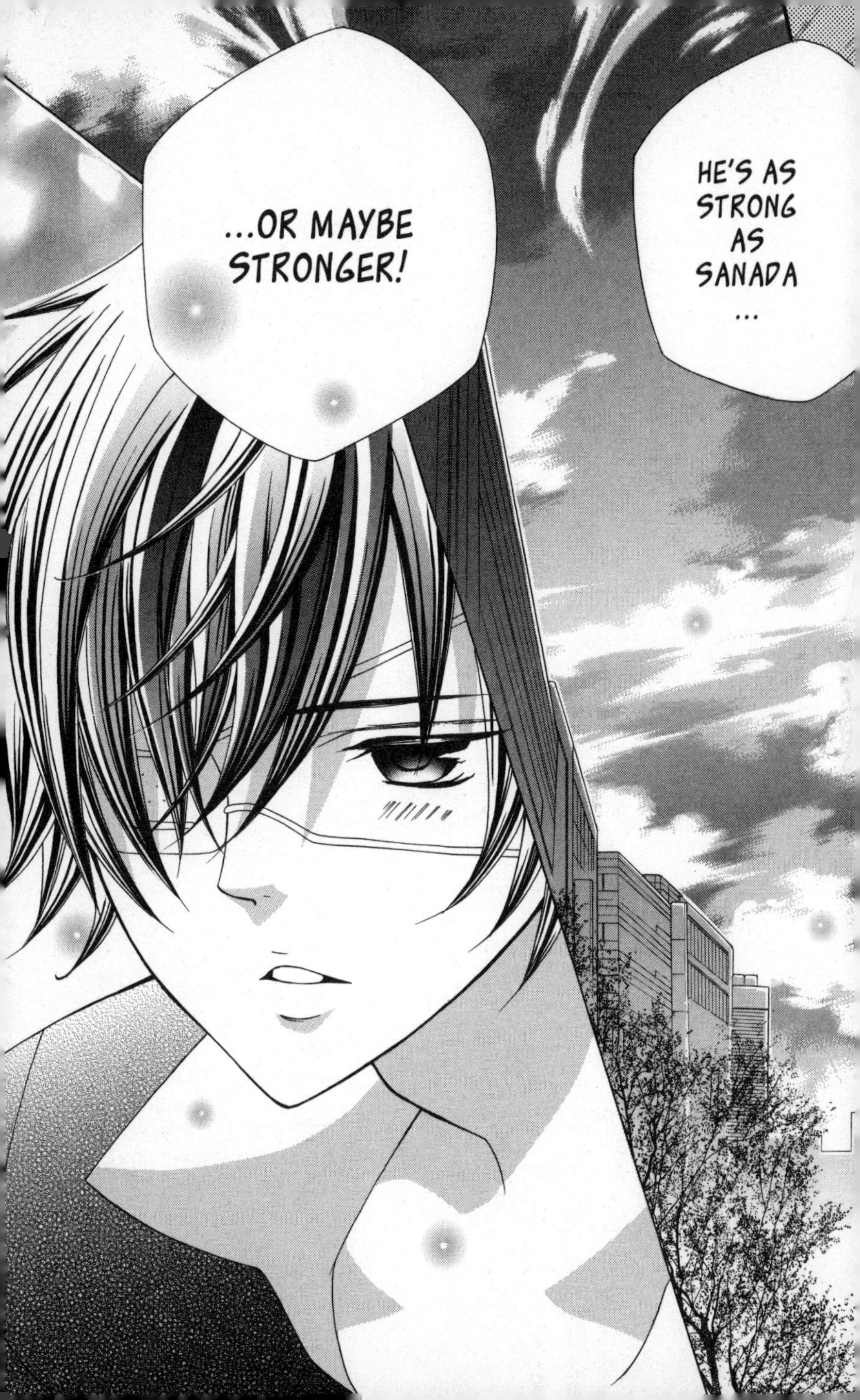
HE'S AS STRONG AS SANADA ...
...OR MAYBE STRONGER!

palet x So Cute! anime DVD theme song, "You Are My Miracle" ♪

THE IDOL GROUP palet SINGS THE THEME SONG OF THE NEW *SO CUTE!* ANIME! ♪ ♪

palet second single, "Keep on Lovin' You"
(also includes "You Are My Miracle")

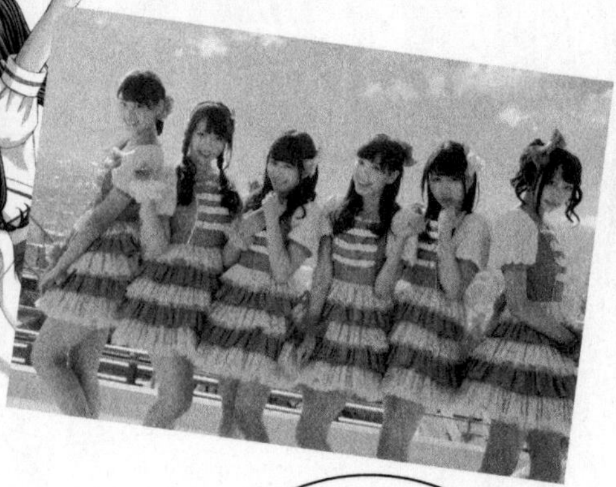

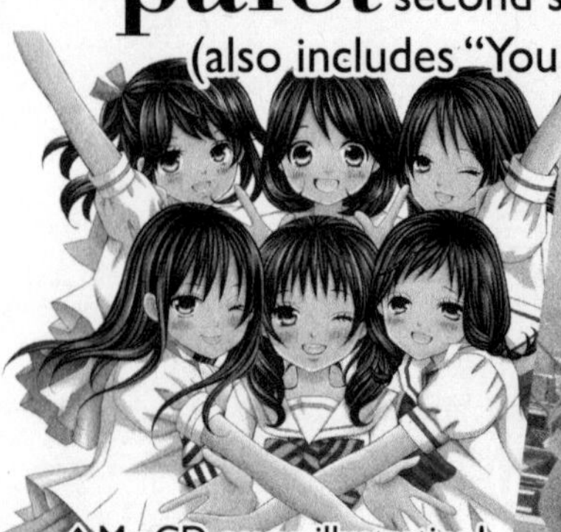

↑ My CD cover illustration!

THE SONG WAS WRITTEN WITH *SO CUTE!* IN MIND! (^O^) I'M MOVED THAT IT'S SUCH A CUTE AND DELIGHTFUL SONG (TOT)!! palet's VERY CUTE BUT POWERFUL SINGING MAKES MY HEART TWINGE AND SINK INTO MY SOUL. ♡♡

THE CD COMES IN THREE VERSIONS, AND I DREW THE COVER FOR THE B VERSION (^O^) ♪ ♪ I WAS VERY NERVOUS DRAWING THE COVER, BUT I REALLY ENJOYED DOING IT, SO I HOPE YOU'LL GET THIS VERSION. ♡♡ I'M REALLY REALLY GRATEFUL TO palet! ♡♡

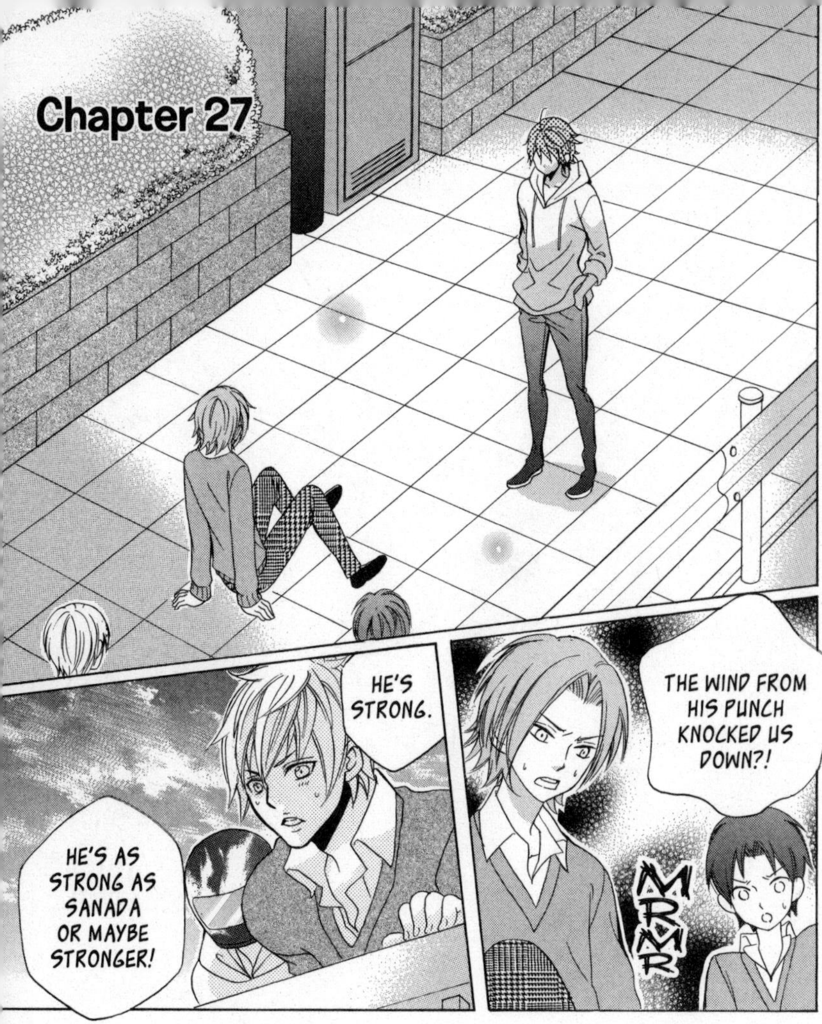
Chapter 27
THE WIND FROM HIS PUNCH KNOCKED US DOWN?!
MRMR
HE'S STRONG.
HE'S AS STRONG AS SANADA OR MAYBE STRONGER!

THE MANGA NOW HAS ITS OFFICIAL TWITTER ACCOUNT! ↓
@kobakawa_info
♡ SO TAKE A LOOK! ♡

THANK YOU FOR SENDING ME LOVELY LETTERS AND DRAWINGS! ♡♡ I WAS VERY HAPPY TO RECEIVE NEW YEAR'S CARDS TOO. ♡♡ (*^_^*)
IT'LL MAKE ME HAPPY IF YOU SEND YOUR THOUGHTS AND DRAWINGS AFTER READING VOLUME 6. ♡

GO IKEYAMADA
C/O SHOJO BEAT
VIZ MEDIA, LLC
P.O. BOX 77010
SAN FRANCISCO, CA
94107

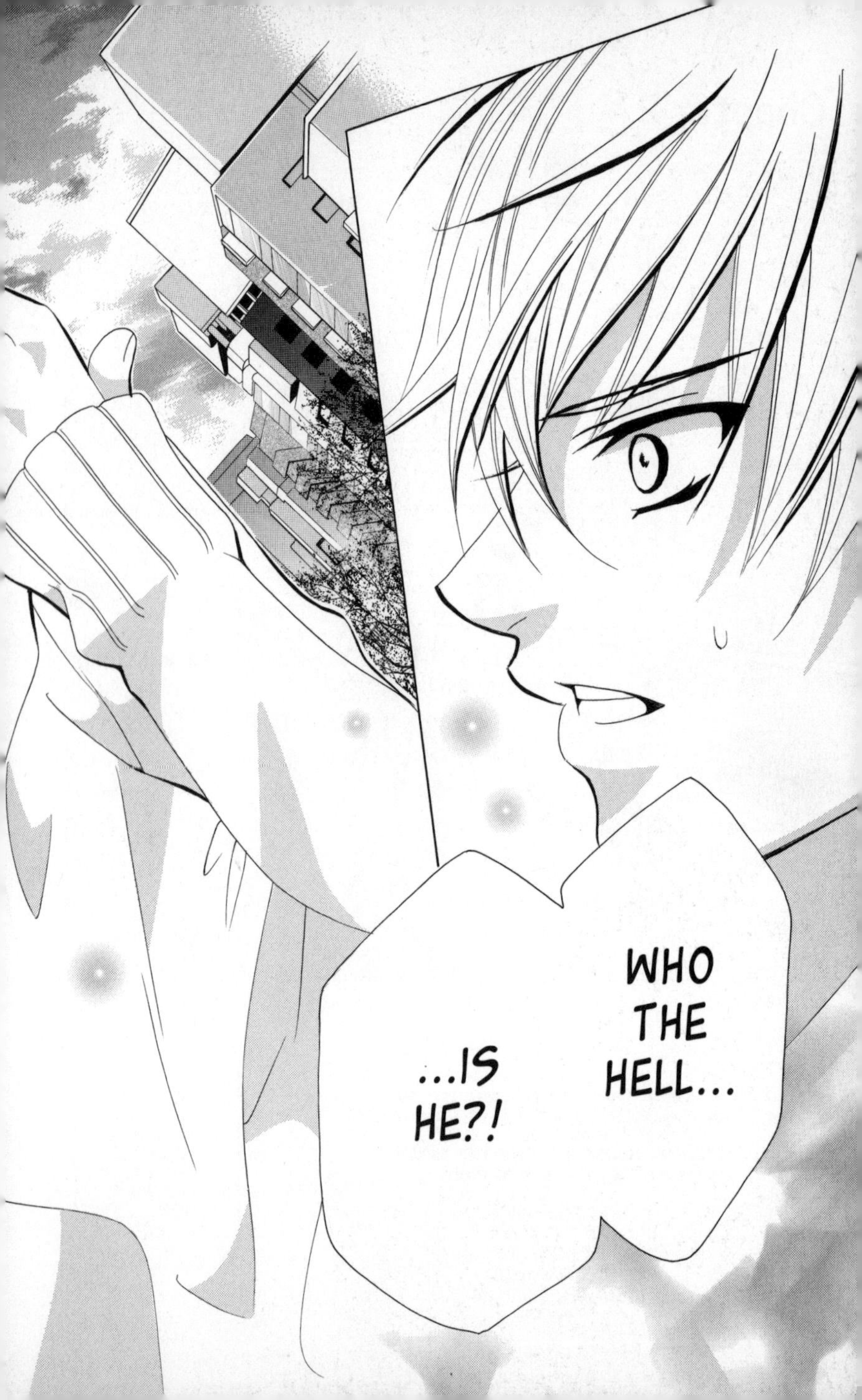
WHO THE HELL...
...IS HE?!

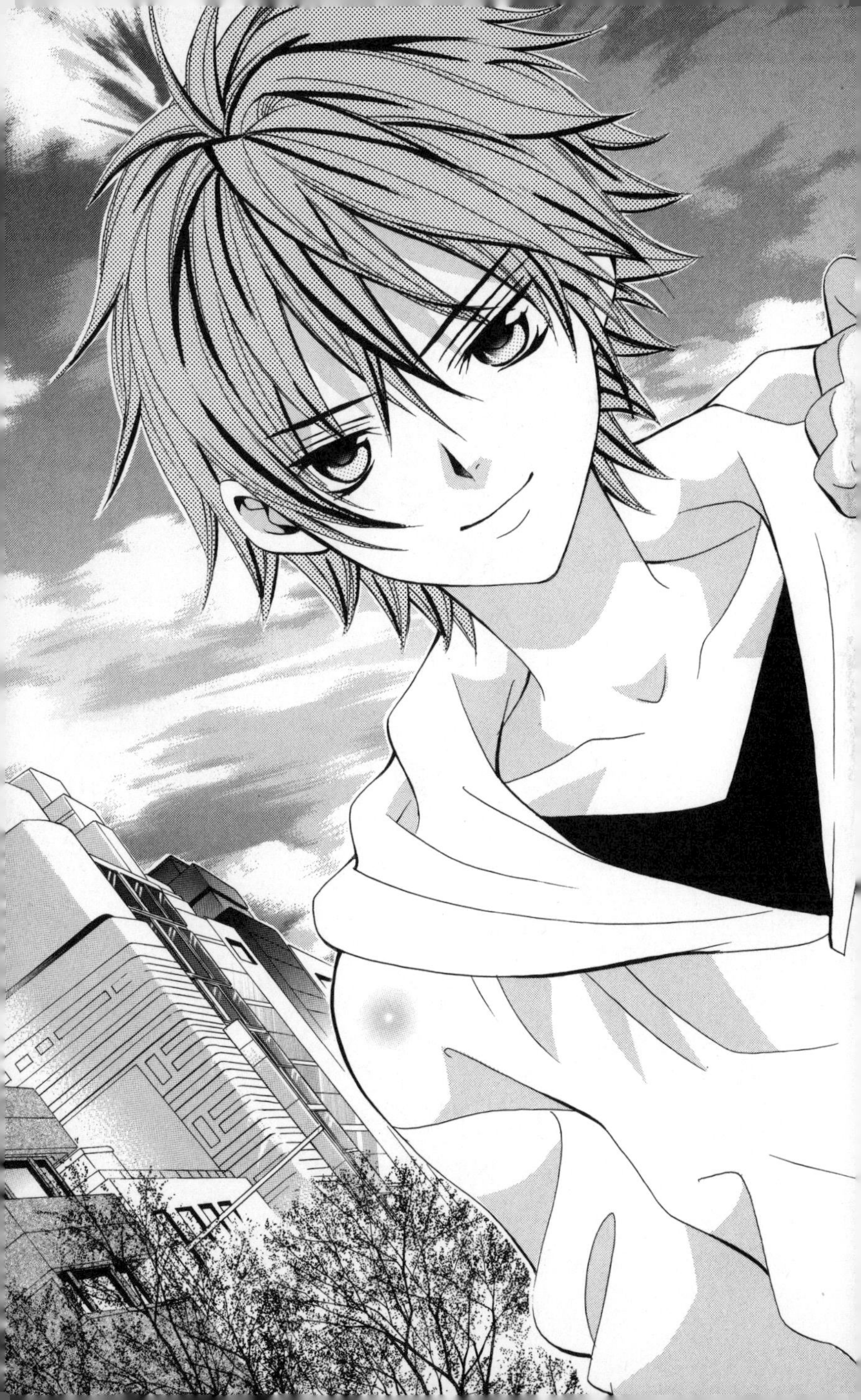

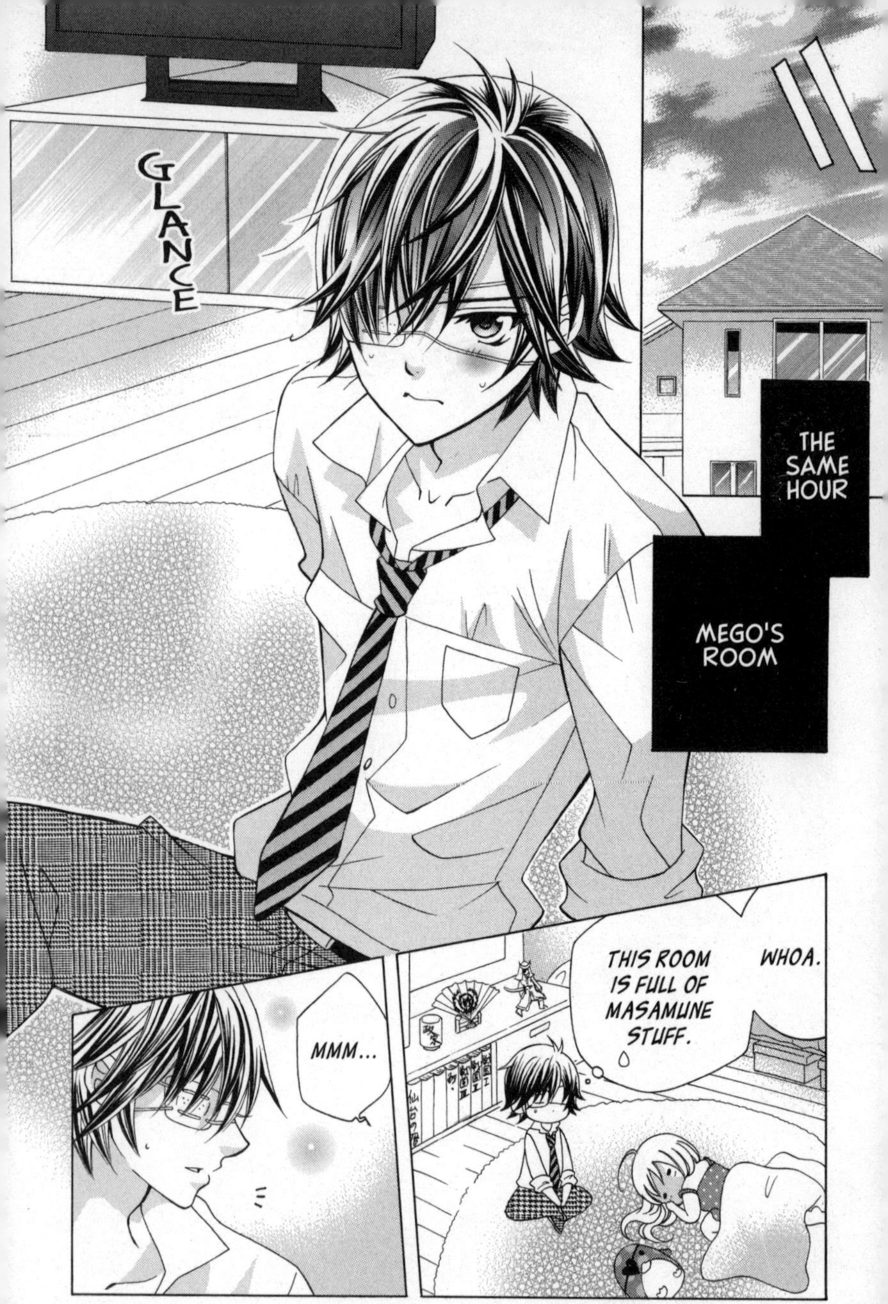
THE SAME HOUR
MEGO'S ROOM
GLANCE
WHOA.
THIS ROOM IS FULL OF MASAMUNE STUFF.
MMM...

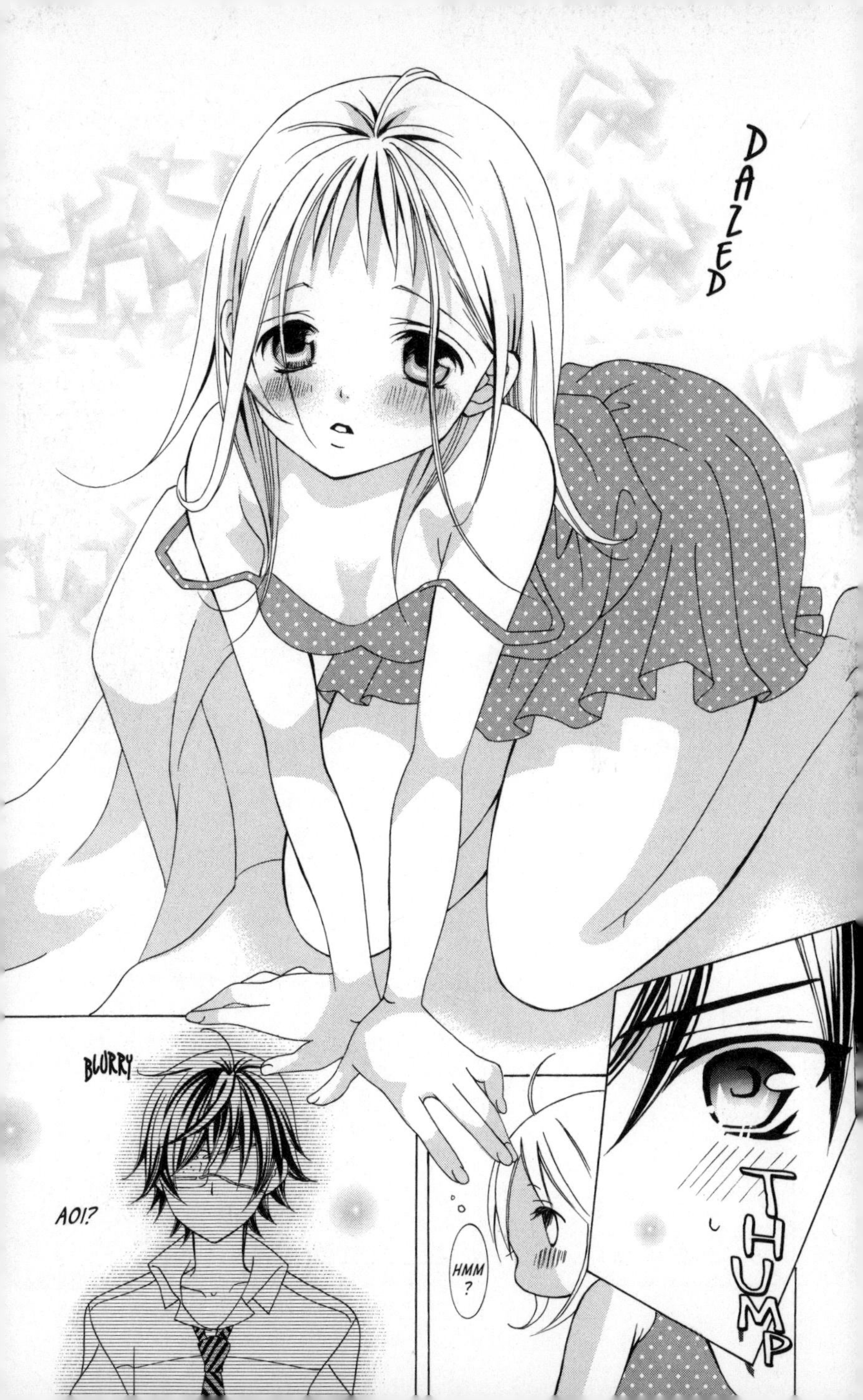
DAZED
THUMP
HMM?
BLURRY
AOI!?

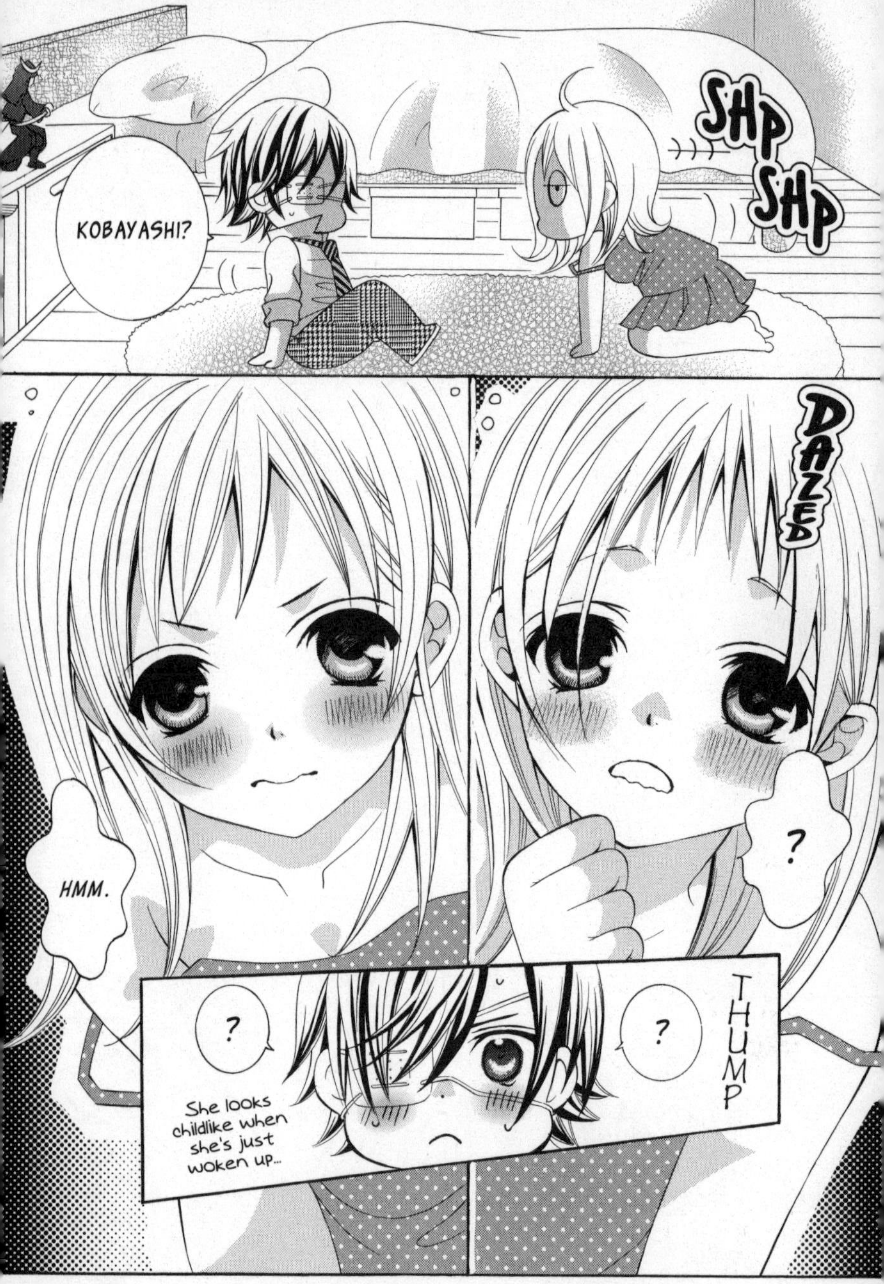
SHP SHP
KOBAYASHI?
DAZED
?
HMM.
THUMP
?
?
She looks childlike when she's just woken up...

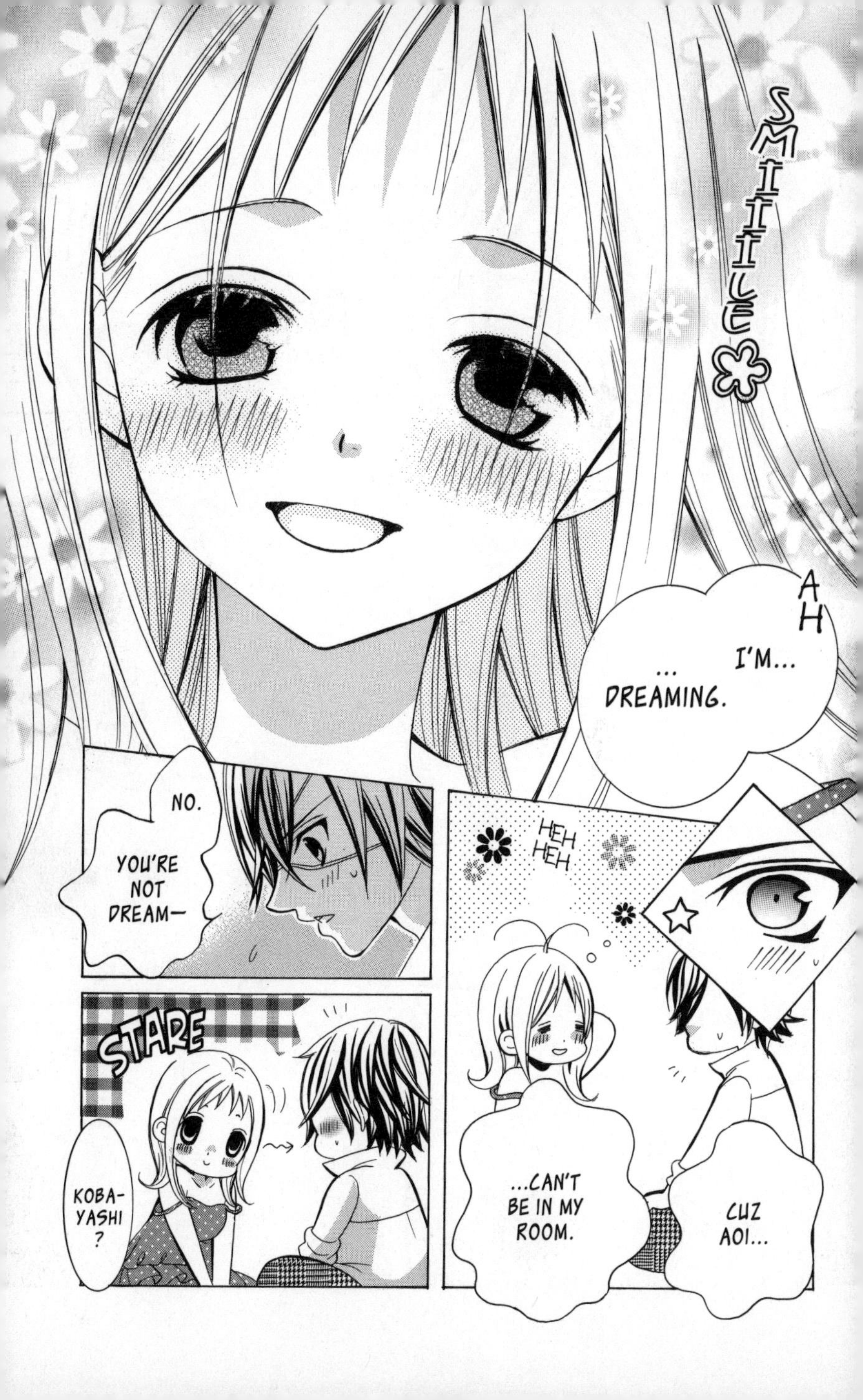
SMIIILE
AH
I'M... ...DREAMING.
HEH HEH
CUZ AOI...
...CAN'T BE IN MY ROOM.
NO. YOU'RE NOT DREAM—
STARE
KOBA-YASHI?

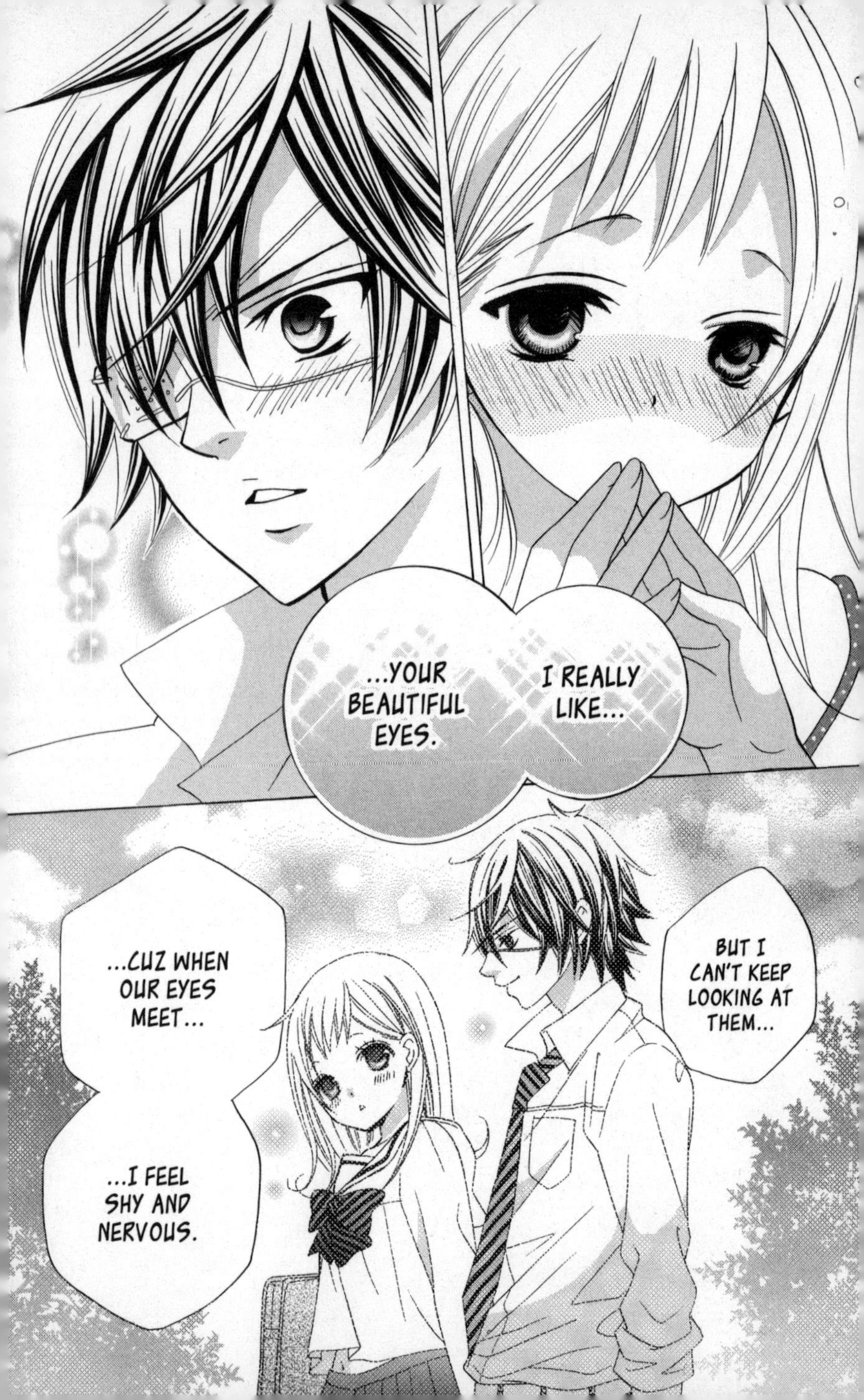
I REALLY LIKE...
...YOUR BEAUTIFUL EYES.
BUT I CAN'T KEEP LOOKING AT THEM...
...CUZ WHEN OUR EYES MEET...
...I FEEL SHY AND NERVOUS.

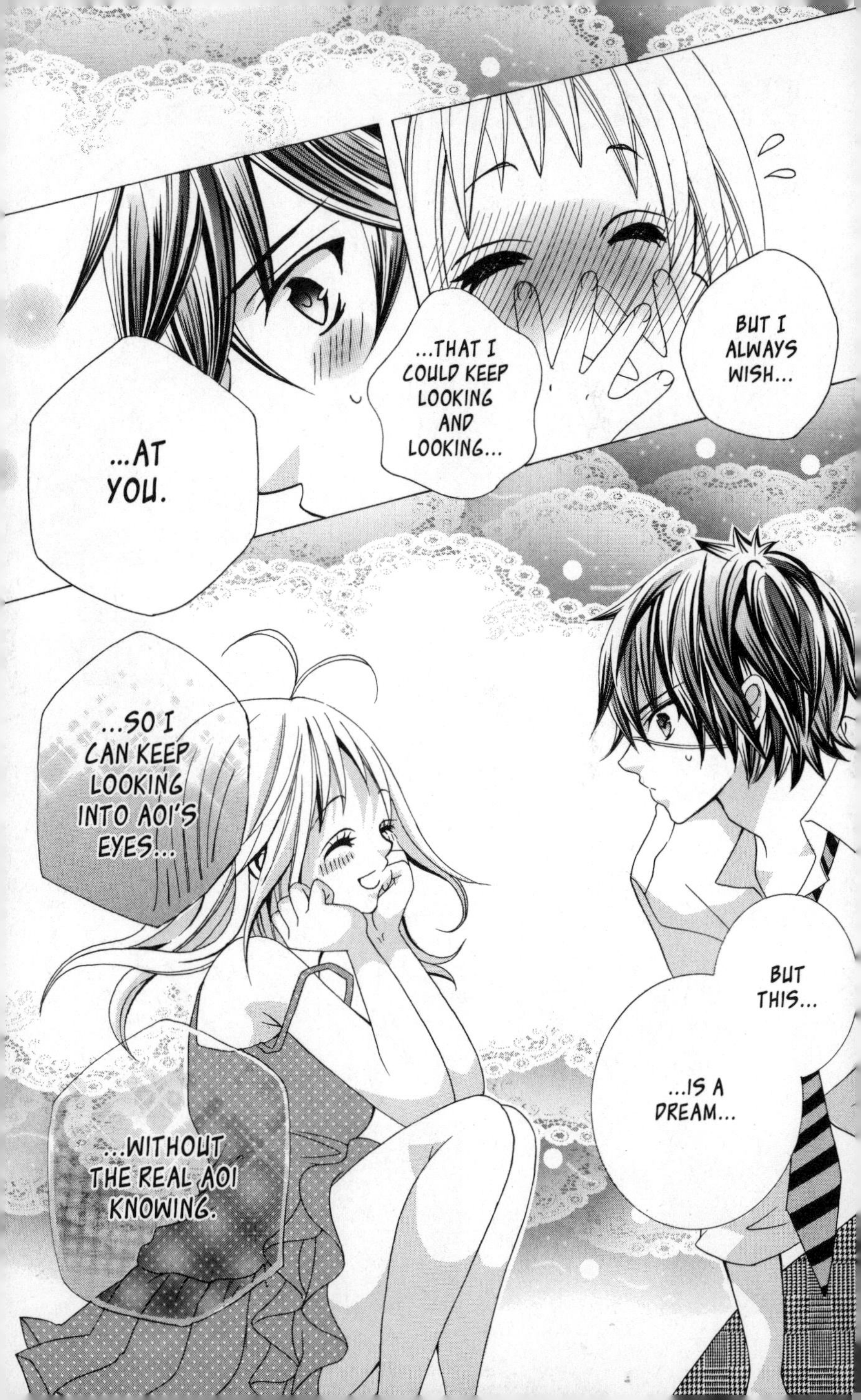
BUT I ALWAYS WISH...
...THAT I COULD KEEP LOOKING AND LOOKING...
...AT YOU.
BUT THIS...
...IS A DREAM...
...SO I CAN KEEP LOOKING INTO AOI'S EYES...
...WITHOUT THE REAL AOI KNOWING.

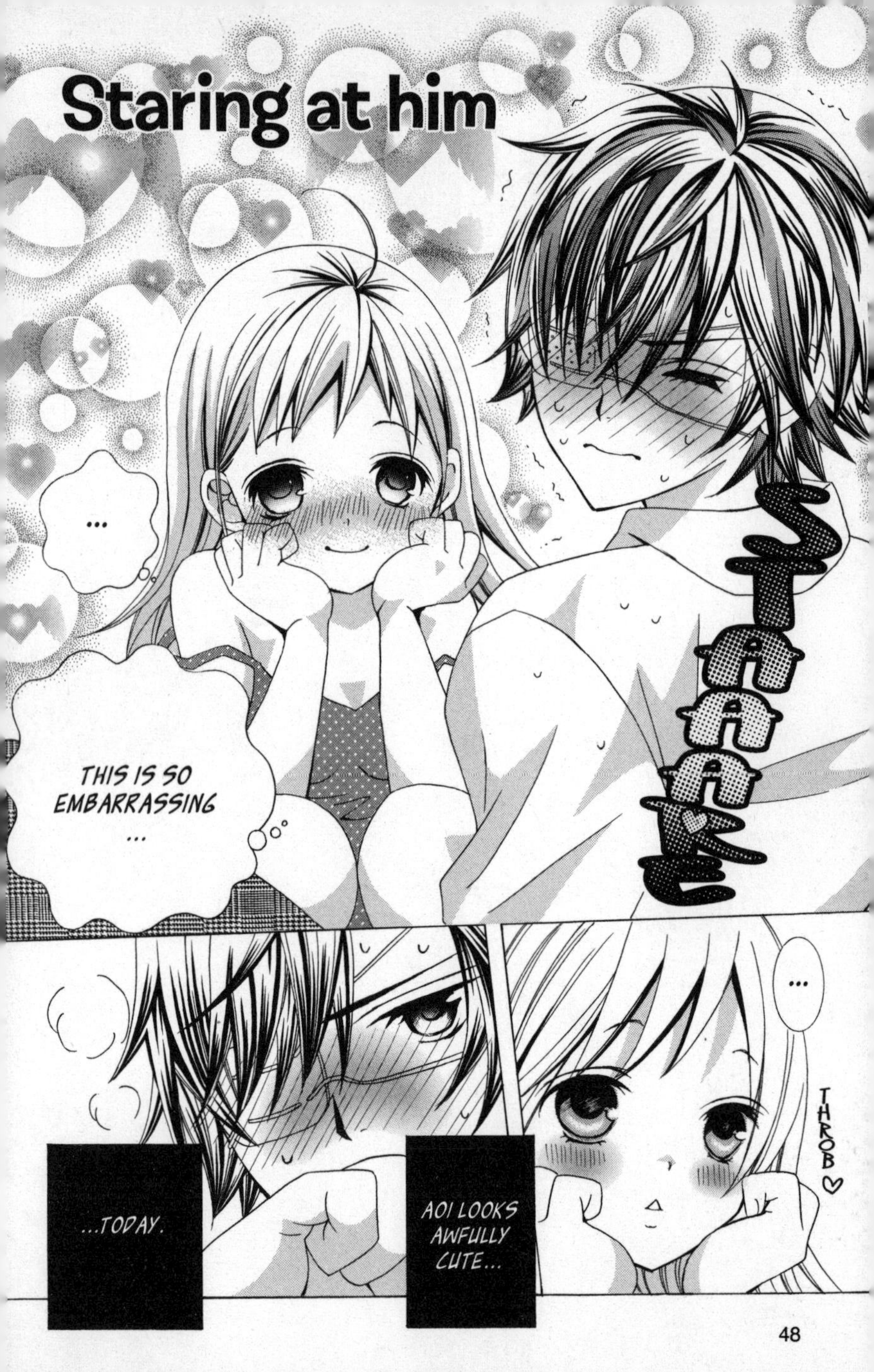
Staring at him
STAAARE
...
THIS IS SO EMBARRASSING...
...
THROB
AOI LOOKS AWFULLY CUTE...
...TODAY.

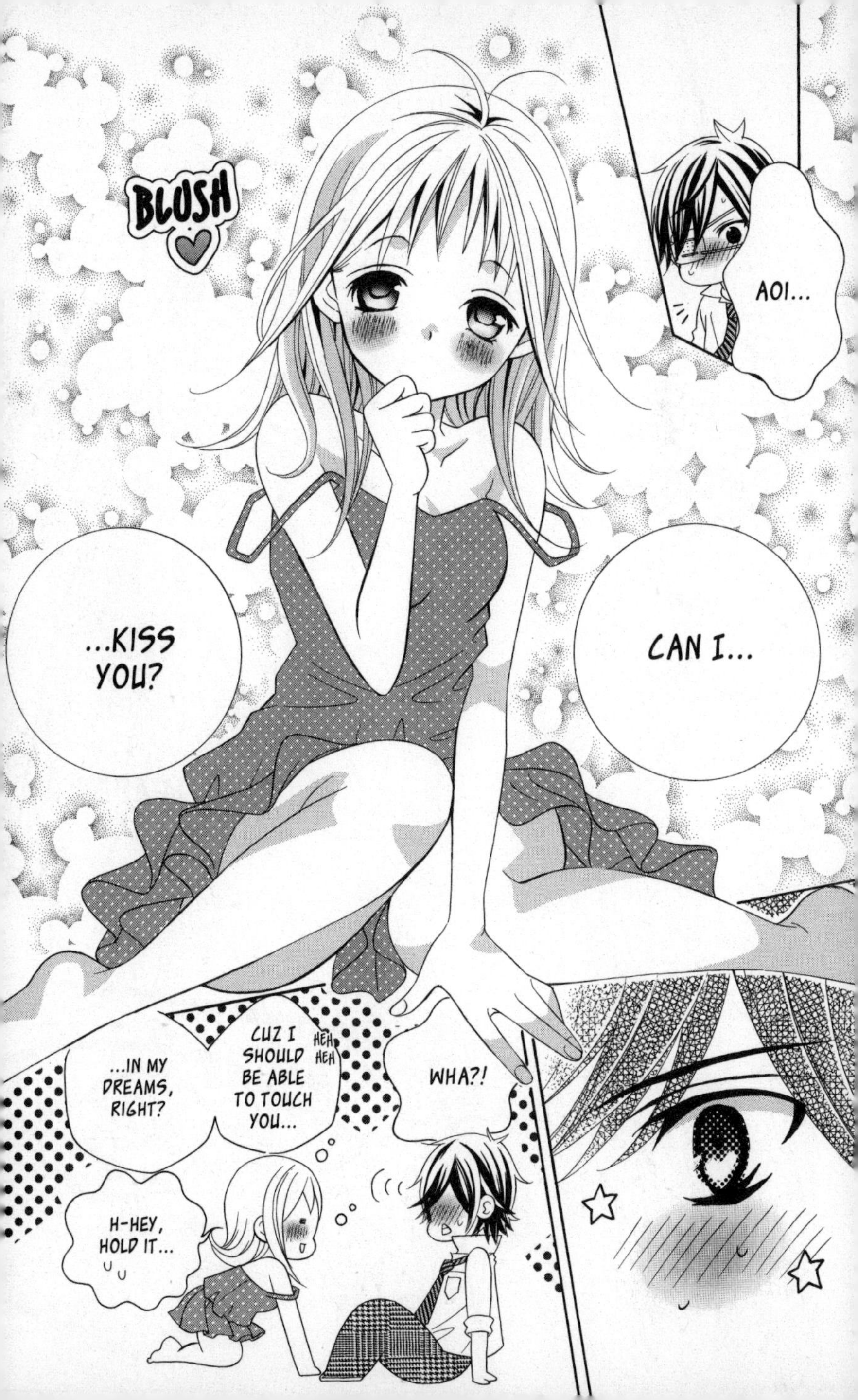
AOI...
CAN I...
...KISS YOU?
BLUSH
WHA?!
CUZ I SHOULD BE ABLE TO TOUCH YOU...
HEH HEH
...IN MY DREAMS, RIGHT?
H-HEY, HOLD IT...

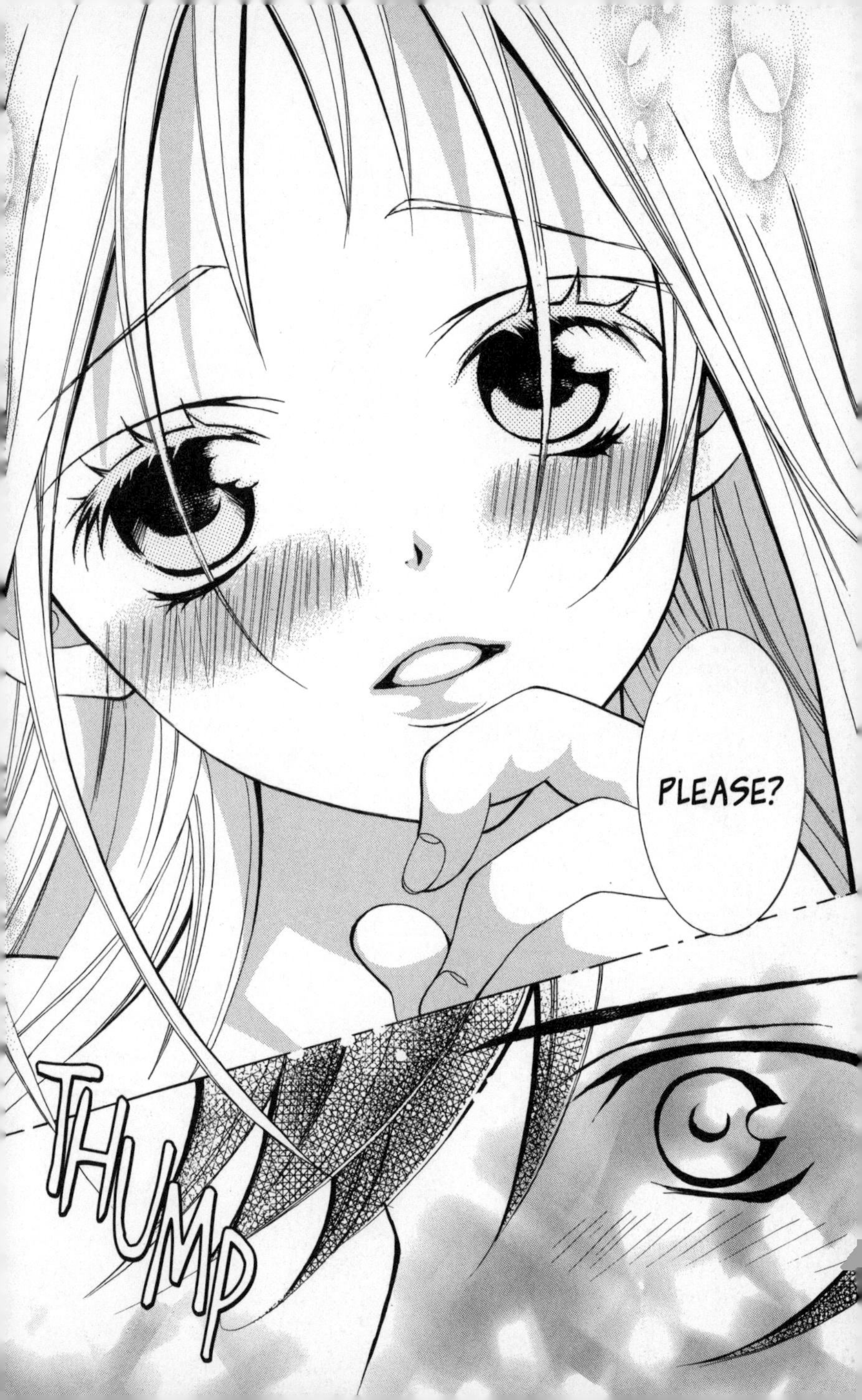
PLEASE?
THUMP

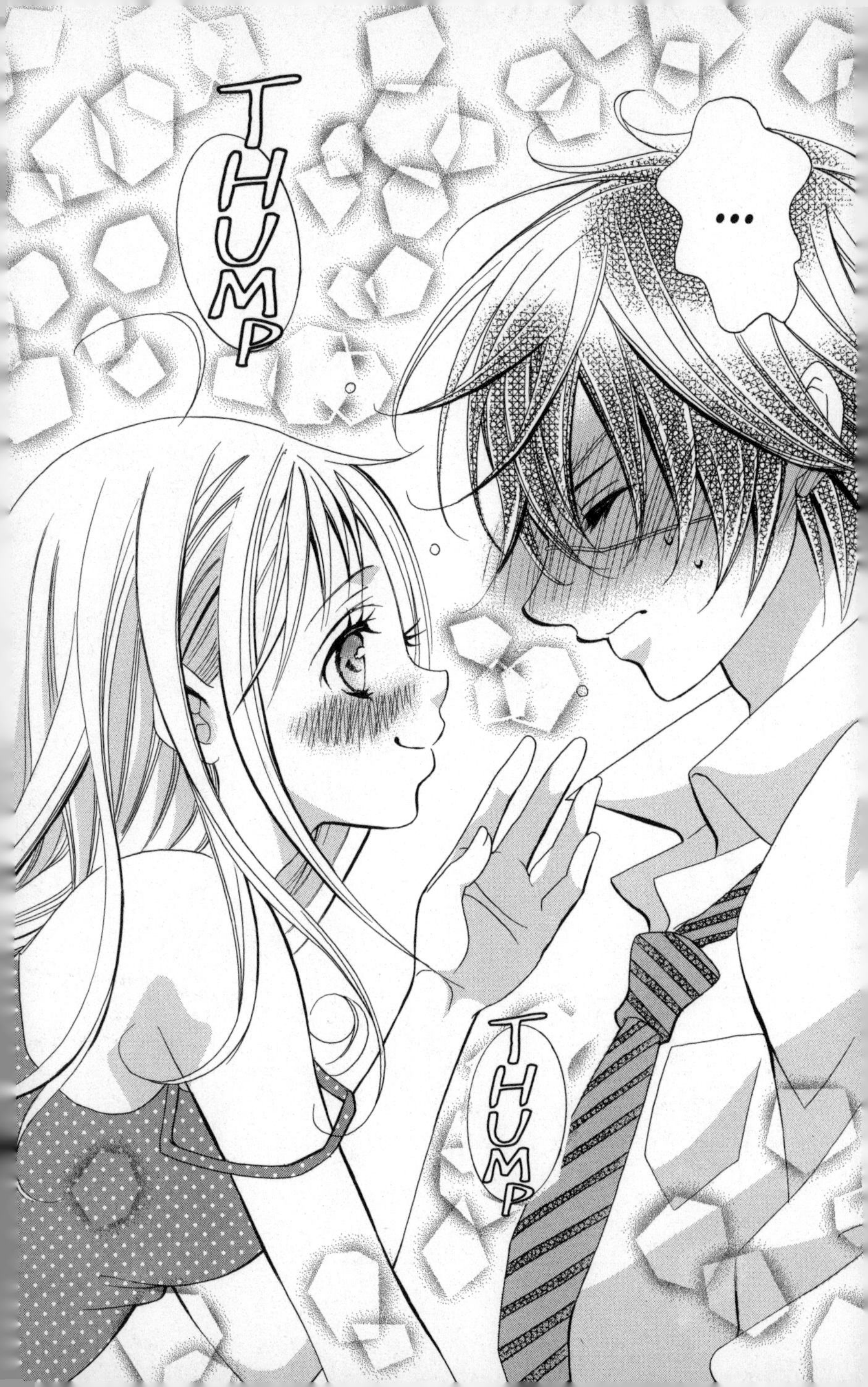
...
THUMP
THUMP

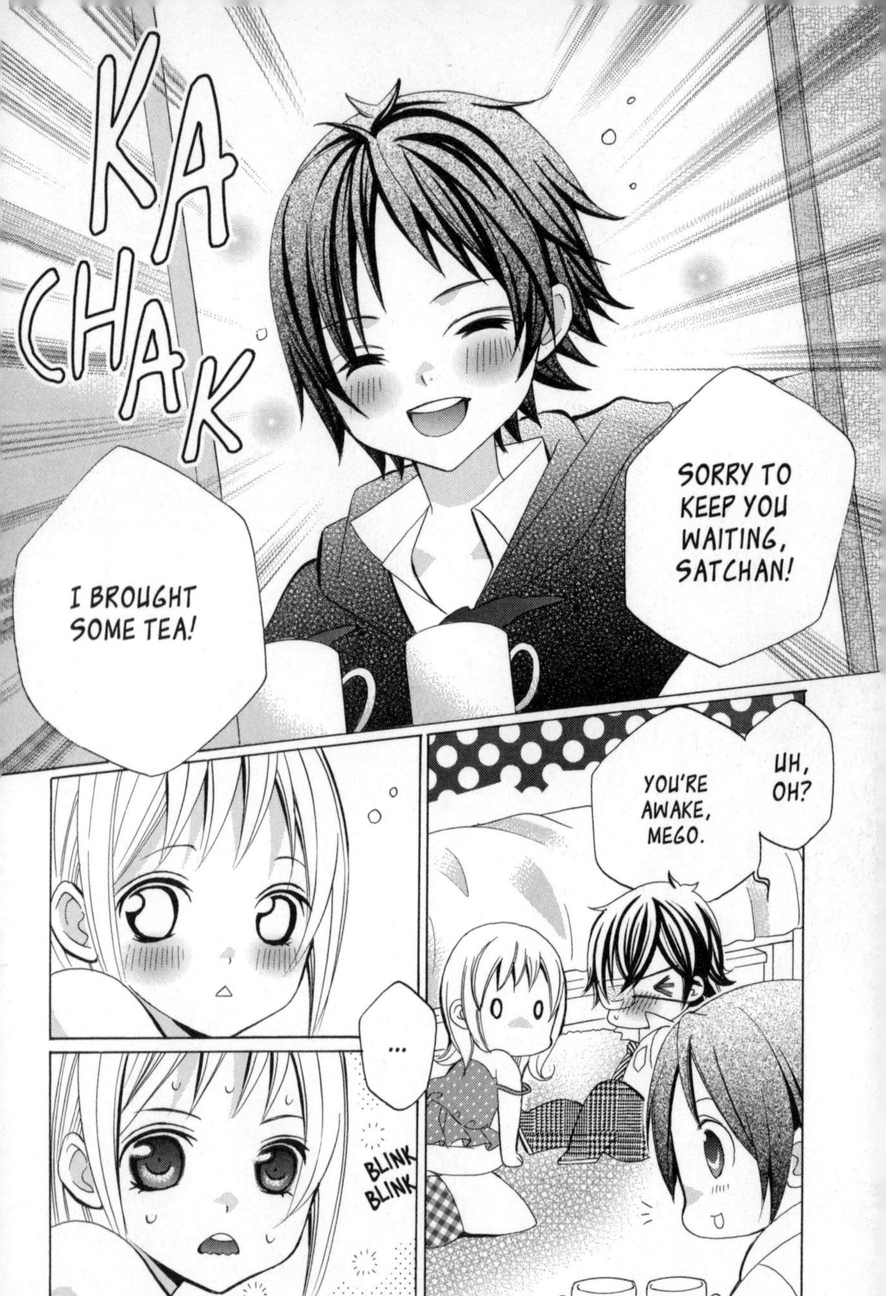
KA CHAK
SORRY TO KEEP YOU WAITING, SATCHAN!
I BROUGHT SOME TEA!
UH, OH?
YOU'RE AWAKE, MEGO.
...
BLINK BLINK

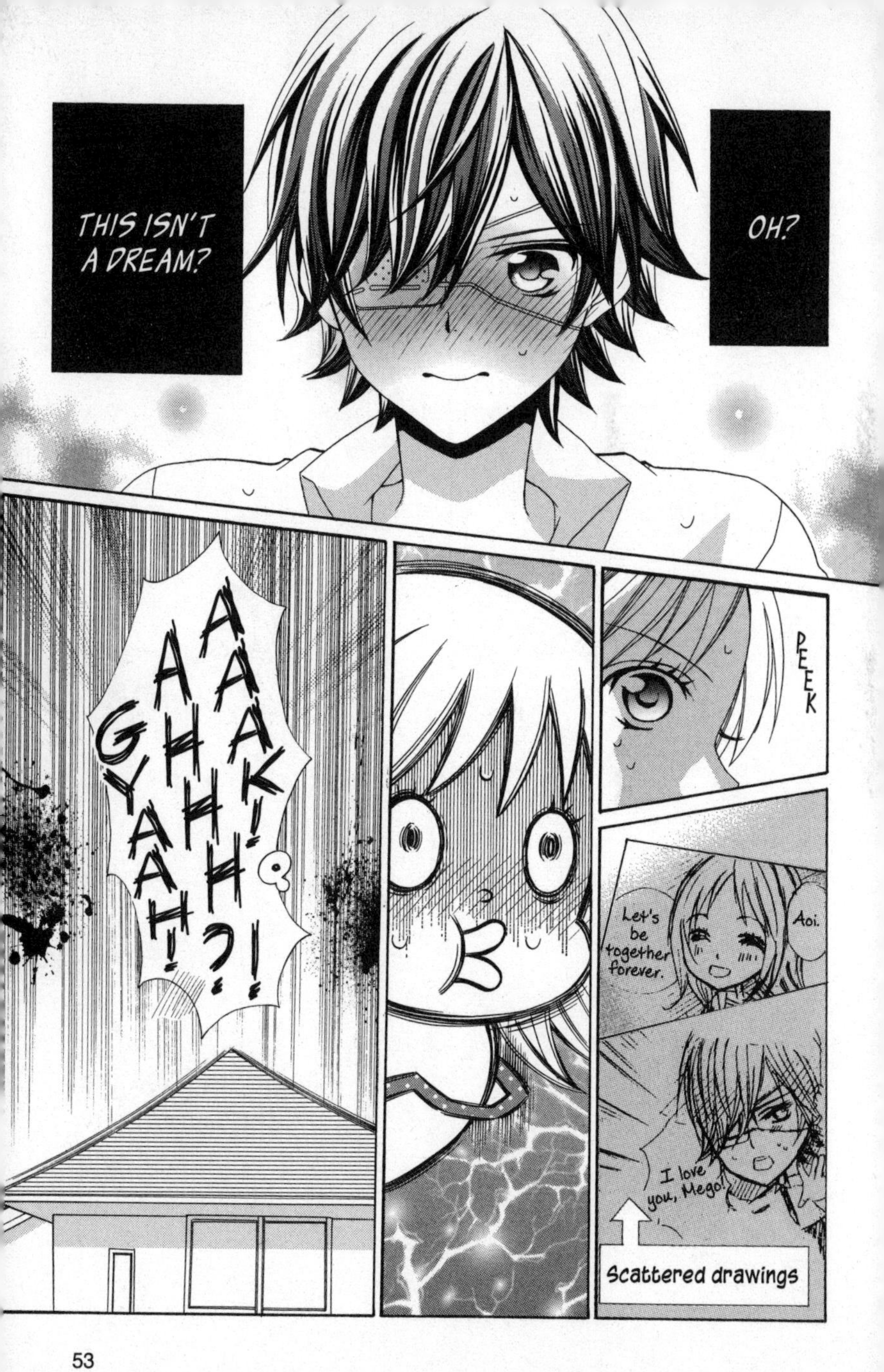
OH?
THIS ISN'T A DREAM?
PEEK
Aoi.
Let's be together forever.
I love you, Mego!
Scattered drawings
AAAK! AHHH?! GYAAH!

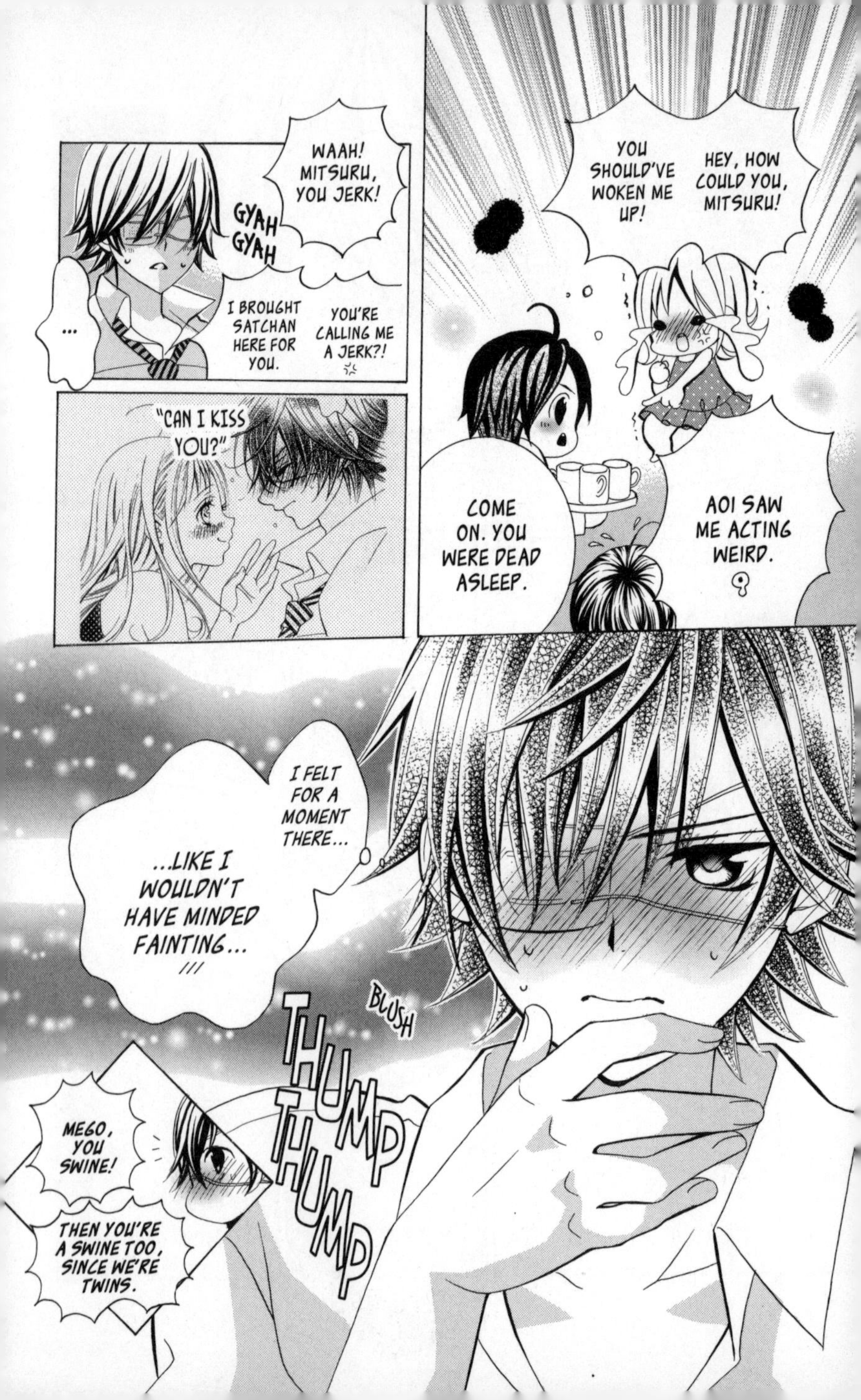
HEY, HOW COULD YOU, MITSURU!
YOU SHOULD'VE WOKEN ME UP!
AOI SAW ME ACTING WEIRD.
COME ON. YOU WERE DEAD ASLEEP.
WAAH! MITSURU, YOU JERK!
GYAH GYAH
YOU'RE CALLING ME A JERK?!
I BROUGHT SATCHAN HERE FOR YOU.
...
"CAN I KISS YOU?"
I FELT FOR A MOMENT THERE...
...LIKE I WOULDN'T HAVE MINDED FAINTING...
BLUSH
THUMP THUMP
MEGO, YOU SWINE!
THEN YOU'RE A SWINE TOO, SINCE WE'RE TWINS.

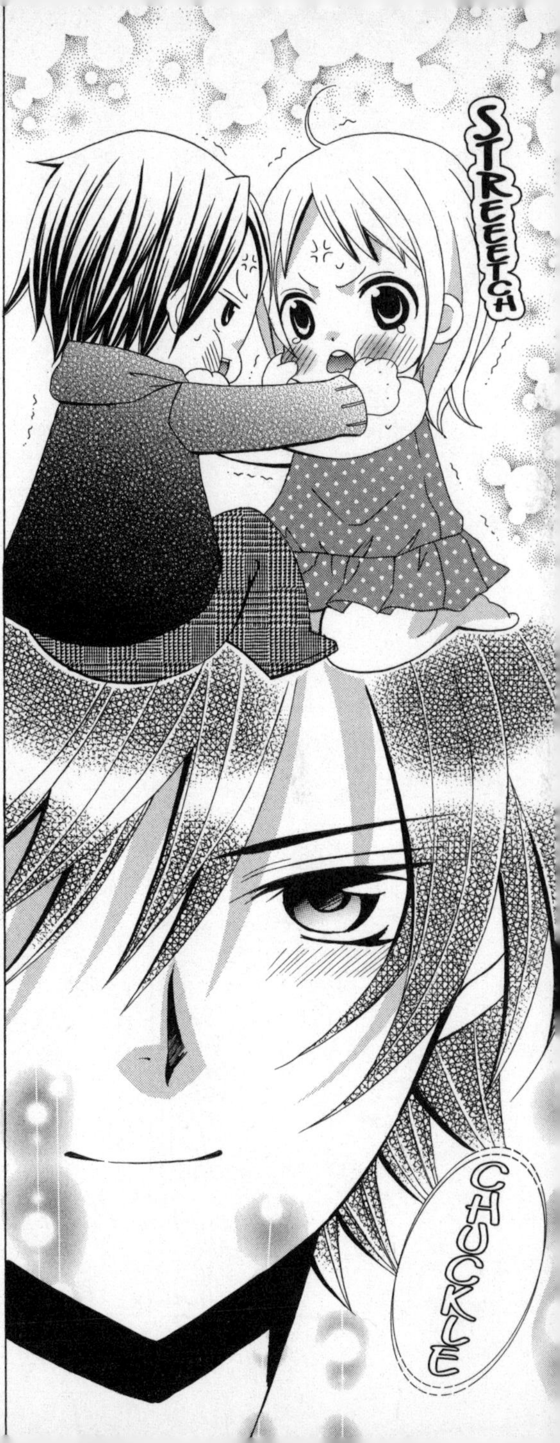
STREEETCH
CHUCKLE

SPECIAL THANKS

Yuka Ito-sama, Rieko Hirai-sama, Kayoko Takahashi-sama, Yukako Kawasaki-sama, Nagisa Sato Sensei.

Rei Nanase Sensei, Arisu Fujishiro Sensei, Mumi Mimura Sensei, Masayo Nagata-sama, Naochan-sama, Asuka Sakura Sensei and many others.

Bookstore Dan Kinshicho Branch, Kinokuniya Shinjuku Branch, LIBRO Ikebukuro Branch, Kinokuniya Hankyu 32-Bangai Branch.

Sendai Hachimonjiya Bookstore, BOOKS HOSHINO Kintetsu Pass'e Branch, Asahiya Tennnoji MiO Branch, Kurashiki Kikuya Bookstore.

Salesperson:
Hata-sama

First salesperson:
Honma-sama

Previous editor:
Nakata-sama

Current editor:
Shoji-sama

My sincerest gratitude to everyone who picked up this volume.

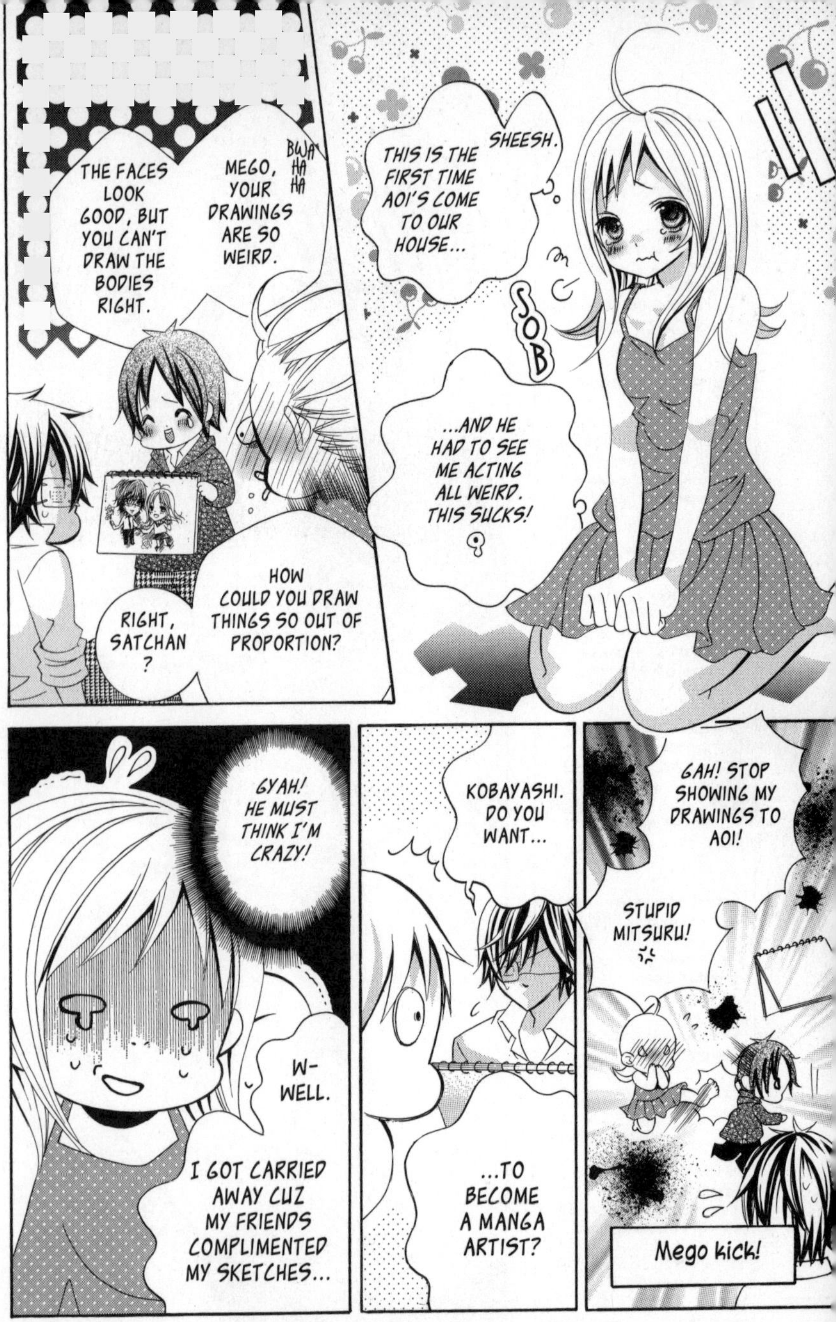
SHEESH.
THIS IS THE FIRST TIME AOI'S COME TO OUR HOUSE...
SOB
...AND HE HAD TO SEE ME ACTING ALL WEIRD. THIS SUCKS!
BWA HA HA
MEGO, YOUR DRAWINGS ARE SO WEIRD.
THE FACES LOOK GOOD, BUT YOU CAN'T DRAW THE BODIES RIGHT.
HOW COULD YOU DRAW THINGS SO OUT OF PROPORTION?
RIGHT, SATCHAN?
GAH! STOP SHOWING MY DRAWINGS TO AOI!
STUPID MITSURU!
Mego kick!
KOBAYASHI. DO YOU WANT...
...TO BECOME A MANGA ARTIST?
GYAH! HE MUST THINK I'M CRAZY!
W-WELL.
I GOT CARRIED AWAY CUZ MY FRIENDS COMPLIMENTED MY SKETCHES...

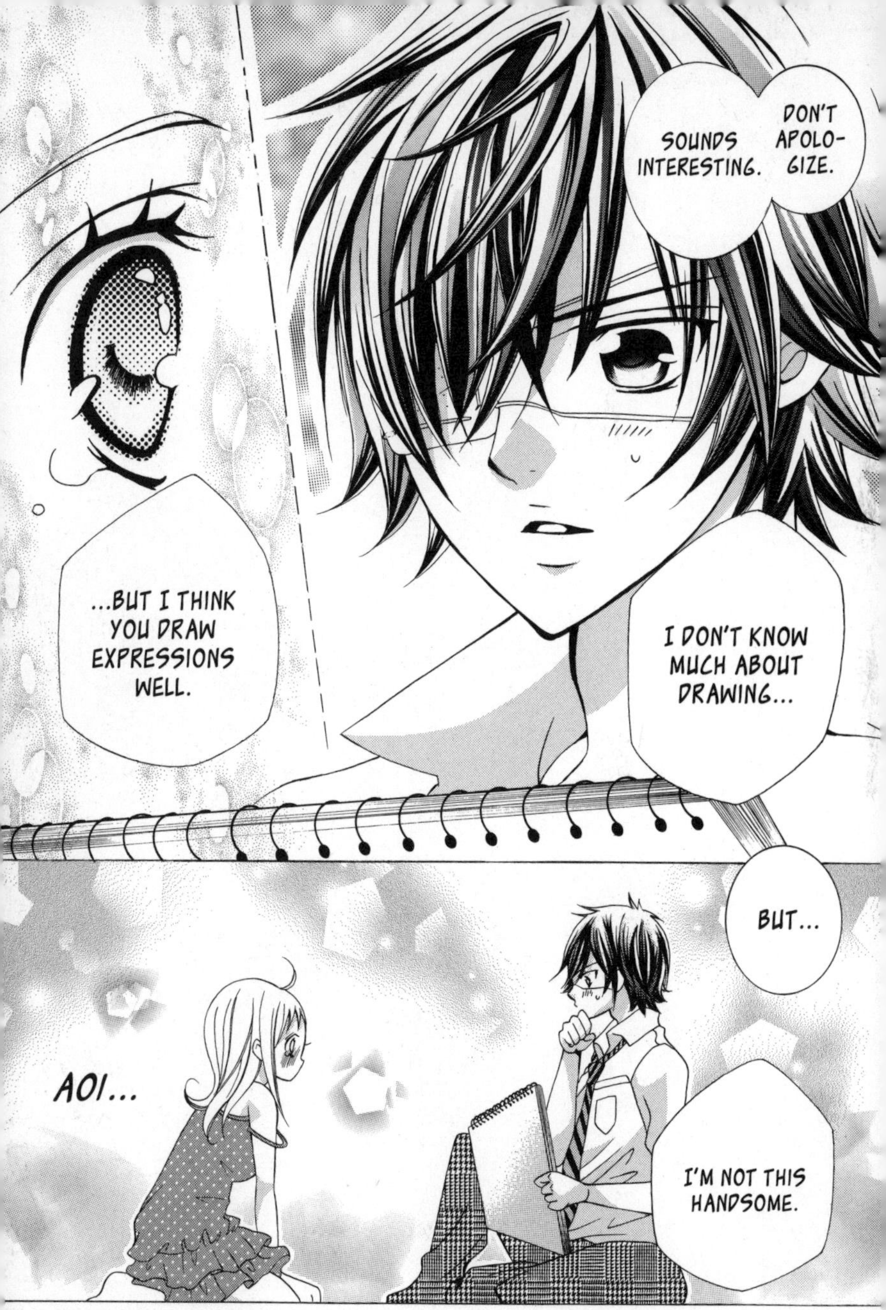
DON'T APOLO-GIZE.
SOUNDS INTERESTING.
I DON'T KNOW MUCH ABOUT DRAWING...
...BUT I THINK YOU DRAW EXPRESSIONS WELL.
BUT...
I'M NOT THIS HANDSOME.
AOI...

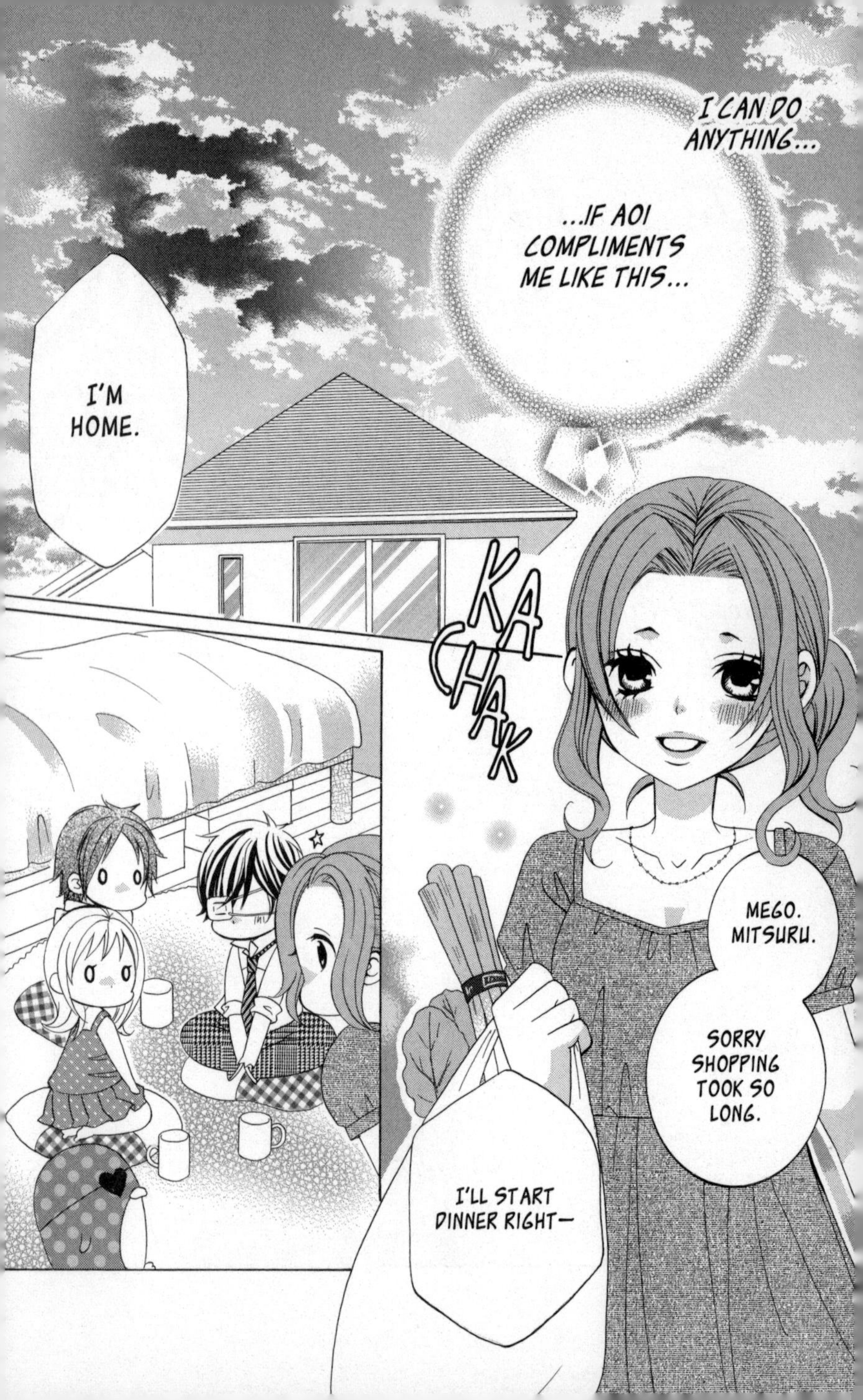
I CAN DO ANYTHING...
...IF AOI COMPLIMENTS ME LIKE THIS...
I'M HOME.
KA CHAK
MEGO. MITSURU.
SORRY SHOPPING TOOK SO LONG.
I'LL START DINNER RIGHT—

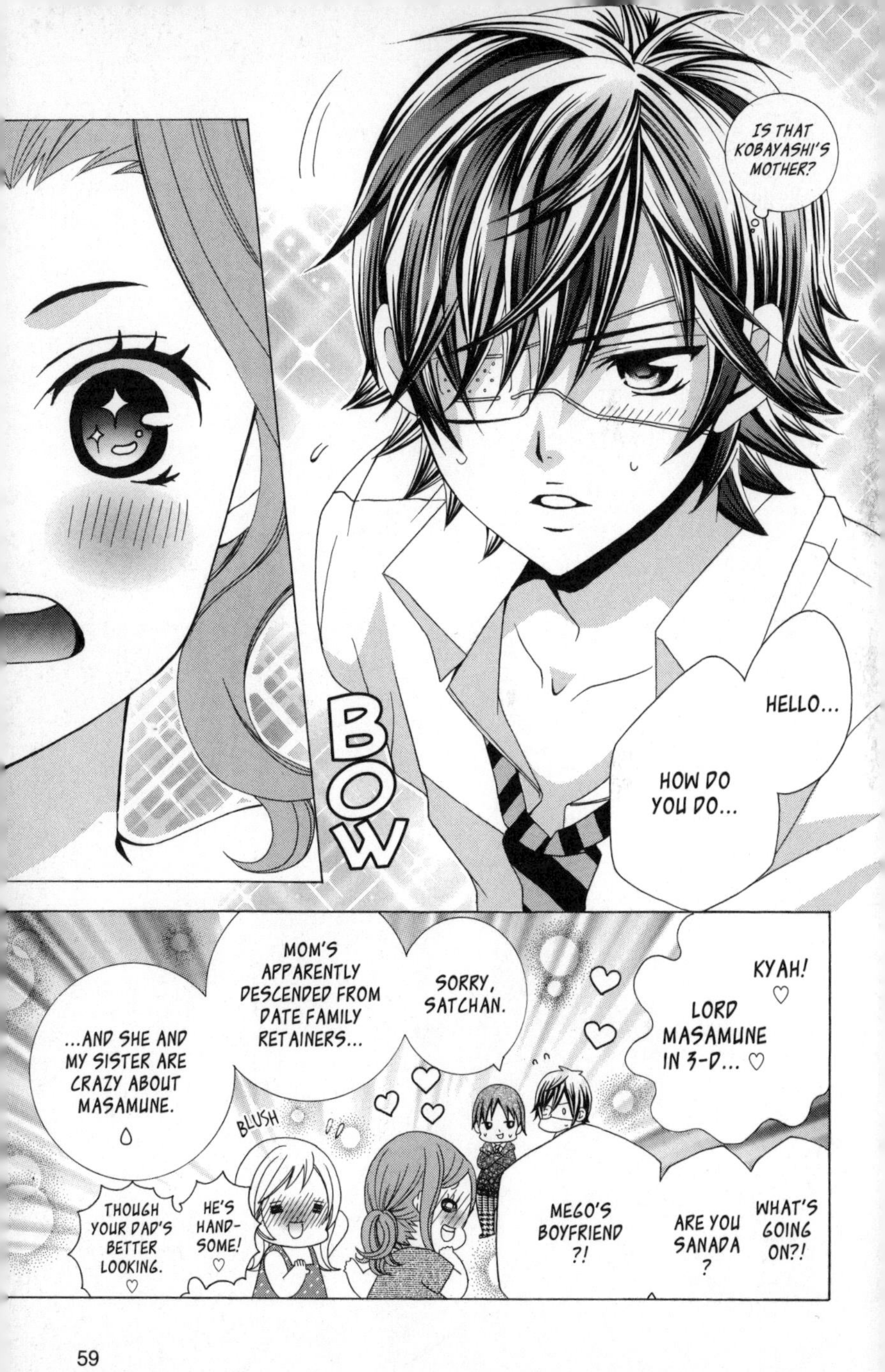
IS THAT KOBAYASHI'S MOTHER?
HELLO...
HOW DO YOU DO...
BOW
KYAH! ♡
LORD MASAMUNE IN 3-D... ♡
SORRY, SATCHAN.
MOM'S APPARENTLY DESCENDED FROM DATE FAMILY RETAINERS...
...AND SHE AND MY SISTER ARE CRAZY ABOUT MASAMUNE.
WHAT'S GOING ON?!
ARE YOU SANADA?
MEGO'S BOYFRIEND?!
HE'S HANDSOME! ♡
BLUSH
THOUGH YOUR DAD'S BETTER LOOKING. ♡

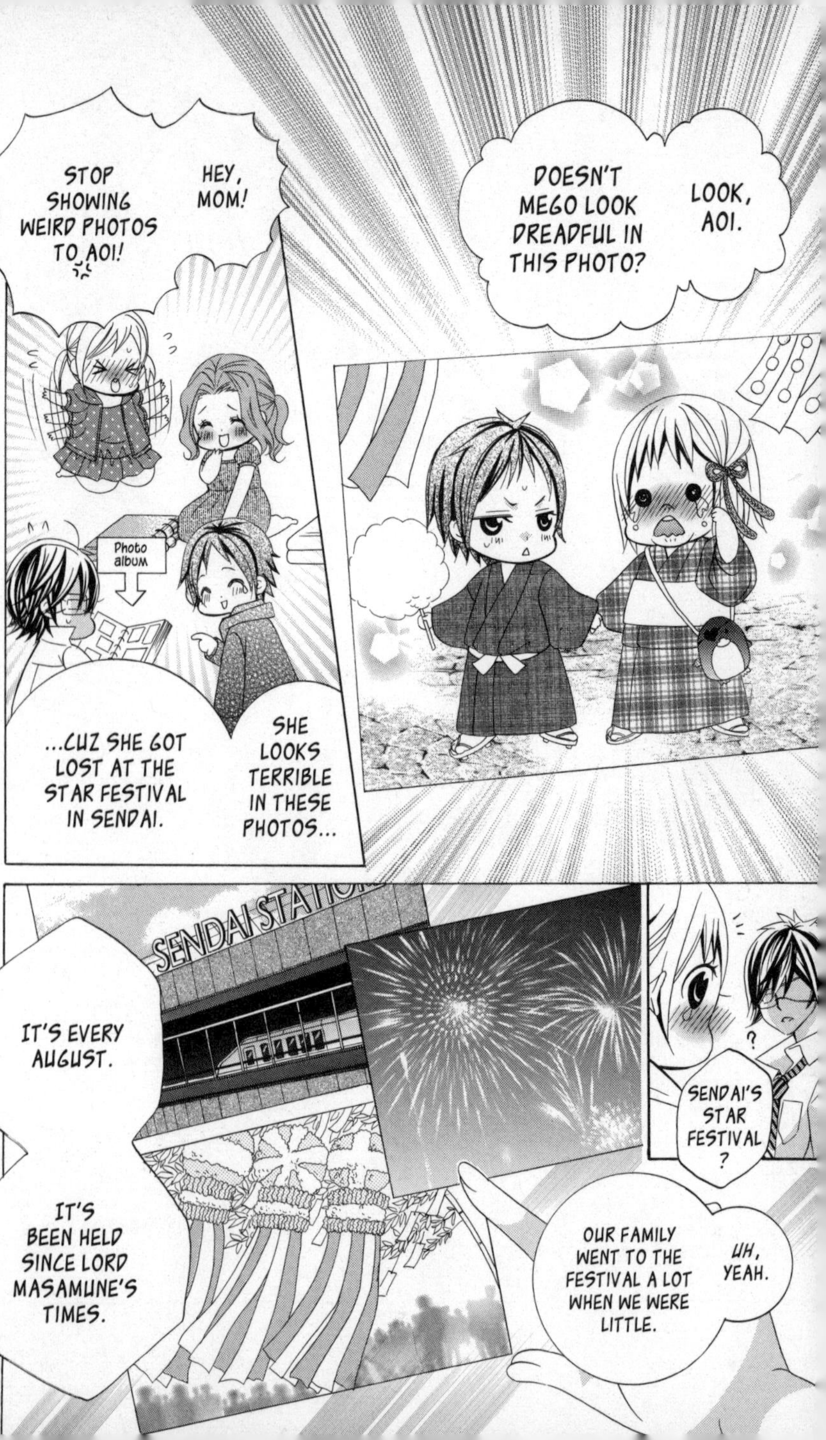
LOOK, AOI.
DOESN'T MEGO LOOK DREADFUL IN THIS PHOTO?
HEY, MOM!
STOP SHOWING WEIRD PHOTOS TO AOI!
Photo album
SHE LOOKS TERRIBLE IN THESE PHOTOS...
...CUZ SHE GOT LOST AT THE STAR FESTIVAL IN SENDAI.
SENDAI'S STAR FESTIVAL?
UH, YEAH.
OUR FAMILY WENT TO THE FESTIVAL A LOT WHEN WE WERE LITTLE.
SENDAI STATION
IT'S EVERY AUGUST.
IT'S BEEN HELD SINCE LORD MASAMUNE'S TIMES.

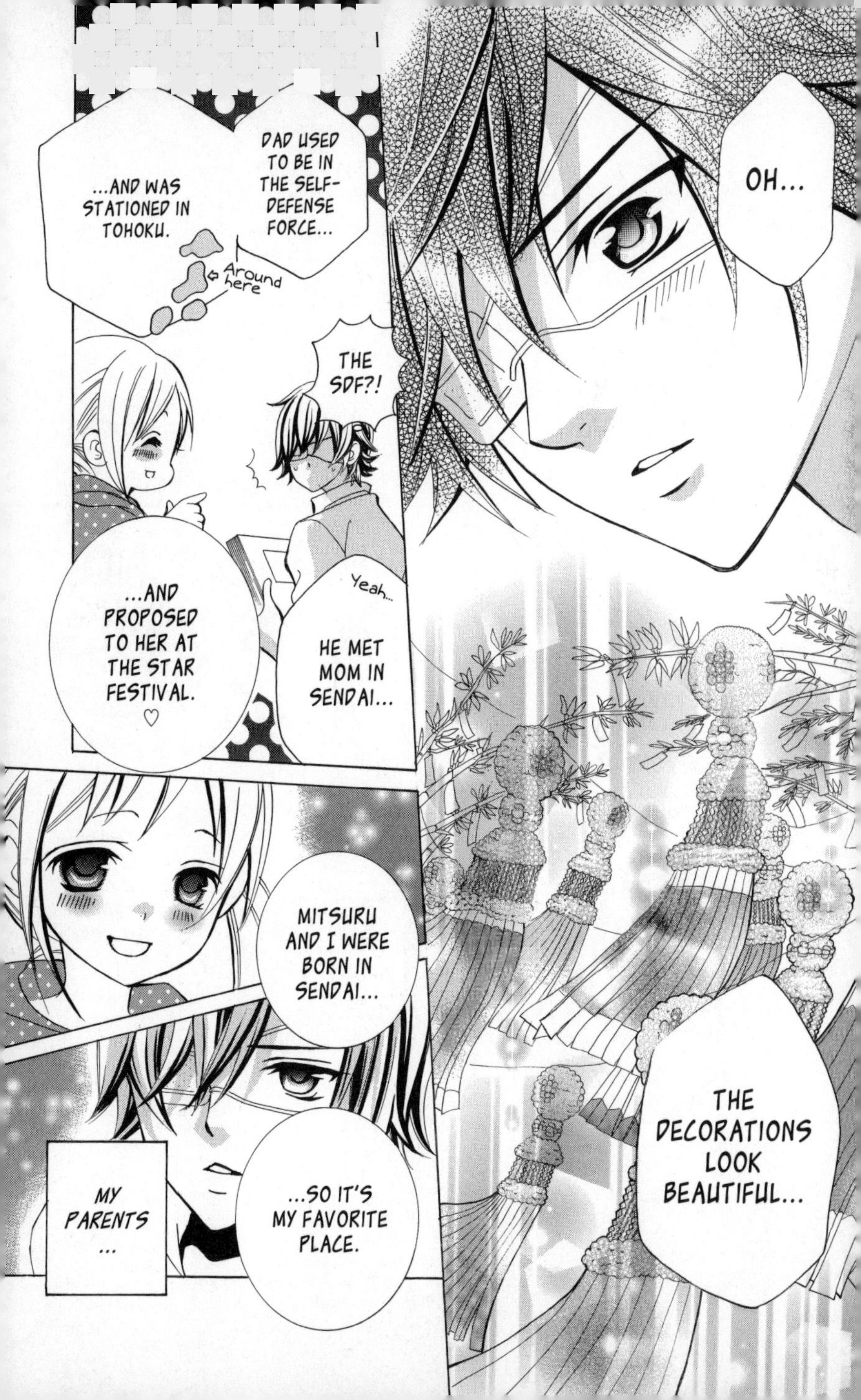
OH...
THE DECORATIONS LOOK BEAUTIFUL...
DAD USED TO BE IN THE SELF-DEFENSE FORCE...
...AND WAS STATIONED IN TOHOKU.
Around here
THE SDF?!
Yeah...
HE MET MOM IN SENDAI...
...AND PROPOSED TO HER AT THE STAR FESTIVAL. ♡
MITSURU AND I WERE BORN IN SENDAI...
...SO IT'S MY FAVORITE PLACE.
MY PARENTS ...

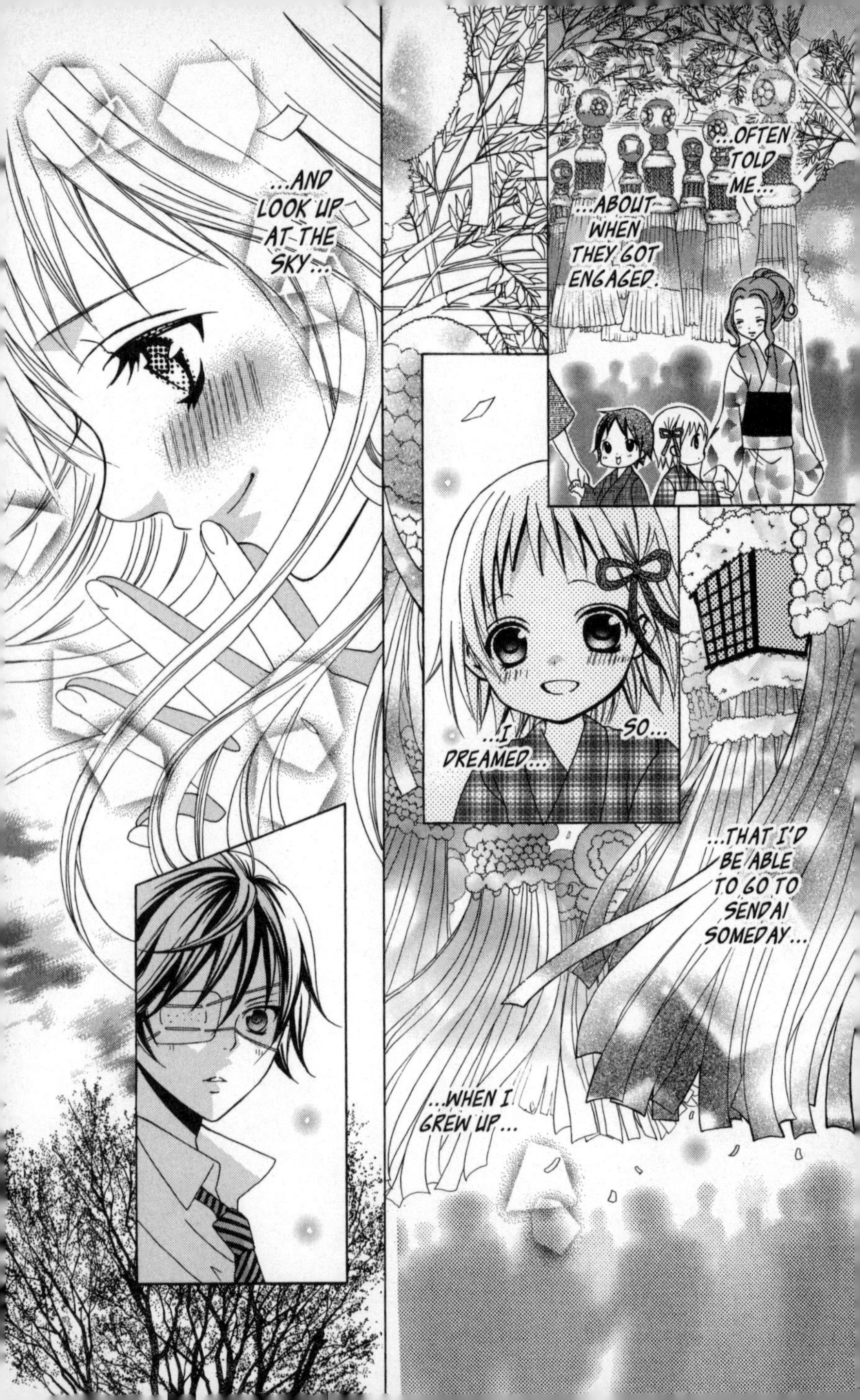
...OFTEN TOLD ME...
...ABOUT WHEN THEY GOT ENGAGED.
SO...
...I DREAMED...
...THAT I'D BE ABLE TO GO TO SENDAI SOMEDAY...
...WHEN I GREW UP...
...AND LOOK UP AT THE SKY...

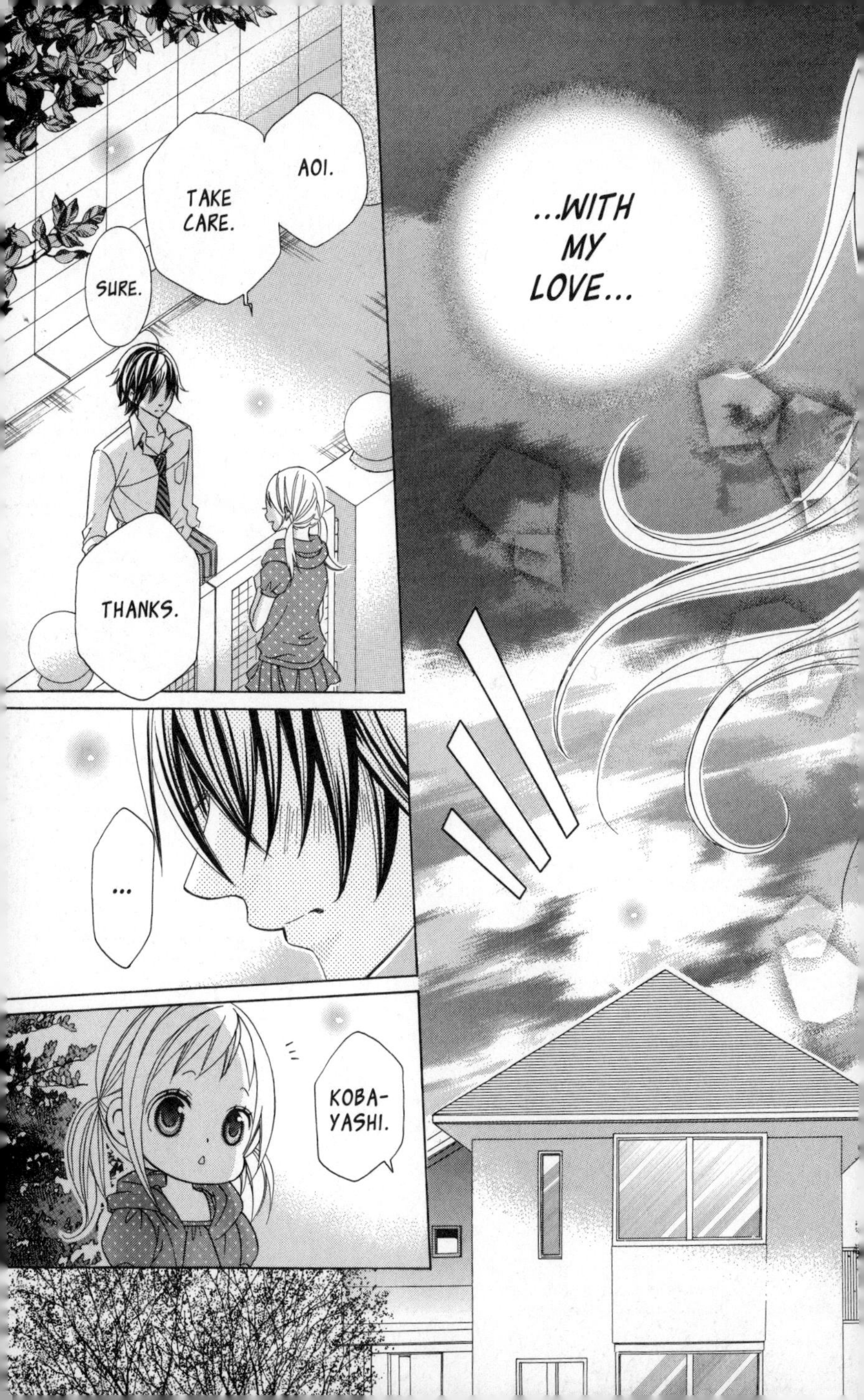
...WITH MY LOVE...
AOI.
TAKE CARE.
SURE.
THANKS.
...
KOBA-YASHI.

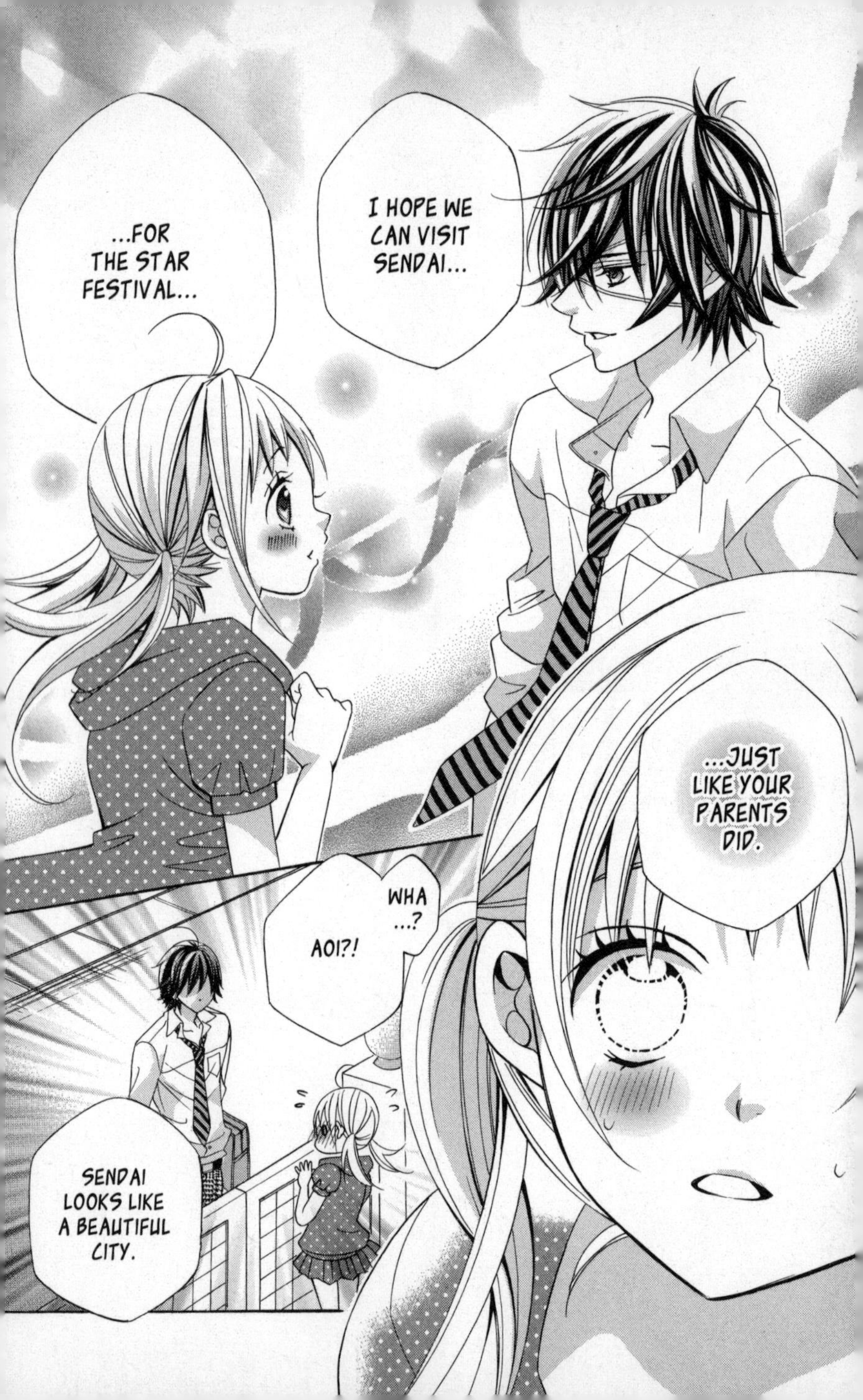
I HOPE WE CAN VISIT SENDAI...
...FOR THE STAR FESTIVAL...
...JUST LIKE YOUR PARENTS DID.
WHA ...?
AOI?!
SENDAI LOOKS LIKE A BEAUTIFUL CITY.

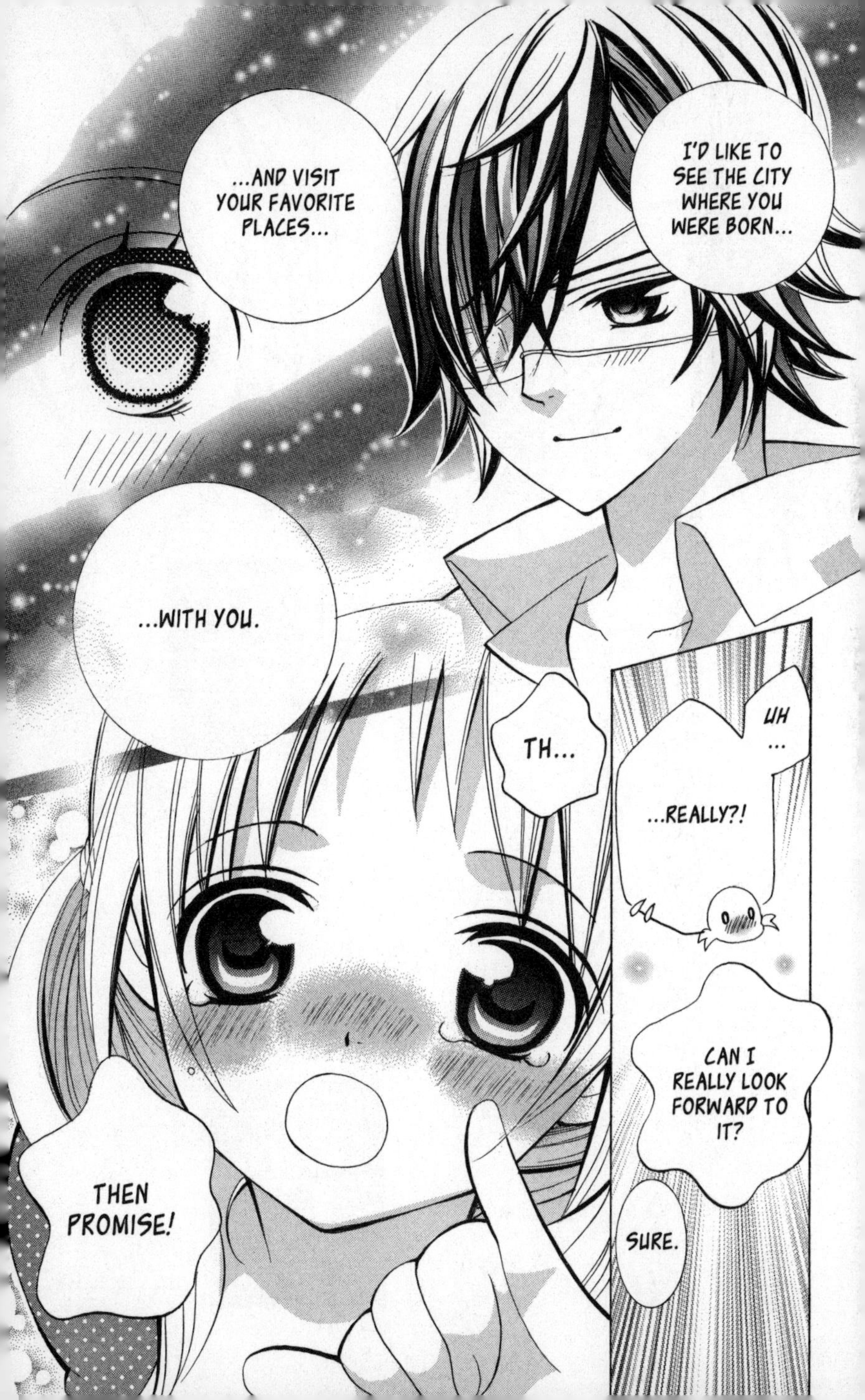
I'D LIKE TO SEE THE CITY WHERE YOU WERE BORN...
...AND VISIT YOUR FAVORITE PLACES...
...WITH YOU.
TH...
UH ...
...REALLY?!
CAN I REALLY LOOK FORWARD TO IT?
SURE.
THEN PROMISE!

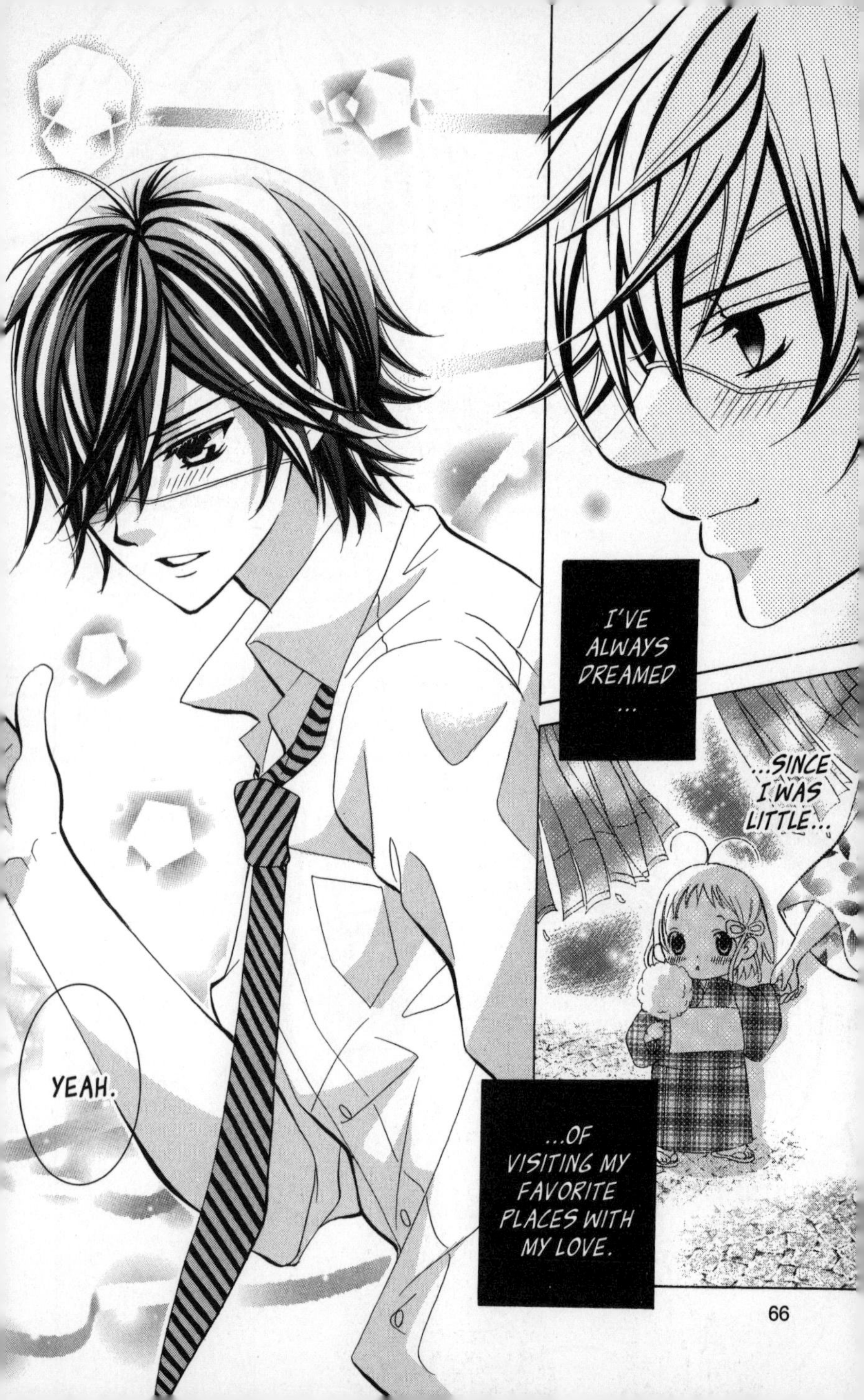
I'VE ALWAYS DREAMED...
...SINCE I WAS LITTLE...
...OF VISITING MY FAVORITE PLACES WITH MY LOVE.
YEAH.

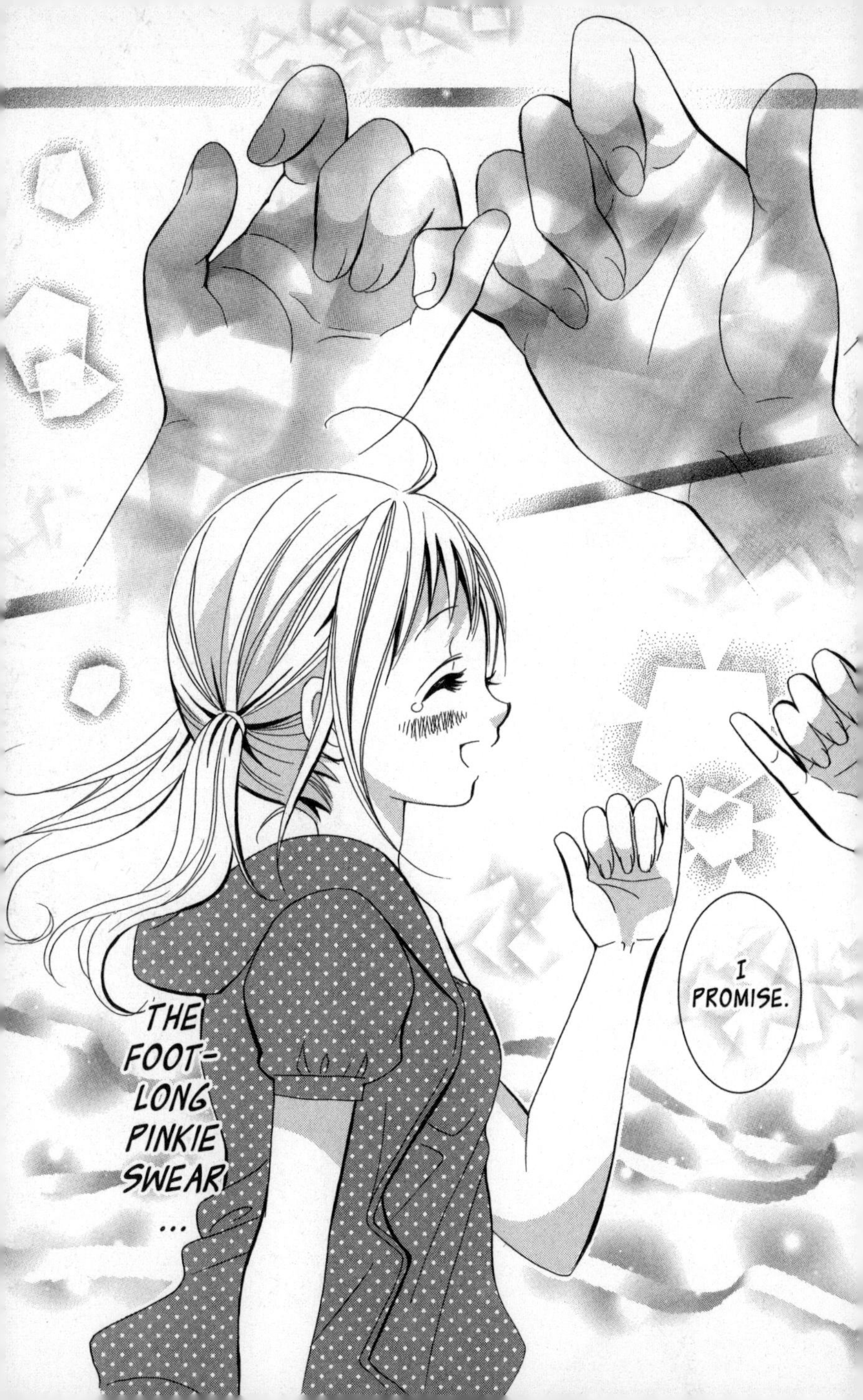
I PROMISE.
THE FOOT-LONG PINKIE SWEAR...

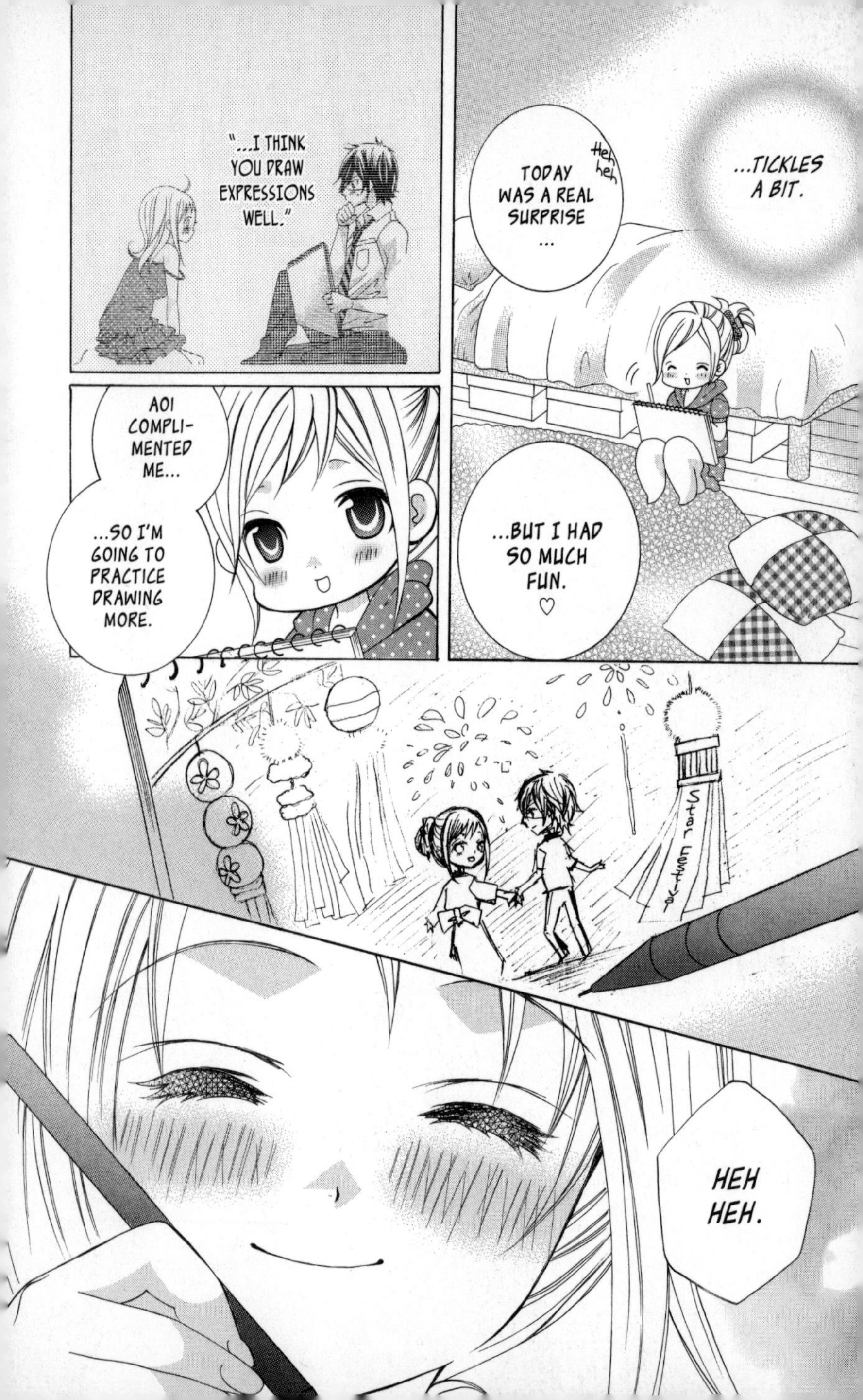
...TICKLES A BIT.
Heh heh
TODAY WAS A REAL SURPRISE...
...BUT I HAD SO MUCH FUN. ♡
"...I THINK YOU DRAW EXPRESSIONS WELL."
AOI COMPLIMENTED ME...
...SO I'M GOING TO PRACTICE DRAWING MORE.
Star Festival
HEH HEH.

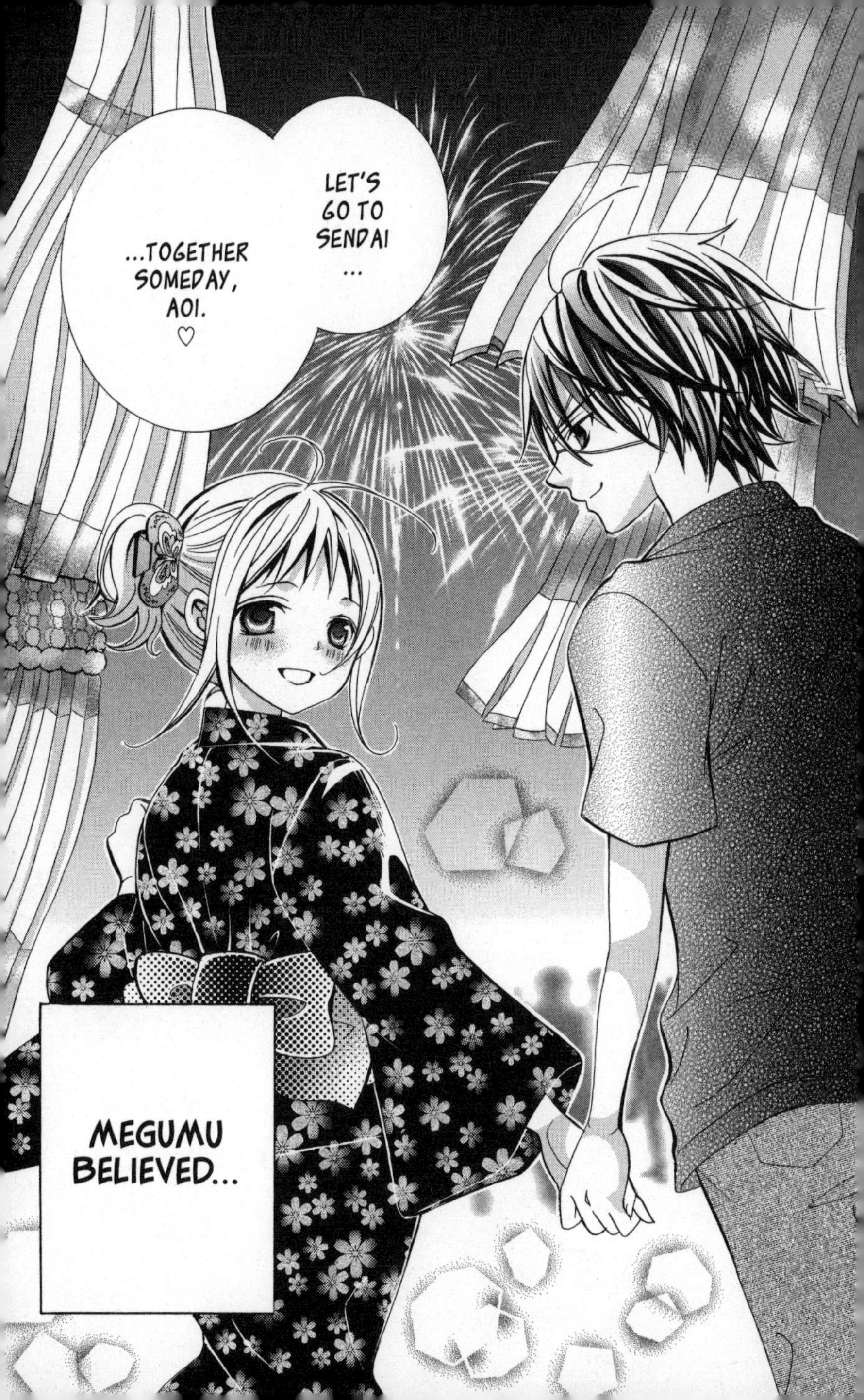
LET'S GO TO SENDAI ...
...TOGETHER SOMEDAY, AOI. ♡
MEGUMU BELIEVED...

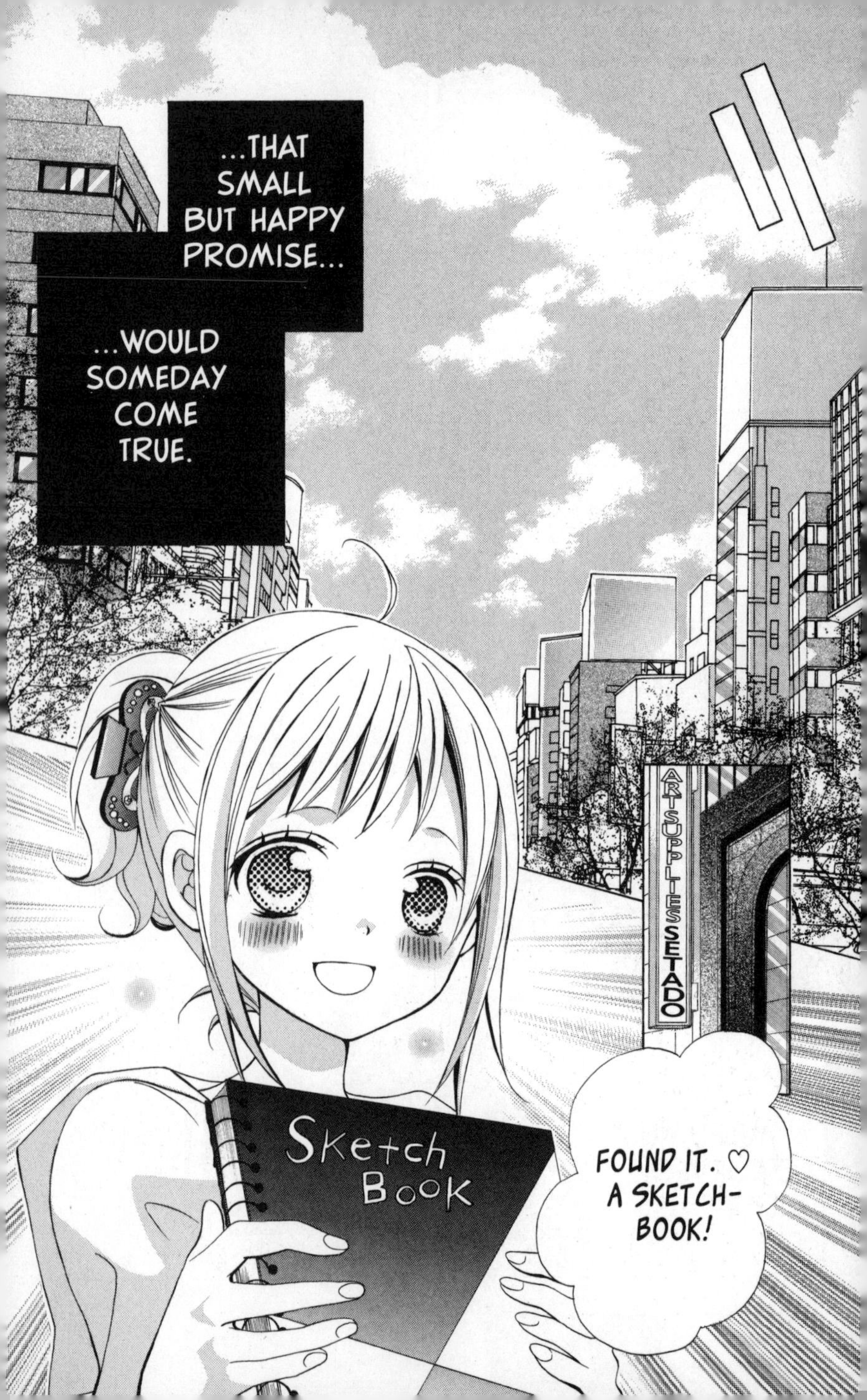
...THAT SMALL BUT HAPPY PROMISE...
...WOULD SOMEDAY COME TRUE.
ART SUPPLIES SETADO
Sketch Book
FOUND IT. ♡ A SKETCH-BOOK!

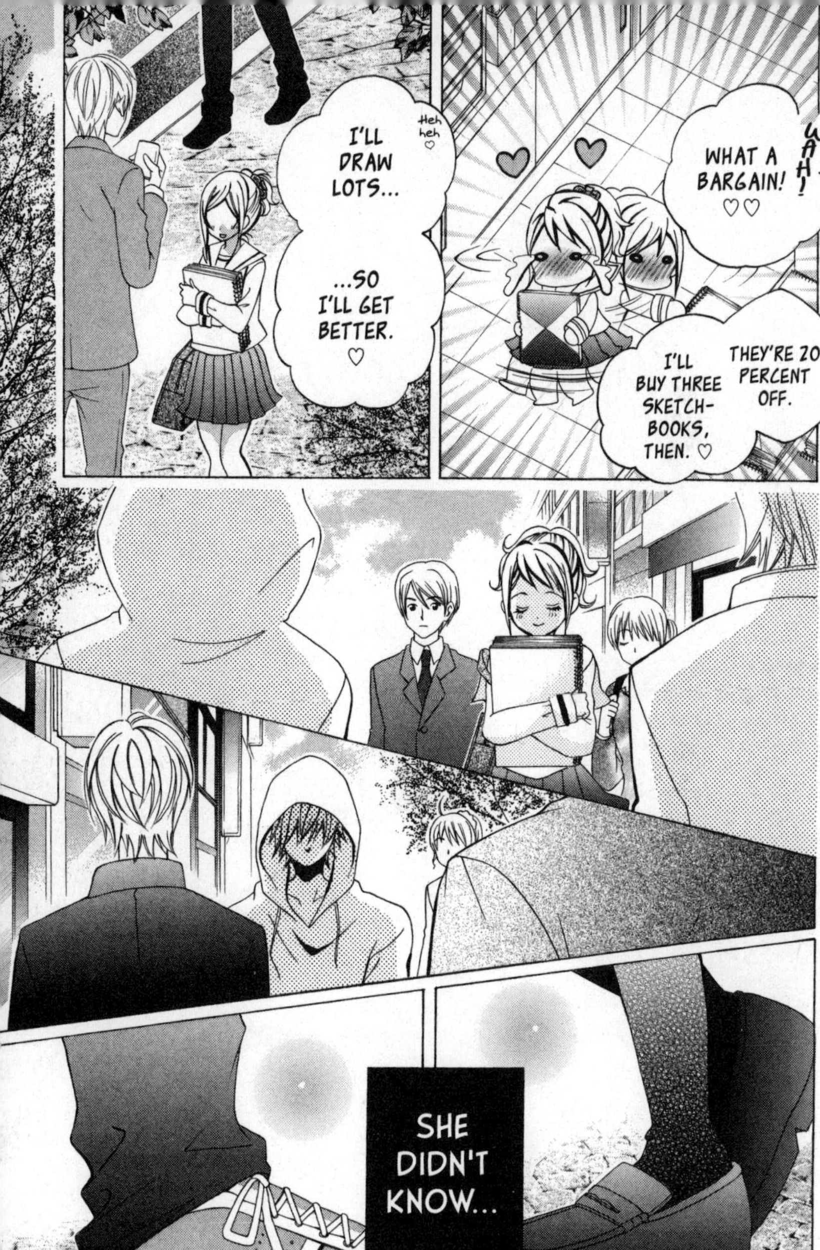
WAH!
WHAT A BARGAIN! ♡♡
THEY'RE 20 PERCENT OFF.
I'LL BUY THREE SKETCH-BOOKS, THEN. ♡
I'LL DRAW LOTS...
Heh heh ♡
...SO I'LL GET BETTER. ♡
SHE DIDN'T KNOW...

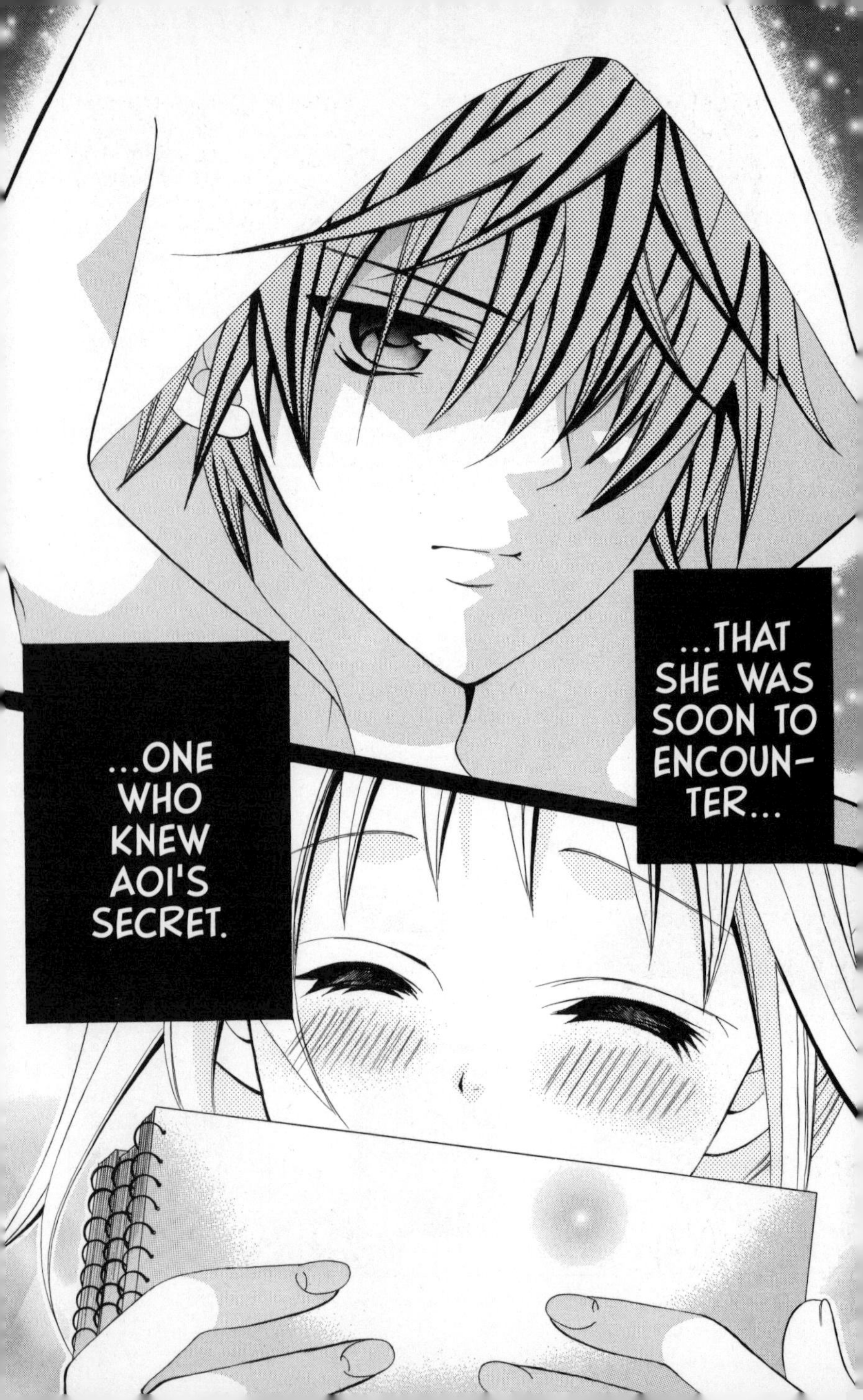
...THAT SHE WAS SOON TO ENCOUN-TER...
...ONE WHO KNEW AOI'S SECRET.

Chapter 28

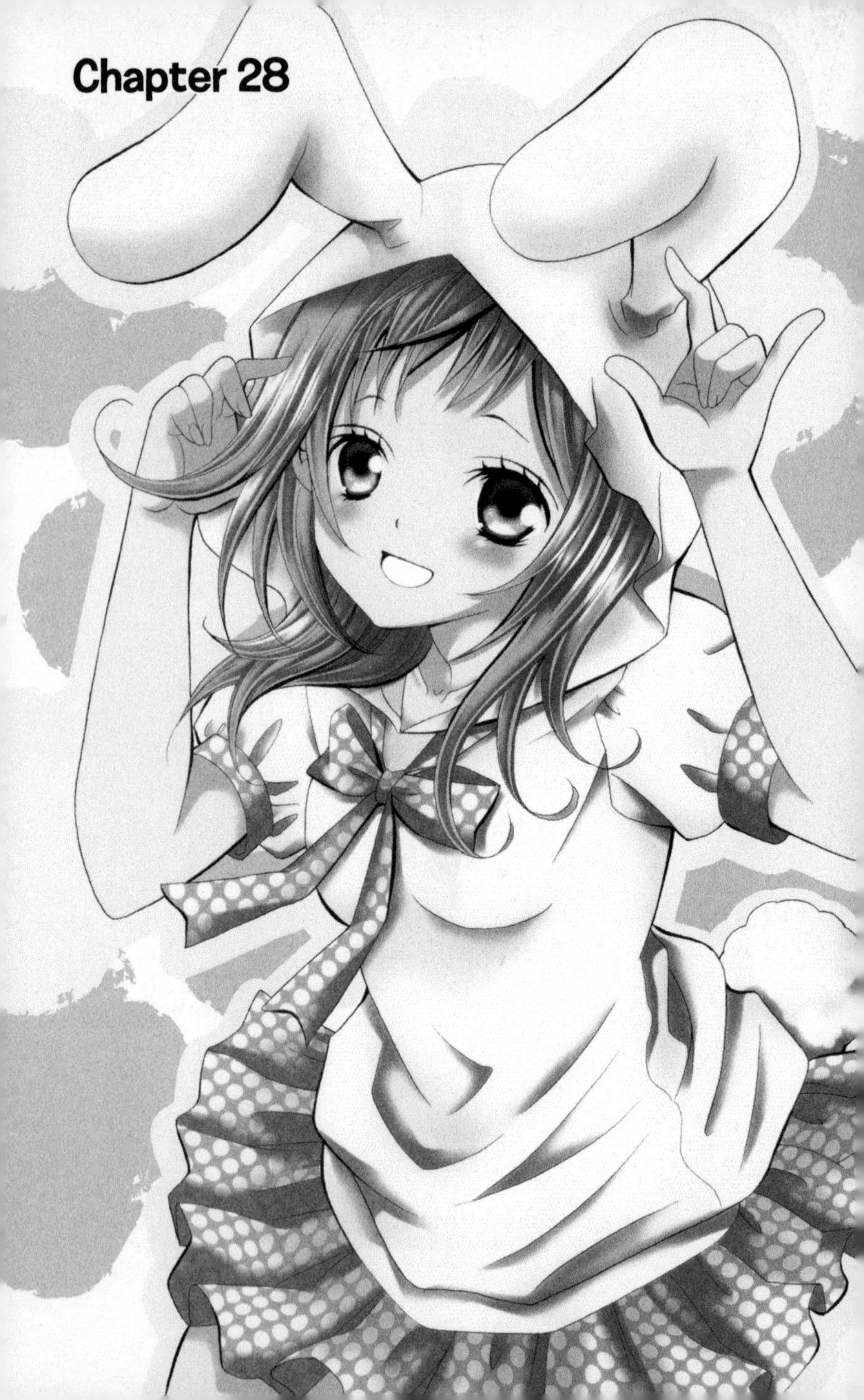

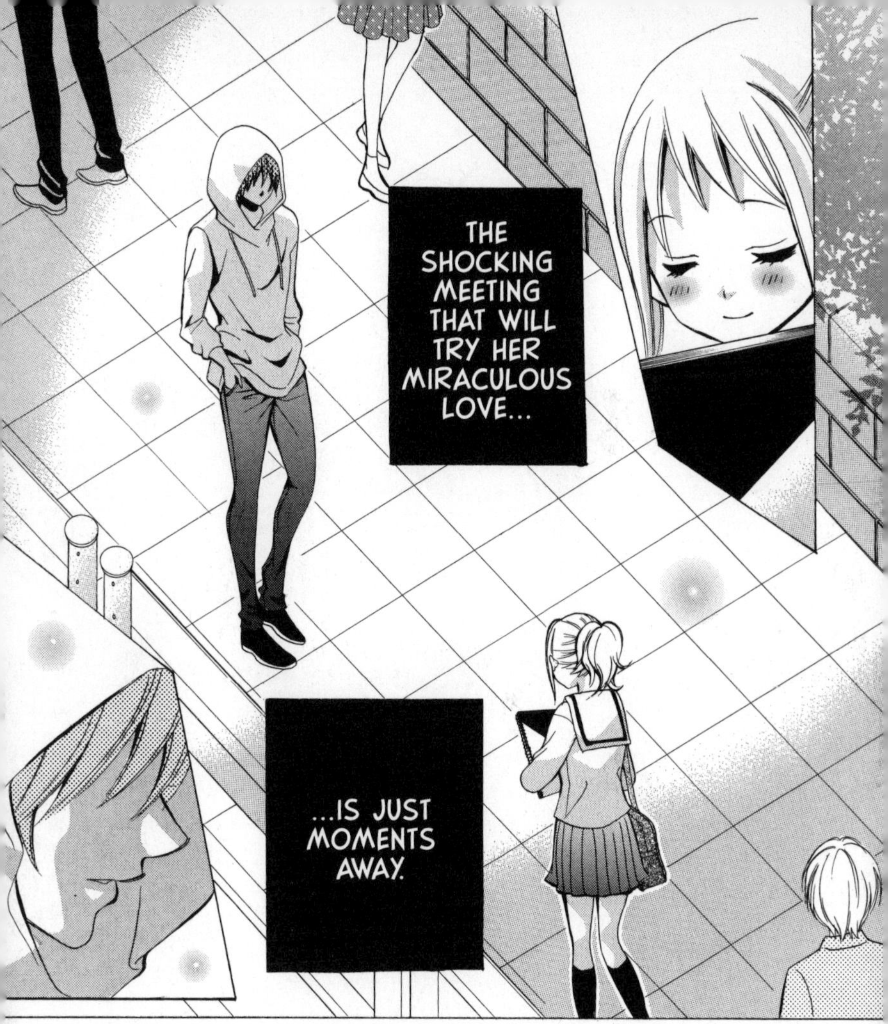
THE SHOCKING MEETING THAT WILL TRY HER MIRACULOUS LOVE...
...IS JUST MOMENTS AWAY.

WHAT'S NEW.

I WATCH KIS-MY-FT2'S *SNOW DOME NO YAKUSOKU* LIVE SHOW ON DVD AND LISTEN TO SEXY ZONE'S SECOND ALBUM AND palet's CD WHEN I'M WORKING. ♪ I ESPECIALLY LIKE "LUV SICK," "TANA KARA BOTAMOCHI," "BUTSUKACCHAUYO," "CONGRATULATION," "SHOURI NO SEAL" AND "LOVE WINTER MEMORIES." I KEEP PLAYING THEM OVER AND OVER. LOL! THEY'RE AMAZING SONGS! (^O^)

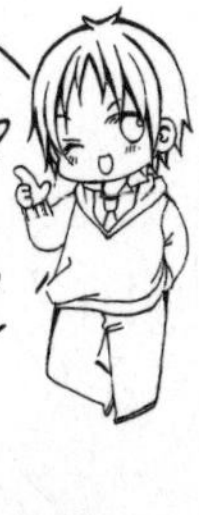

I WENT TO IMPERIAL THEATRE TO SEE *JOHNNYS' 2020 WORLD* WITH MY ASSISTANTS AT THE END OF LAST YEAR. ♪ ABC-Z'S LIVE ACROBATICS WERE SO, SO COOL! KENTY SENPAI PLAYING TEN ROLES WAS THE BEST! (^O^)

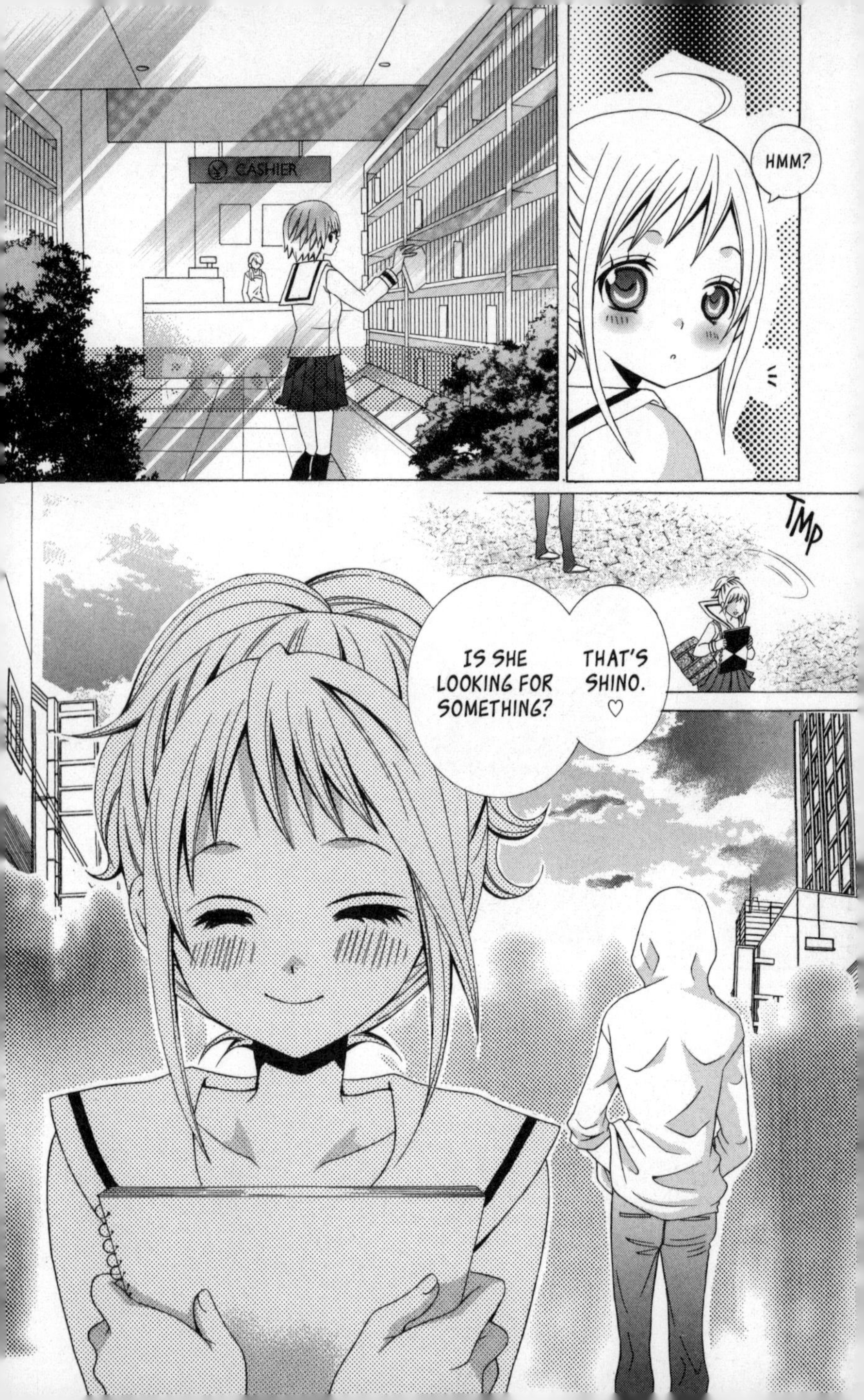
HMM?
CASHIER
TMP
THAT'S SHINO. ♡
IS SHE LOOKING FOR SOMETHING?

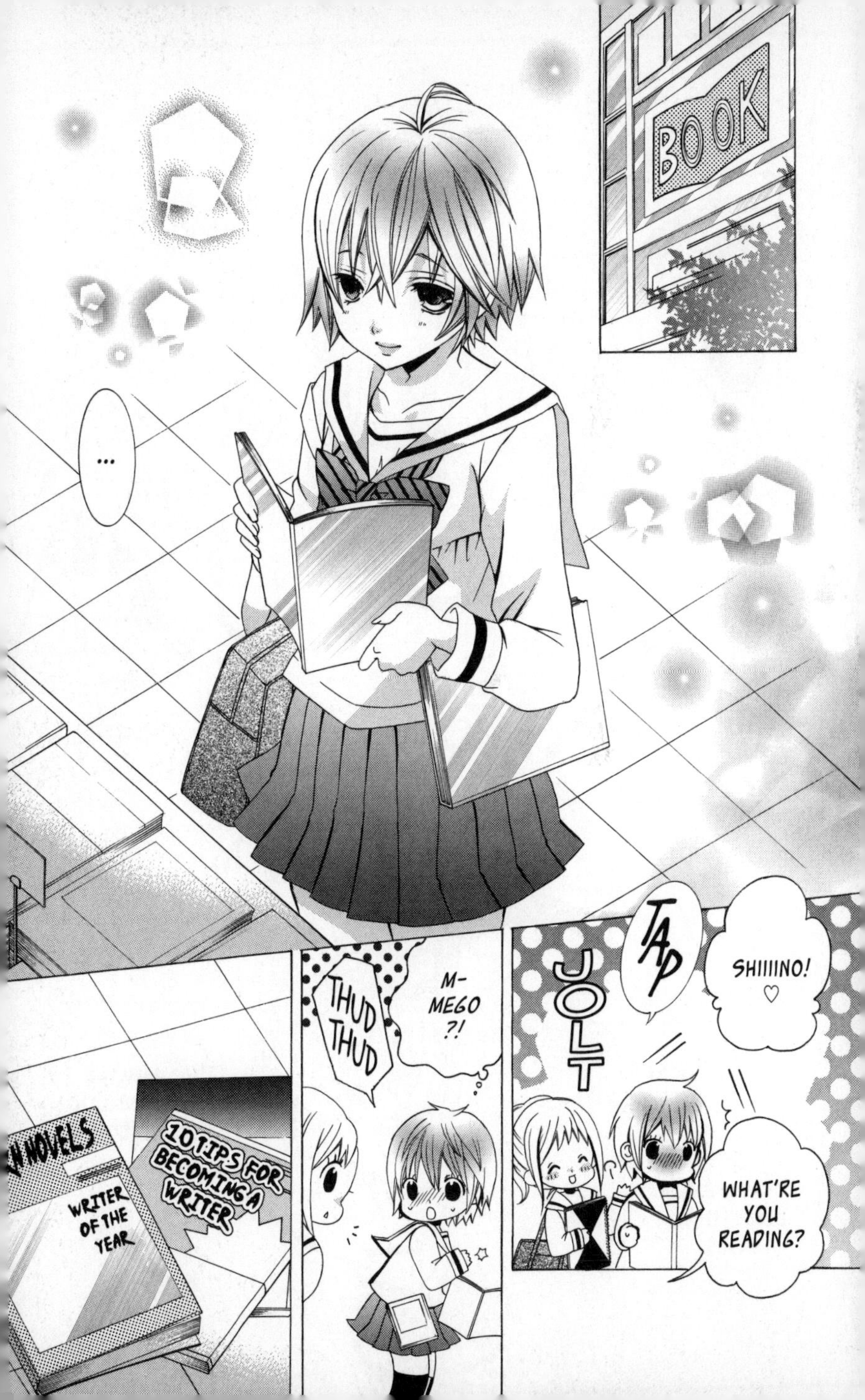
BOOK
...
TAP
JOLT
SHIIIINO! ♡
WHAT'RE YOU READING?
THUD THUD
M-MEGO ?!
NOVELS
WRITER OF THE YEAR
101 TIPS FOR BECOMING A WRITER

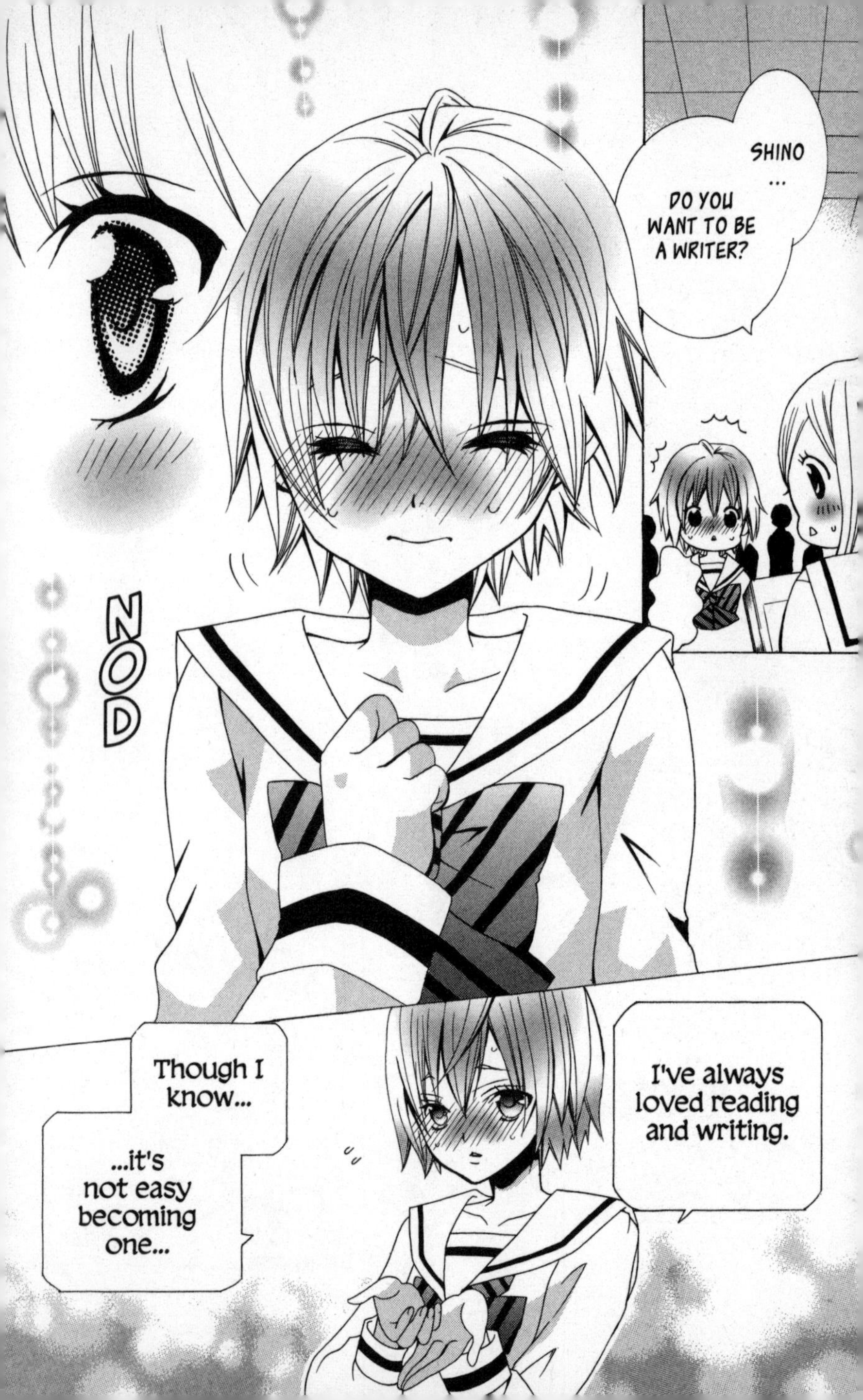
SHINO ...
DO YOU WANT TO BE A WRITER?
NOD
I've always loved reading and writing.
Though I know...
...it's not easy becoming one...

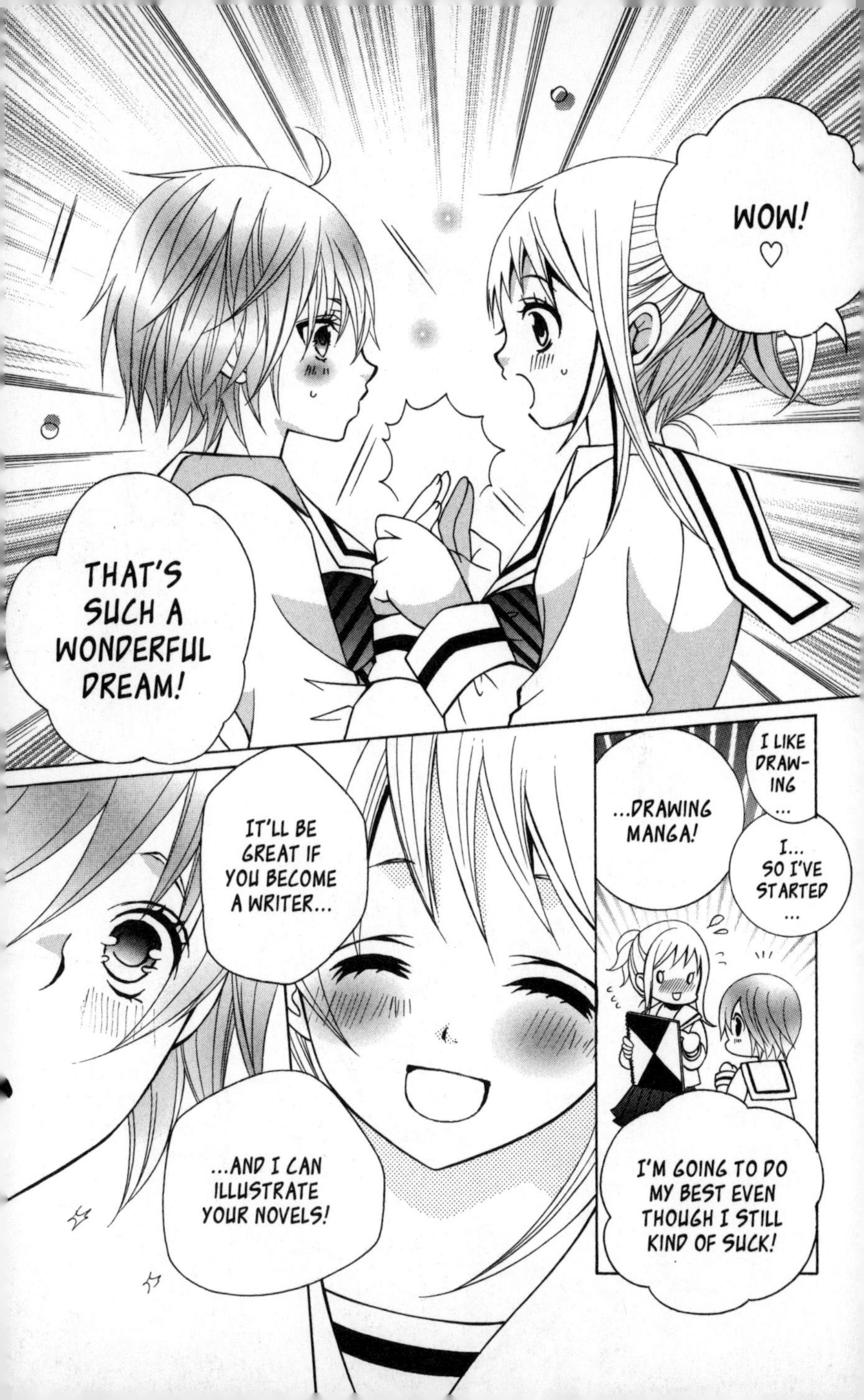
WOW! ♡
THAT'S SUCH A WONDERFUL DREAM!
I LIKE DRAWING...
I... SO I'VE STARTED...
...DRAWING MANGA!
I'M GOING TO DO MY BEST EVEN THOUGH I STILL KIND OF SUCK!
IT'LL BE GREAT IF YOU BECOME A WRITER...
...AND I CAN ILLUSTRATE YOUR NOVELS!

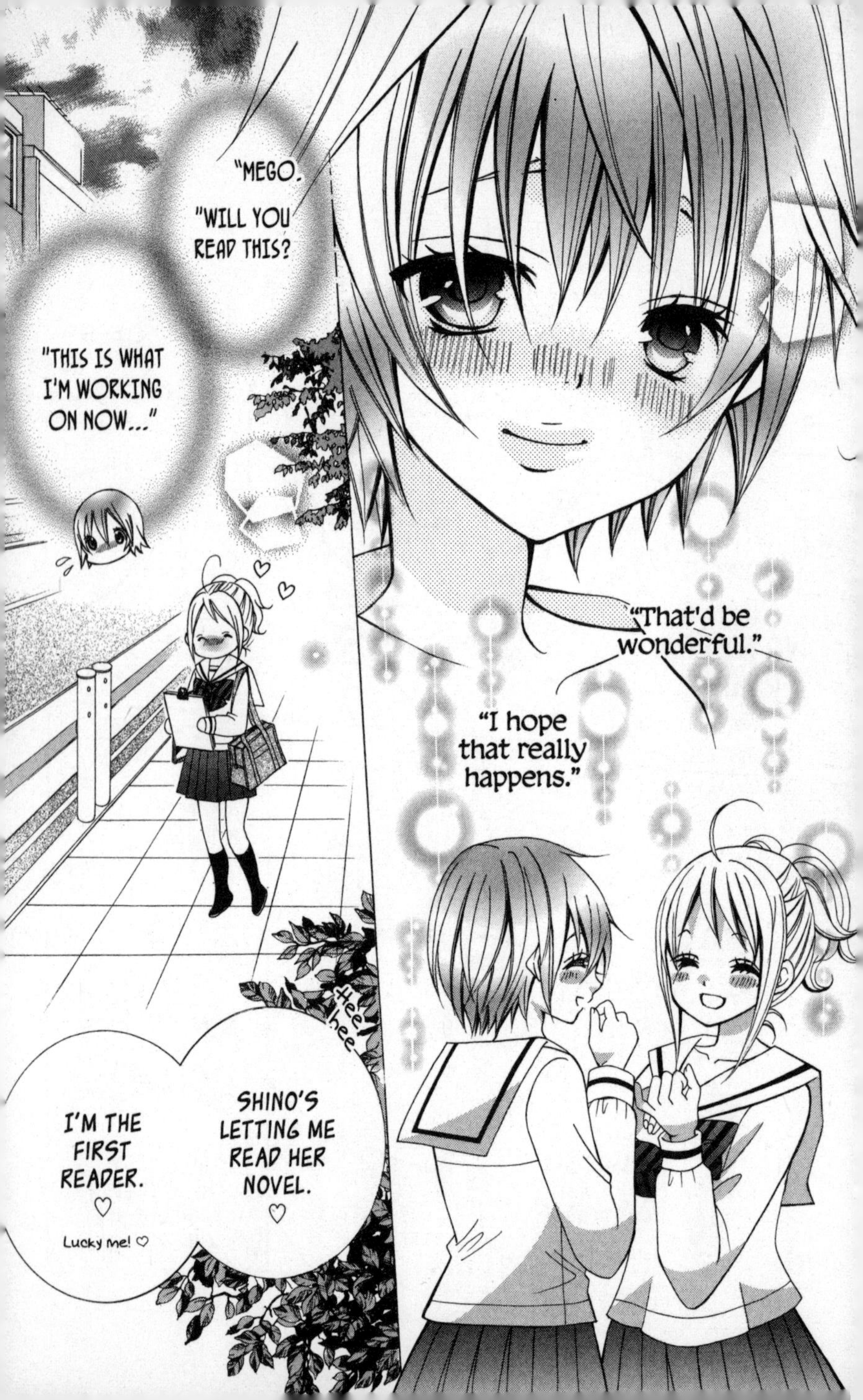
"That'd be wonderful."
"I hope that really happens."
Hee hee
"MEGO.
"WILL YOU READ THIS?
"THIS IS WHAT I'M WORKING ON NOW..."
SHINO'S LETTING ME READ HER NOVEL. ♡
I'M THE FIRST READER. ♡
Lucky me! ♡

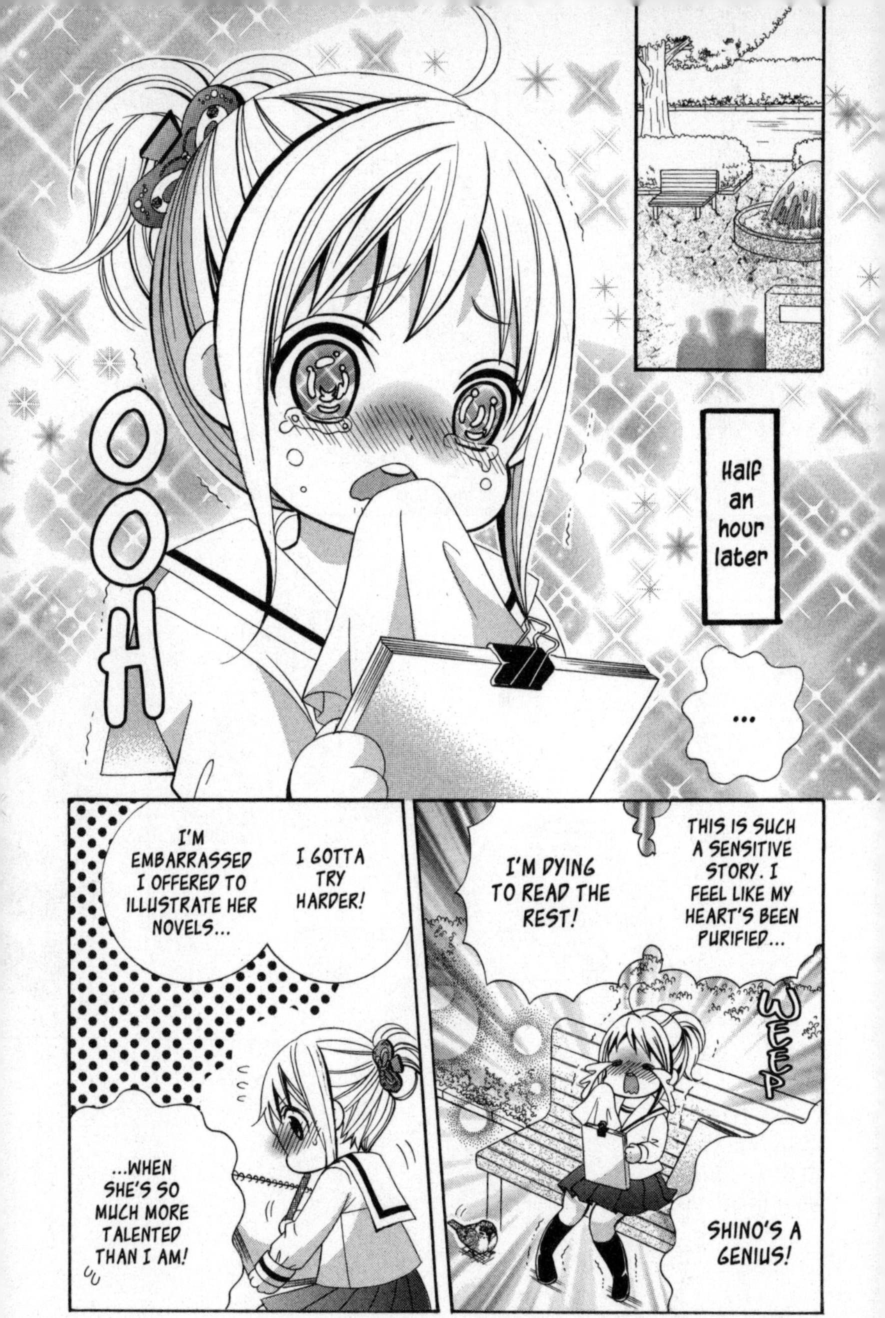
Half an hour later
...
OOOH
THIS IS SUCH A SENSITIVE STORY. I FEEL LIKE MY HEART'S BEEN PURIFIED...
I'M DYING TO READ THE REST!
WEEP
SHINO'S A GENIUS!
I GOTTA TRY HARDER!
I'M EMBARRASSED I OFFERED TO ILLUSTRATE HER NOVELS...
...WHEN SHE'S SO MUCH MORE TALENTED THAN I AM!

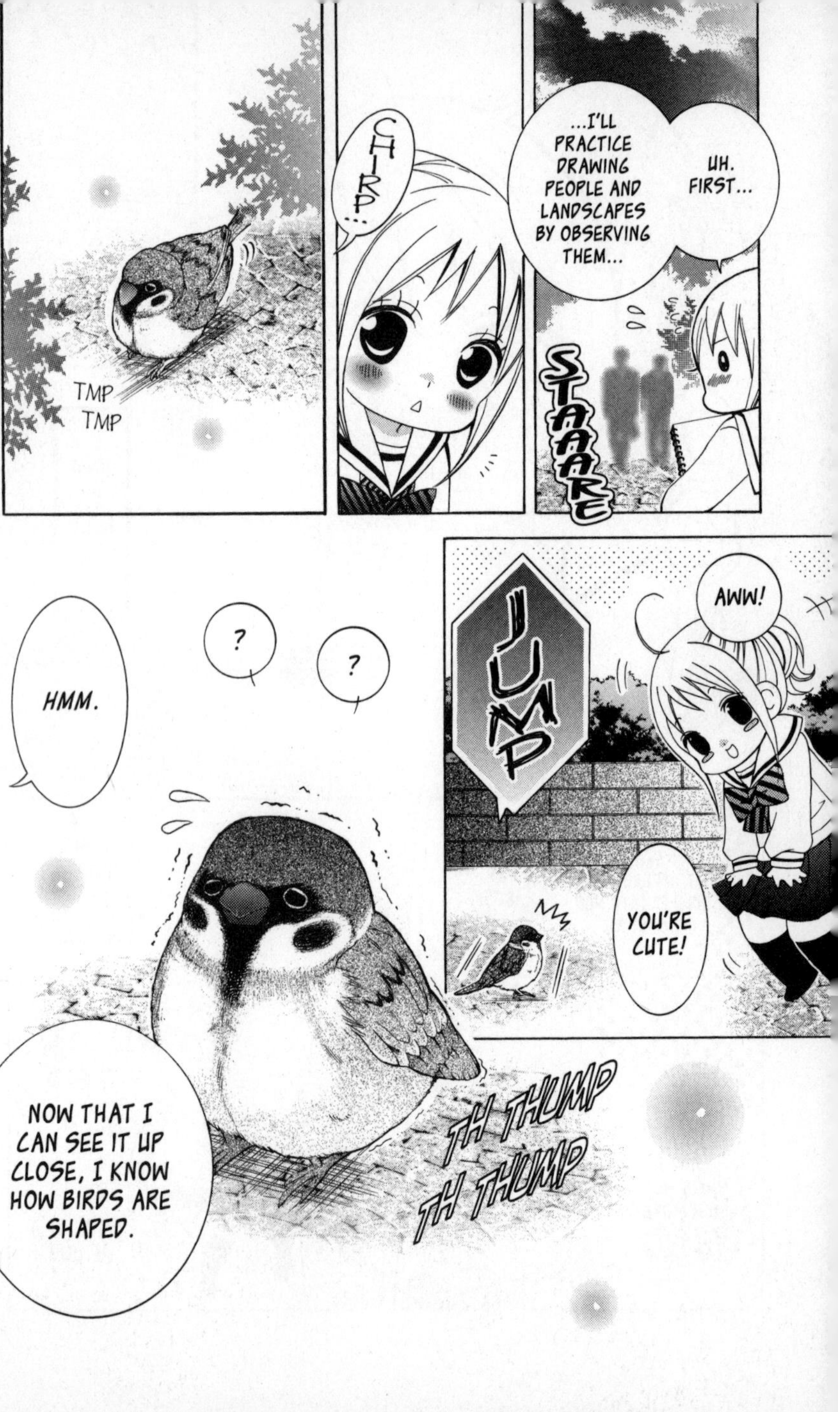
UH. FIRST...
...I'LL PRACTICE DRAWING PEOPLE AND LANDSCAPES BY OBSERVING THEM...
STAAARE
CHIRP...
TMP TMP
AWW!
JUMP
YOU'RE CUTE!
?
?
HMM.
NOW THAT I CAN SEE IT UP CLOSE, I KNOW HOW BIRDS ARE SHAPED.
TH THUMP TH THUMP

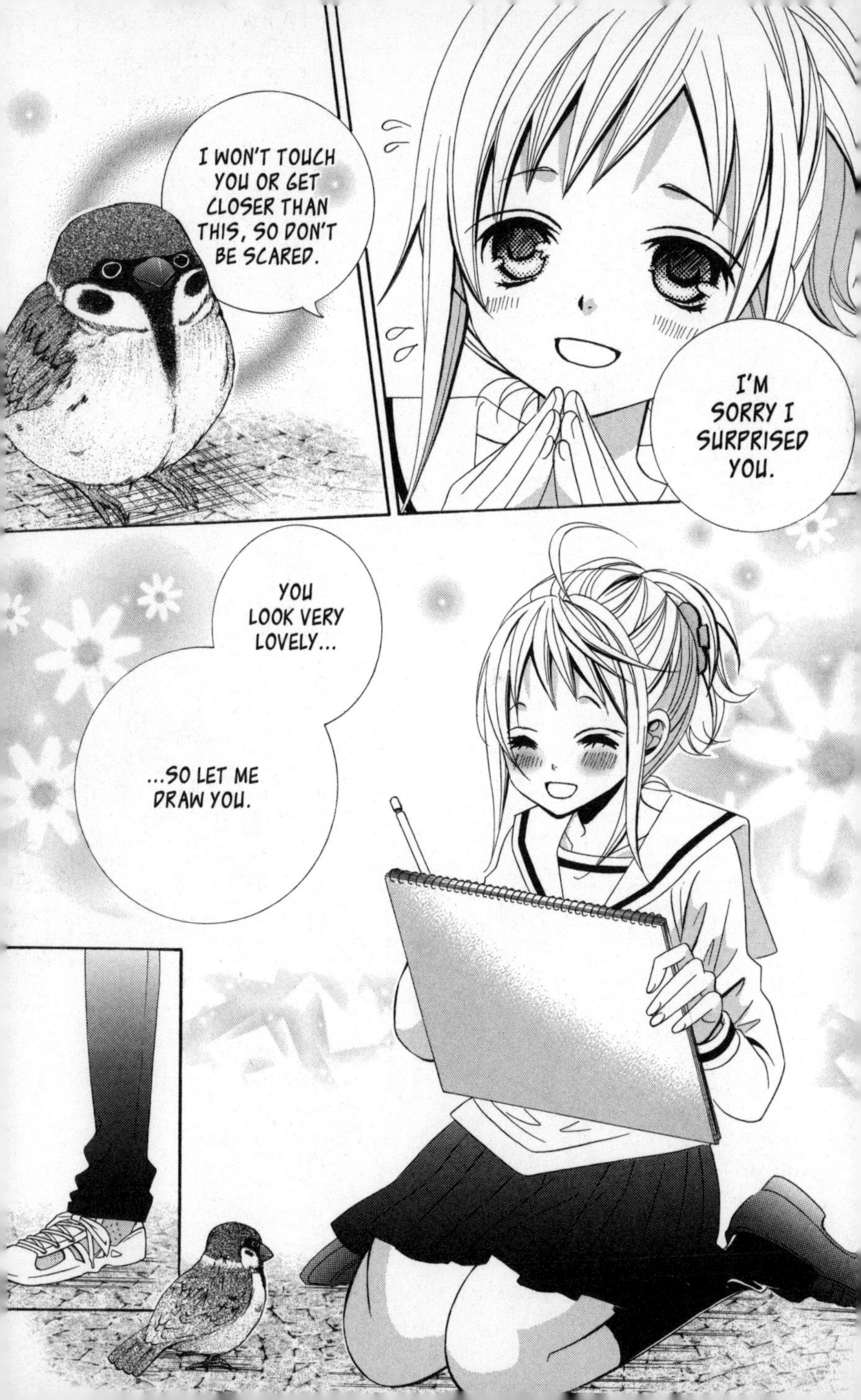
I'M SORRY I SURPRISED YOU.
I WON'T TOUCH YOU OR GET CLOSER THAN THIS, SO DON'T BE SCARED.
YOU LOOK VERY LOVELY...
...SO LET ME DRAW YOU.

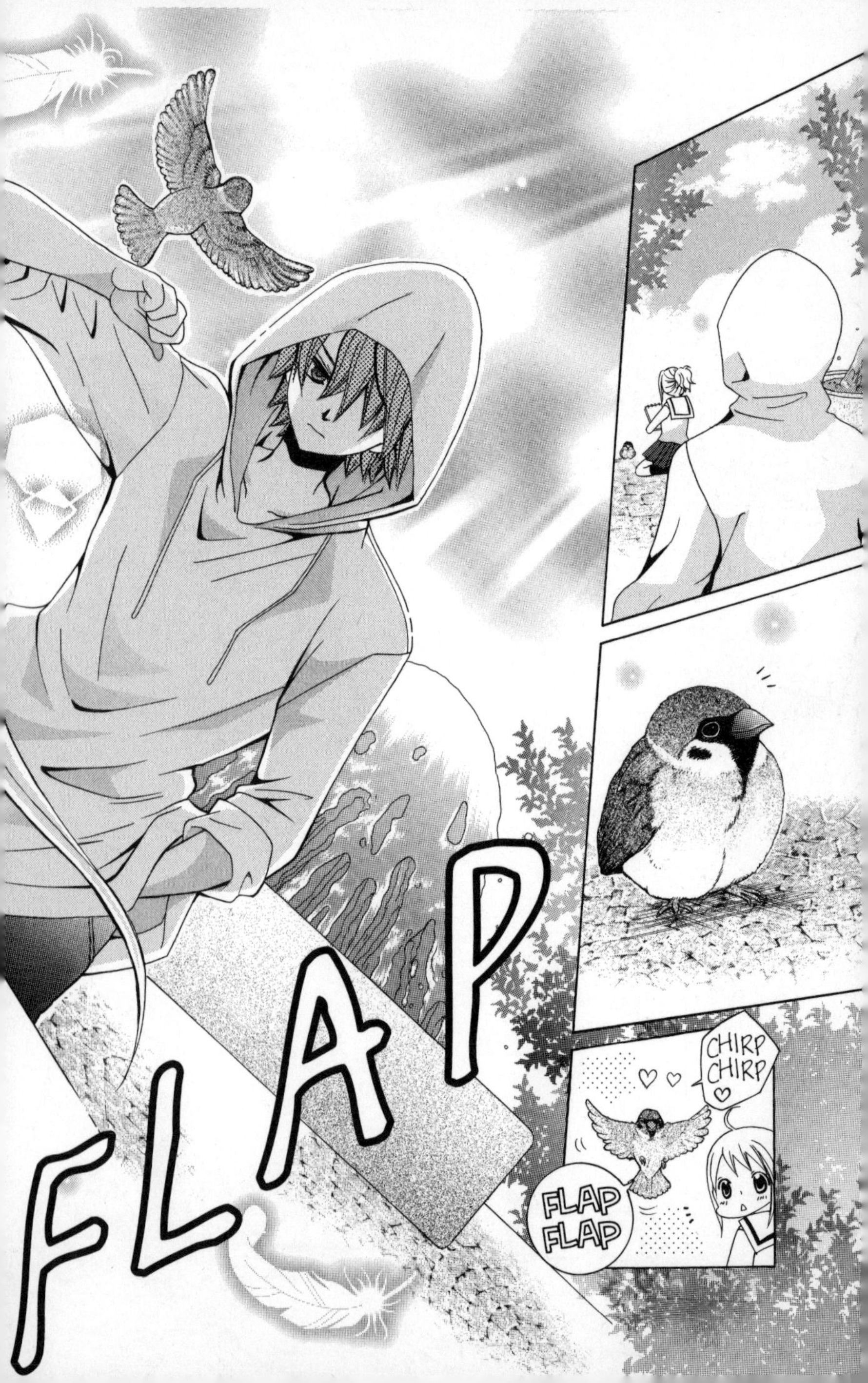
FLAP
CHIRP CHIRP ♡
FLAP FLAP

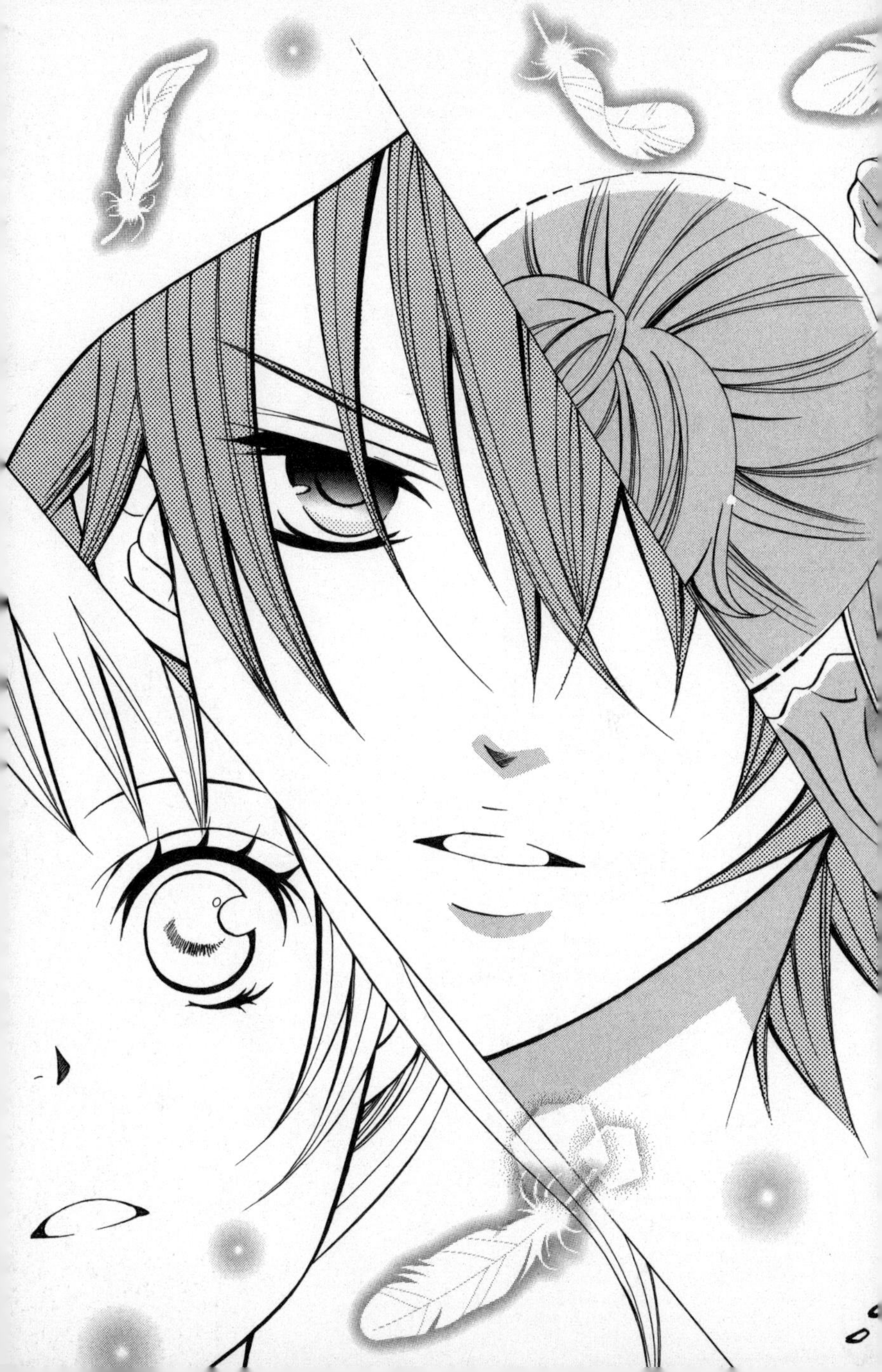

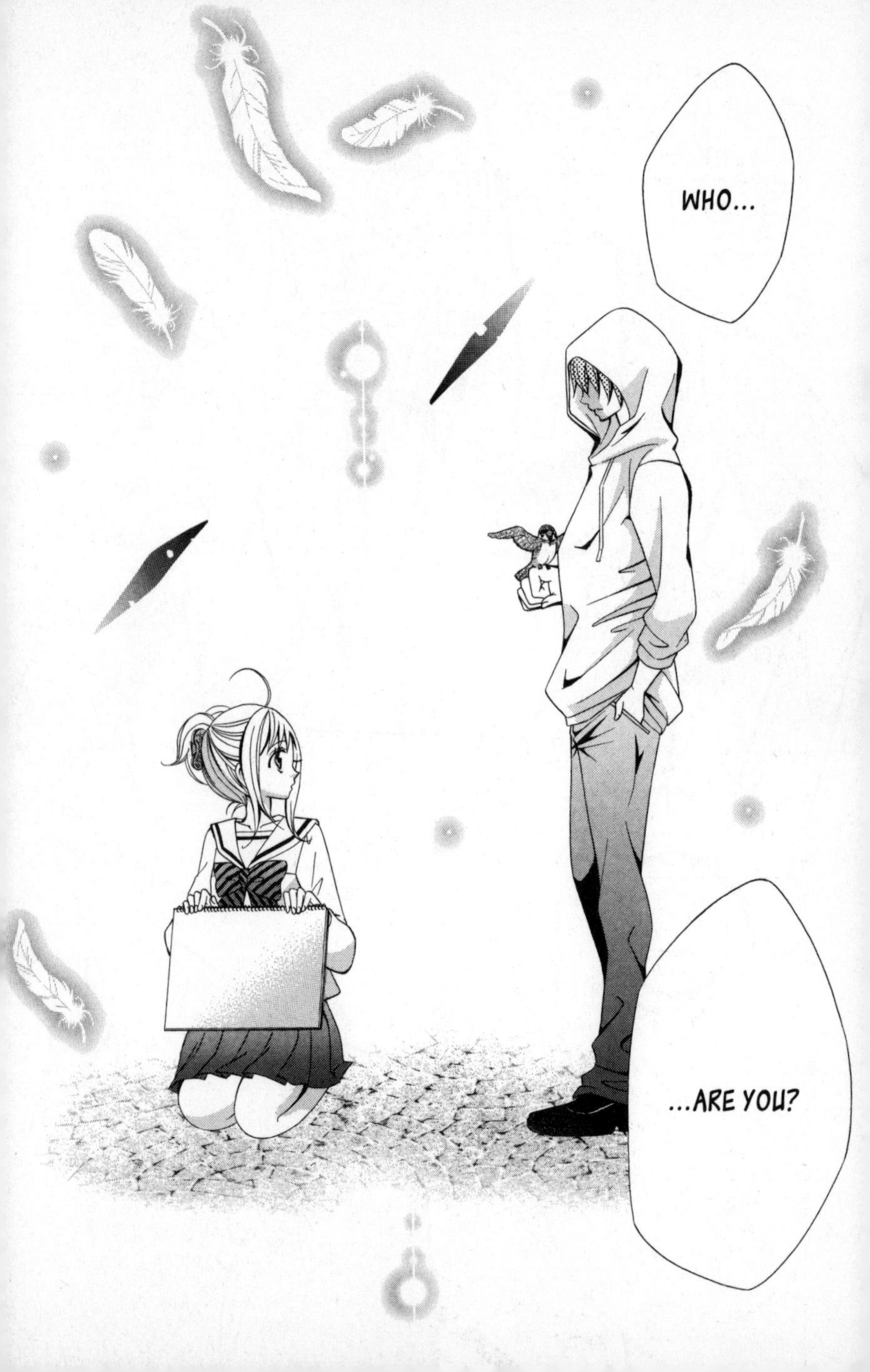
WHO...
...ARE YOU?

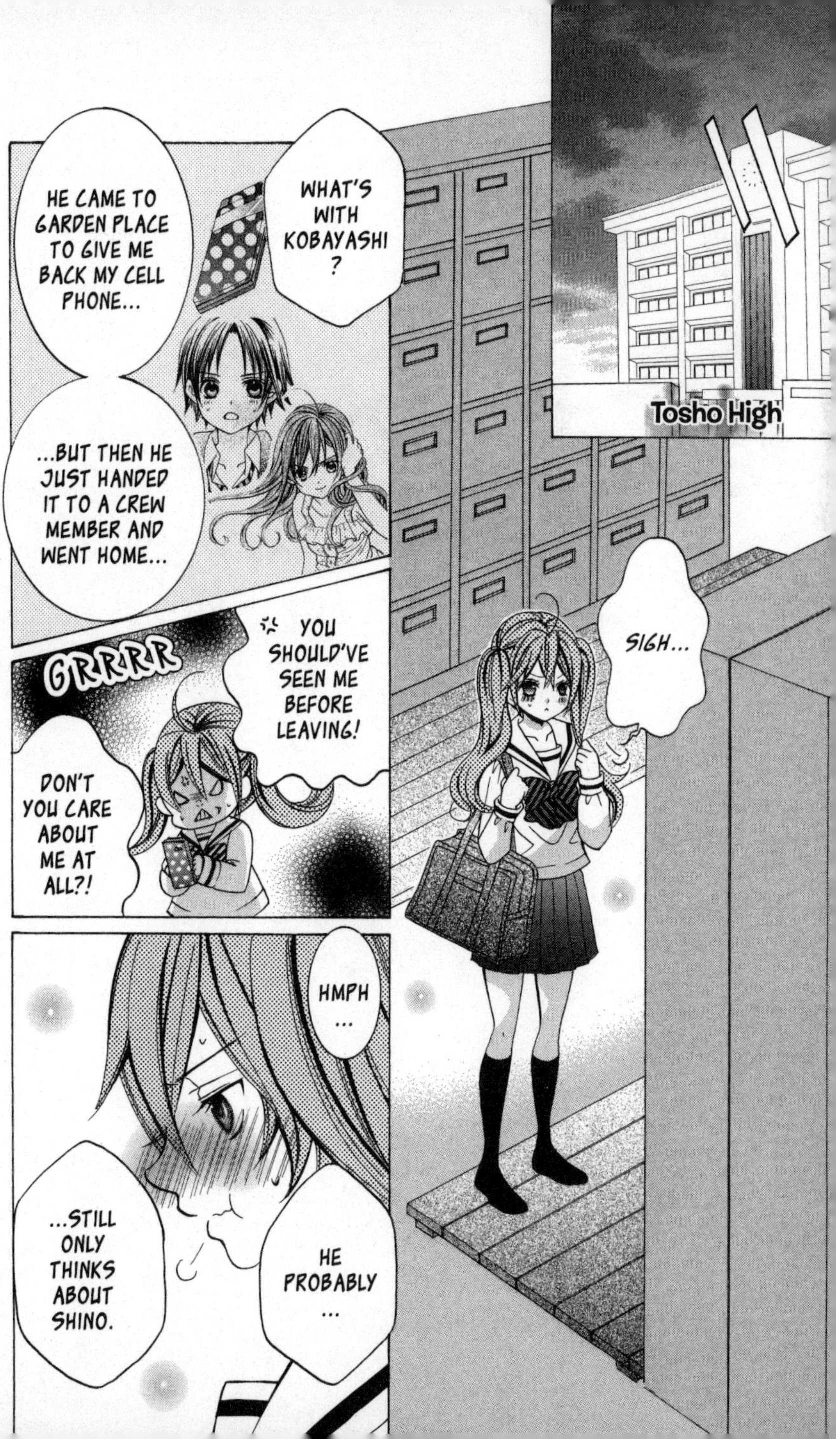
Tosho High
SIGH...
WHAT'S WITH KOBAYASHI?
HE CAME TO GARDEN PLACE TO GIVE ME BACK MY CELL PHONE...
...BUT THEN HE JUST HANDED IT TO A CREW MEMBER AND WENT HOME...
GRRRR
YOU SHOULD'VE SEEN ME BEFORE LEAVING!
DON'T YOU CARE ABOUT ME AT ALL?!
HMPH...
HE PROBABLY...
...STILL ONLY THINKS ABOUT SHINO.

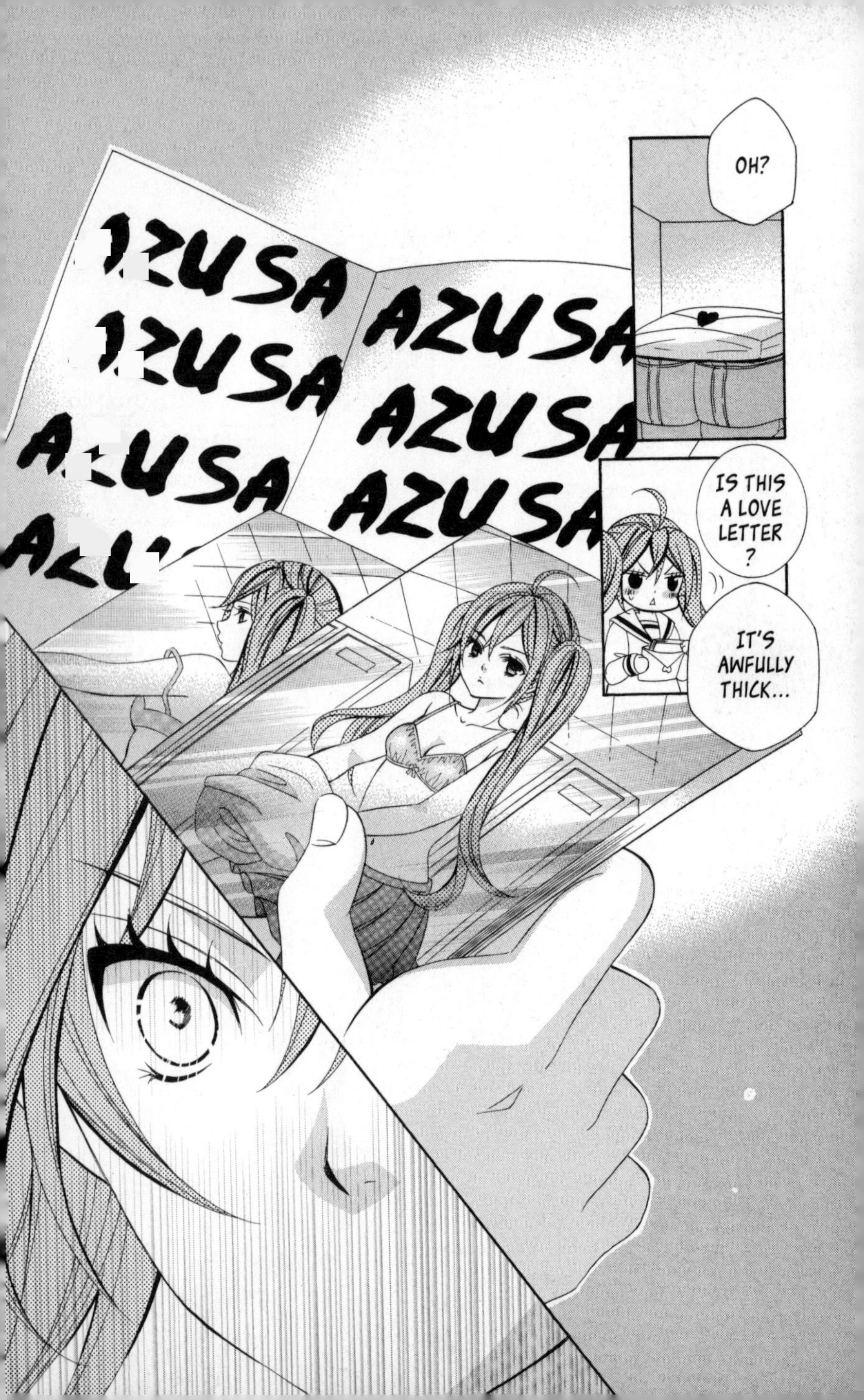
OH?
IS THIS A LOVE LETTER?
IT'S AWFULLY THICK...
AZUSA
AZUSA
AZUSA
AZUSA

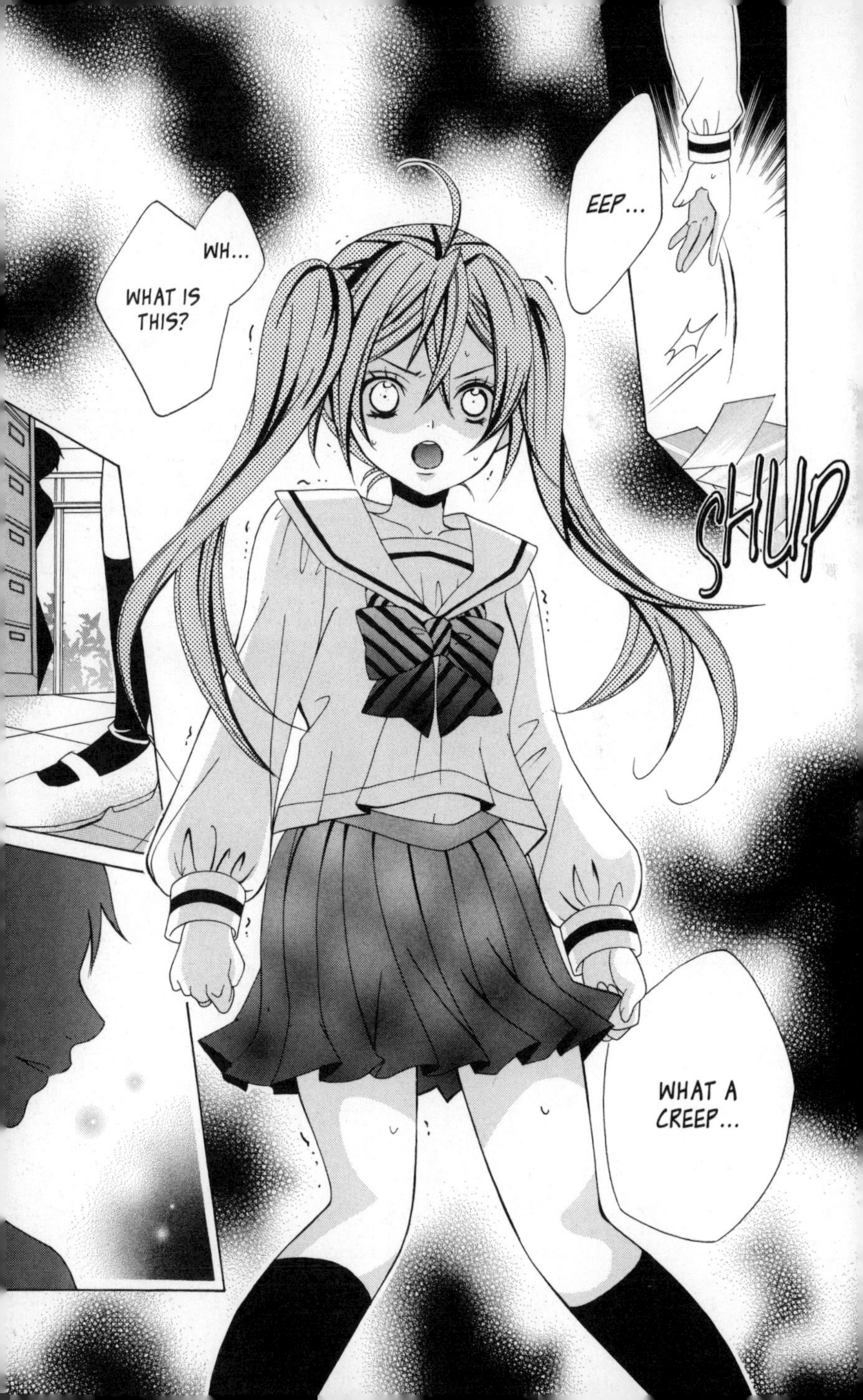
EEP...
SHUP
WH... WHAT IS THIS?
WHAT A CREEP...

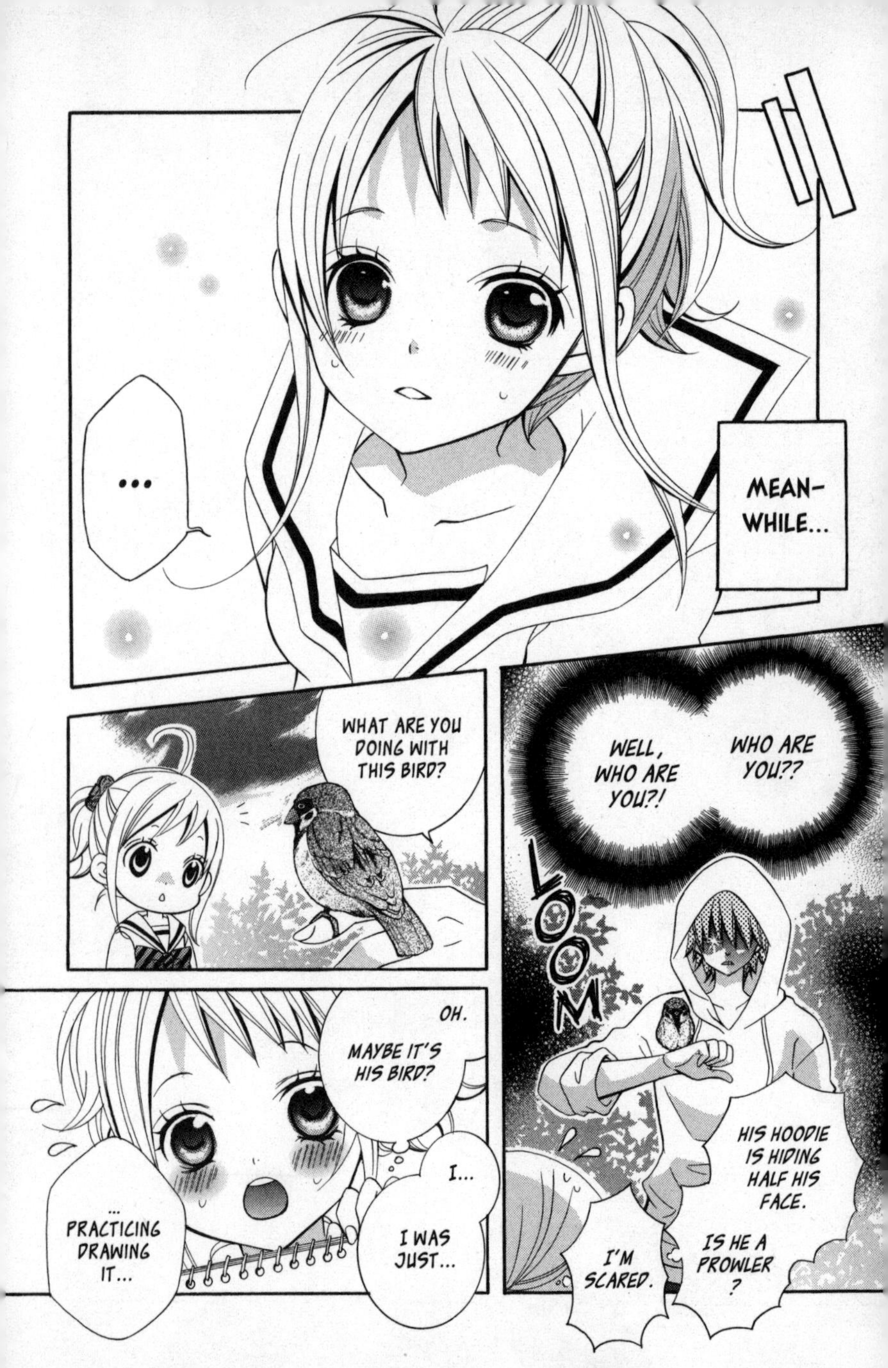
MEAN-WHILE...
...
WHO ARE YOU??
WELL, WHO ARE YOU?!
LOOM
HIS HOODIE IS HIDING HALF HIS FACE.
IS HE A PROWLER?
I'M SCARED.
WHAT ARE YOU DOING WITH THIS BIRD?
OH.
MAYBE IT'S HIS BIRD?
I...
I WAS JUST...
...PRACTICING DRAWING IT...

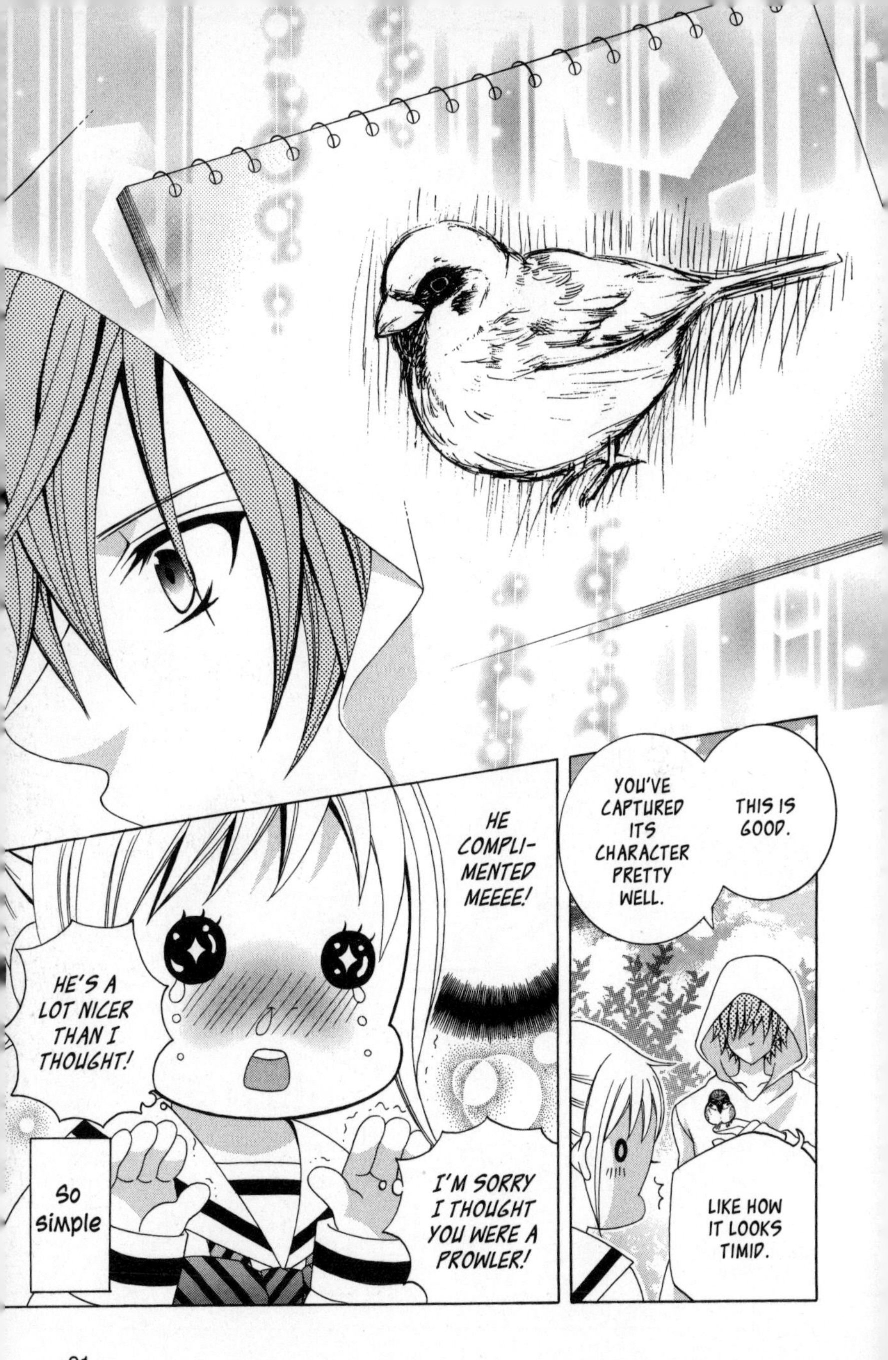
THIS IS GOOD.
YOU'VE CAPTURED ITS CHARACTER PRETTY WELL.
LIKE HOW IT LOOKS TIMID.
HE COMPLI-MENTED MEEEE!
HE'S A LOT NICER THAN I THOUGHT!
I'M SORRY I THOUGHT YOU WERE A PROWLER!
So simple

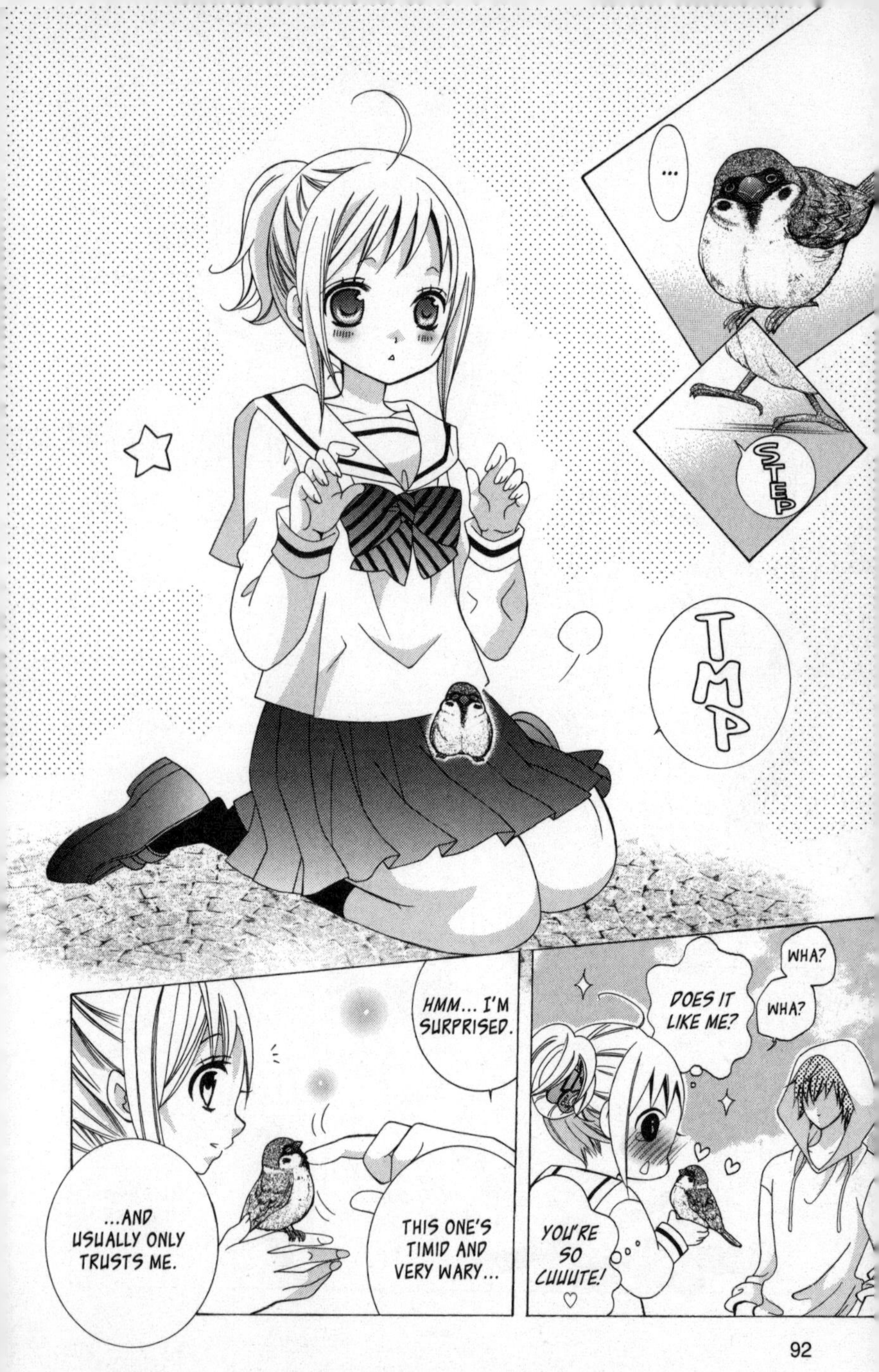
...
STEP
TMP
WHA?
WHA?
DOES IT LIKE ME?
YOU'RE SO CUUUTE! ♡
HMM... I'M SURPRISED.
THIS ONE'S TIMID AND VERY WARY...
...AND USUALLY ONLY TRUSTS ME.

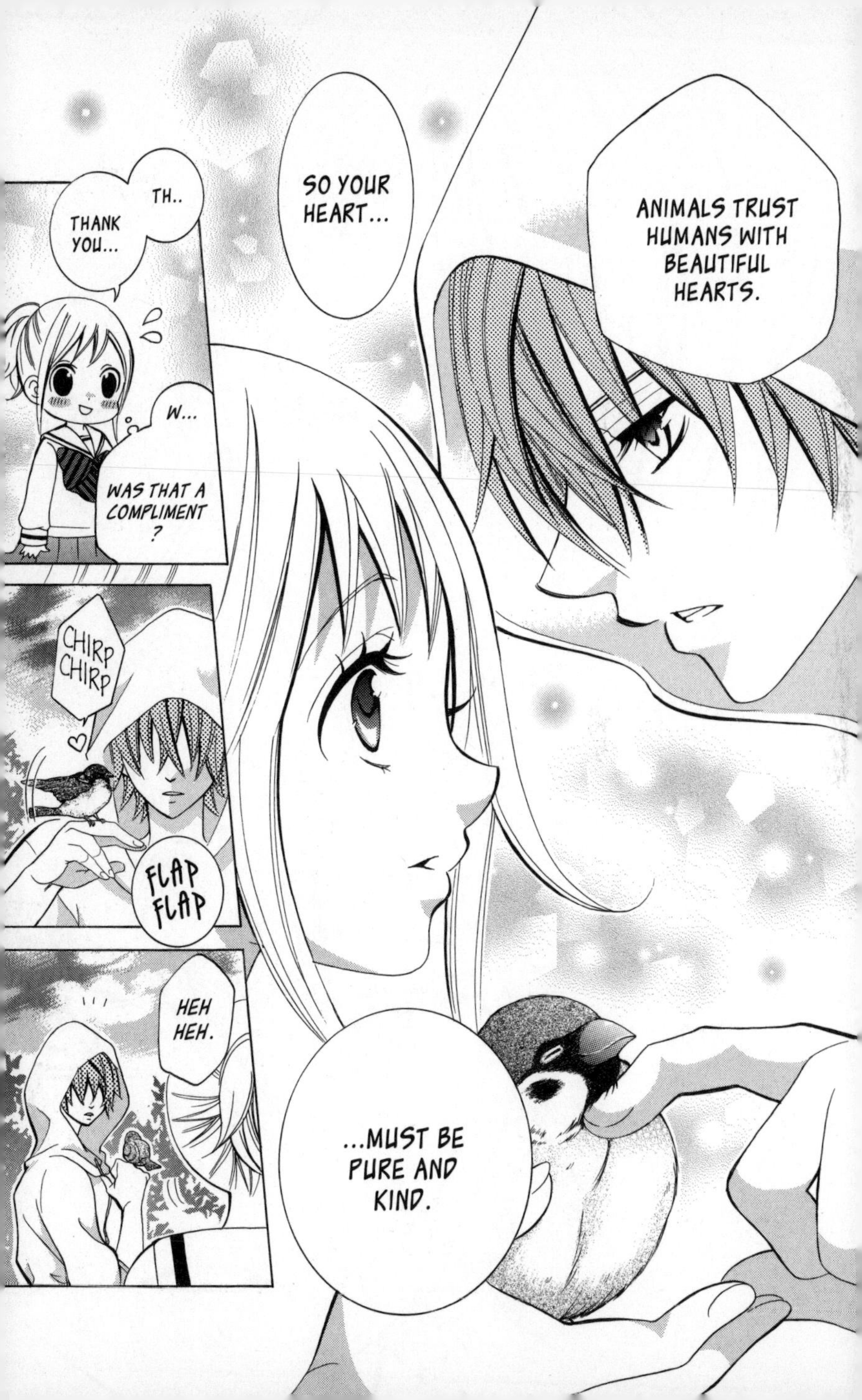
ANIMALS TRUST HUMANS WITH BEAUTIFUL HEARTS.
SO YOUR HEART...
...MUST BE PURE AND KIND.
TH.. THANK YOU...
W... WAS THAT A COMPLIMENT ?
CHIRP CHIRP
FLAP FLAP
HEH HEH.

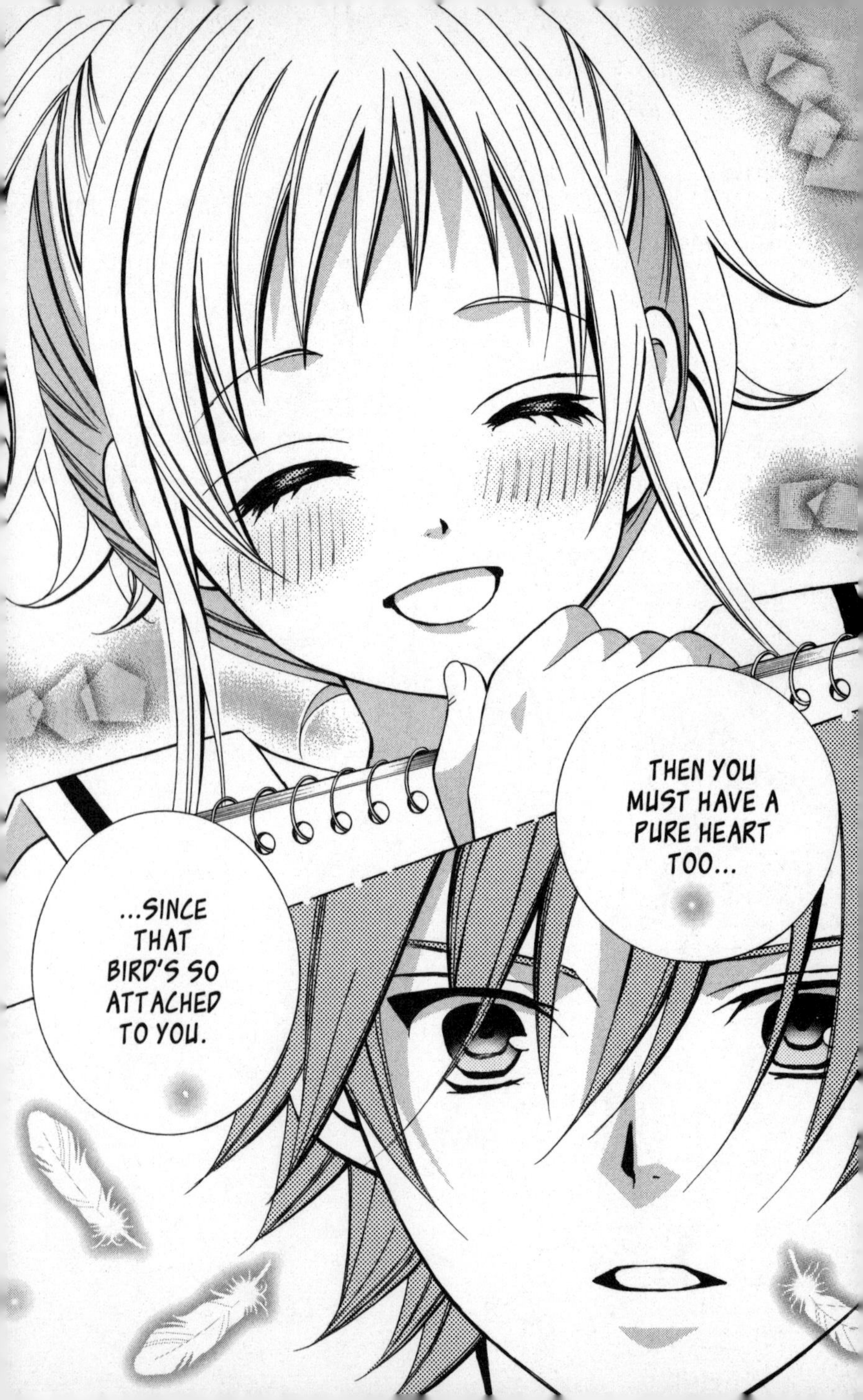
THEN YOU MUST HAVE A PURE HEART TOO...
...SINCE THAT BIRD'S SO ATTACHED TO YOU.

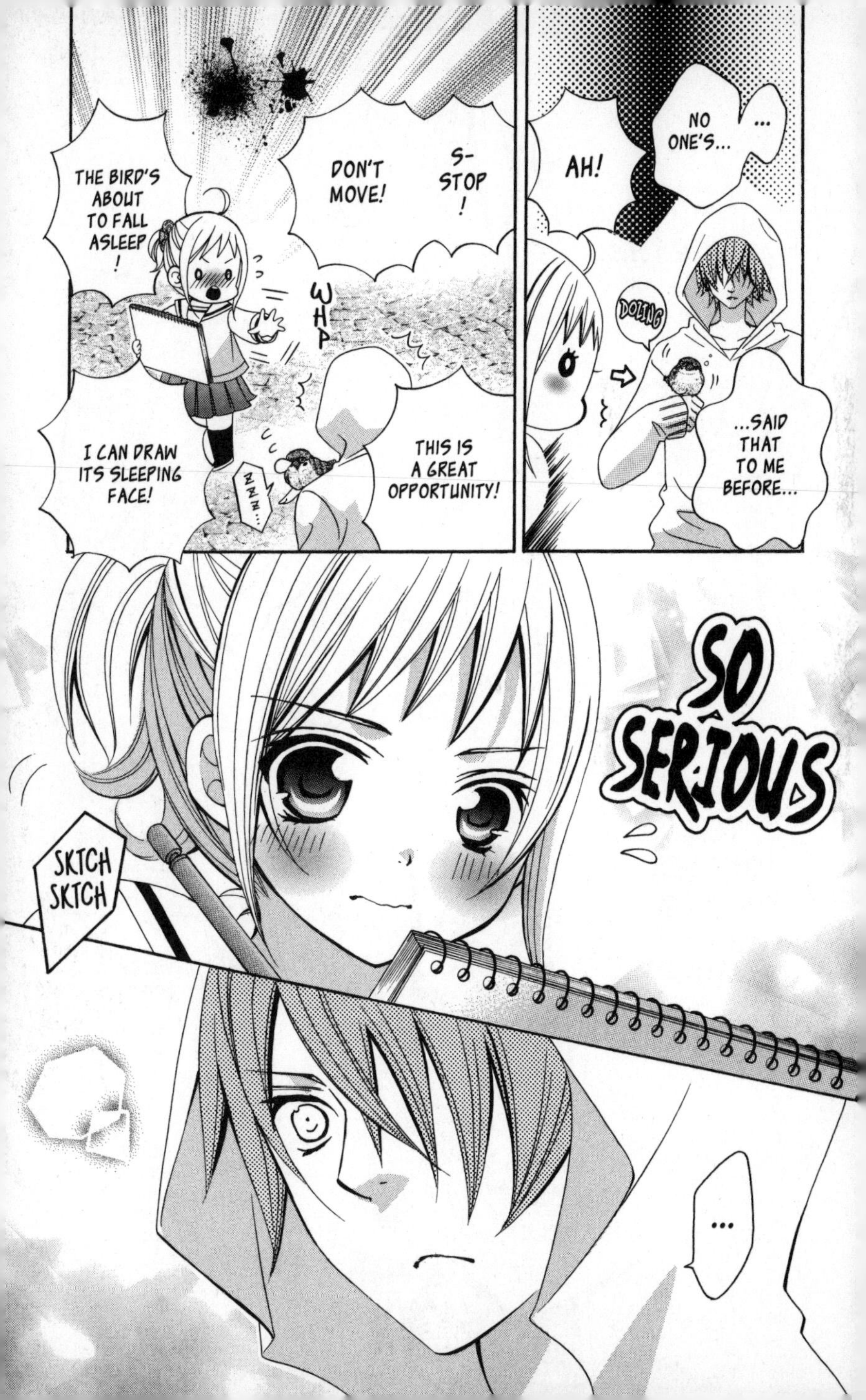
...
NO ONE'S...
AH!
DOLING
...SAID THAT TO ME BEFORE...
S-STOP!
DON'T MOVE!
THE BIRD'S ABOUT TO FALL ASLEEP!
WHP
THIS IS A GREAT OPPORTUNITY!
I CAN DRAW ITS SLEEPING FACE!
ZZZ...
SO SERIOUS
SKTCH SKTCH
...

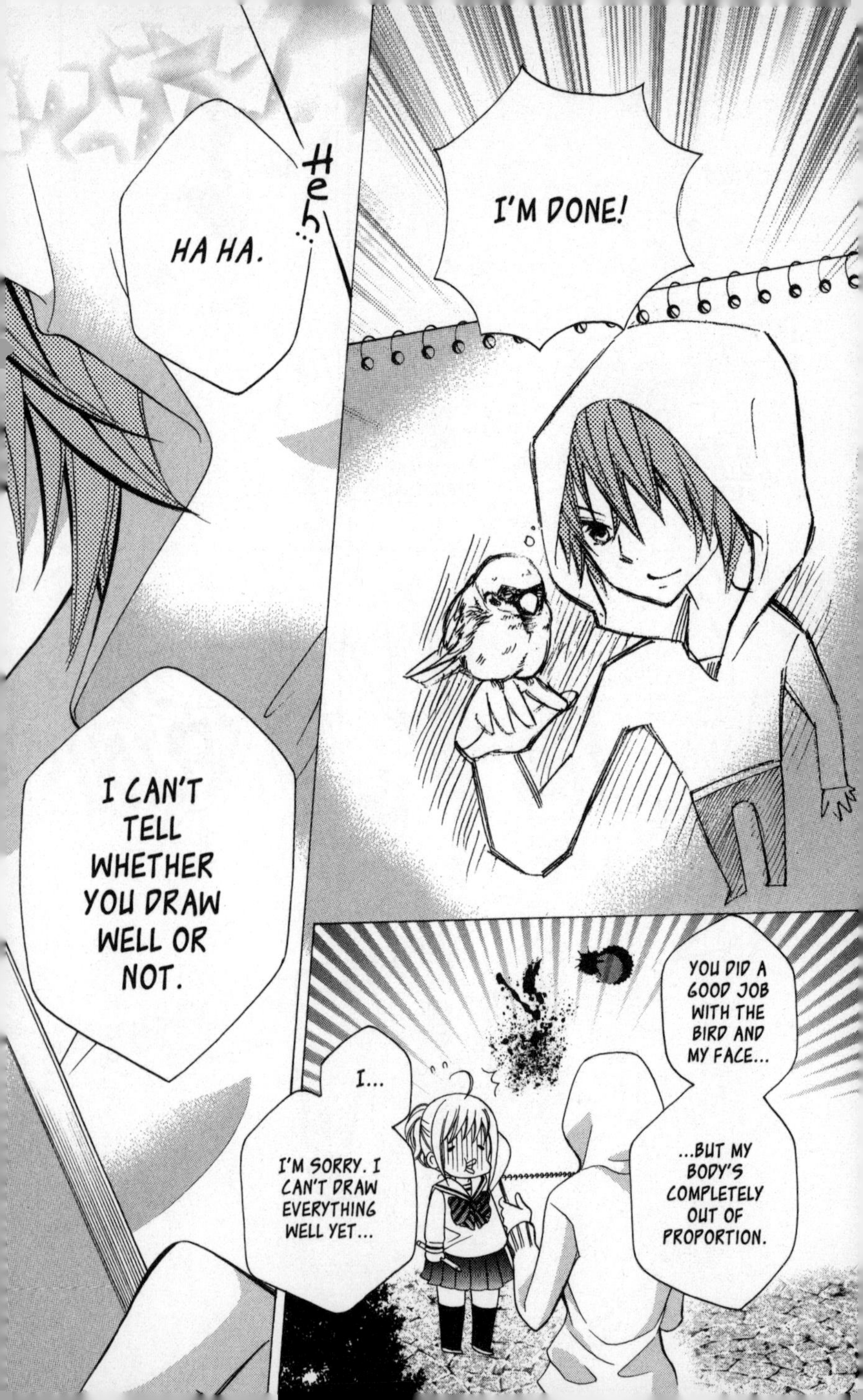
I'M DONE!
YOU DID A GOOD JOB WITH THE BIRD AND MY FACE...
...BUT MY BODY'S COMPLETELY OUT OF PROPORTION.
I...
I'M SORRY. I CAN'T DRAW EVERYTHING WELL YET...
Heh...
HA HA.
I CAN'T TELL WHETHER YOU DRAW WELL OR NOT.

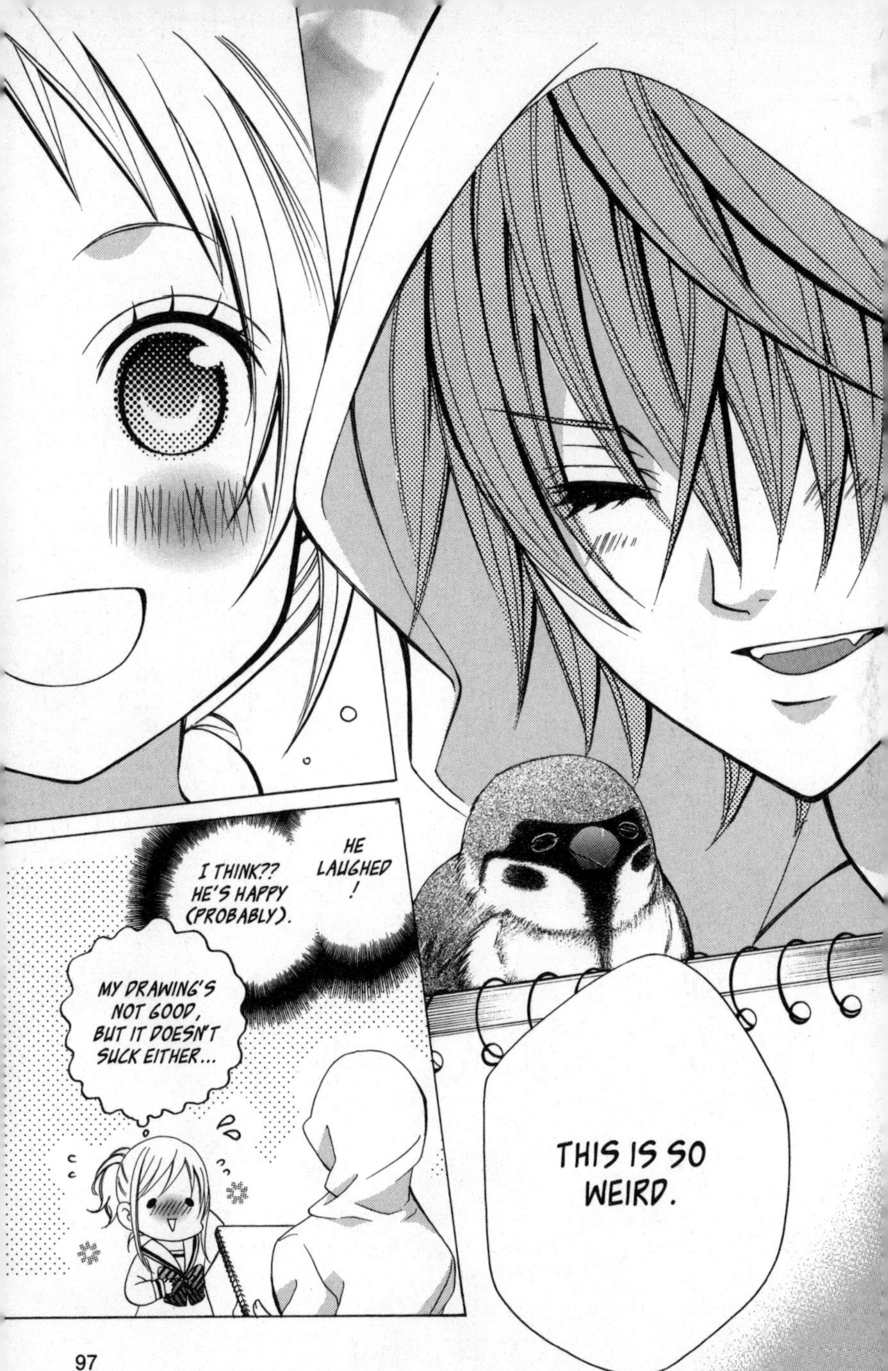
THIS IS SO WEIRD.
HE LAUGHED!
I THINK?? HE'S HAPPY (PROBABLY).
MY DRAWING'S NOT GOOD, BUT IT DOESN'T SUCK EITHER...

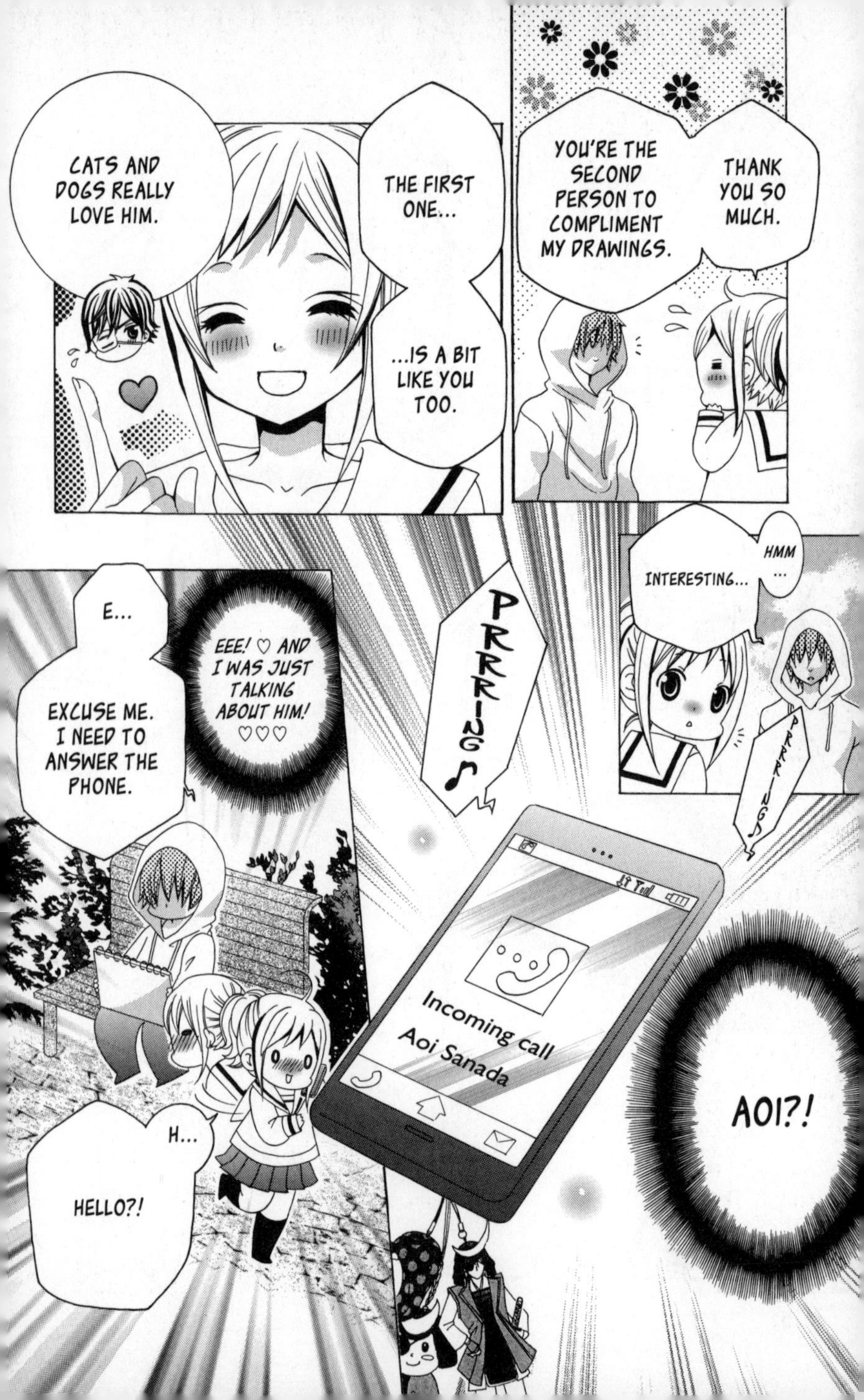
THANK YOU SO MUCH.
YOU'RE THE SECOND PERSON TO COMPLIMENT MY DRAWINGS.
THE FIRST ONE...
...IS A BIT LIKE YOU TOO.
CATS AND DOGS REALLY LOVE HIM.
HMM...
INTERESTING...
PRRRING♪
PRRRING♪
AOI?!
Incoming call
Aoi Sanada
EEE! ♡ AND I WAS JUST TALKING ABOUT HIM! ♡♡♡
E...
EXCUSE ME. I NEED TO ANSWER THE PHONE.
H...
HELLO?!

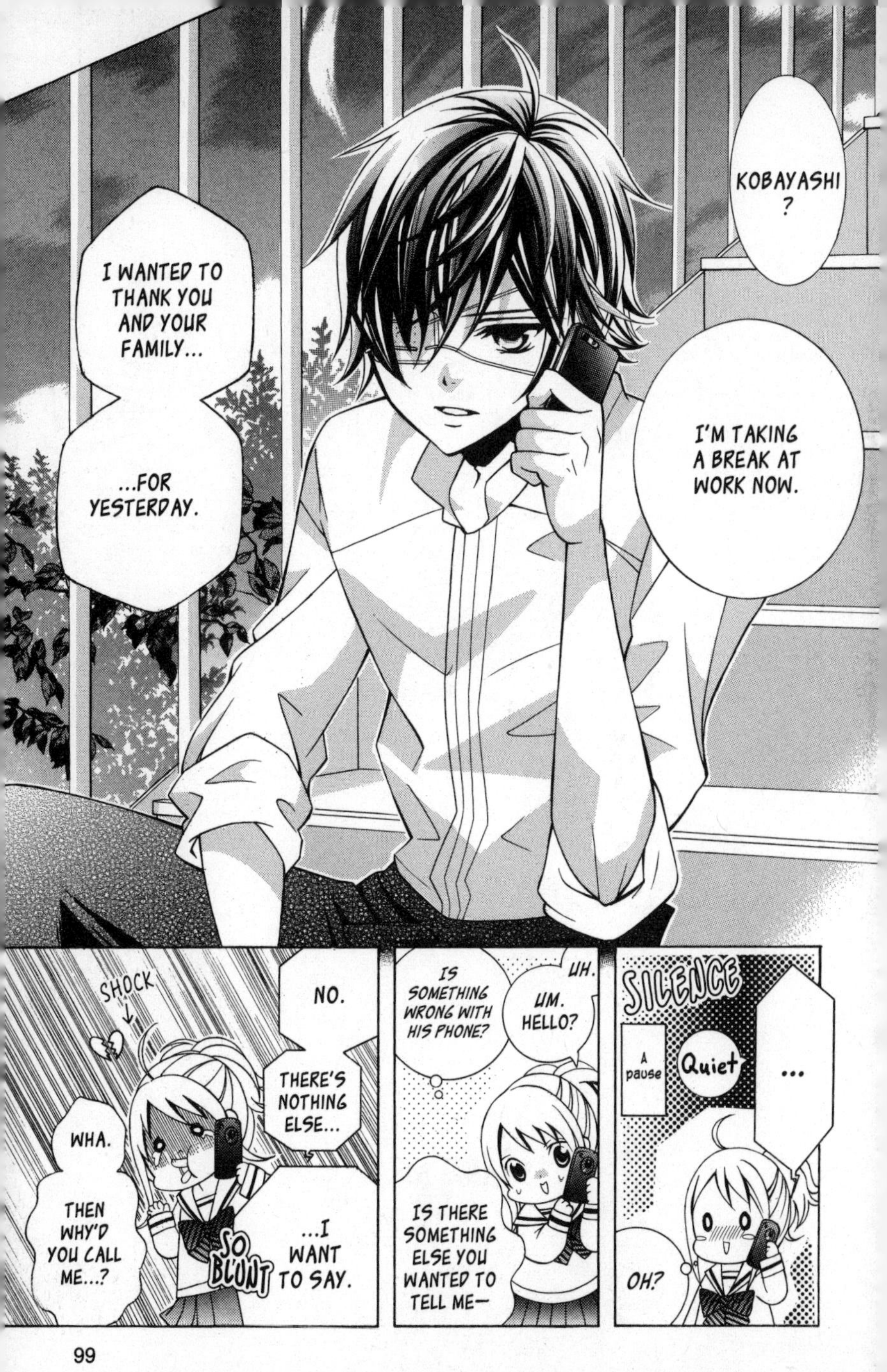
KOBAYASHI ?
I'M TAKING A BREAK AT WORK NOW.
I WANTED TO THANK YOU AND YOUR FAMILY...
...FOR YESTERDAY.
SILENCE
...
A pause
Quiet
OH?
UH.
UM. HELLO?
IS SOMETHING WRONG WITH HIS PHONE?
IS THERE SOMETHING ELSE YOU WANTED TO TELL ME—
NO.
THERE'S NOTHING ELSE...
...I WANT TO SAY.
SHOCK
WHA.
THEN WHY'D YOU CALL ME...?
SO BLUNT

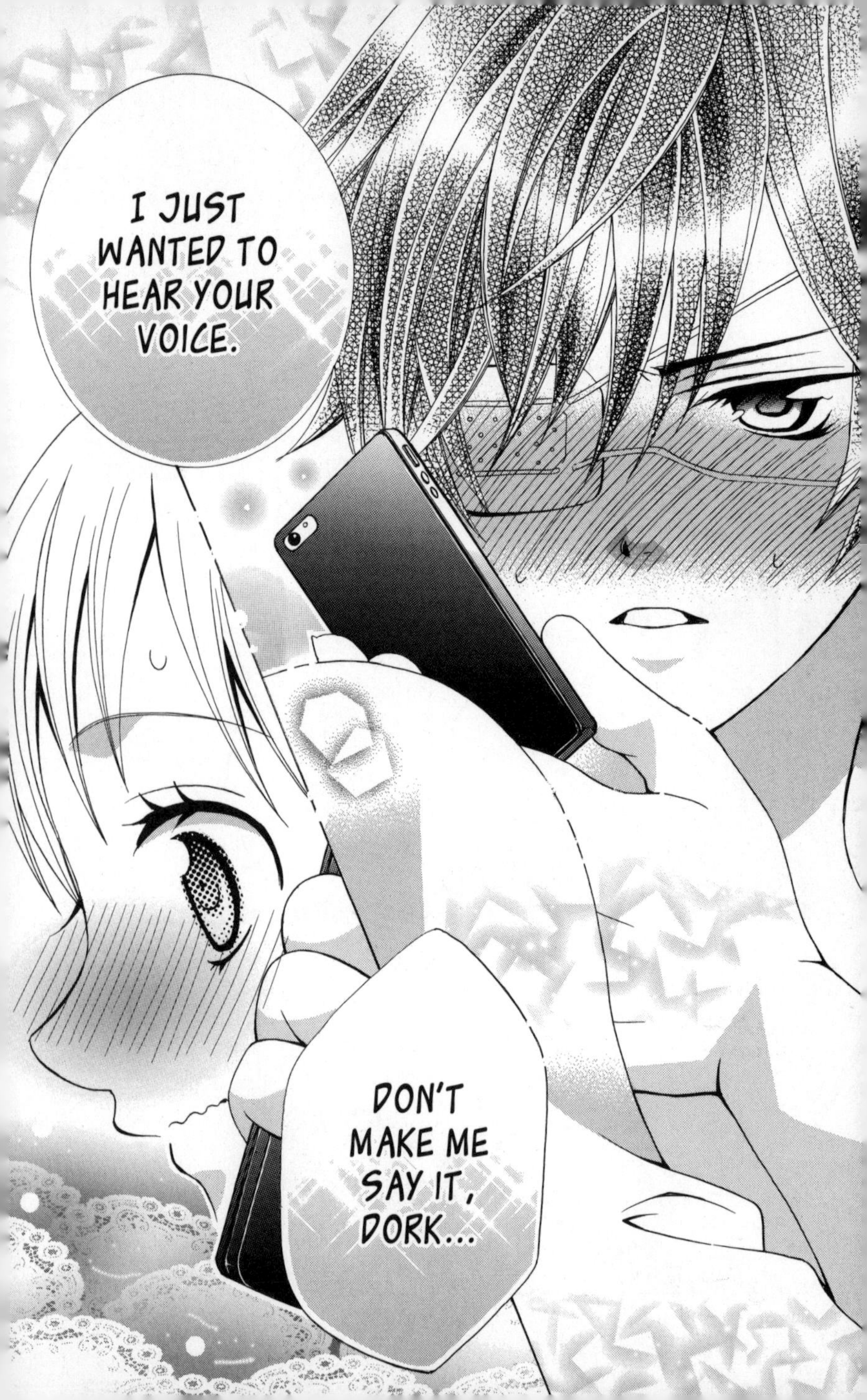
I JUST WANTED TO HEAR YOUR VOICE.
DON'T MAKE ME SAY IT, DORK...

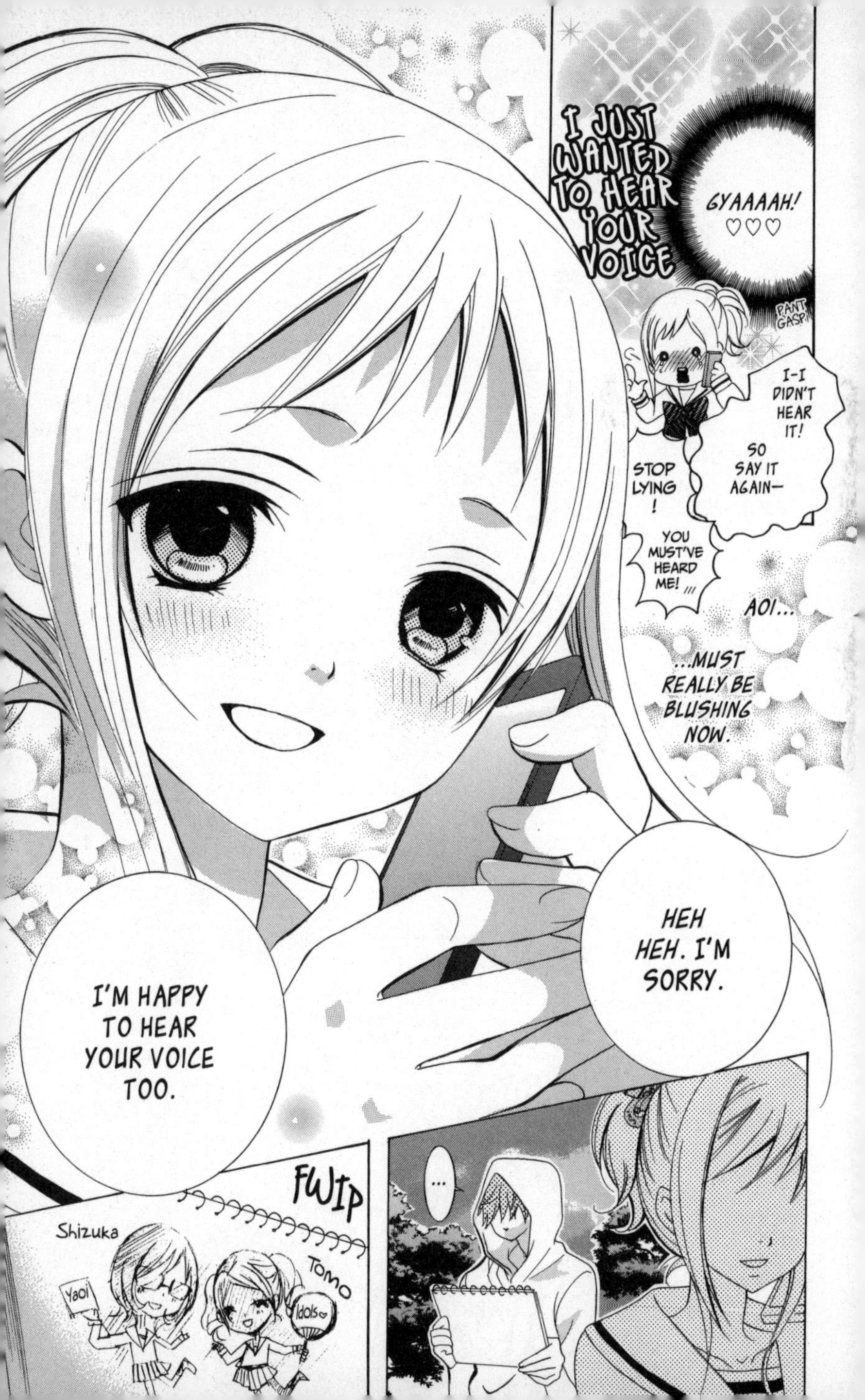
I JUST WANTED TO HEAR YOUR VOICE
GYAAAAH! ♡♡♡
PANT GASP
I-I DIDN'T HEAR IT!
SO SAY IT AGAIN—
STOP LYING!
YOU MUST'VE HEARD ME!
AOI...
...MUST REALLY BE BLUSHING NOW.
HEH HEH. I'M SORRY.
I'M HAPPY TO HEAR YOUR VOICE TOO.
...
FWIP
Tomo
Idols♡
Shizuka
Yaoi

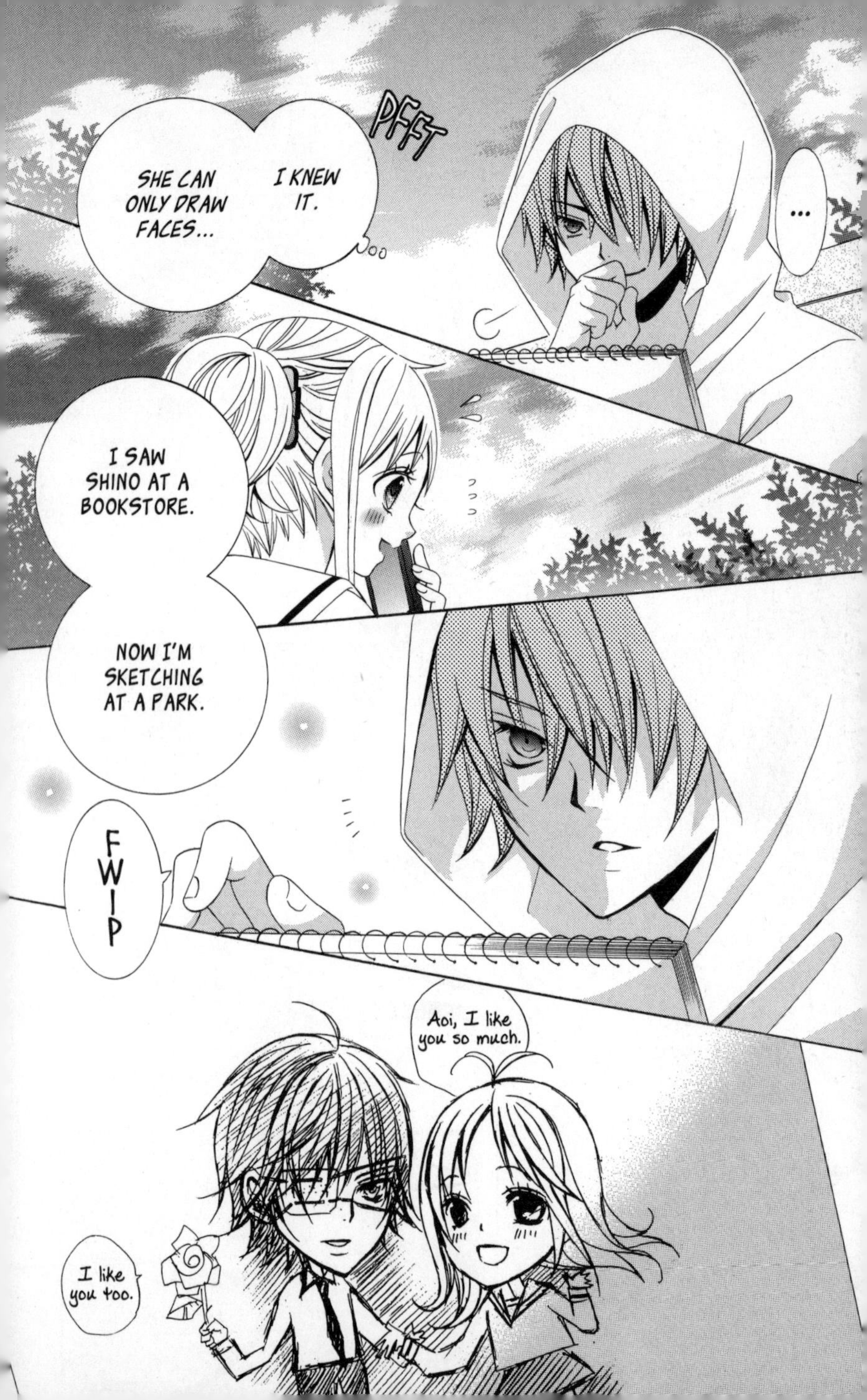
...
PFFT
I KNEW IT.
SHE CAN ONLY DRAW FACES...
I SAW SHINO AT A BOOKSTORE.
NOW I'M SKETCHING AT A PARK.
FWIP
Aoi, I like you so much.
I like you too.

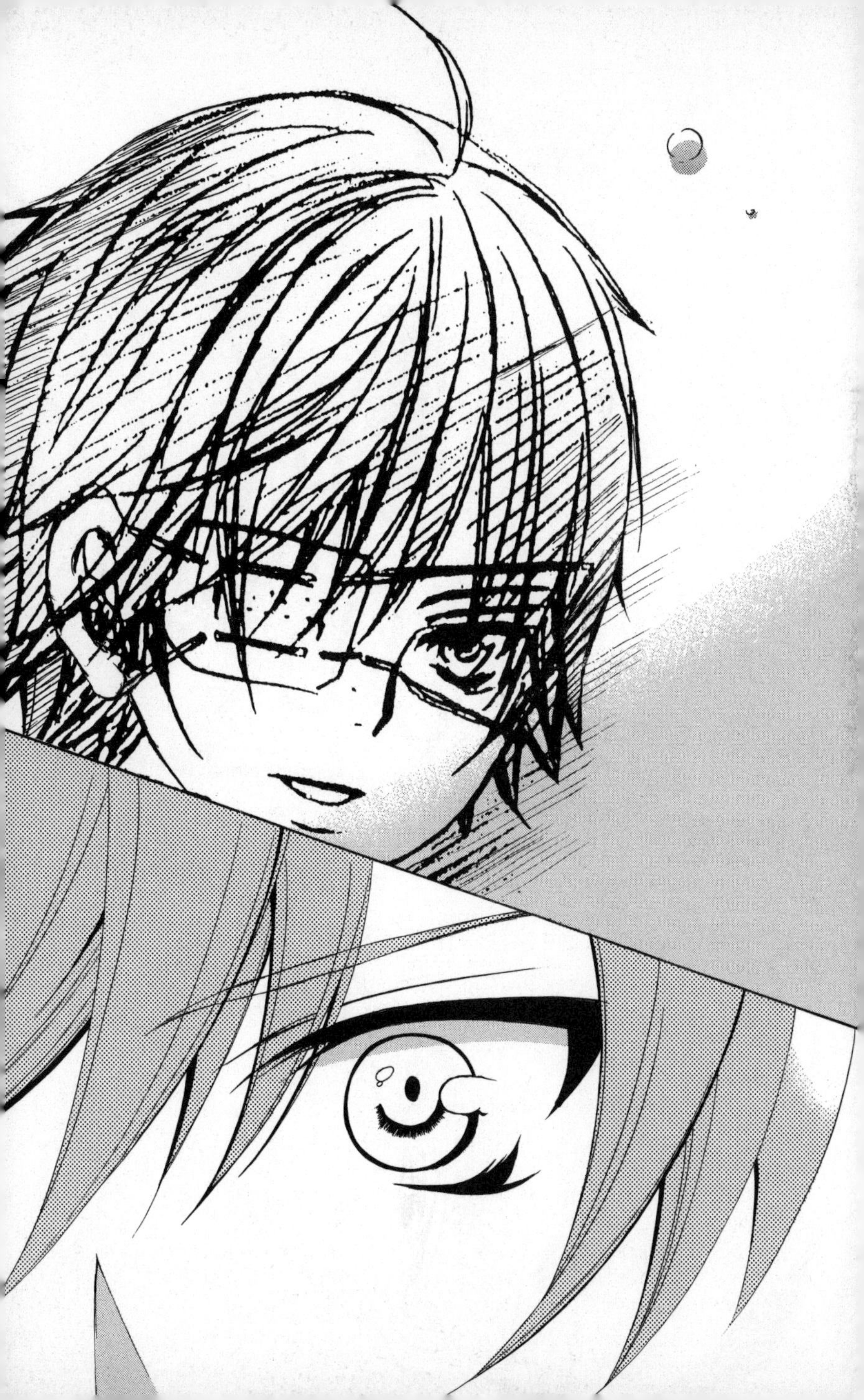

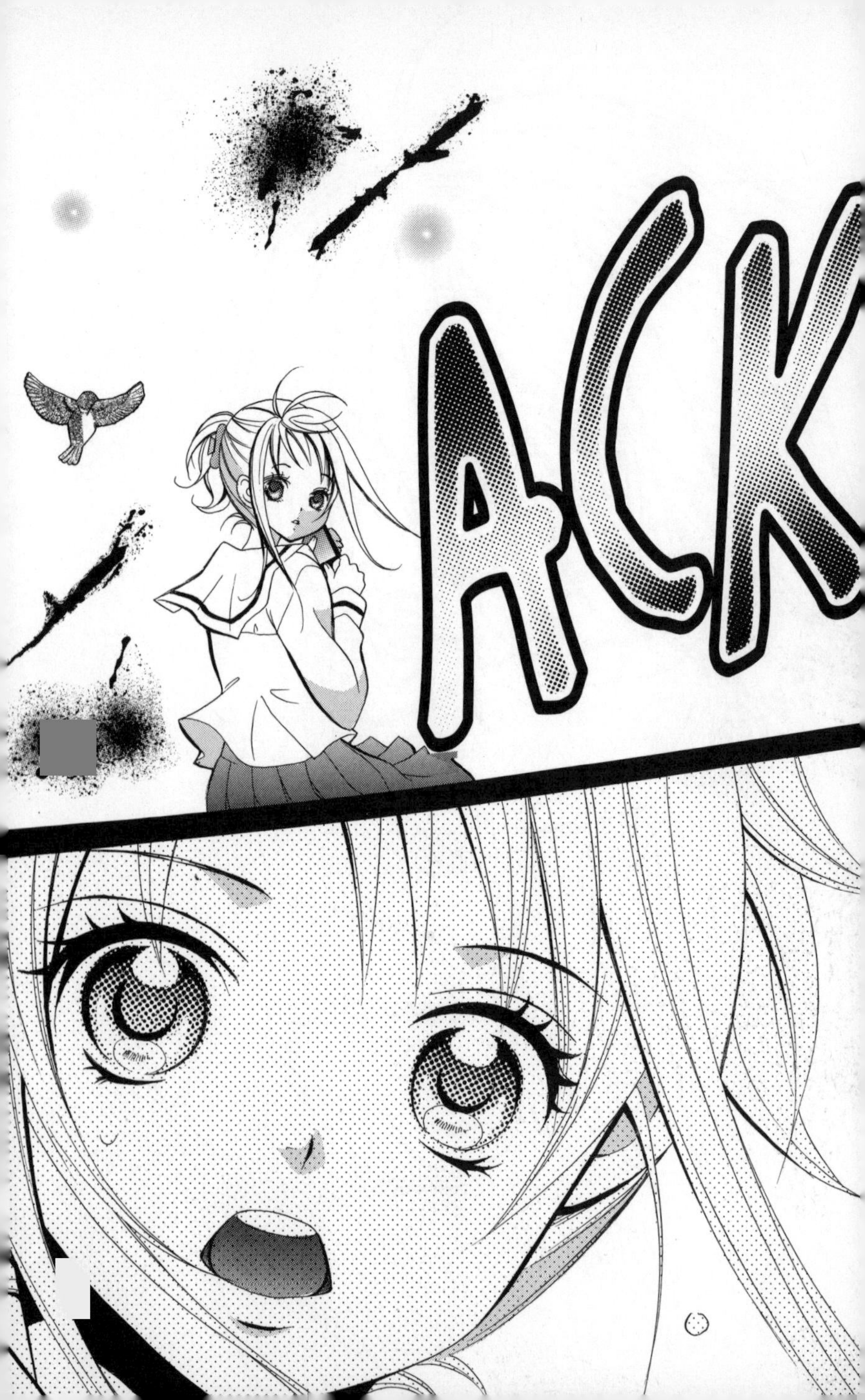
ACK

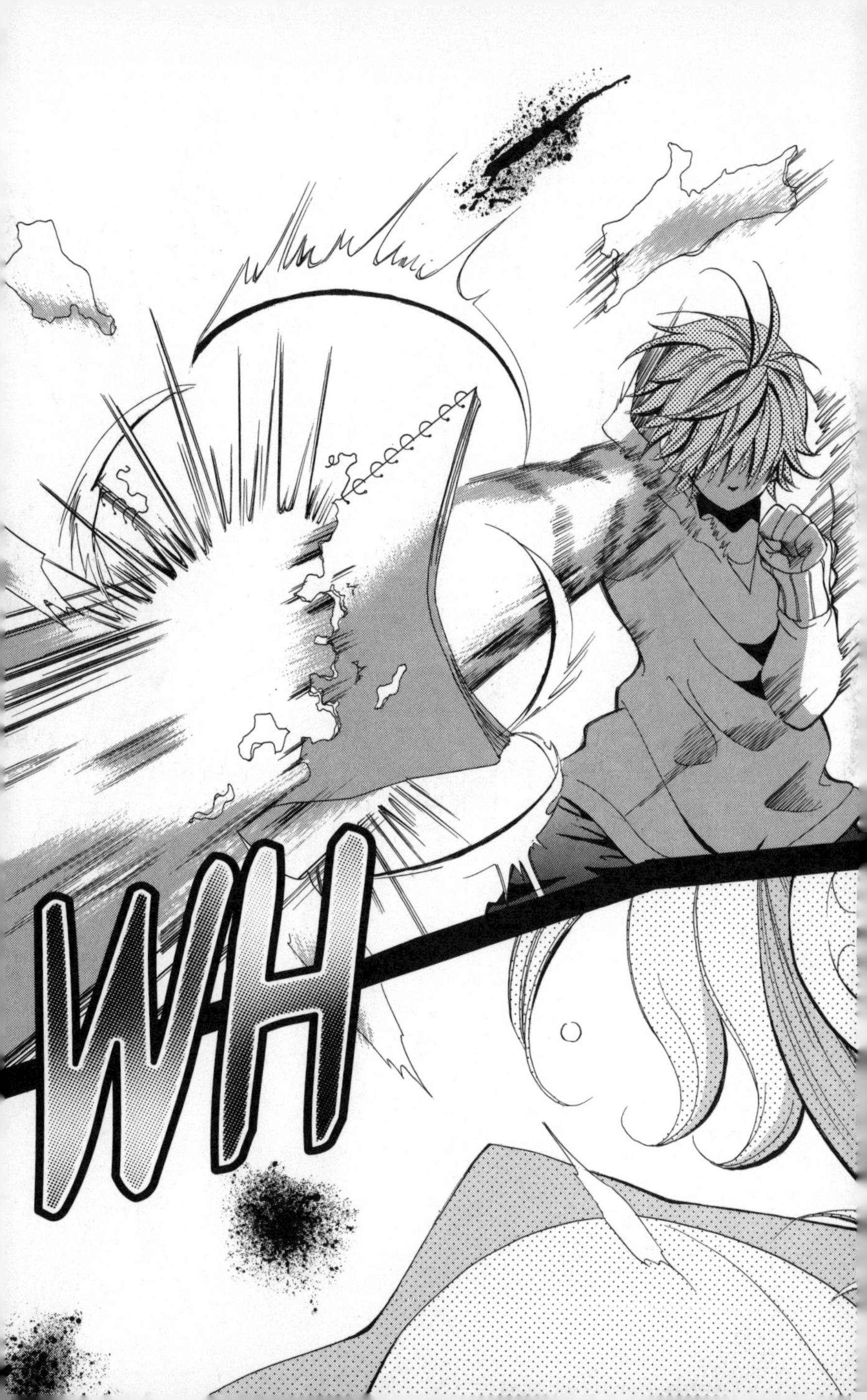
WH

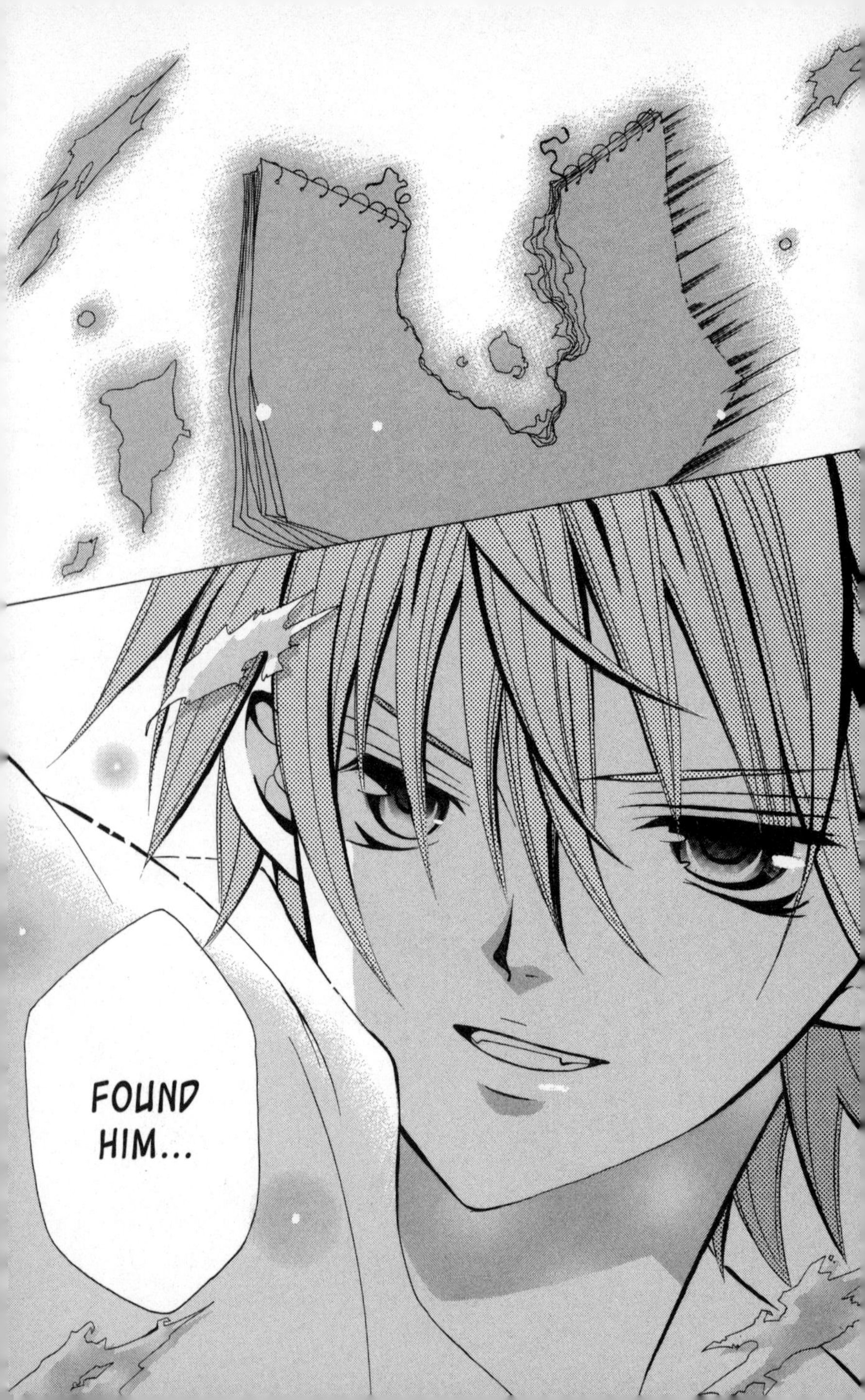
FOUND HIM...

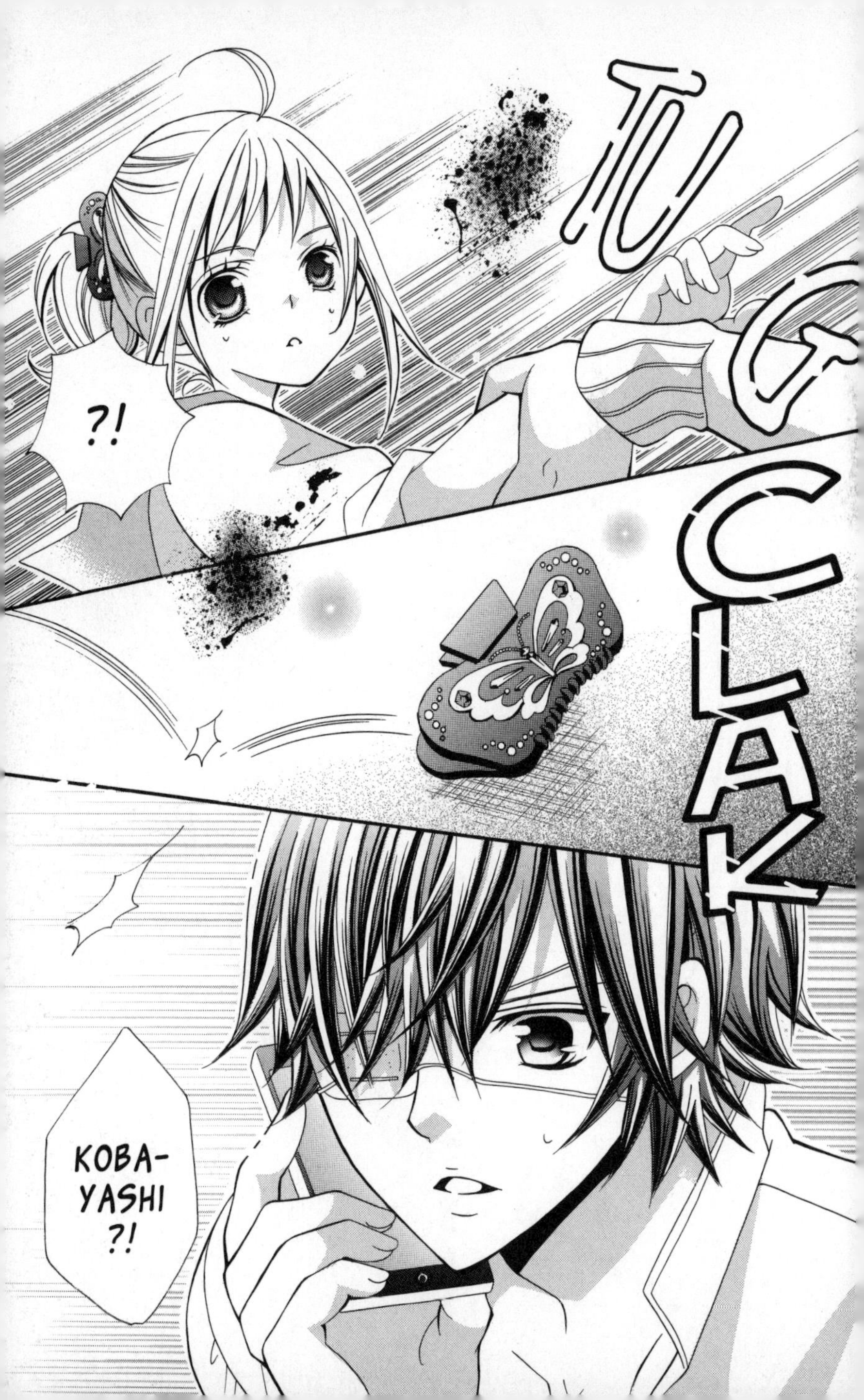
TUG
?!
CLAK
KOBA-YASHI ?!

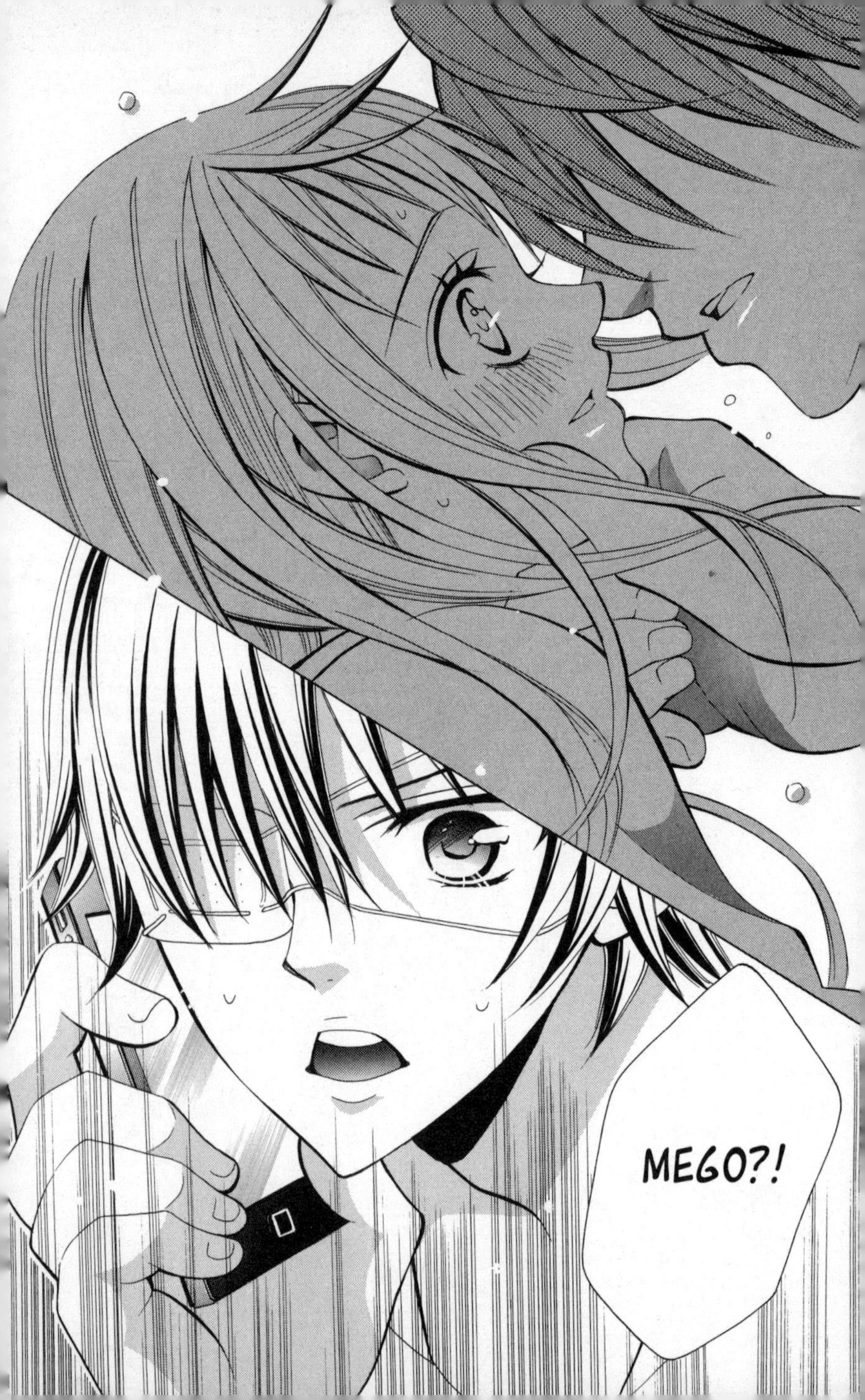
MEGO?!

Chapter 29

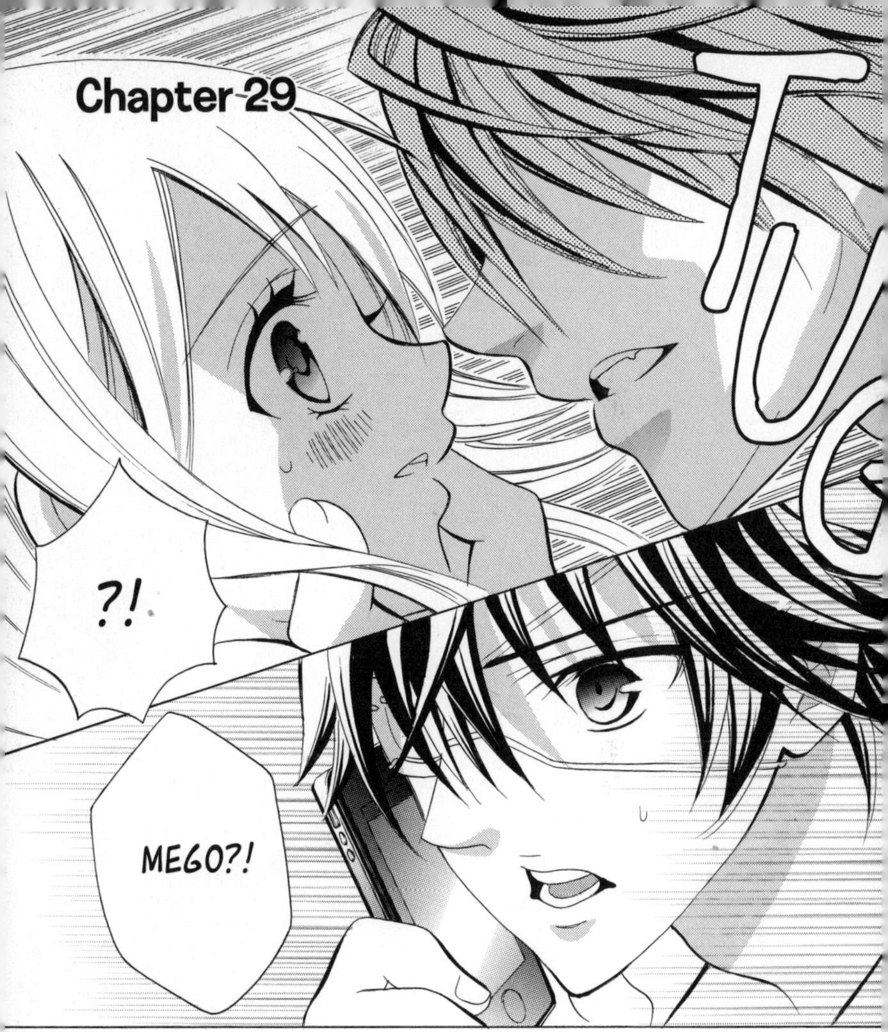
?!
MEGO?!

MANGA AND ANIME

SILVER SPOON, A VERY POPULAR MANGA THAT RUNS IN *SHONEN SUNDAY* MAGAZINE, HAS BECOME A LIVE-ACTION MOVIE! I REALLY LOVE THE MANGA BECAUSE IT'S DELIGHTFUL, BUT I ALSO ENJOYED THE MOVIE AND LAUGHED AND CRIED! I WAS MOVED BY YUZU'S "HIDAMARI" (THE MOVIE THEME SONG). IT'S SUCH A GREAT SONG. ♪♪

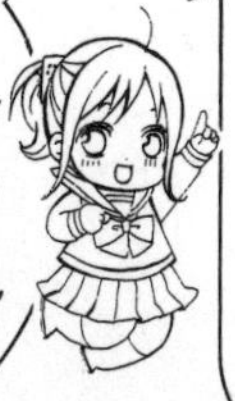

HAIKYU! AND THE THIRD SEASON OF *JOJO'S BIZARRE ADVENTURE* AIR IN JAPAN IN APRIL! I'M LOOKING FORWARD TO *JOJO'S* BECAUSE MR. DAISUKE ONO IS JOTARO THE HERO! MR. ONO, WHO DOES A WONDERFUL JOB WITH AOI'S VOICE, WILL BE THE THIRD JOJO! (*TEARS*) I'M SURE HE'LL BE EVEN MORE WONDERFUL AS JOJO, AND I'M VERY MUCH LOOKING FORWARD TO IT! I'M ALSO LOOKING FORWARD TO WATCHING *KAKYOIN*. ♪ I WANNA WATCH THE ANIME QUICK! LOL.

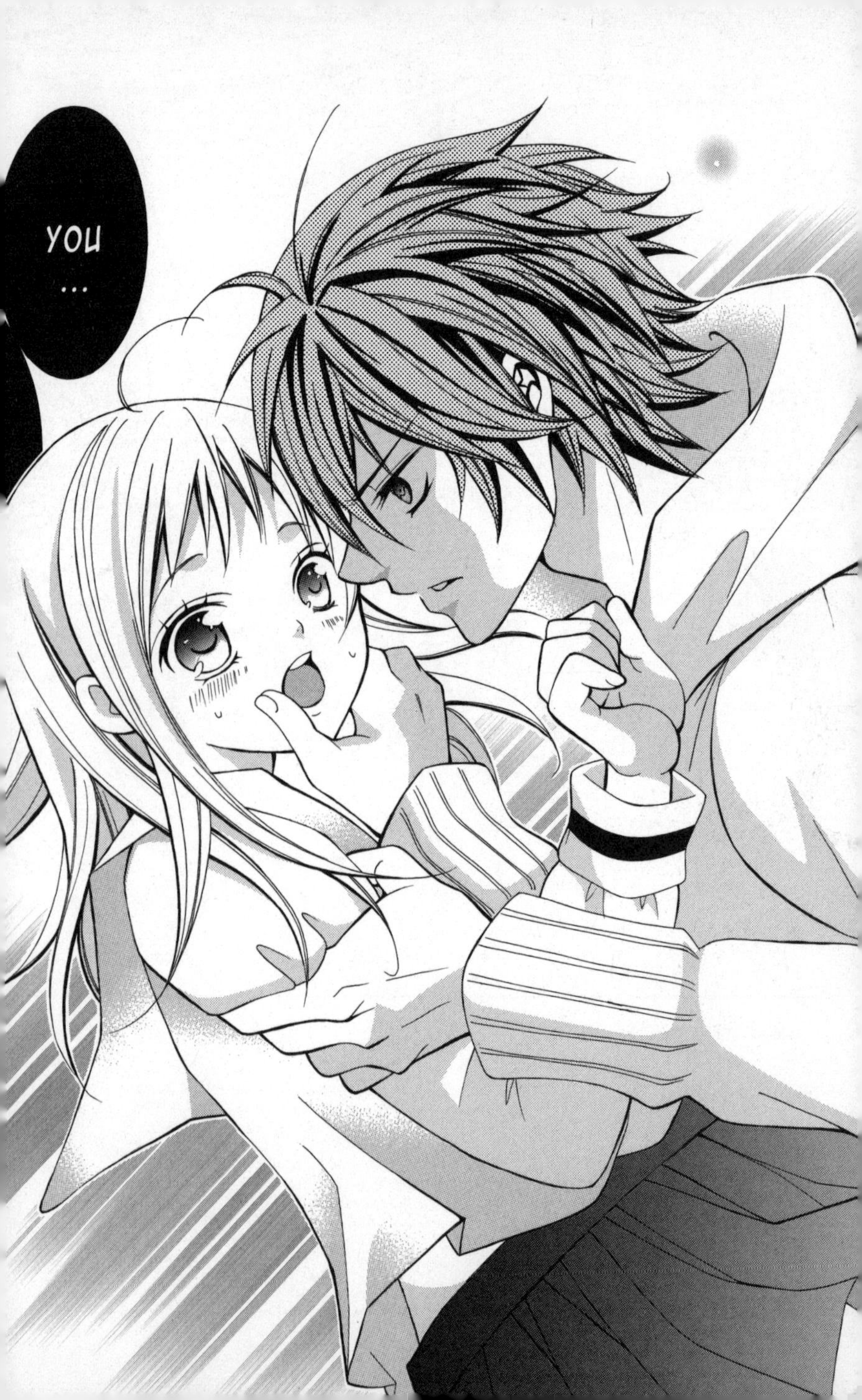
YOU ...

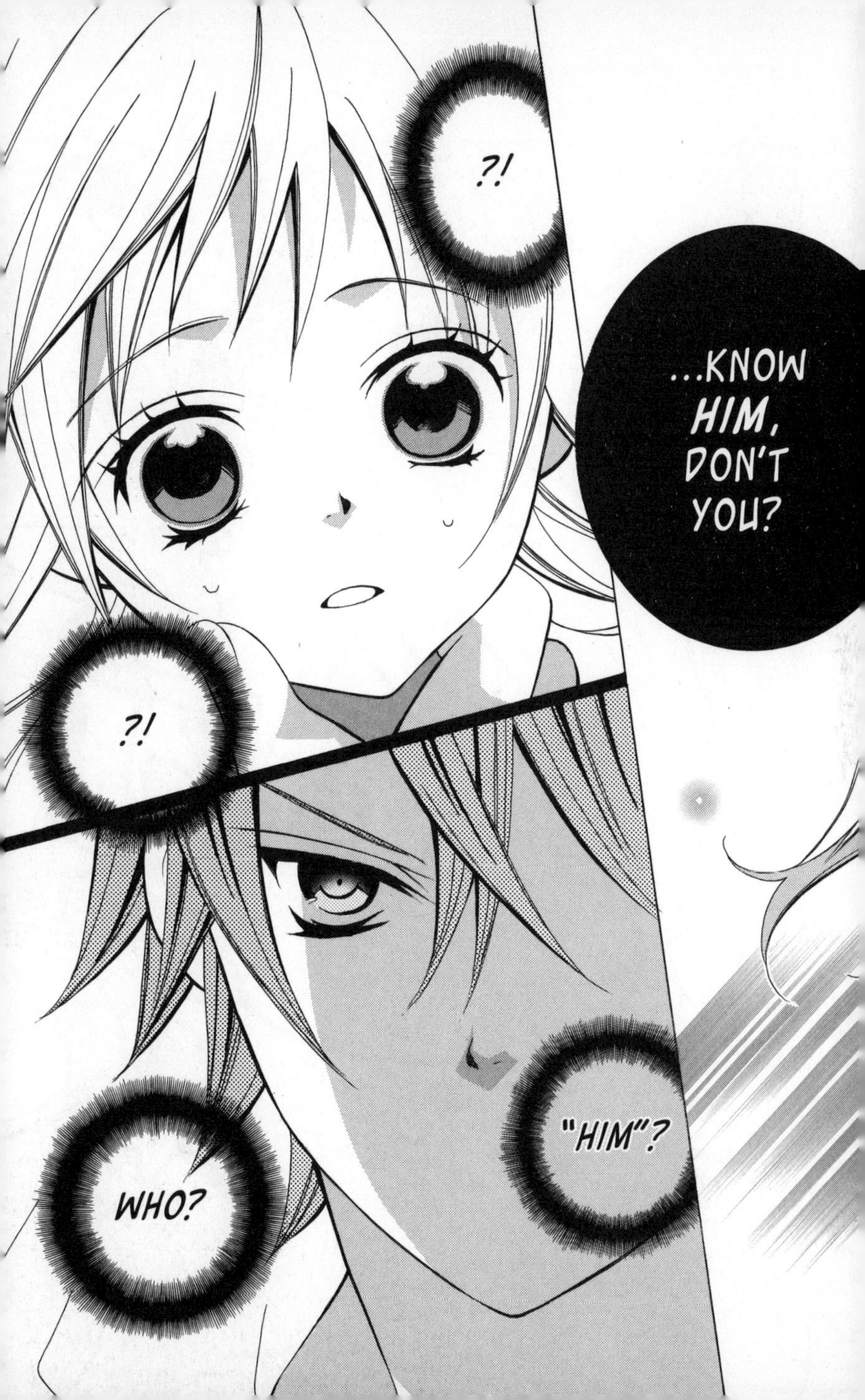
...KNOW HIM, DON'T YOU?
?!
?!
"HIM"?
WHO?

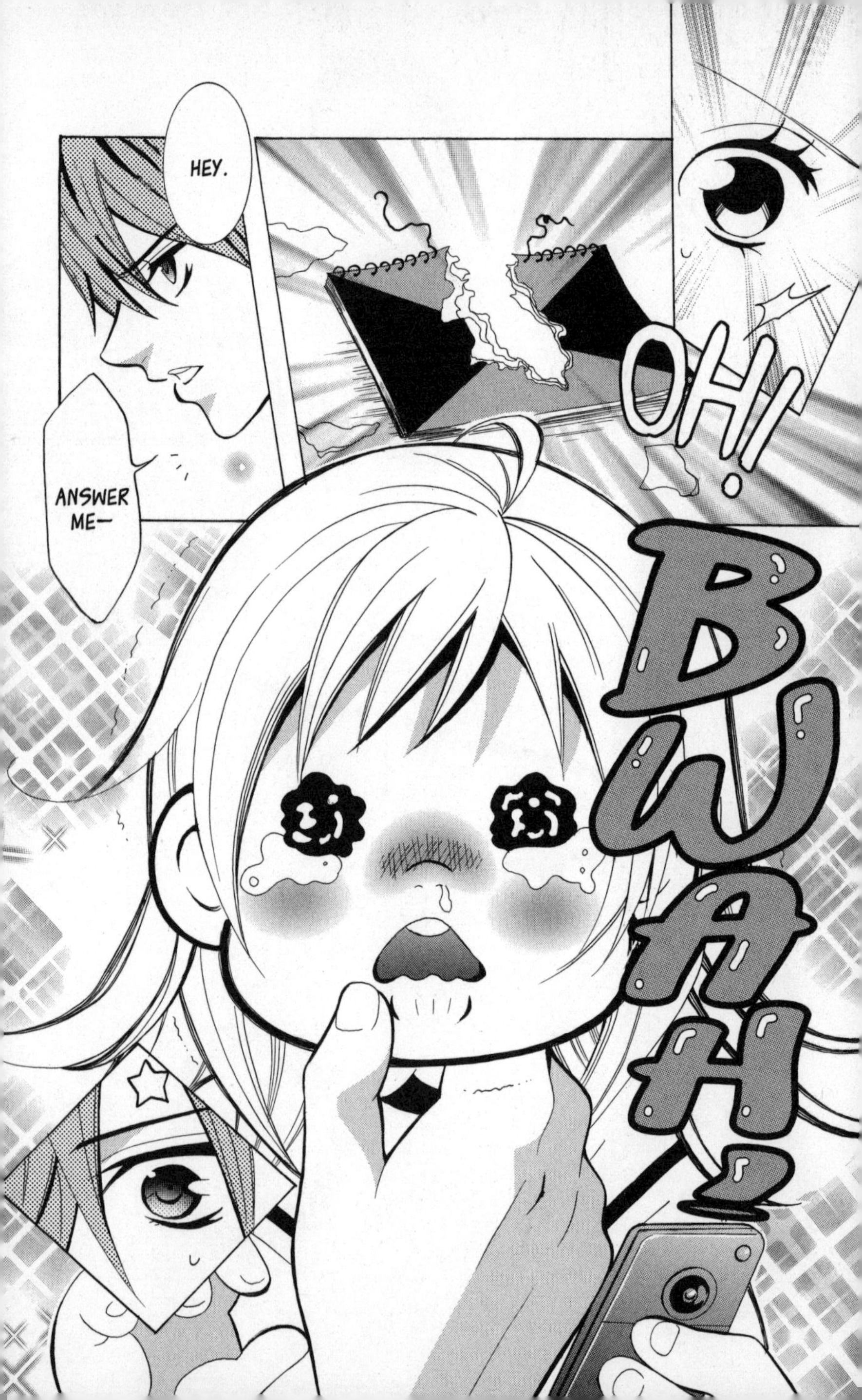
OH!
HEY.
ANSWER ME—
BWAAH?

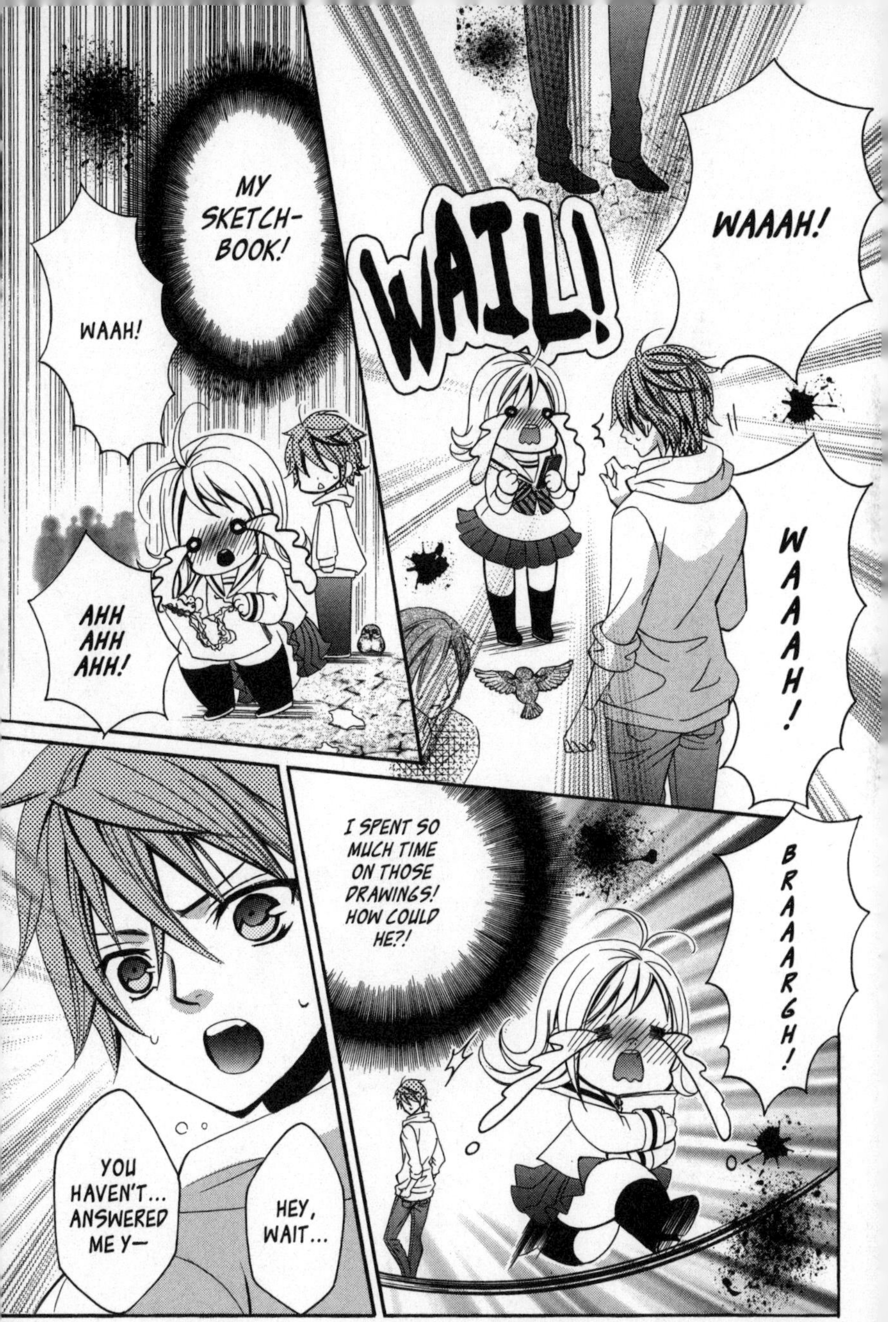
WAAAH!
WAIL!
WAAAAH!
MY SKETCH-BOOK!
WAAH!
AHH AHH AHH!
BRAAAARGH!
I SPENT SO MUCH TIME ON THOSE DRAWINGS! HOW COULD HE?!
HEY, WAIT...
YOU HAVEN'T... ANSWERED ME Y—

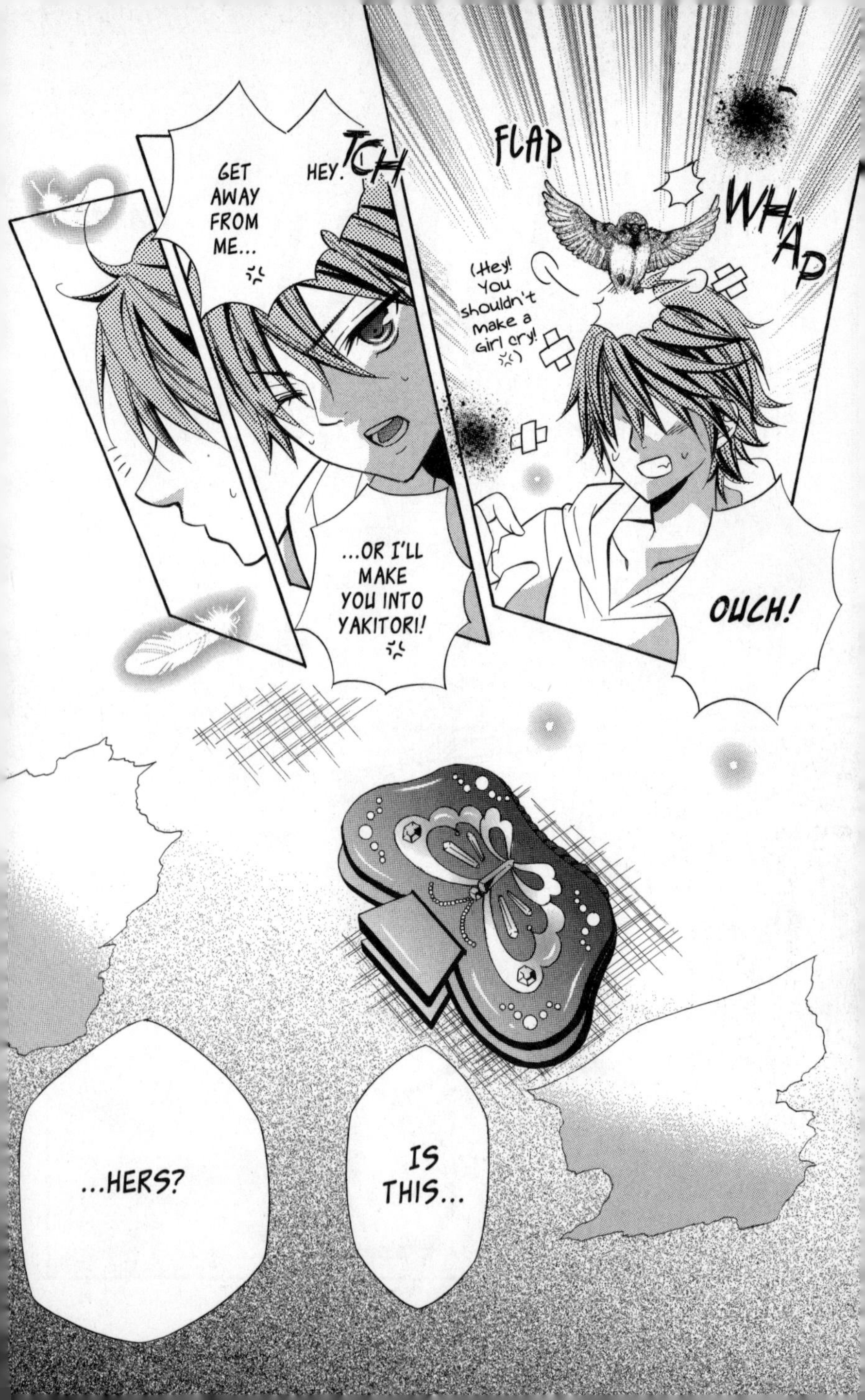
FLAP
WHAP
(Hey! You shouldn't make a girl cry!)
OUCH!
TCH
HEY.
GET AWAY FROM ME...
...OR I'LL MAKE YOU INTO YAKITORI!
IS THIS...
...HERS?

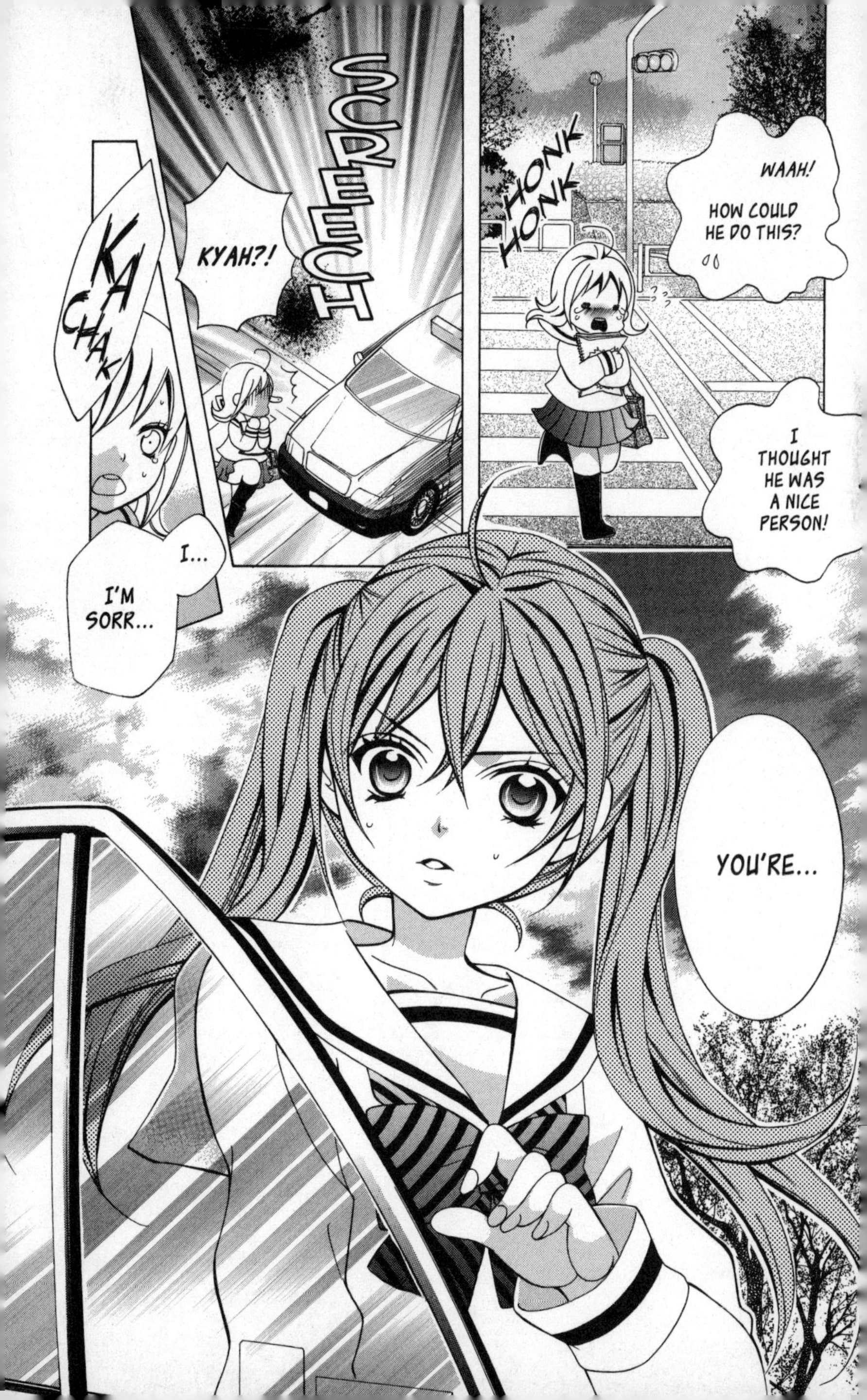
WAAH!
HOW COULD HE DO THIS?
HONK HONK
I THOUGHT HE WAS A NICE PERSON!
SCREECH
KYAH?!
KA CHAK
I...
I'M SORR...
YOU'RE...

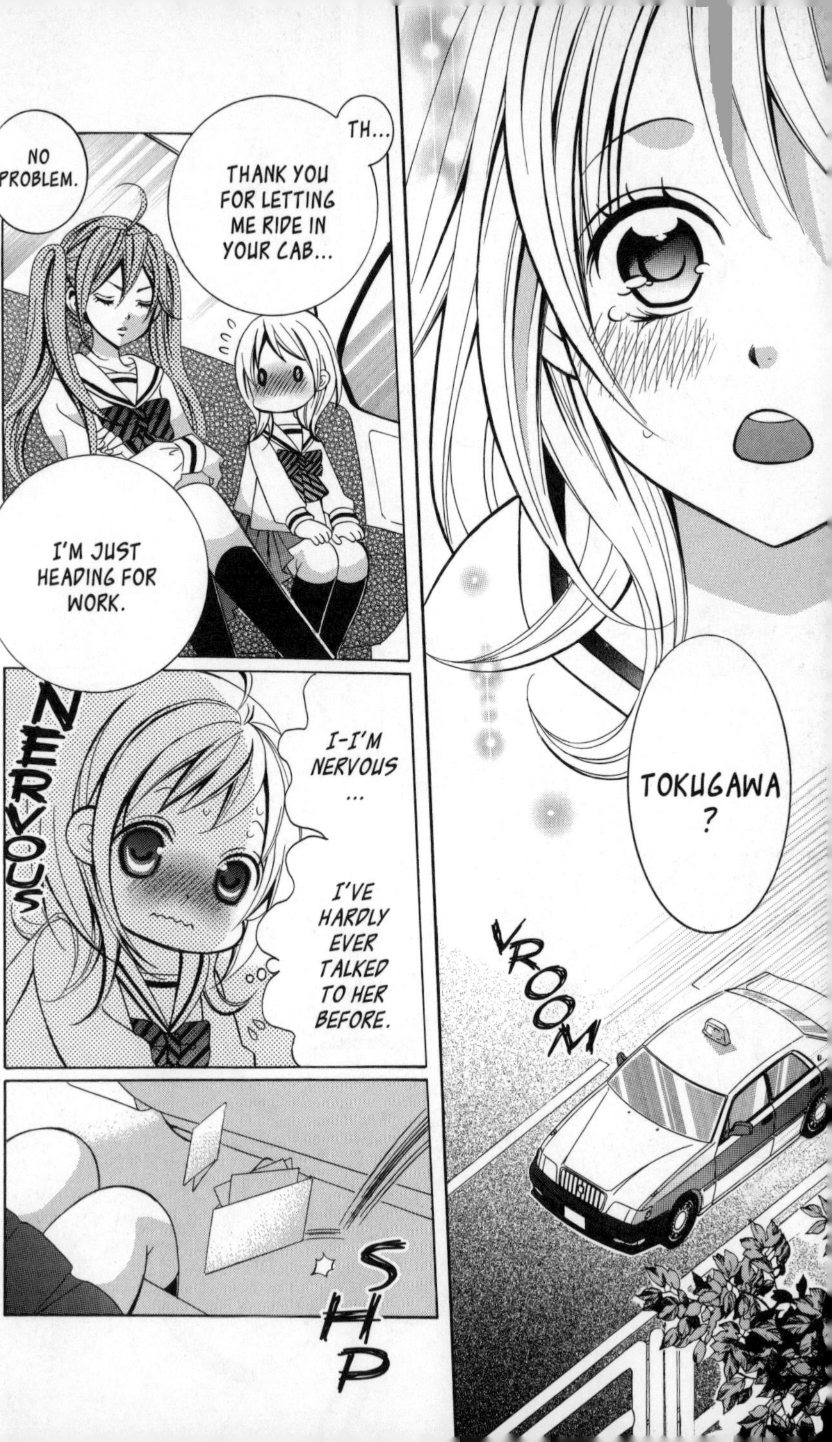
TOKUGAWA ?
VROOM
TH...
THANK YOU FOR LETTING ME RIDE IN YOUR CAB...
NO PROBLEM.
I'M JUST HEADING FOR WORK.
I-I'M NERVOUS ...
I'VE HARDLY EVER TALKED TO HER BEFORE.
NERVOUS
SHP

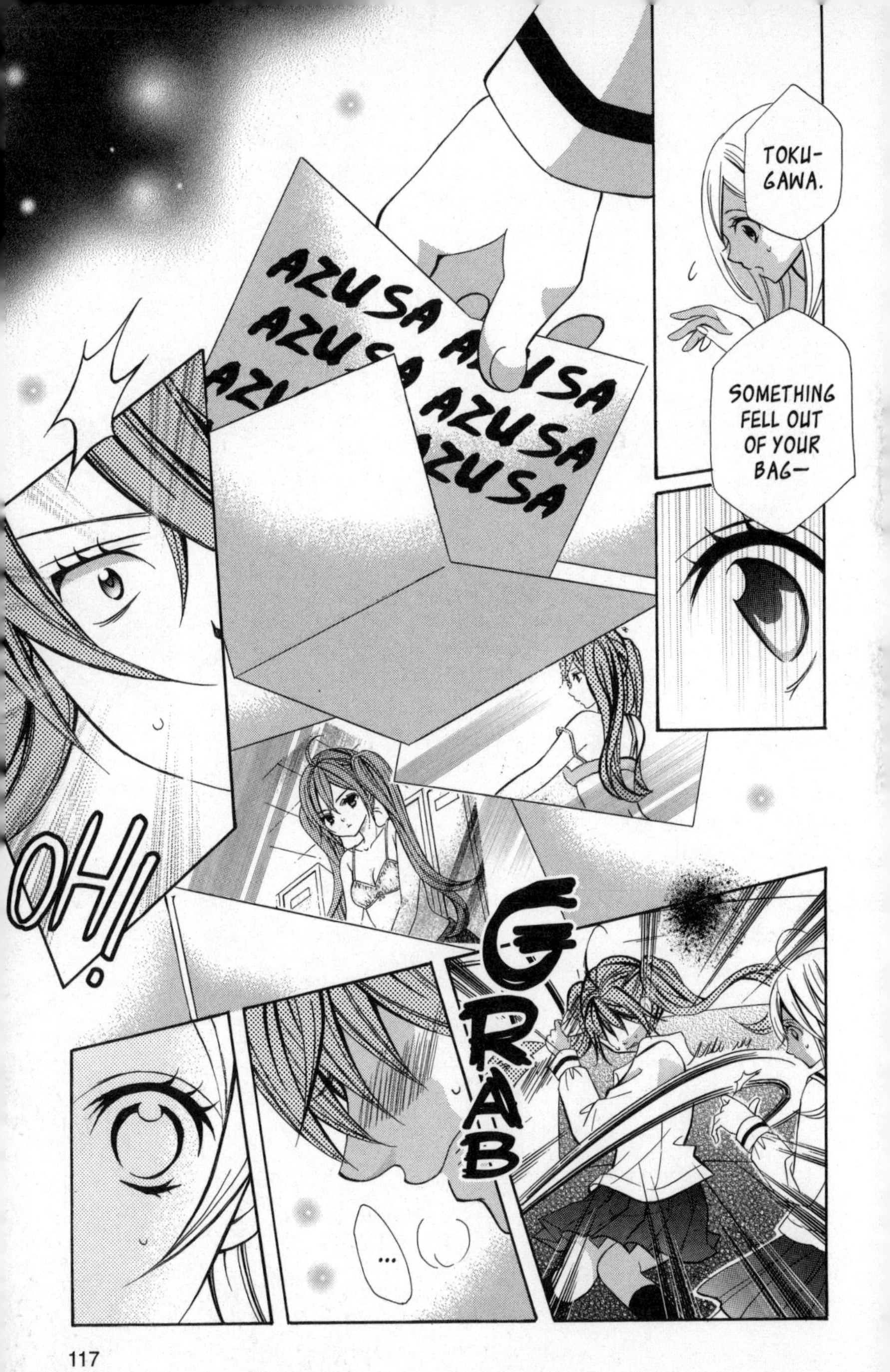
TOKU-GAWA.
SOMETHING FELL OUT OF YOUR BAG—
AZUSA AZUSA AZUSA AZUSA AZUSA AZUSA
OH!
GRAB
...

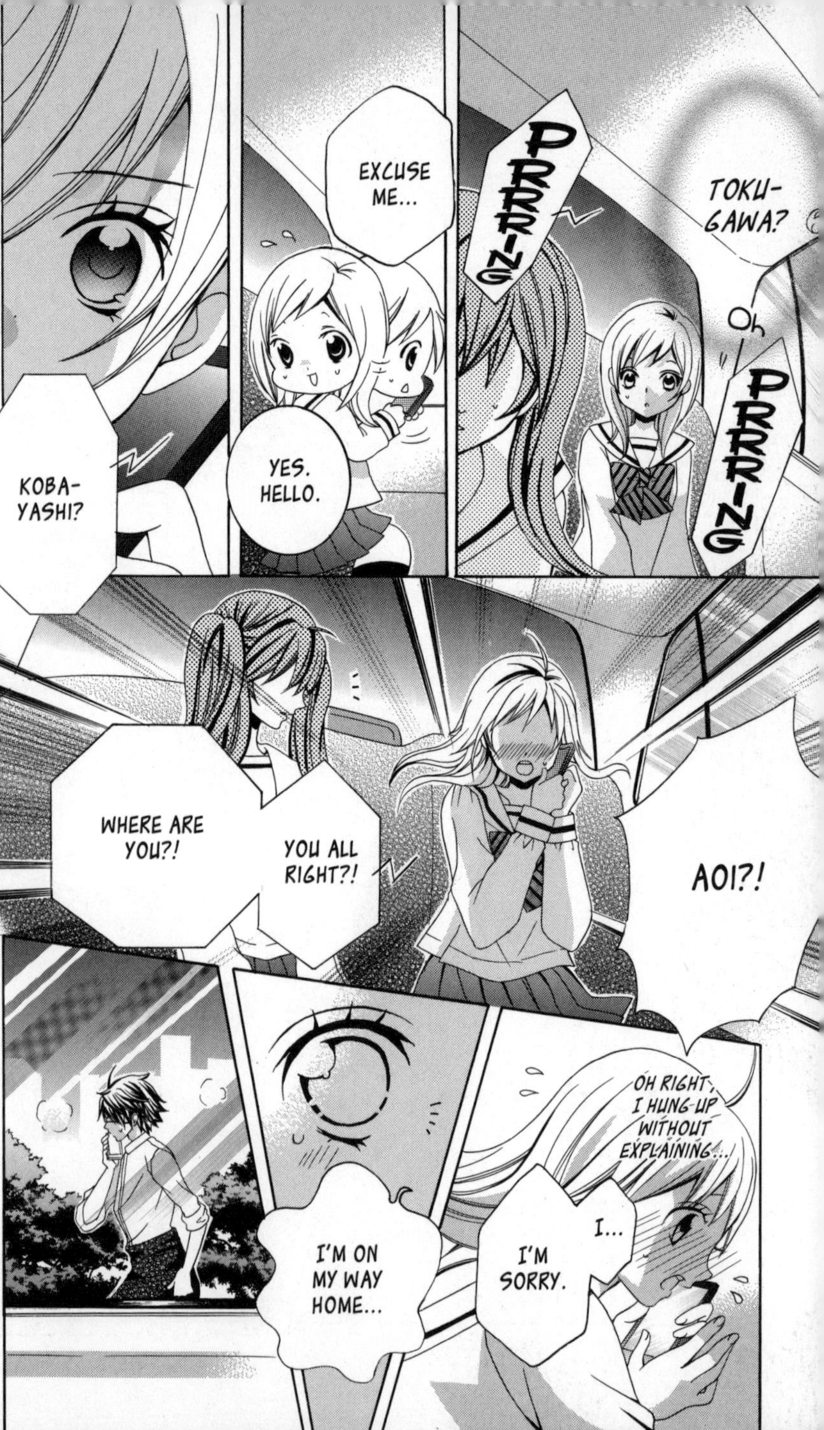
TOKU-GAWA?
PRRRING
Oh
PRRRING
EXCUSE ME...
YES. HELLO.
KOBA-YASHI?
AOI?!
YOU ALL RIGHT?!
WHERE ARE YOU?!
OH RIGHT, I HUNG-UP WITHOUT EXPLAINING...
I...
I'M SORRY.
I'M ON MY WAY HOME...

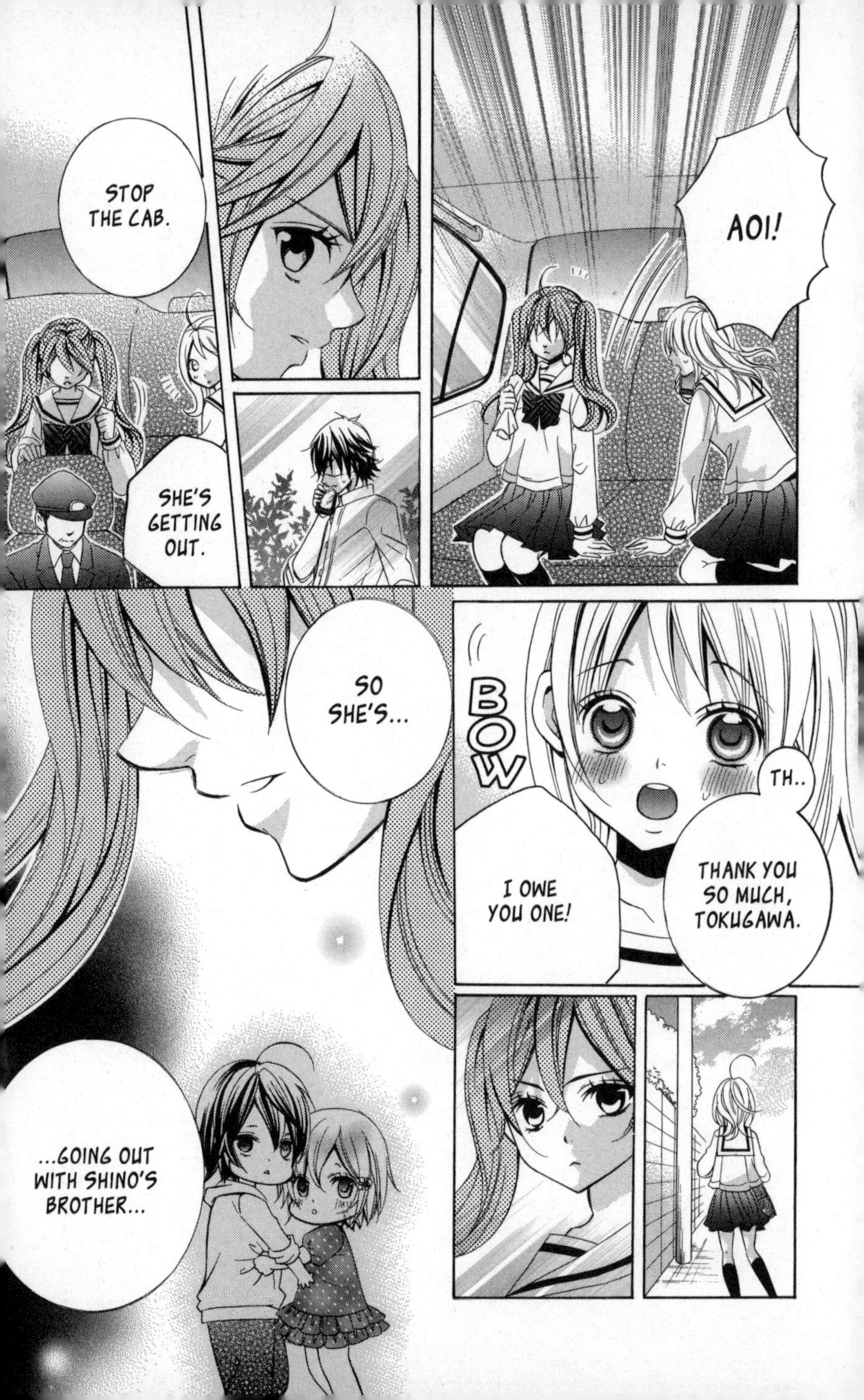
AOI!
STOP THE CAB.
SHE'S GETTING OUT.
BOW
TH..
THANK YOU SO MUCH, TOKUGAWA.
I OWE YOU ONE!
SO SHE'S...
...GOING OUT WITH SHINO'S BROTHER...

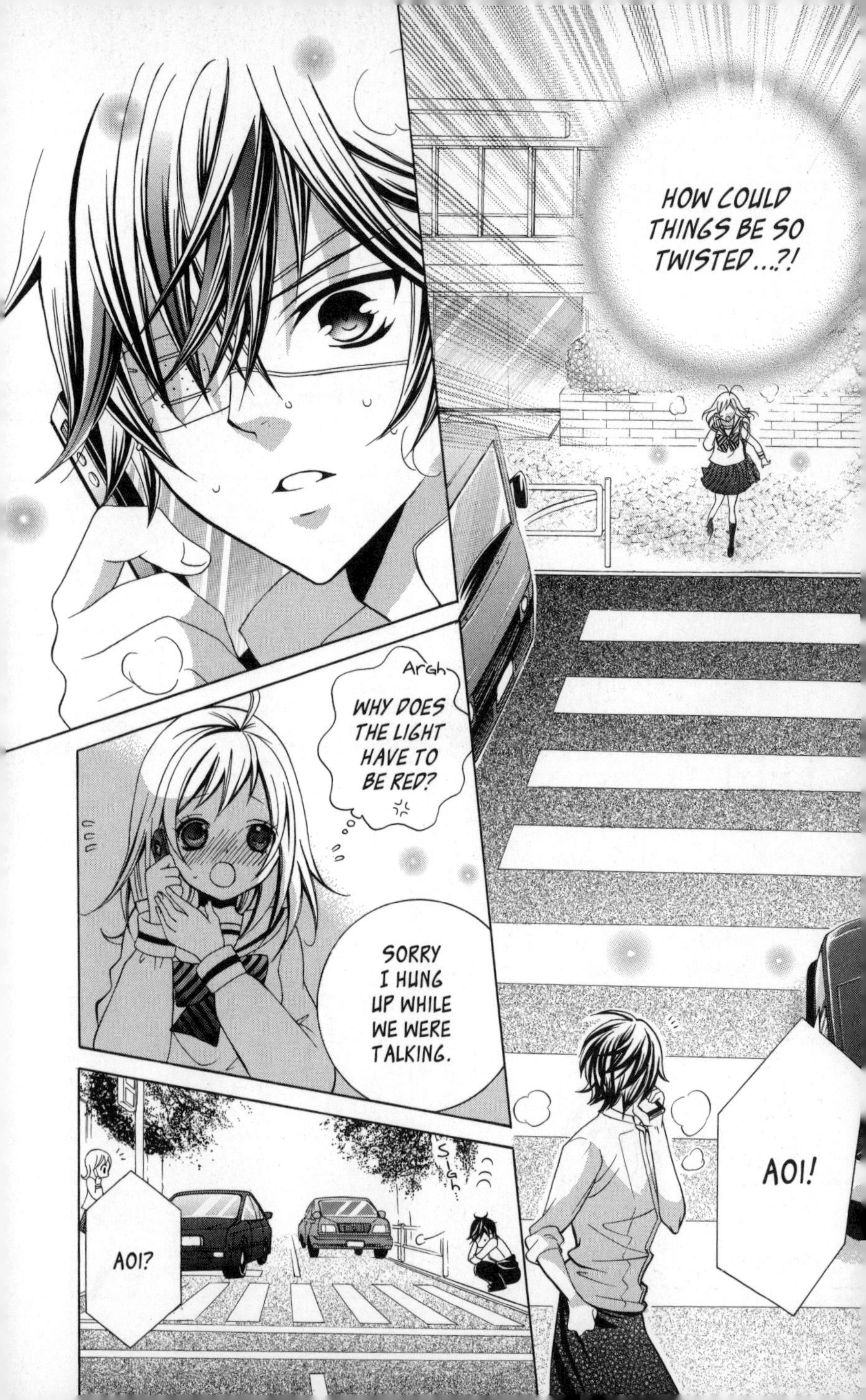
HOW COULD THINGS BE SO TWISTED...?!
AOI!
Argh
WHY DOES THE LIGHT HAVE TO BE RED?
SORRY I HUNG UP WHILE WE WERE TALKING.
Sigh...
AOI?

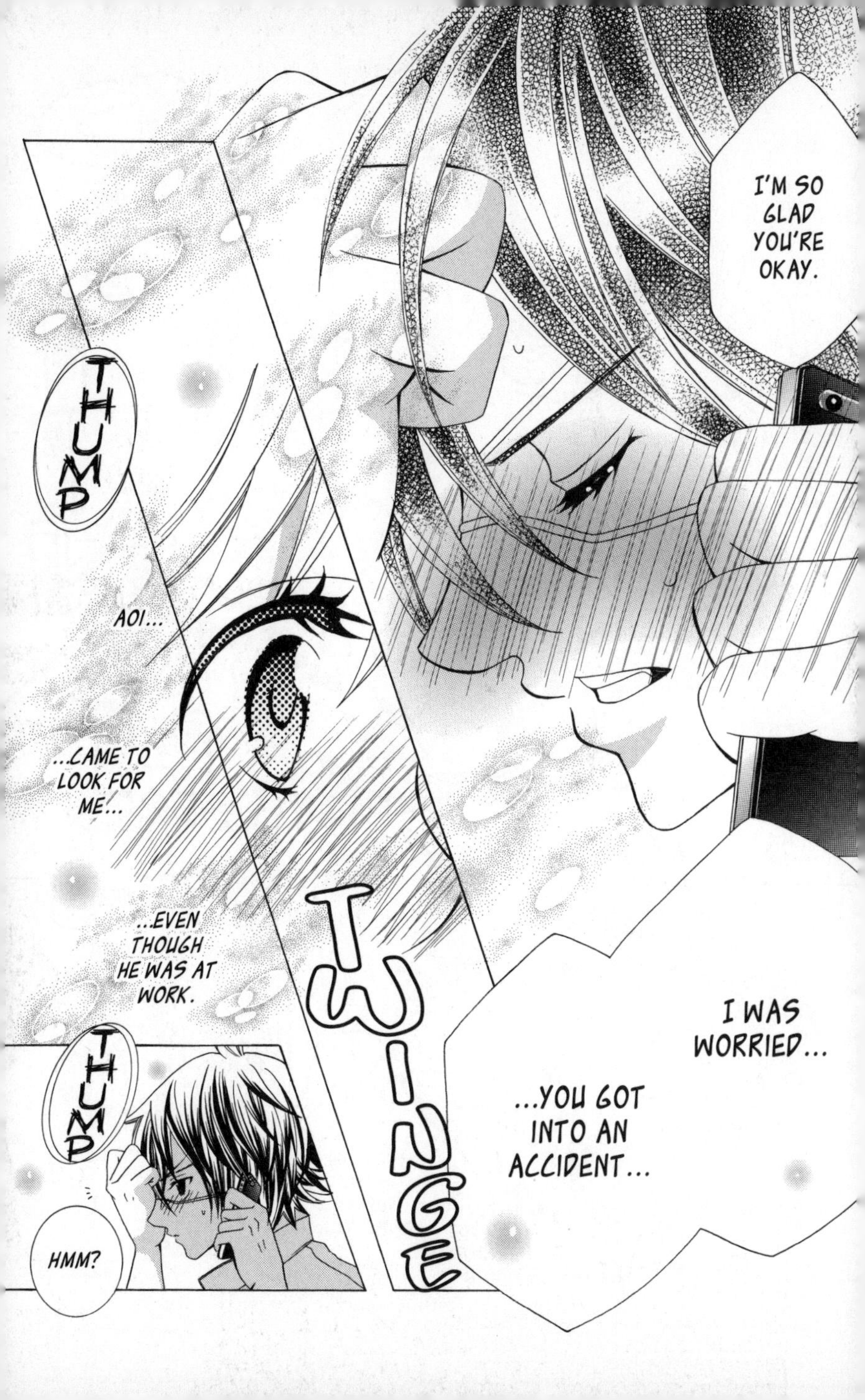
I'M SO GLAD YOU'RE OKAY.
I WAS WORRIED...
...YOU GOT INTO AN ACCIDENT...
TWINGE
THUMP
AOI...
...CAME TO LOOK FOR ME...
...EVEN THOUGH HE WAS AT WORK.
THUMP
HMM?

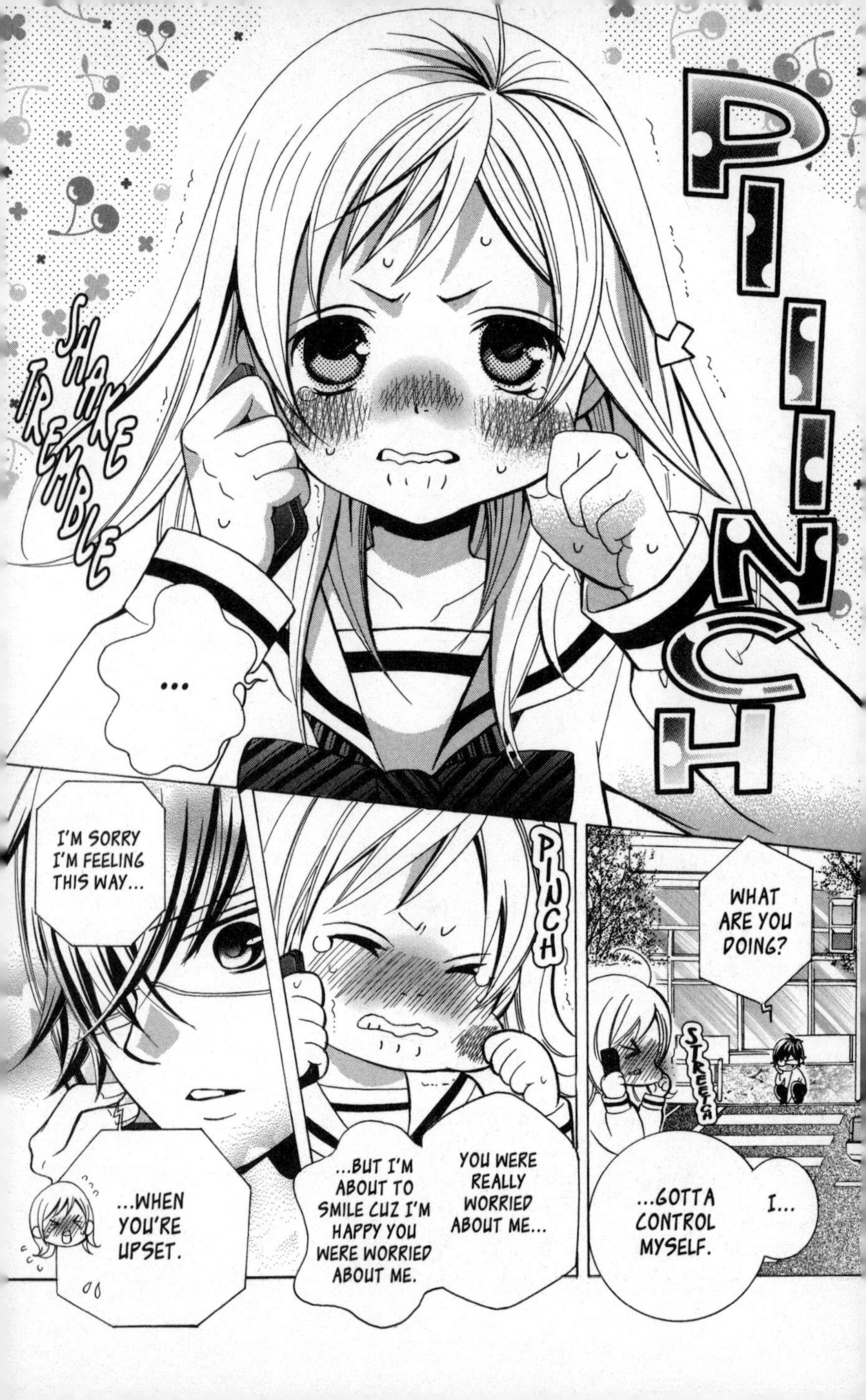
PINCH
SHAKE
TREMBLE
...
WHAT ARE YOU DOING?
STREEEGH
I...
...GOTTA CONTROL MYSELF.
PINCH
YOU WERE REALLY WORRIED ABOUT ME...
...BUT I'M ABOUT TO SMILE CUZ I'M HAPPY YOU WERE WORRIED ABOUT ME.
I'M SORRY I'M FEELING THIS WAY...
...WHEN YOU'RE UPSET.

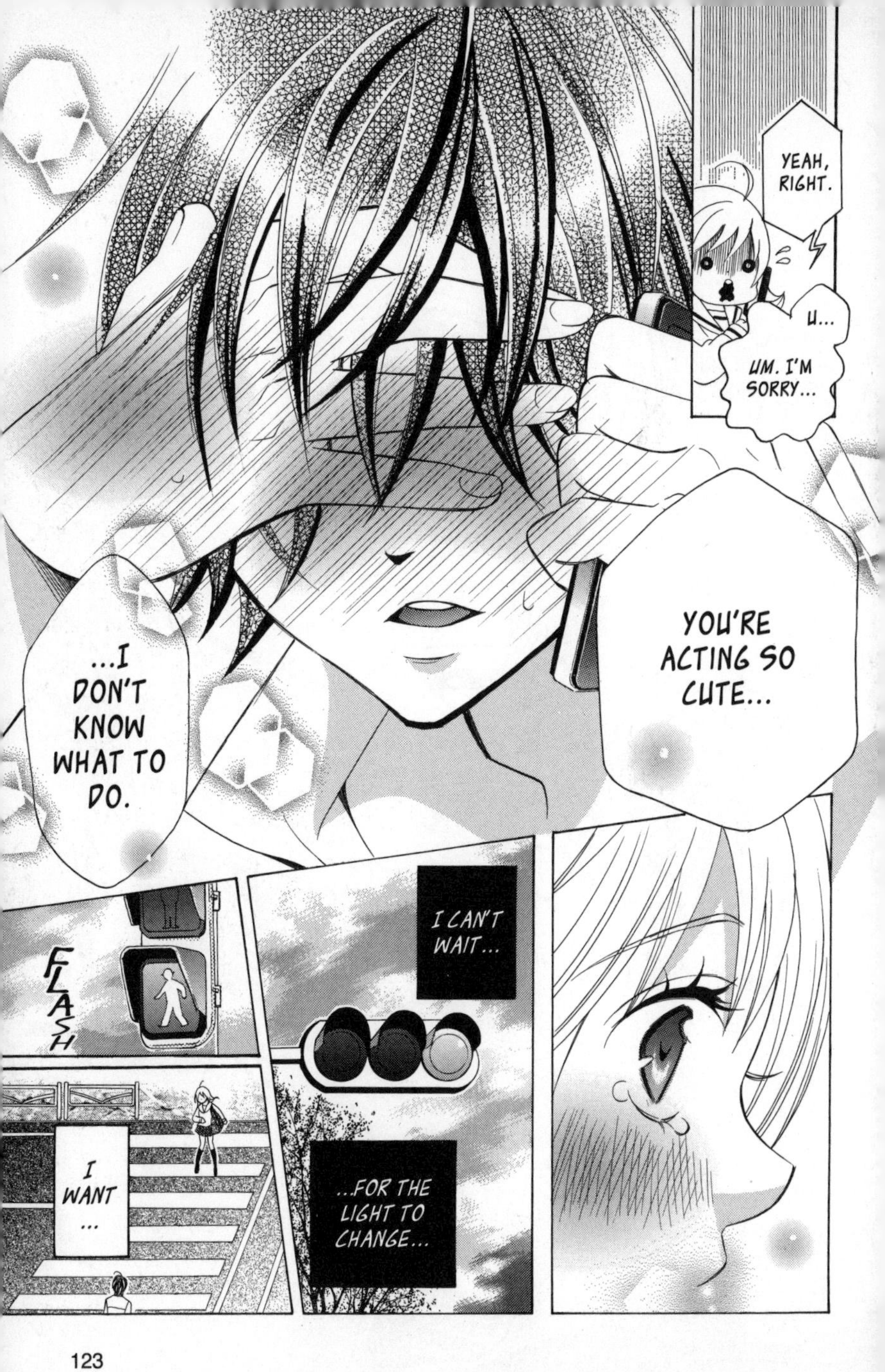
YEAH, RIGHT.
U...
UM. I'M SORRY...
YOU'RE ACTING SO CUTE...
...I DON'T KNOW WHAT TO DO.
I CAN'T WAIT...
...FOR THE LIGHT TO CHANGE...
FLASH
I WANT ...

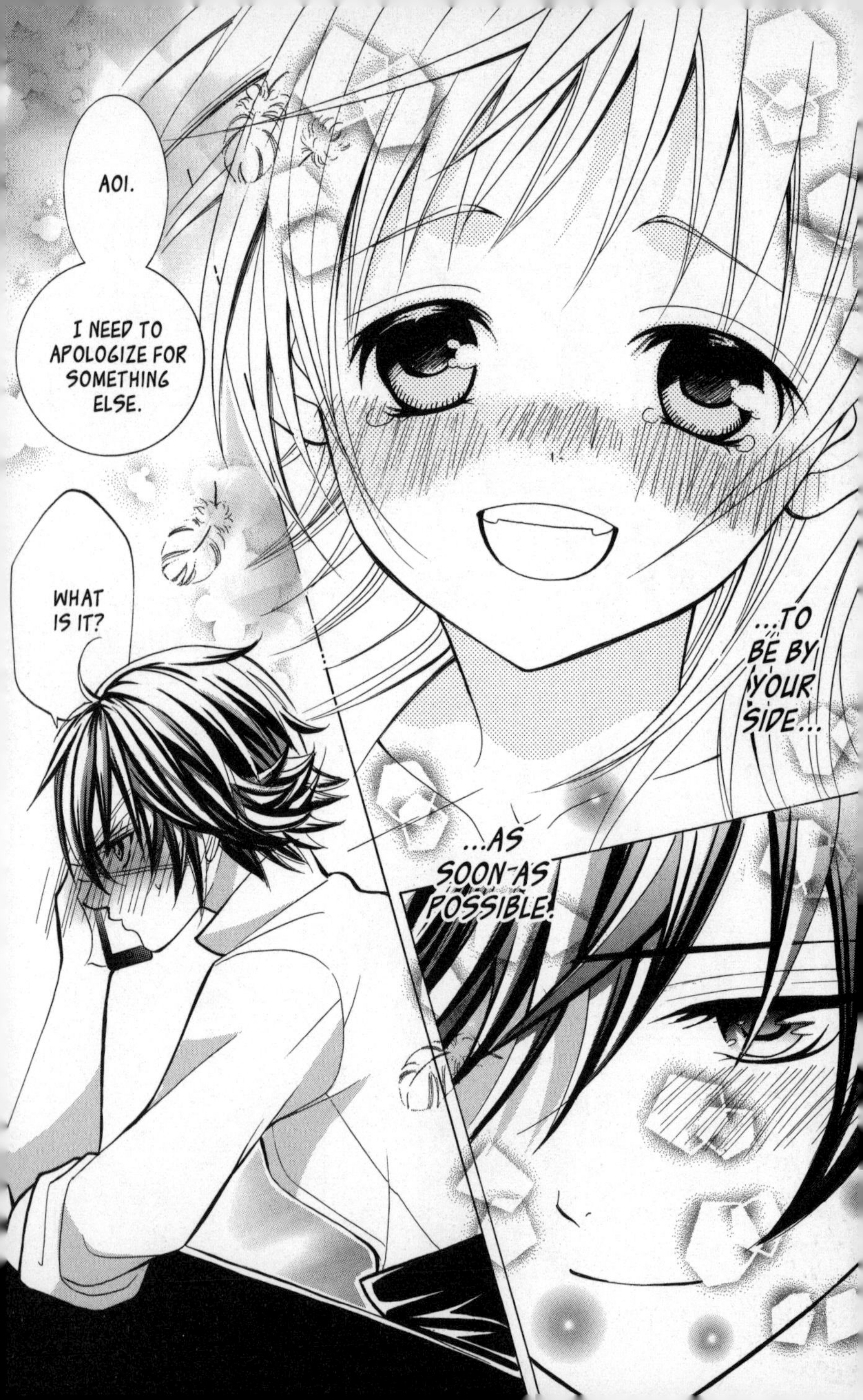
AOI.
I NEED TO APOLOGIZE FOR SOMETHING ELSE.
WHAT IS IT?
...TO BE BY YOUR SIDE...
...AS SOON AS POSSIBLE!

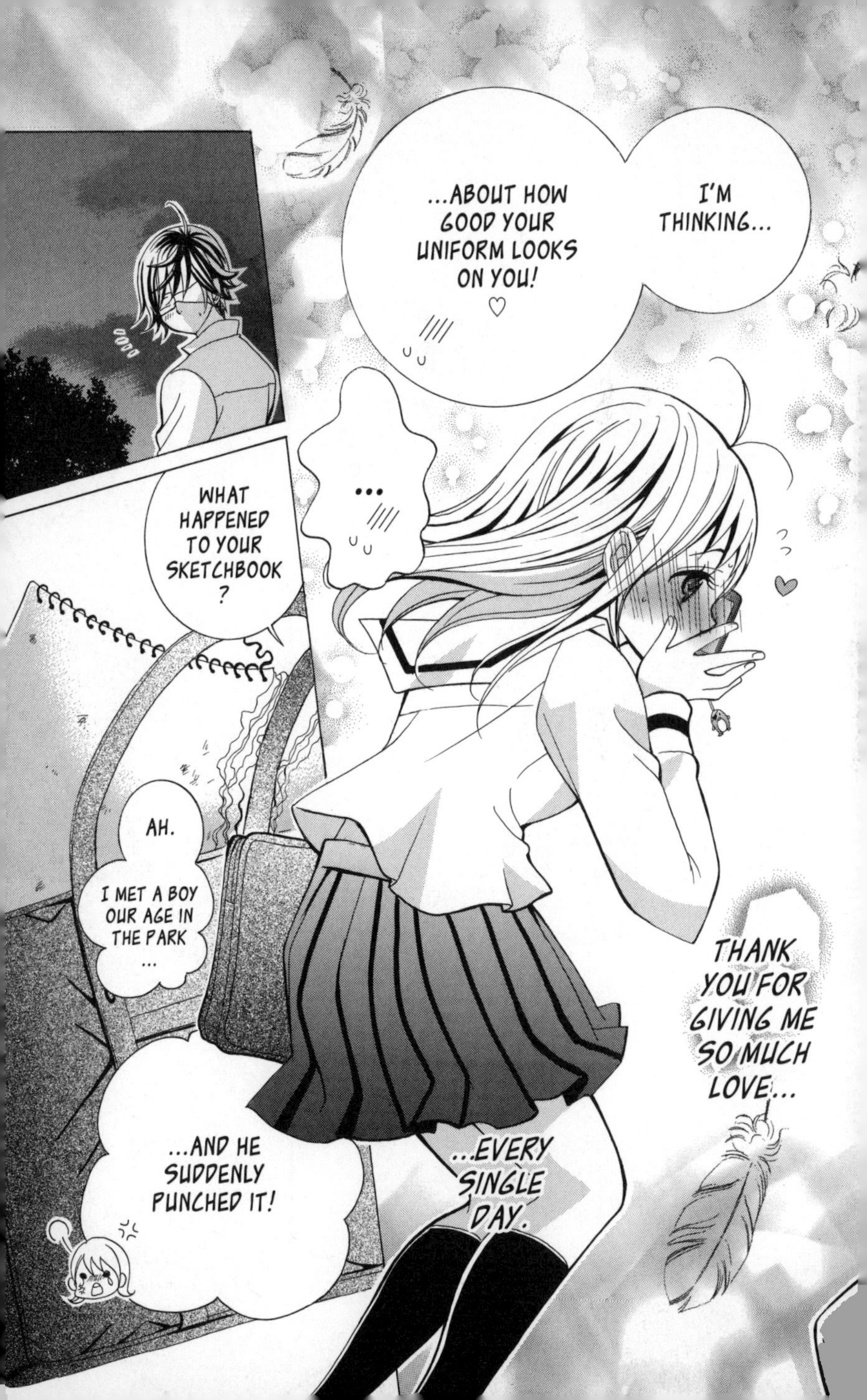
I'M THINKING...
...ABOUT HOW GOOD YOUR UNIFORM LOOKS ON YOU! ♡
...
WHAT HAPPENED TO YOUR SKETCHBOOK?
AH.
I MET A BOY OUR AGE IN THE PARK ...
...AND HE SUDDENLY PUNCHED IT!
THANK YOU FOR GIVING ME SO MUCH LOVE...
...EVERY SINGLE DAY.

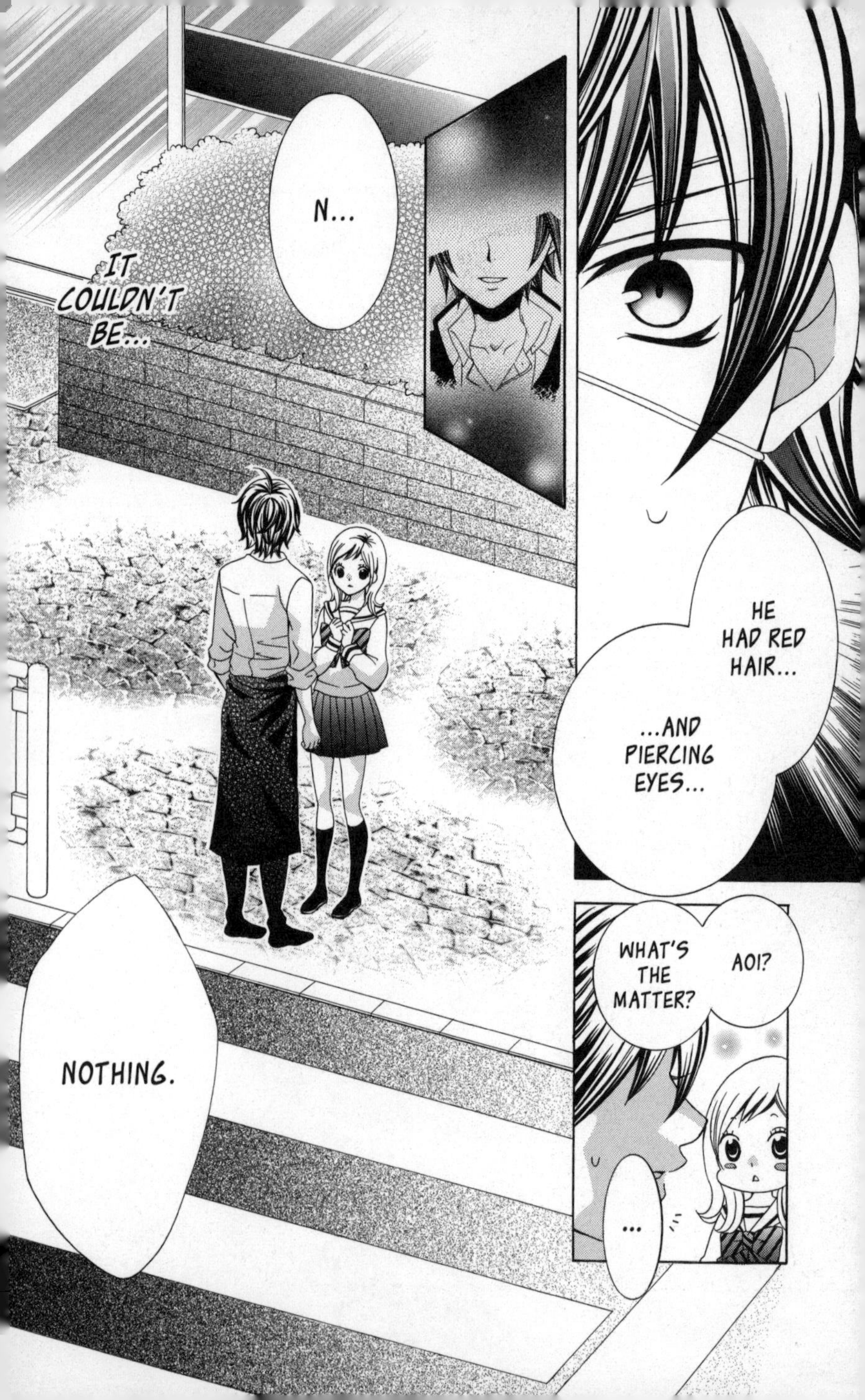
HE HAD RED HAIR...
...AND PIERCING EYES...
AOI?
WHAT'S THE MATTER?
...
N...
IT COULDN'T BE...
NOTHING.

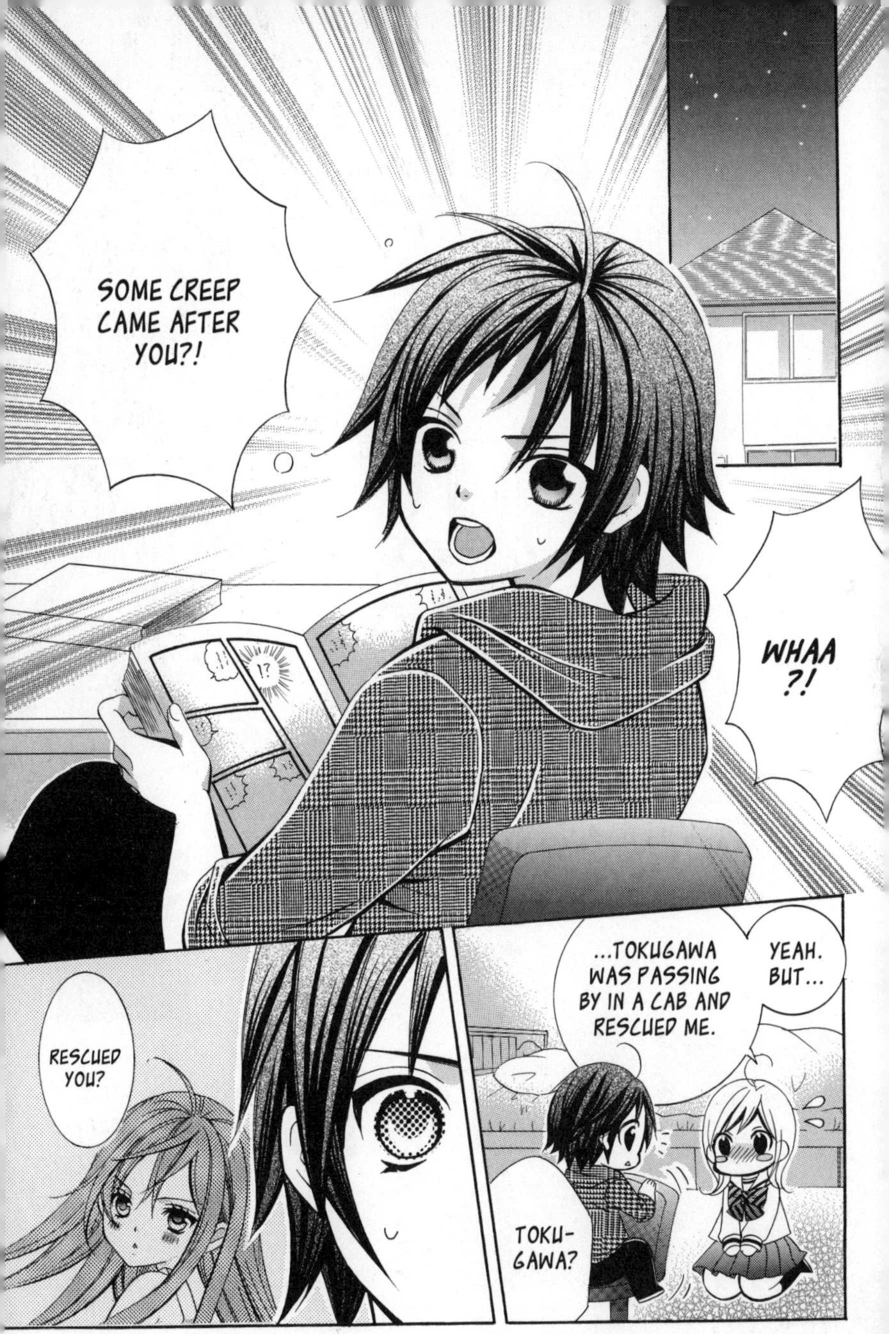
WHAA ?!
SOME CREEP CAME AFTER YOU?!
YEAH. BUT...
...TOKUGAWA WAS PASSING BY IN A CAB AND RESCUED ME.
TOKU-GAWA?
RESCUED YOU?

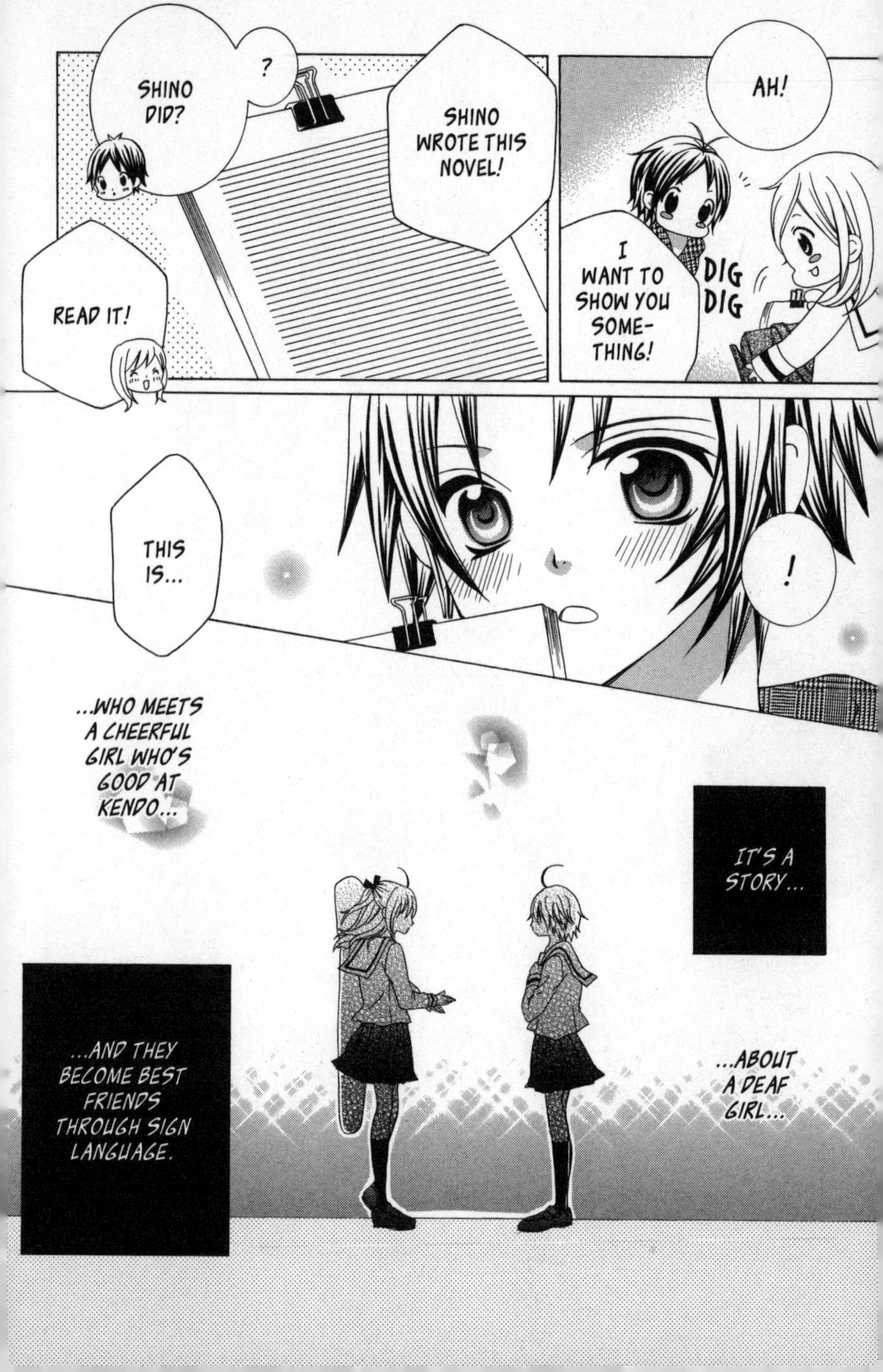
AH!
I WANT TO SHOW YOU SOME-THING!
DIG DIG
SHINO WROTE THIS NOVEL!
?
SHINO DID?
READ IT!
!
THIS IS...
IT'S A STORY...
...ABOUT A DEAF GIRL...
...WHO MEETS A CHEERFUL GIRL WHO'S GOOD AT KENDO...
...AND THEY BECOME BEST FRIENDS THROUGH SIGN LANGUAGE.

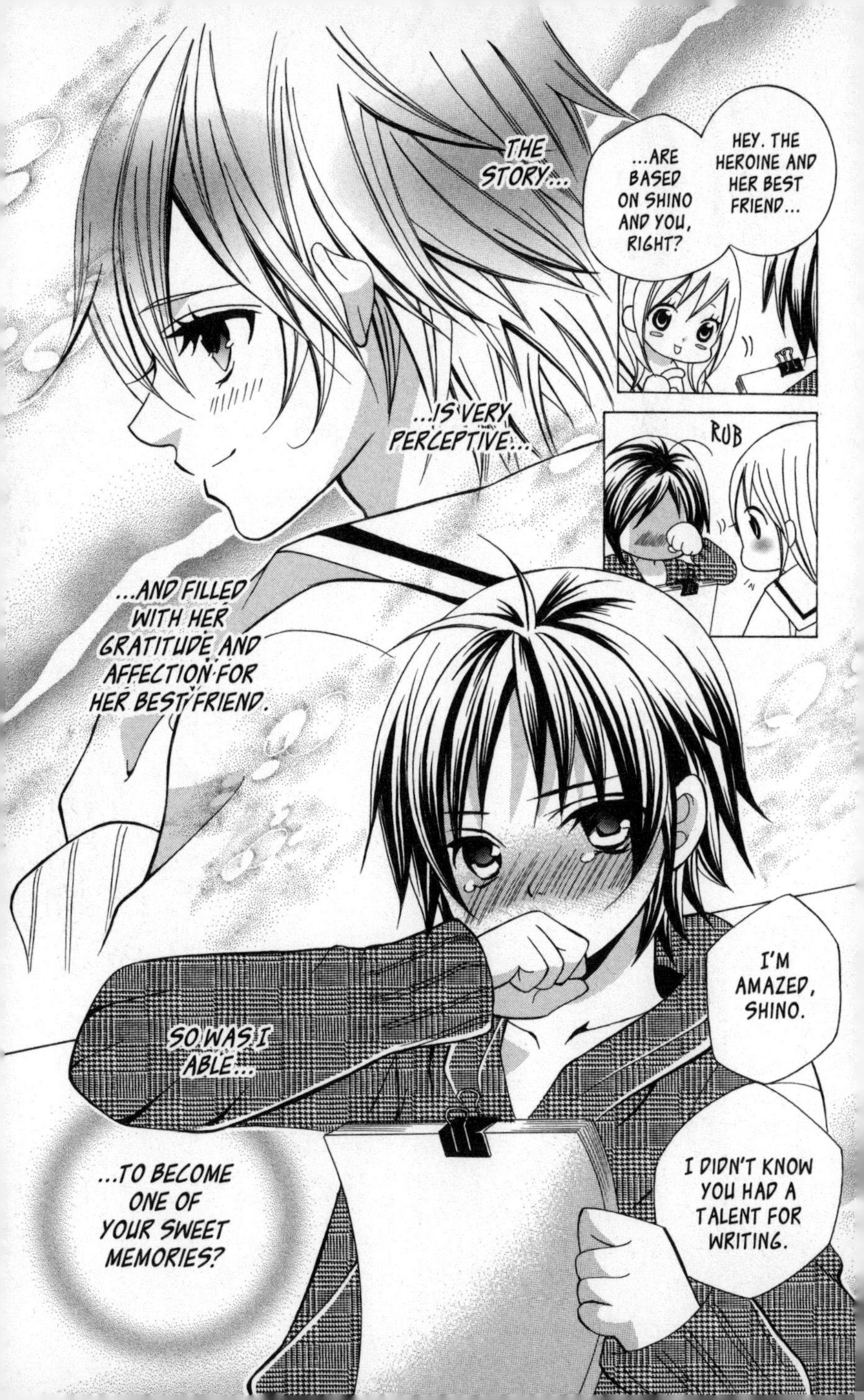
HEY. THE HEROINE AND HER BEST FRIEND... ...ARE BASED ON SHINO AND YOU, RIGHT?
RUB
THE STORY...
...IS VERY PERCEPTIVE...
...AND FILLED WITH HER GRATITUDE AND AFFECTION FOR HER BEST FRIEND.
I'M AMAZED, SHINO.
I DIDN'T KNOW YOU HAD A TALENT FOR WRITING.
SO WAS I ABLE...
...TO BECOME ONE OF YOUR SWEET MEMORIES?

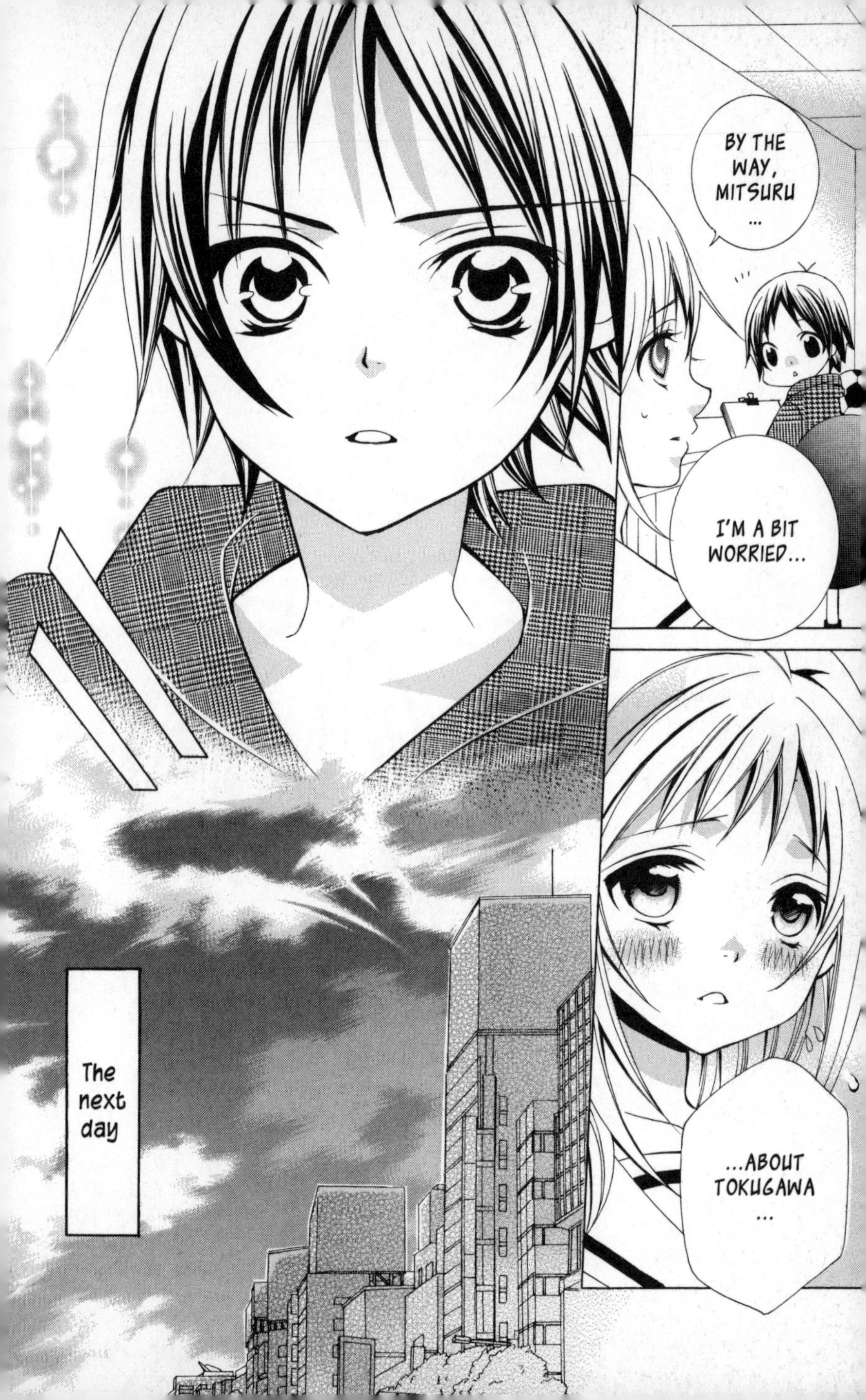
BY THE WAY, MITSURU...
I'M A BIT WORRIED...
...ABOUT TOKUGAWA...
The next day

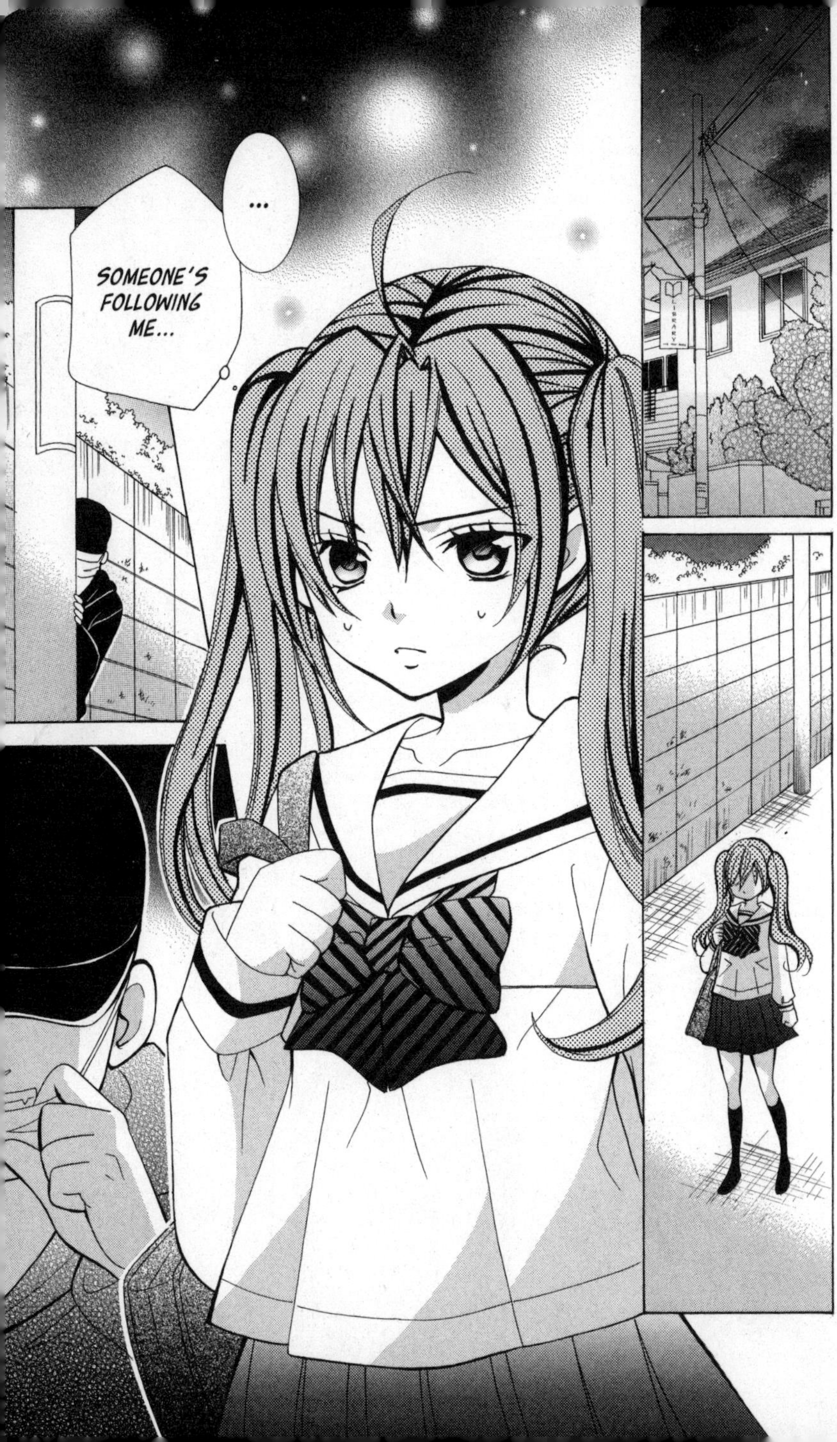
...
SOMEONE'S FOLLOWING ME...

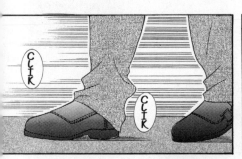

CLIK
CLIK

TMP
TMP

GRAB

IS HE THE ONE WHO SENT ME THAT LETTER?!

ZUSA AZUS
ZUSA AZUS
ZUSA AZU

WHAT A CREEP...

DASH

...

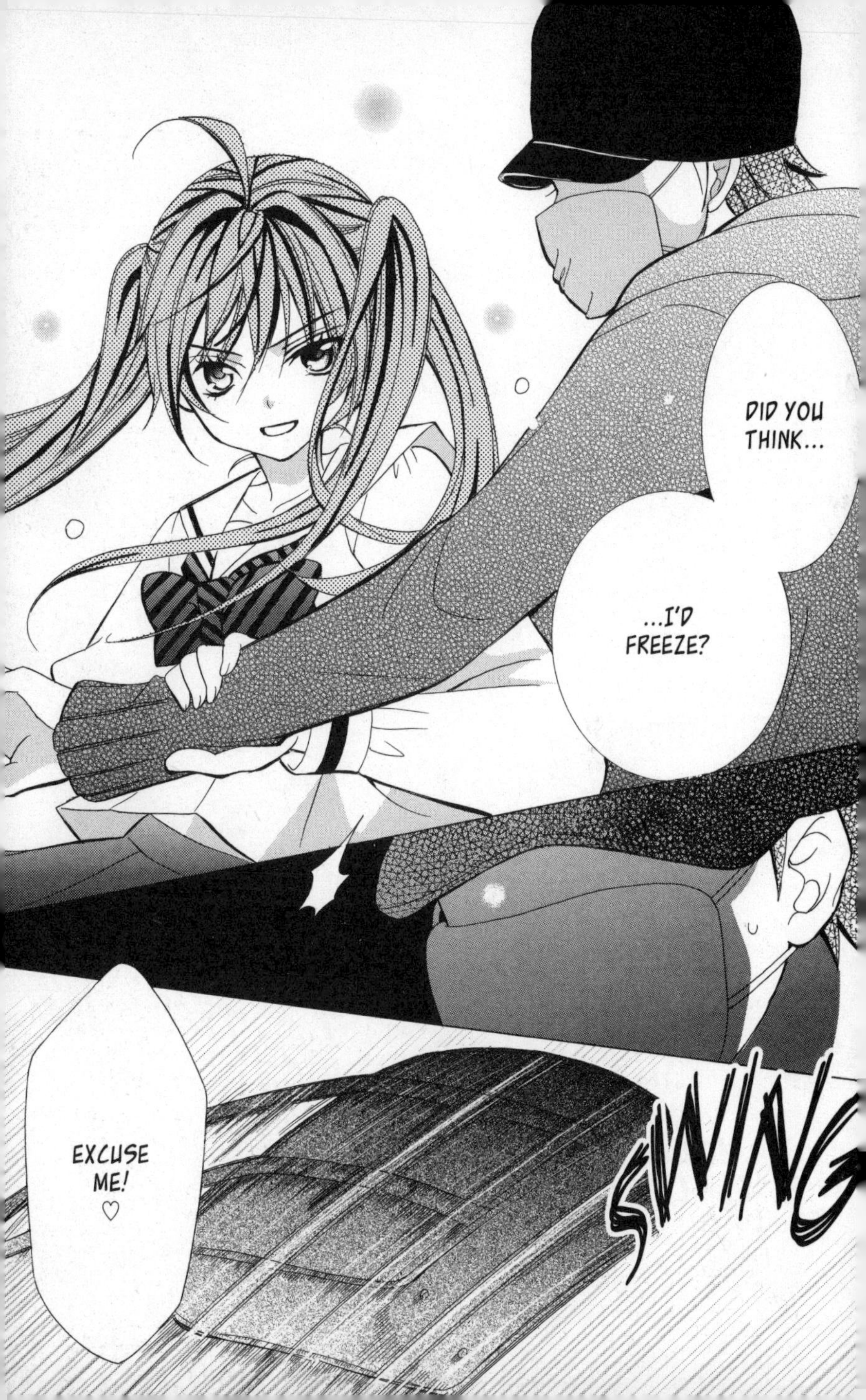
DID YOU THINK...
...I'D FREEZE?
SWING
EXCUSE ME! ♡

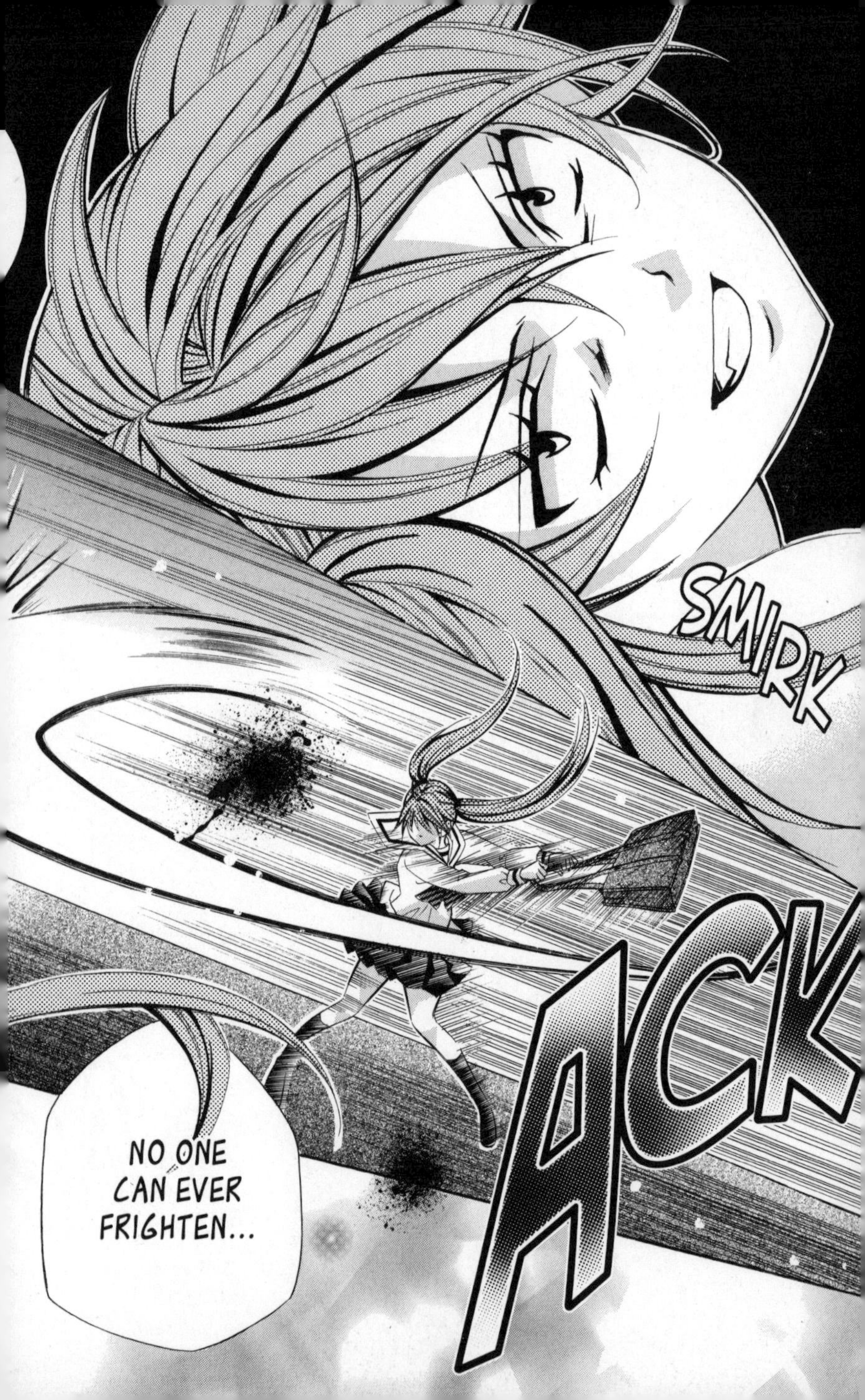
SMIRK
ACK
NO ONE CAN EVER FRIGHTEN...

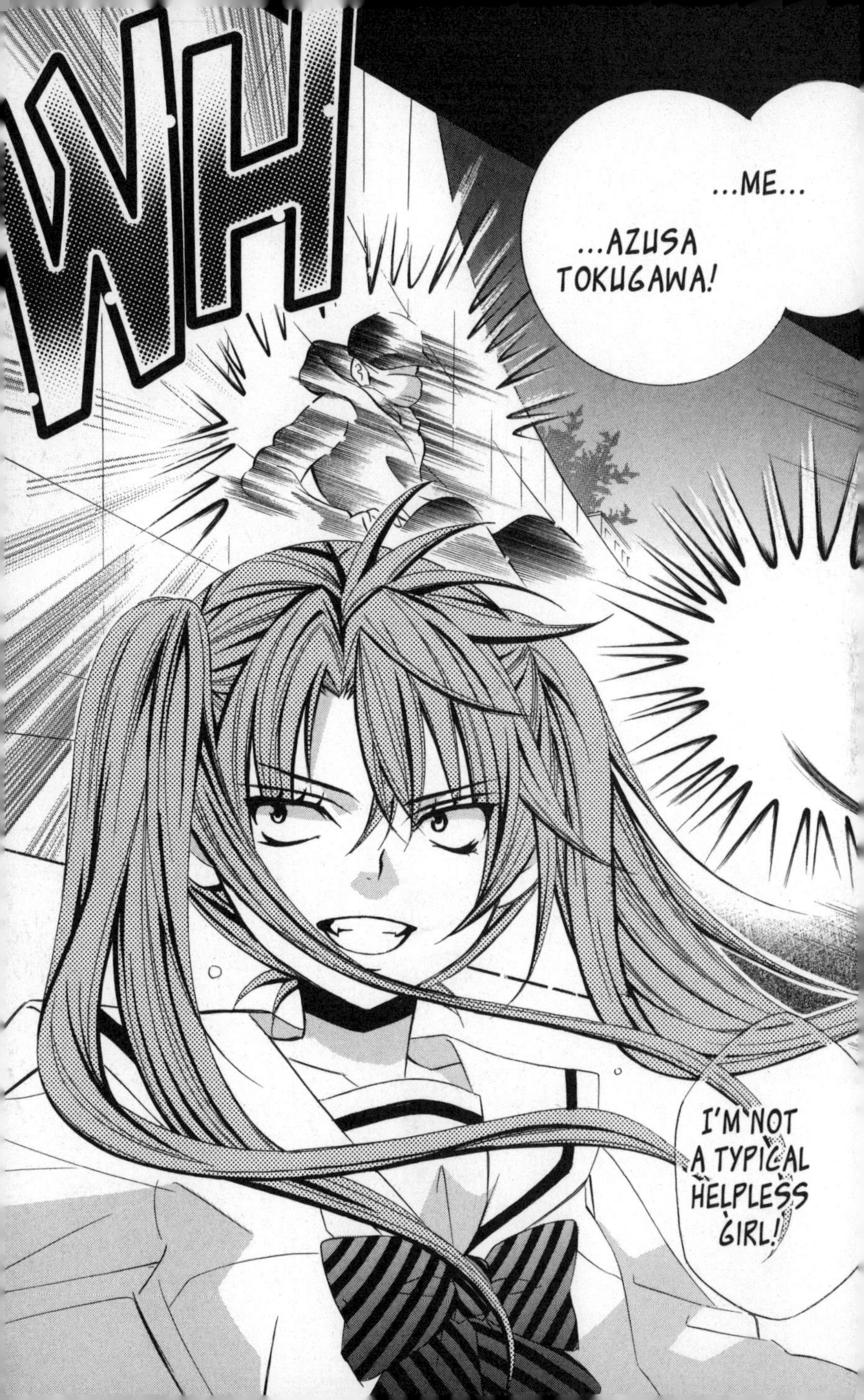
...ME...
...AZUSA TOKUGAWA!
WH
I'M NOT A TYPICAL HELPLESS GIRL!

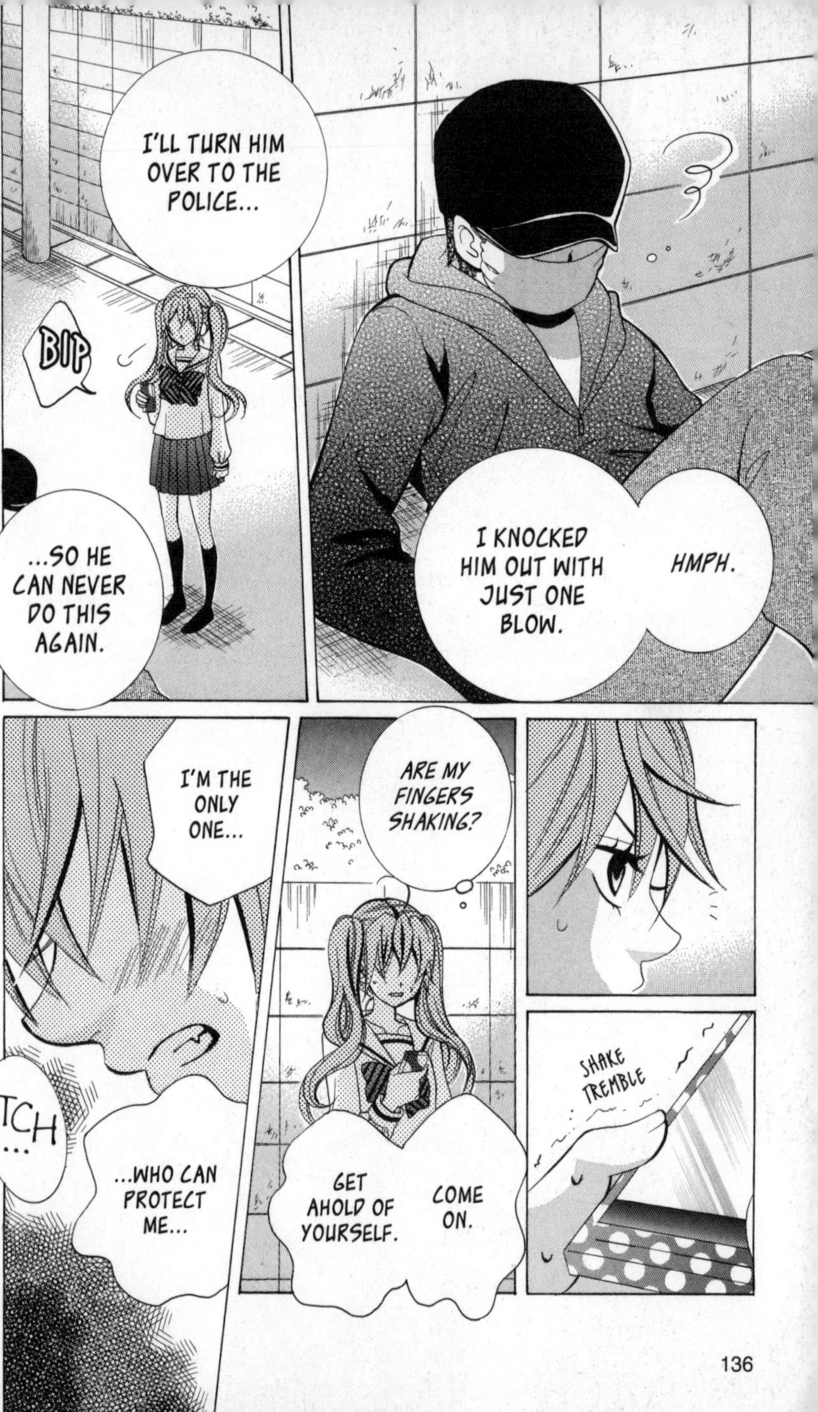
HMPH.
I KNOCKED HIM OUT WITH JUST ONE BLOW.
I'LL TURN HIM OVER TO THE POLICE...
BIP
...SO HE CAN NEVER DO THIS AGAIN.
SHAKE TREMBLE
ARE MY FINGERS SHAKING?
COME ON.
GET AHOLD OF YOURSELF.
I'M THE ONLY ONE...
...WHO CAN PROTECT ME...
TCH...

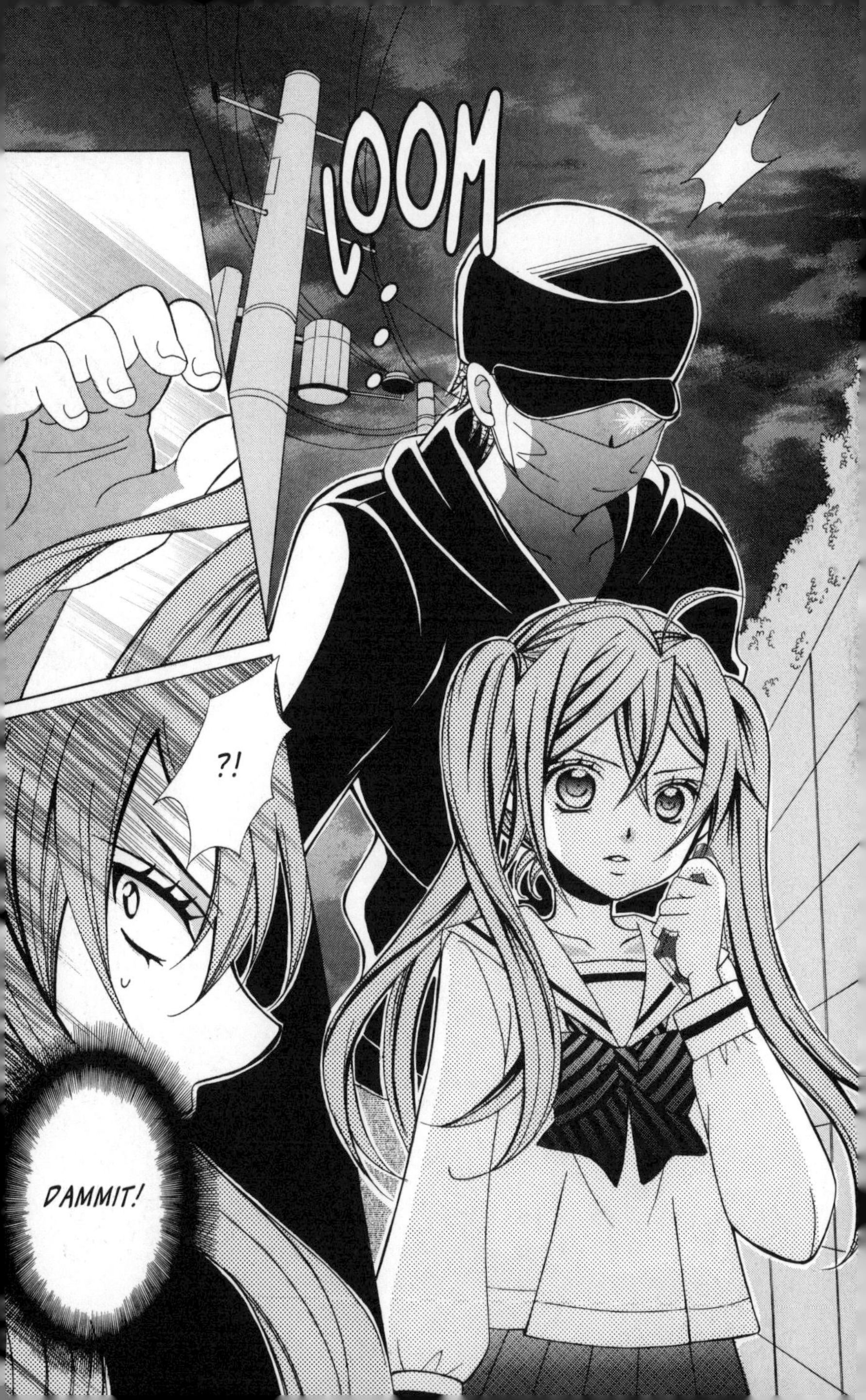
LOOM
?!
DAMMIT!

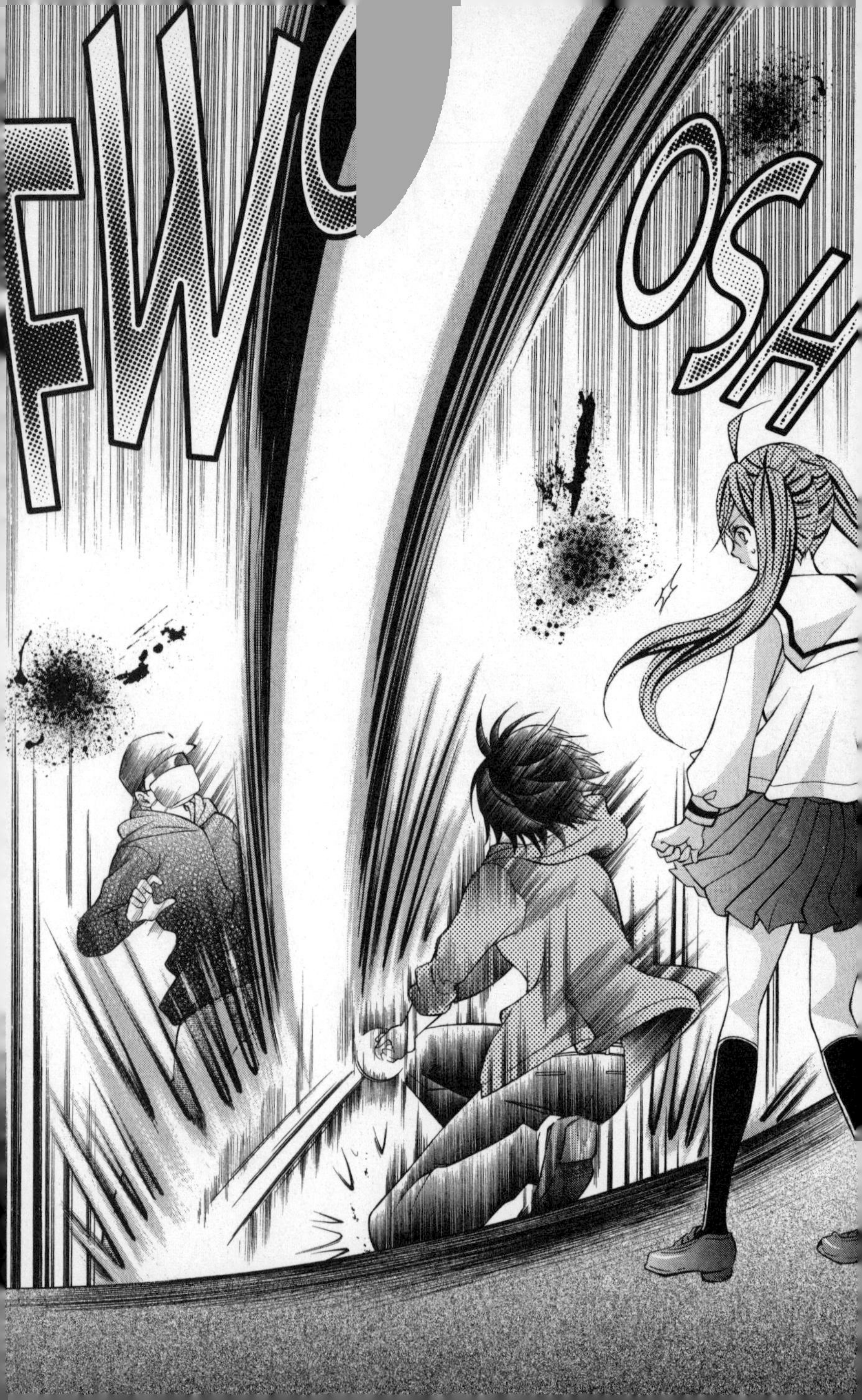
FW
OSH

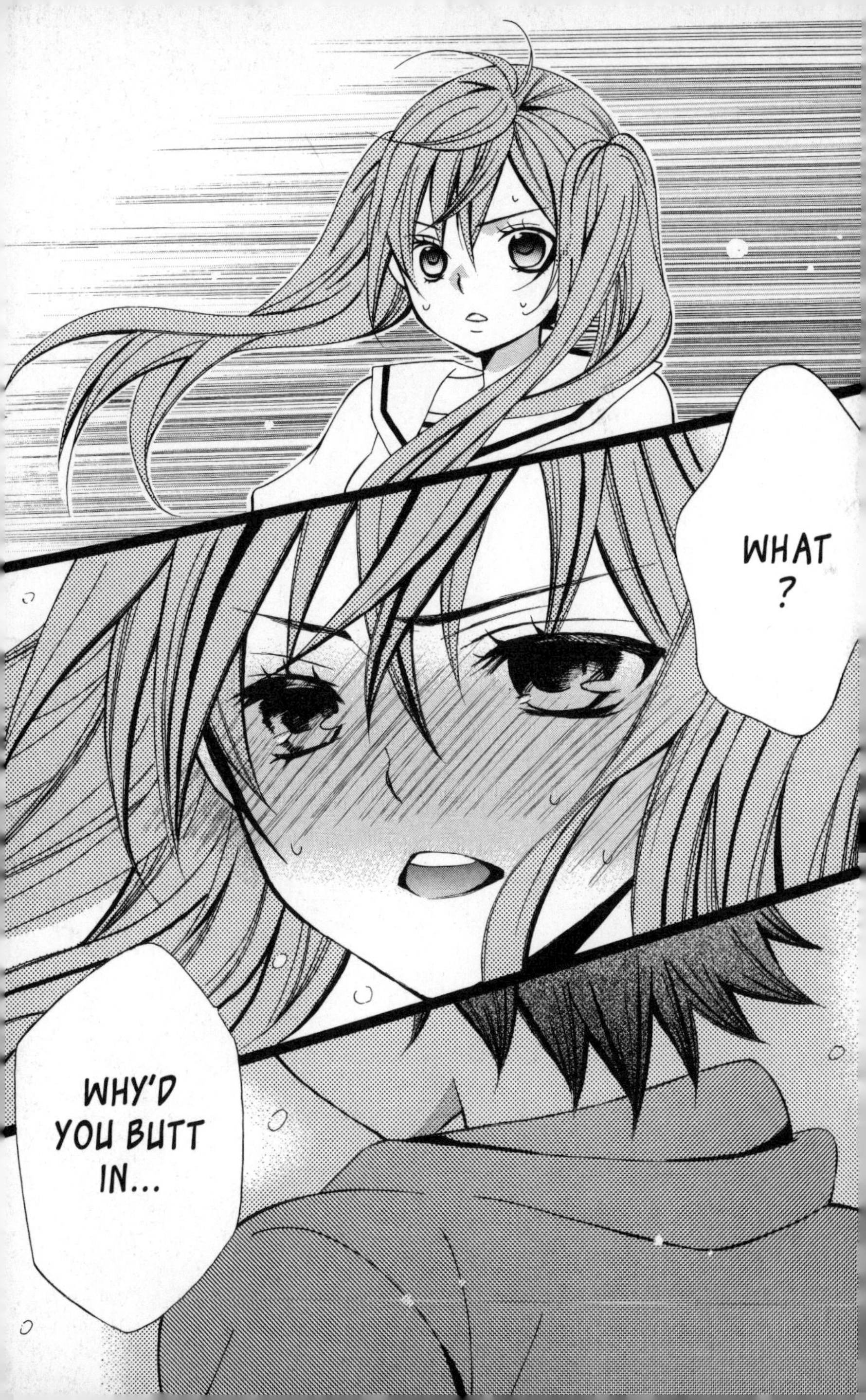
WHAT?
WHY'D YOU BUTT IN...

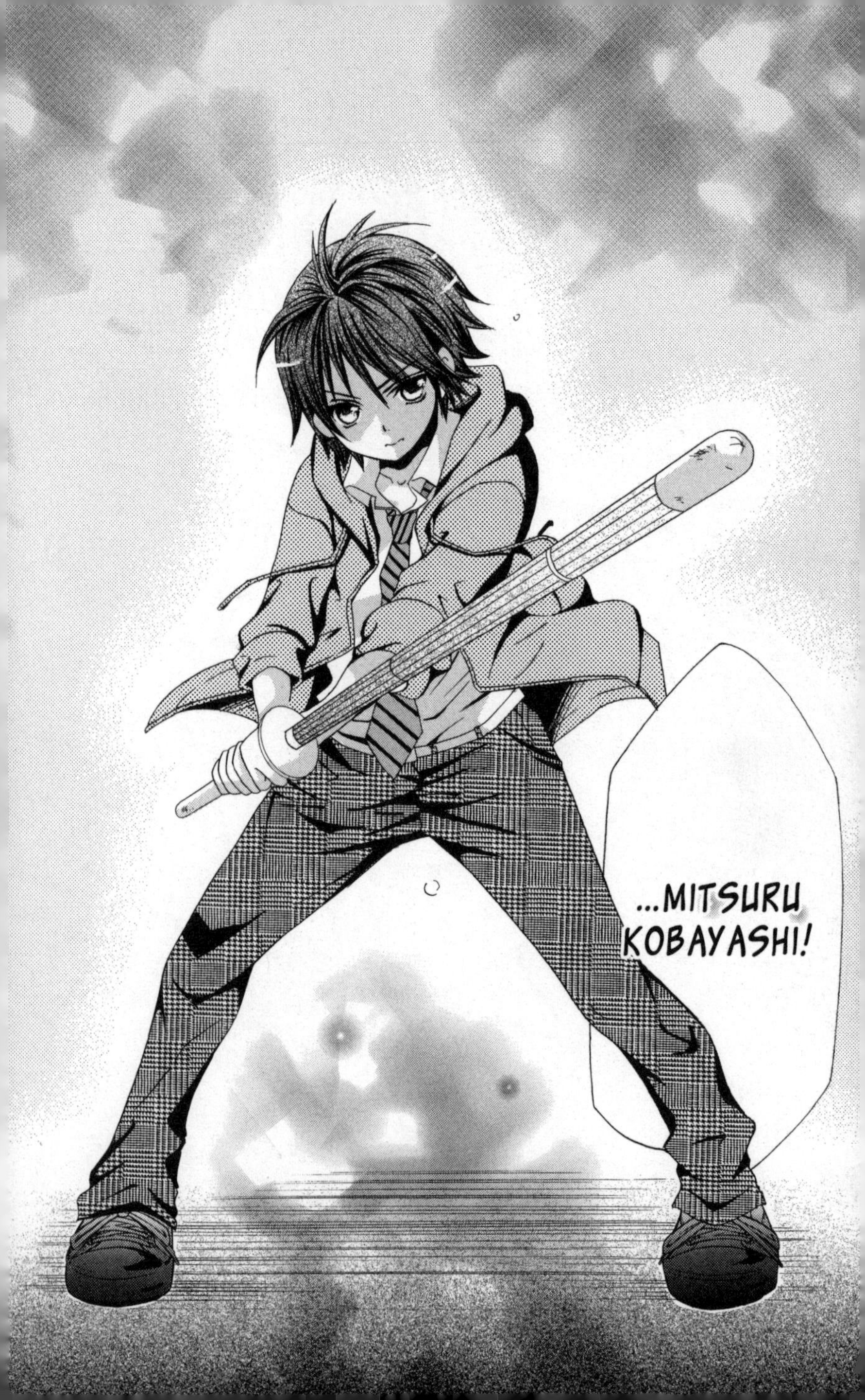
...MITSURU KOBAYASHI!

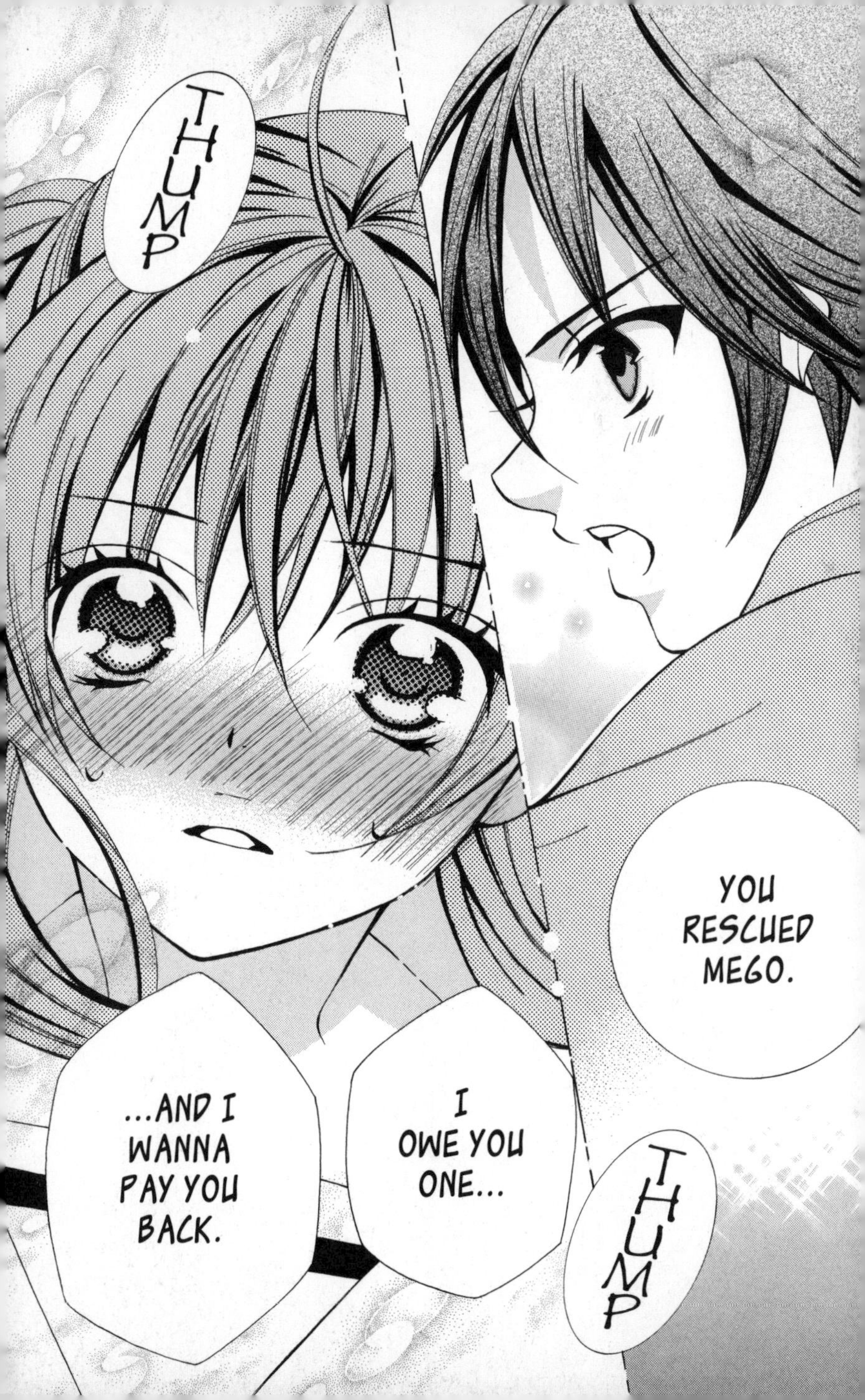
THUMP
YOU RESCUED MEGO.
THUMP
I OWE YOU ONE...
...AND I WANNA PAY YOU BACK.

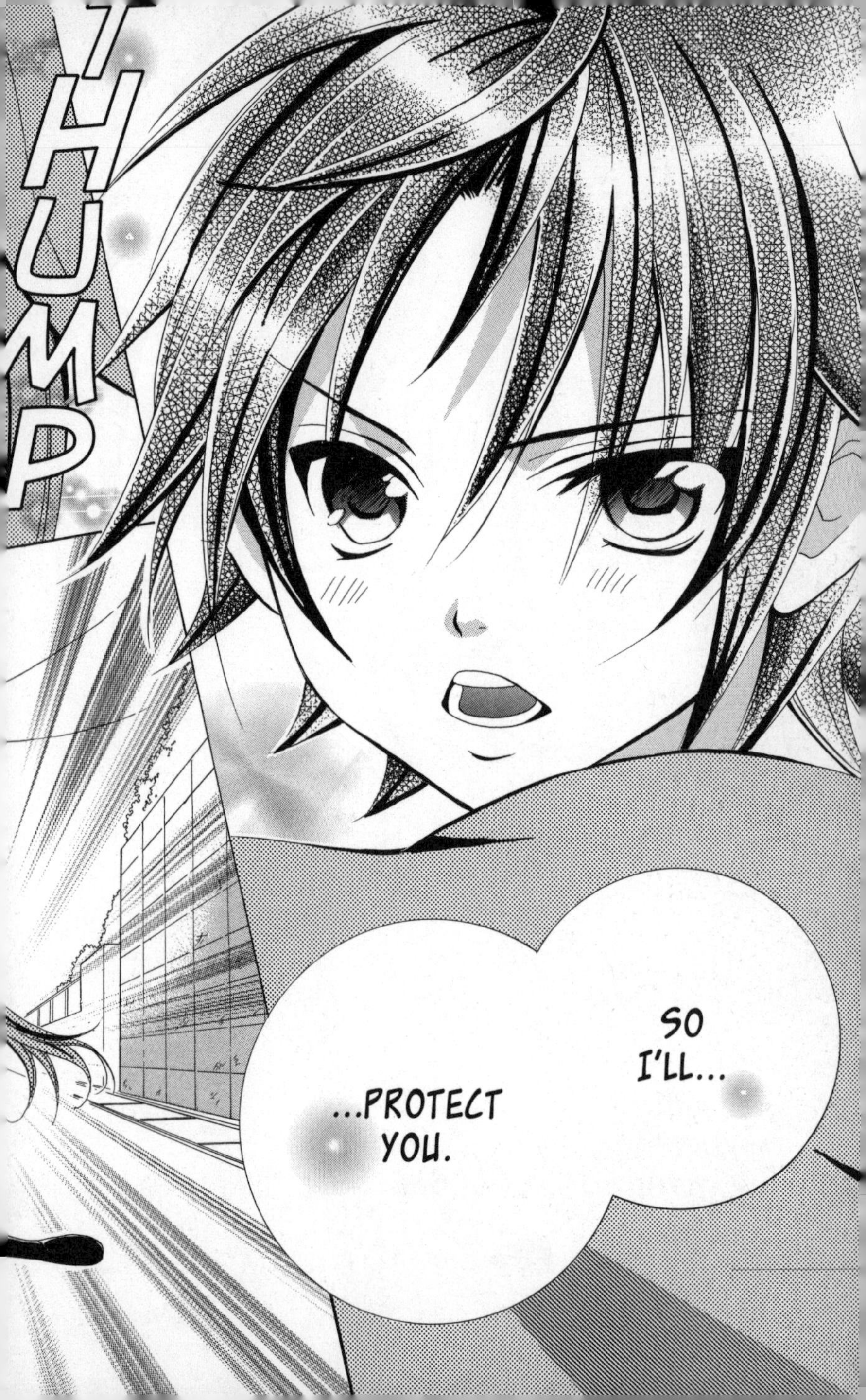
THUMP
SO I'LL...
...PROTECT YOU.

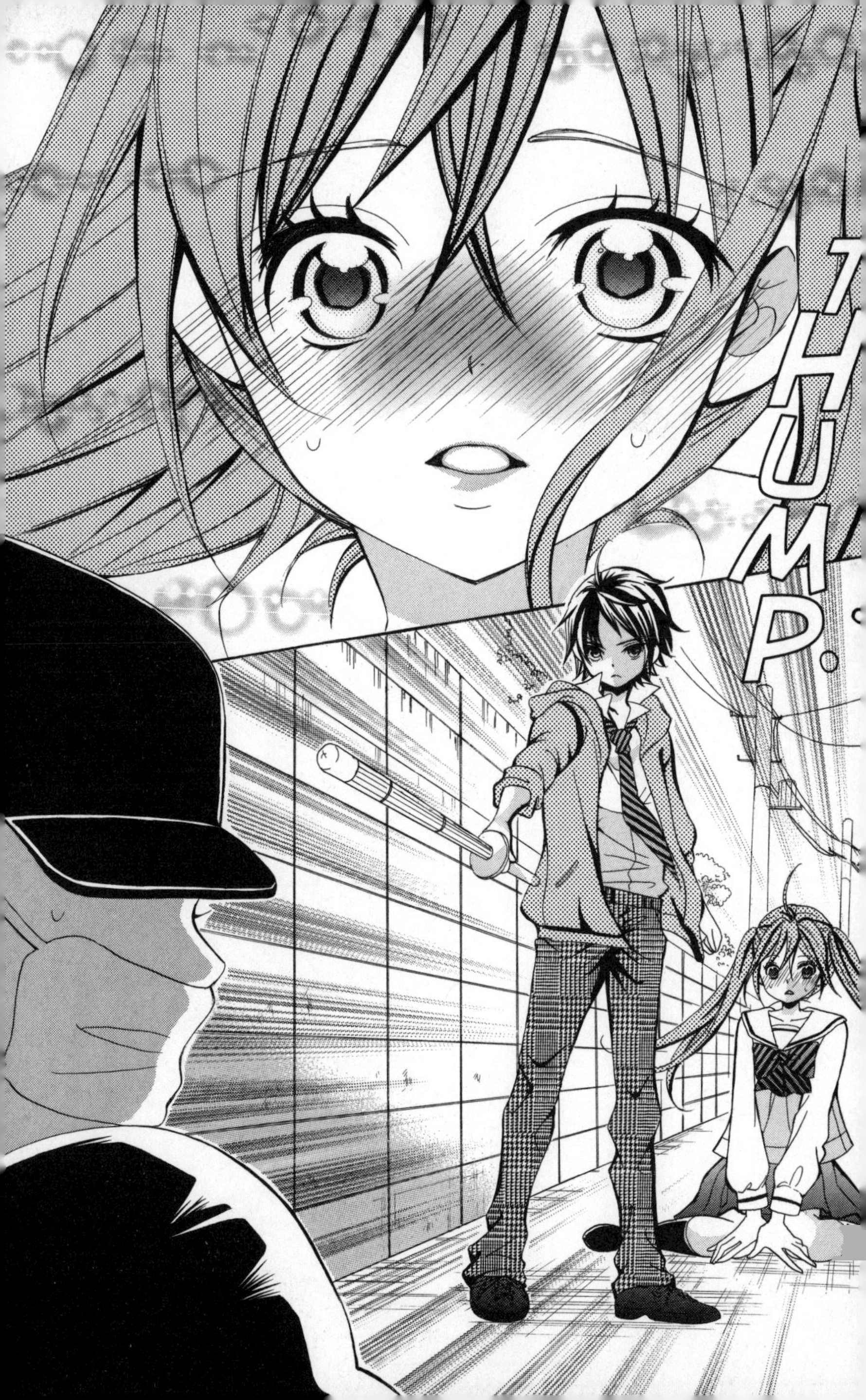
THUMP.

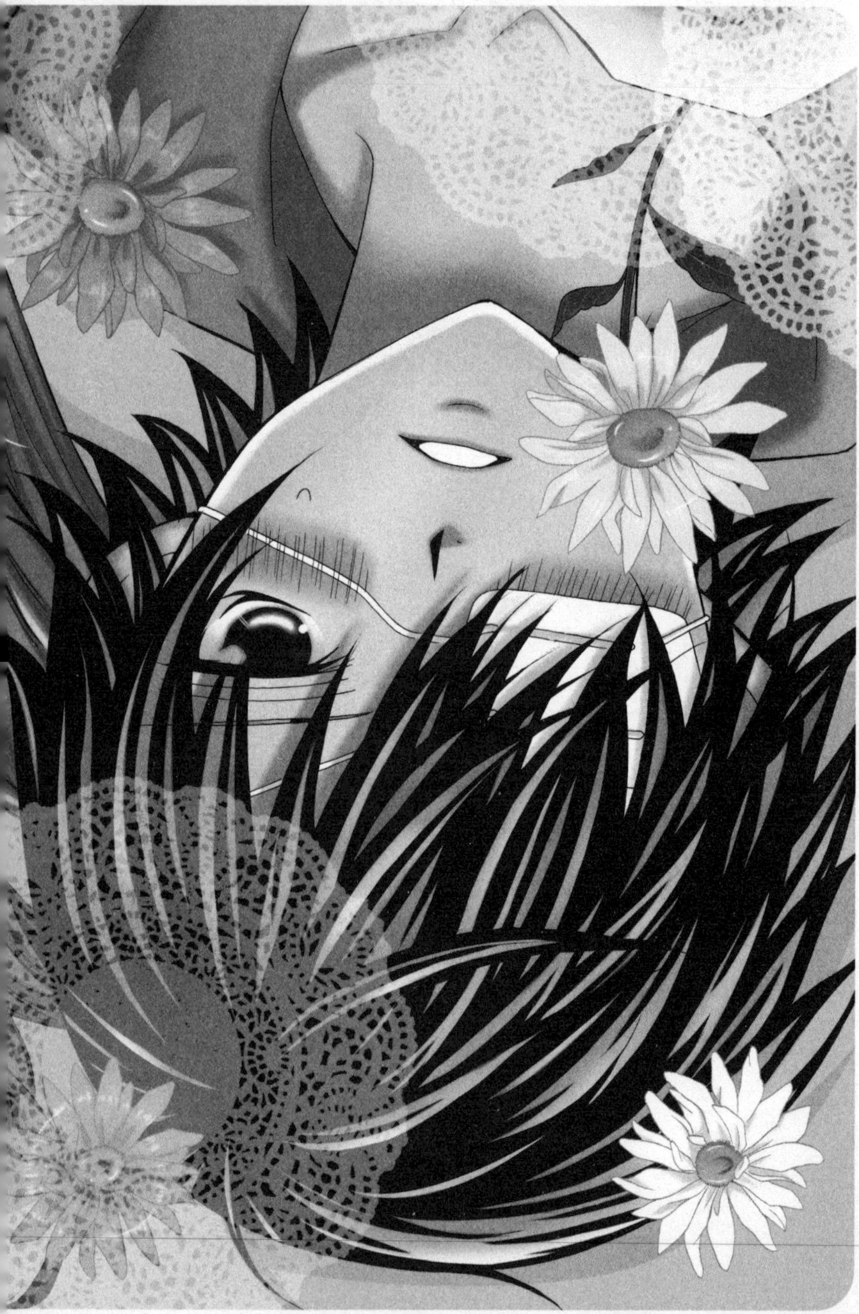

Chapter 30

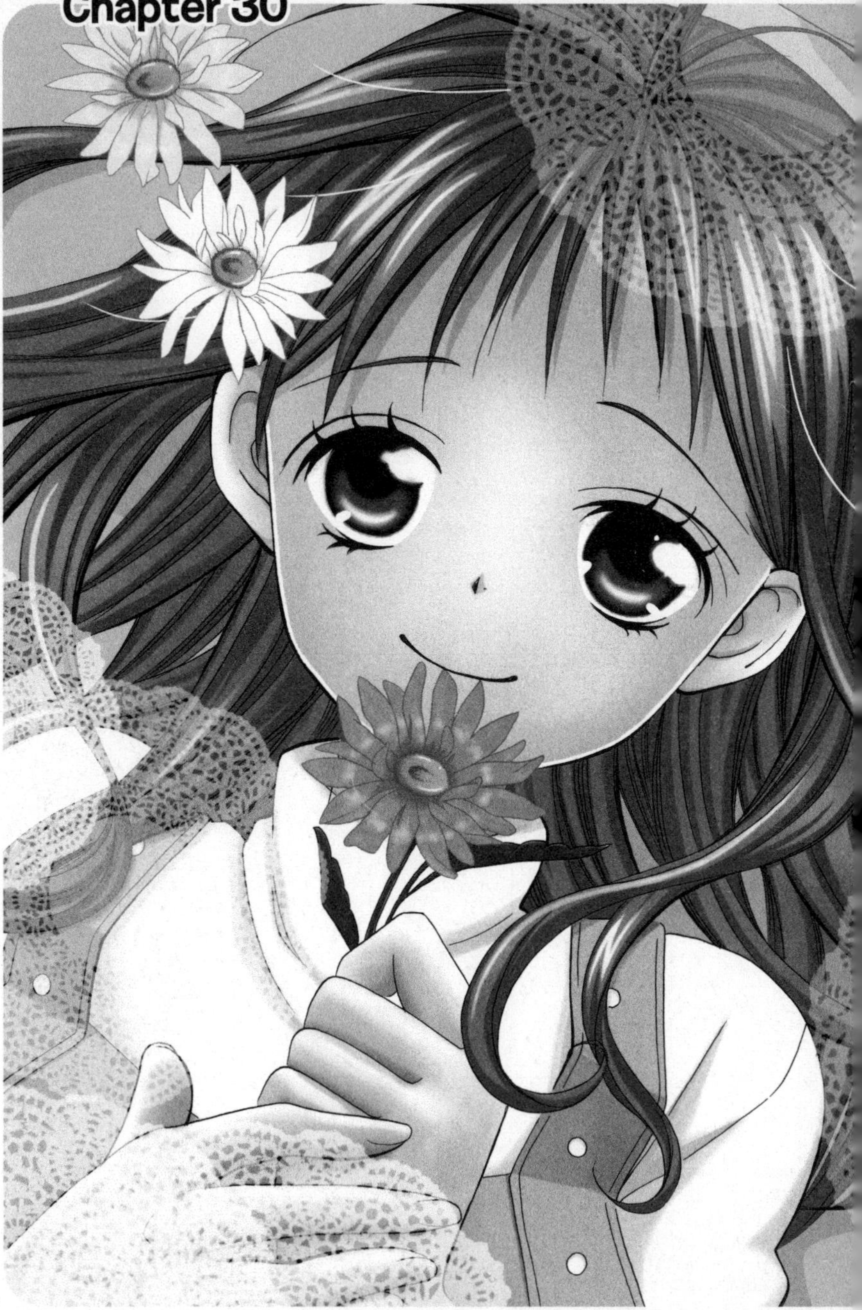

EVERYONE'S DRAWINGS ARE SO CUTE, THEY HURT!!

SO CUTE! FAN ART FEATURE ♥

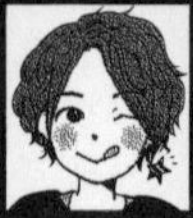

Editor: Shoji

Here we show you everyone's fan art. ♪
Editor Shojii has commented on each one this time too!!

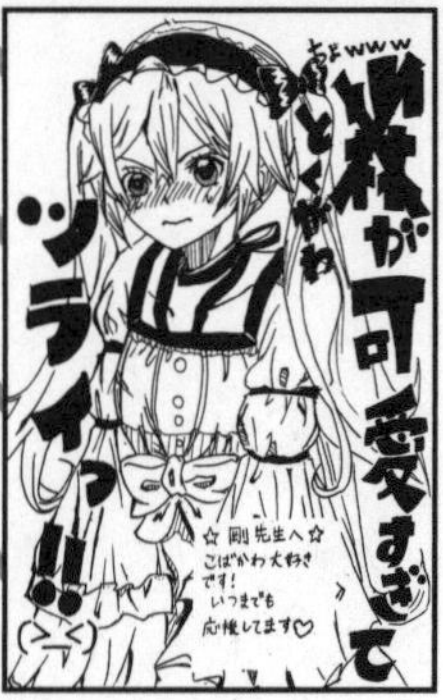

小林が可愛すぎてツライっ!!

Editor: I-is the title changing because Azusa's the heroine now?!

Haruna Ookawa (Fukui) ←

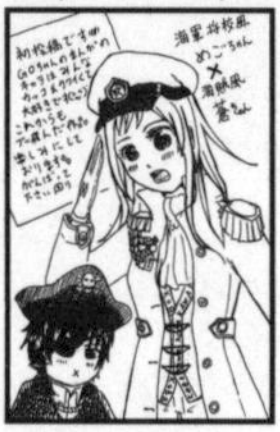

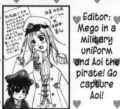

↑ Saika Kushida (Hyogo)

Editor: Mego in a military uniform and Aoi the pirate! Go capture Aoi!

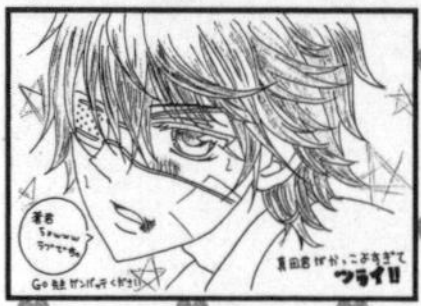

Yui Tanaka (Fukui) ↑

Editor: There're lots of Aoi addicts!

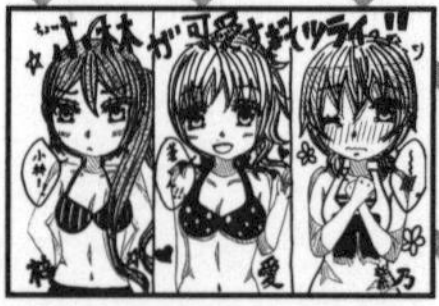

↑ Atchan (Wakayama)

Editor: !!!! The three heroines in swimsuits. (>_<)

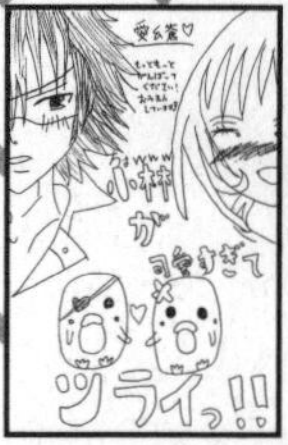

Editor: The penguins are just like Aoi and Mego. ♥ The couples are way too cute!!

↑ Miku Shimamura (Aichi)

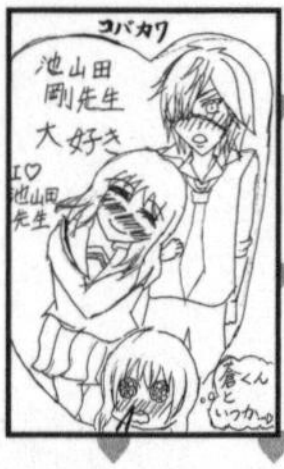

Editor: A girl's fantasy is exploding! (>_<)

Mitchan (Saga) ←

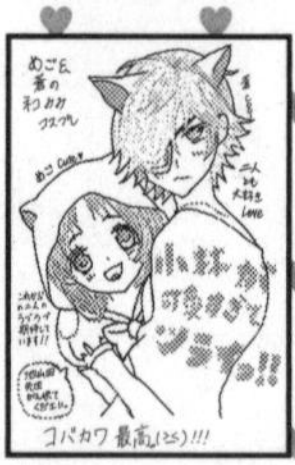

Editor: The cat-eared couple is so cute. ♪

Hizuki (Hyogo) ←

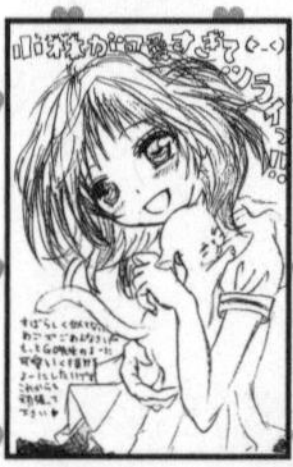

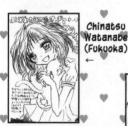

Chinatsu Watanabe (Fukuoka) ←

Editor: The cats play a big part in the anime DVD that comes with the limited edition version of volume 6!

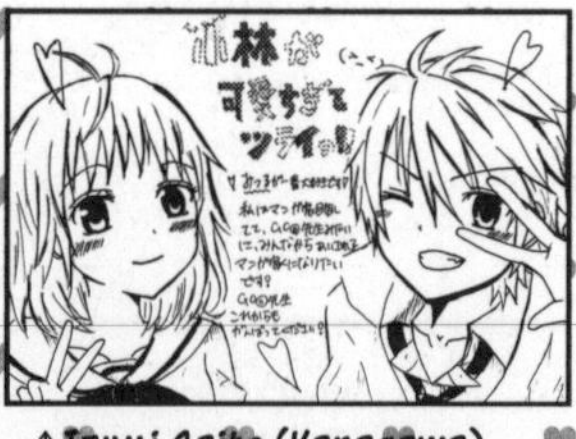

↑ Izumi Saito (Kanagawa)

Editor: The twins' double V signs. ♪

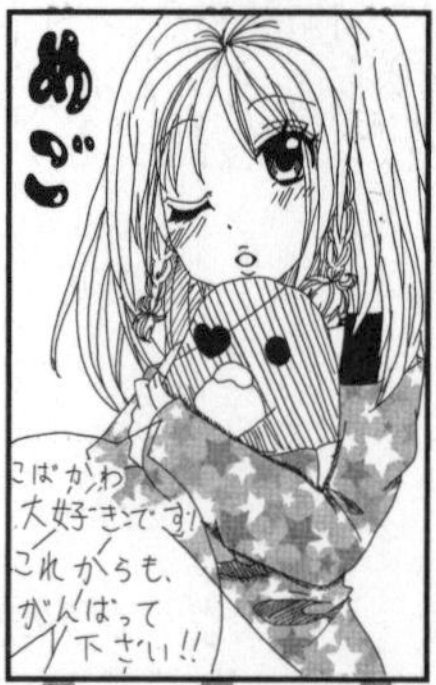

めご
こばかわ大好きです!
これからも、がんばって下さい!!

↑ Shimaneko (Fukushima)

Editor: Holding the eye-patch penguin in place of Aoi. ♥

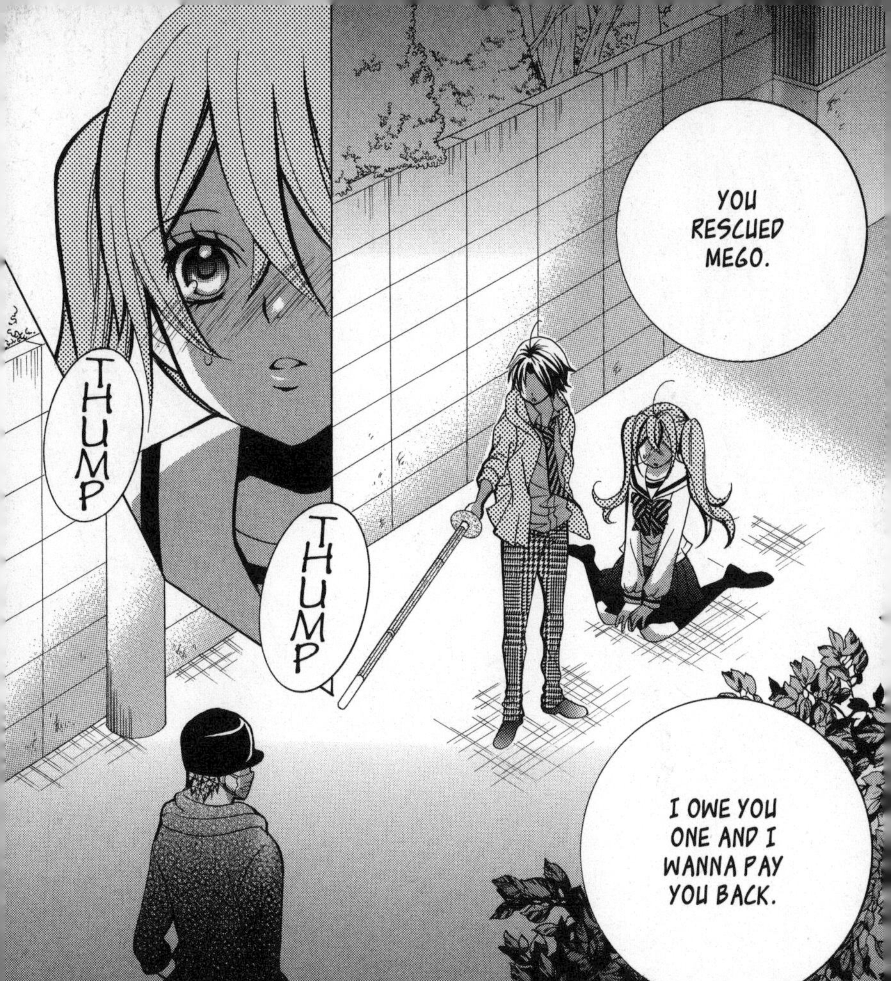
YOU RESCUED MEGO.
I OWE YOU ONE AND I WANNA PAY YOU BACK.
THUMP
THUMP

IT'S A BIT EARLY, BUT THIS IS THE AFTERWORD. THANK YOU FOR READING VOLUME 6 OF *SO CUTE IT HURTS!!* ♡

MY EDITOR AND I ARE BOTH FROM SENDAI CITY, MIYAGI PREFECTURE, SO WE TALKED ABOUT INCLUDING SENDAI'S STAR FESTIVAL IN THE STORY BEFORE THE SERIES BEGAN, AND I WAS FINALLY ABLE TO DO THAT IN THIS VOLUME. I ALSO DECIDED BEFORE THE SERIES BEGAN THAT SHINO WANTS TO BE A WRITER AND MEGO WANTS TO BE A MANGAKA, SO I'M HAPPY THE STORY HAS PROGRESSED THIS FAR. (MEGO'S HOLDING COPIC MARKERS IN THE CHAPTER 1 TITLE PAGE. [*SMILE*])

UESUGI, THE NEW CHARACTER WHO KNOWS AOI'S PAST, ENDED UP BEING FRIENDS WITH A BIRD I INCLUDED FOR NO PARTICULAR REASON. (*SMILE*) I LIKE THE PAIR AND THINK THEY MAKE A PRETTY GOOD TEAM. LOL.

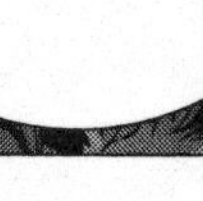

PLEASE LOOK FORWARD TO AOI AND MEGO'S RELATIONSHIP DEVELOPMENTS NOW THAT UESUGI HAS APPEARED. (^0^) AZUSA AND MITSURU'S RELATIONSHIP IS CHANGING QUITE A BIT IN THE MAGAZINE INSTALLMENTS, SO I HOPE YOU LOOK FORWARD TO THAT TOO. ♡

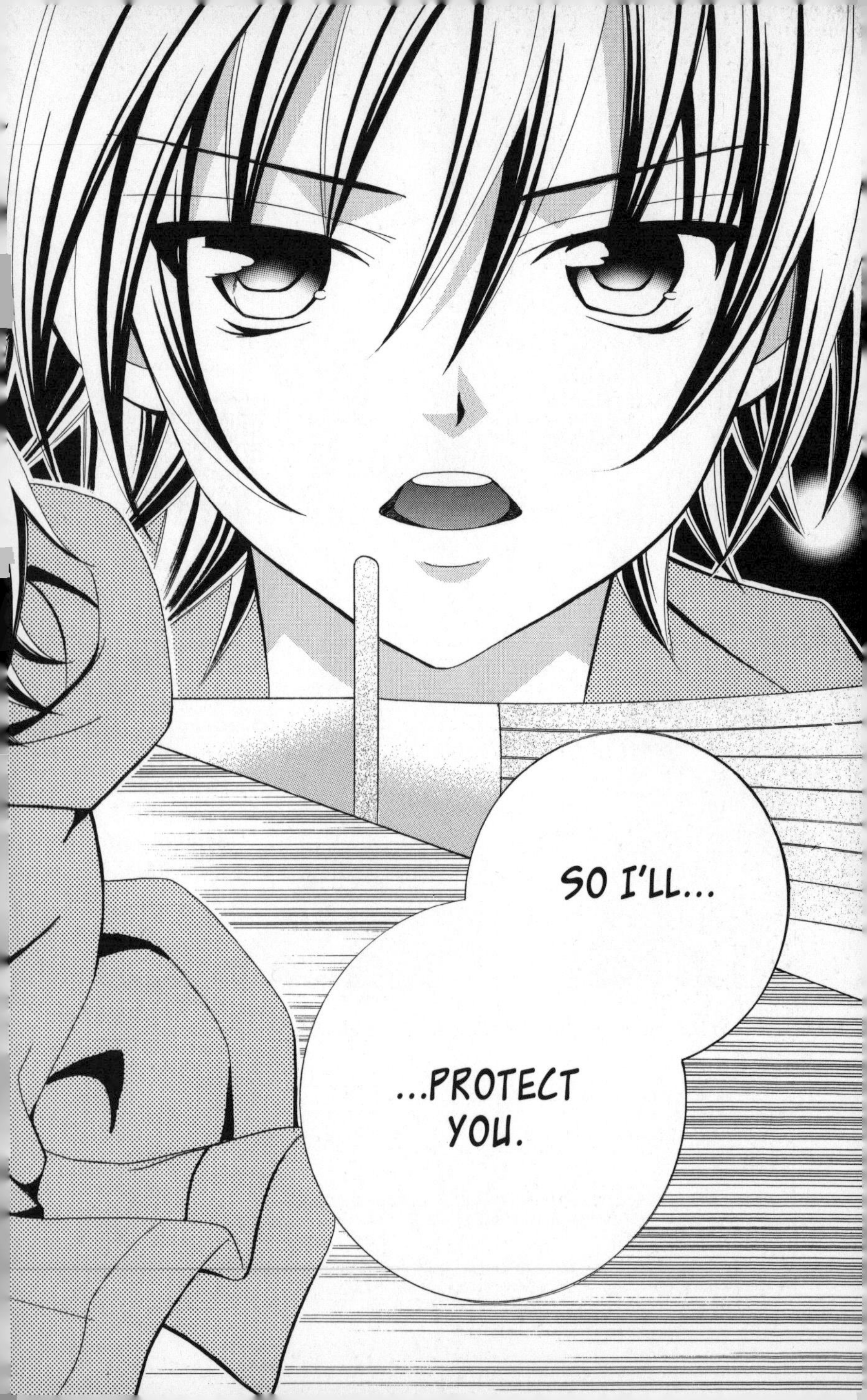
SO I'LL...
...PROTECT YOU.

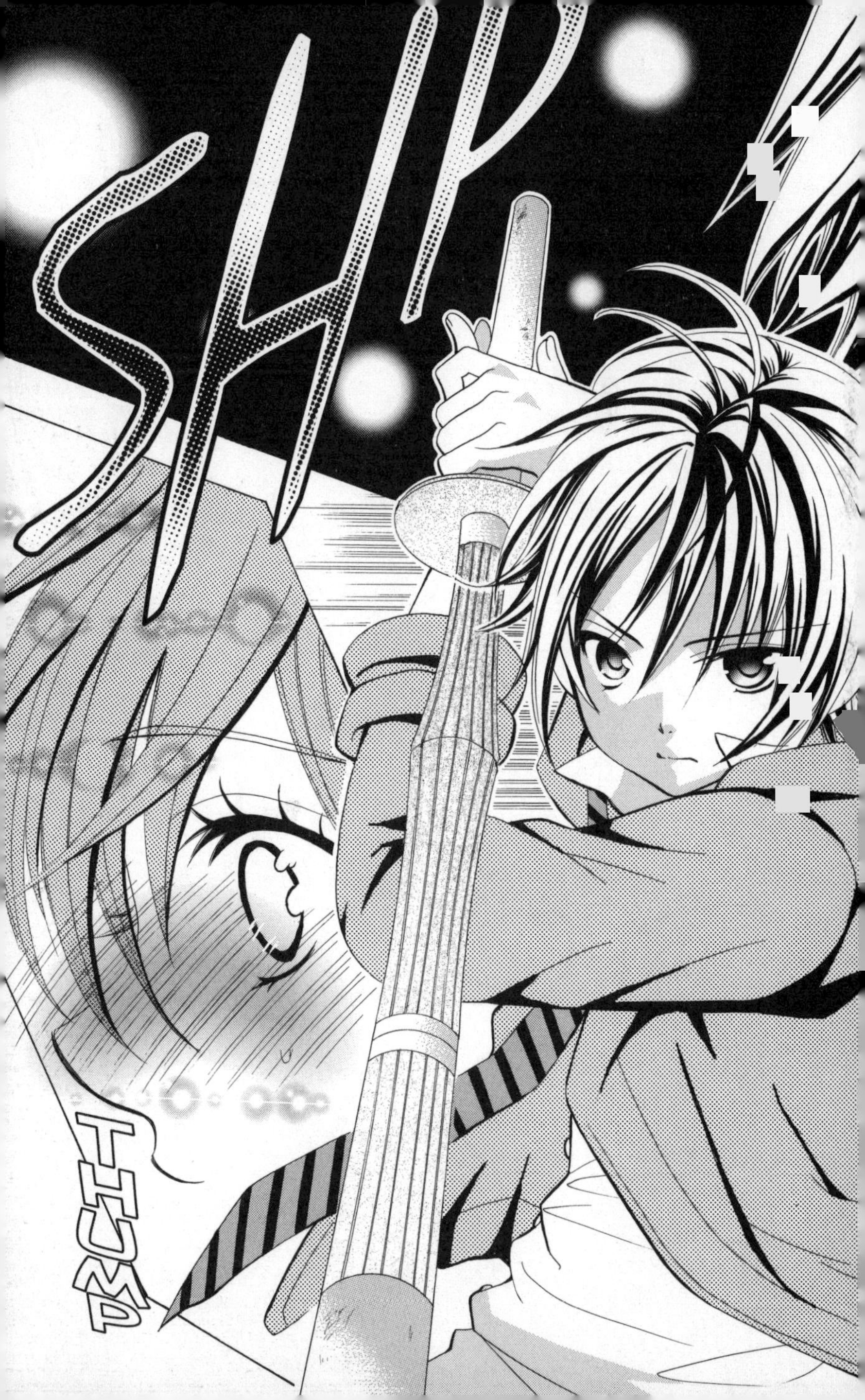
SHIP
THUMP

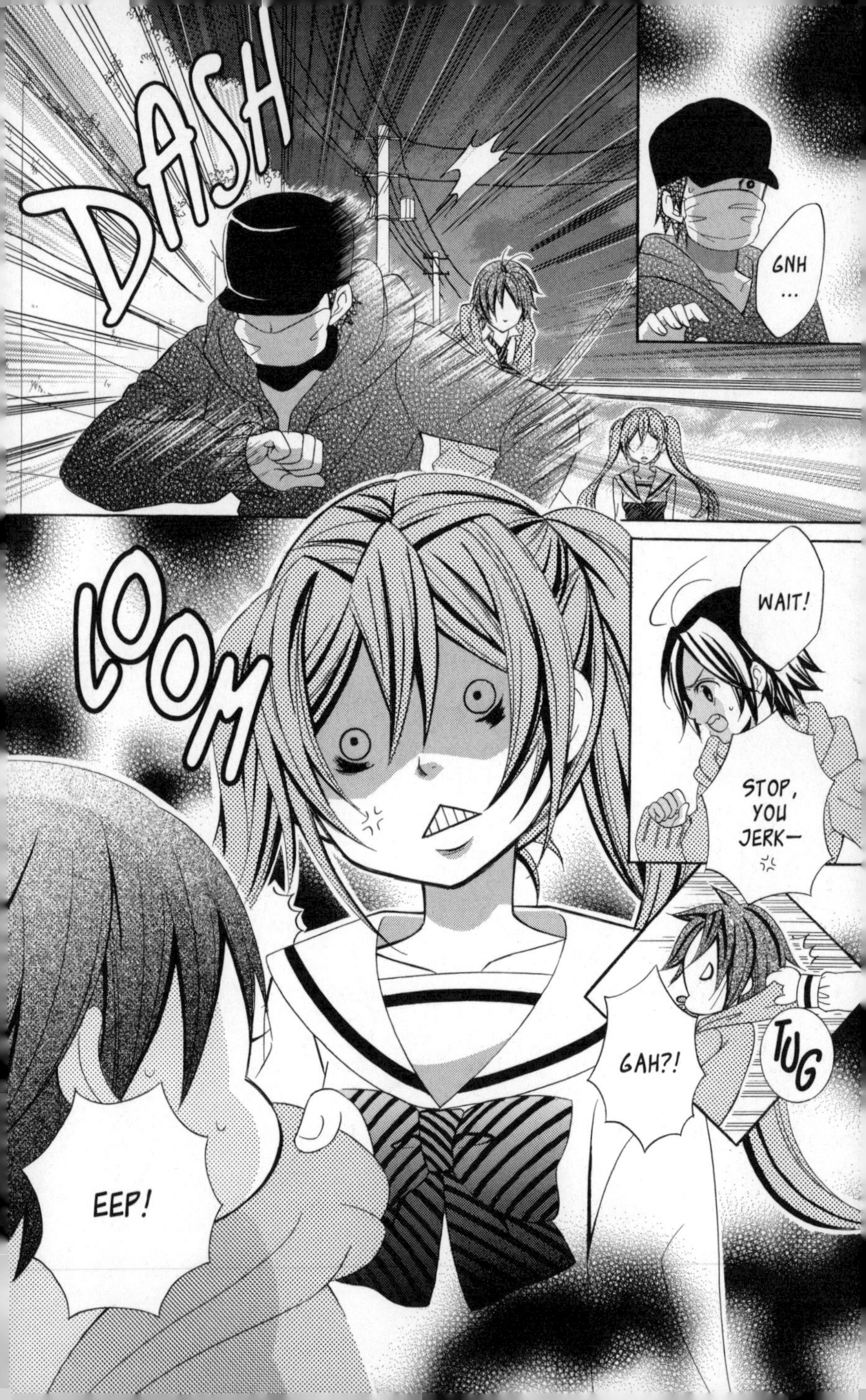
GNH ...
DASH
WAIT!
STOP, YOU JERK—
TUG
GAH?!
LOOM
EEP!

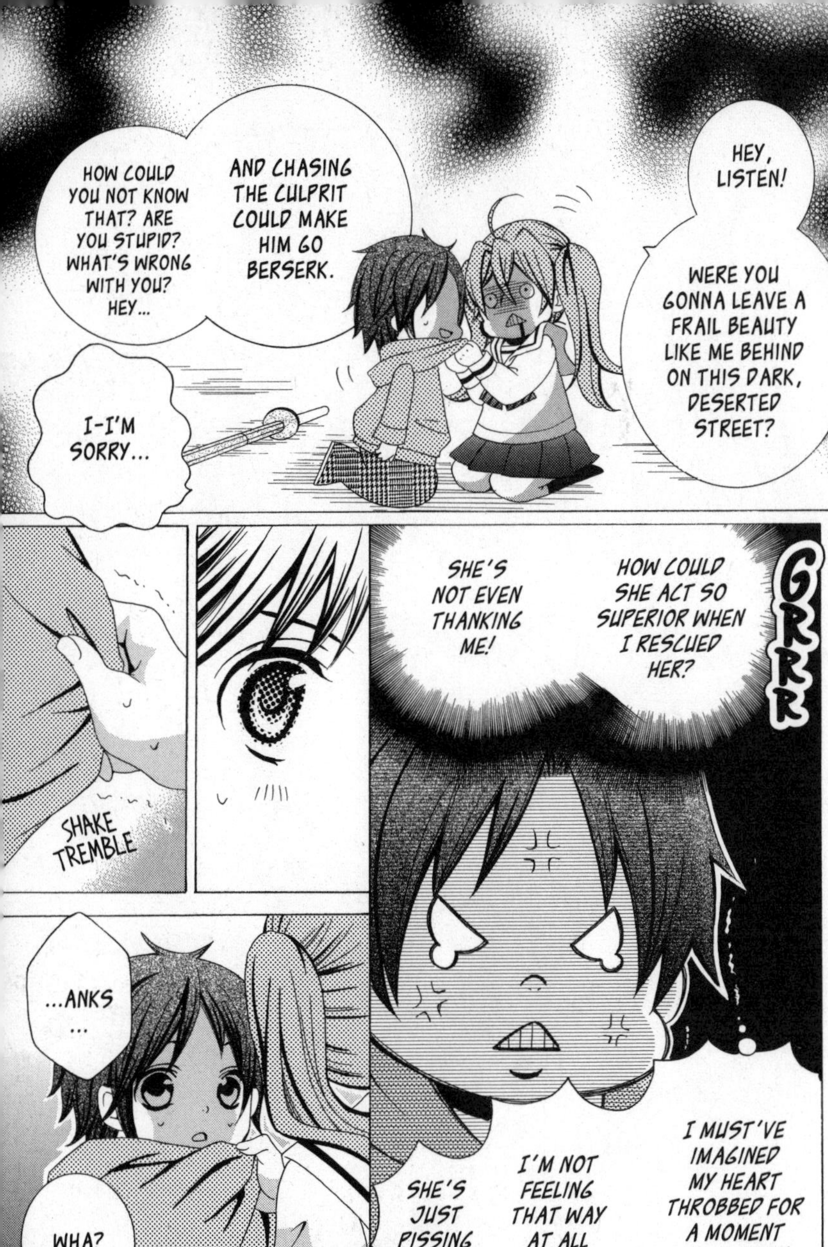
HEY, LISTEN!
WERE YOU GONNA LEAVE A FRAIL BEAUTY LIKE ME BEHIND ON THIS DARK, DESERTED STREET?
AND CHASING THE CULPRIT COULD MAKE HIM GO BERSERK.
HOW COULD YOU NOT KNOW THAT? ARE YOU STUPID? WHAT'S WRONG WITH YOU? HEY...
I-I'M SORRY...
GRRR
HOW COULD SHE ACT SO SUPERIOR WHEN I RESCUED HER?
SHE'S NOT EVEN THANKING ME!
I MUST'VE IMAGINED MY HEART THROBBED FOR A MOMENT THAT TIME!
I'M NOT FEELING THAT WAY AT ALL NOW!
SHE'S JUST PISSING ME OFF!
SHAKE TREMBLE
...ANKS ...
WHA?

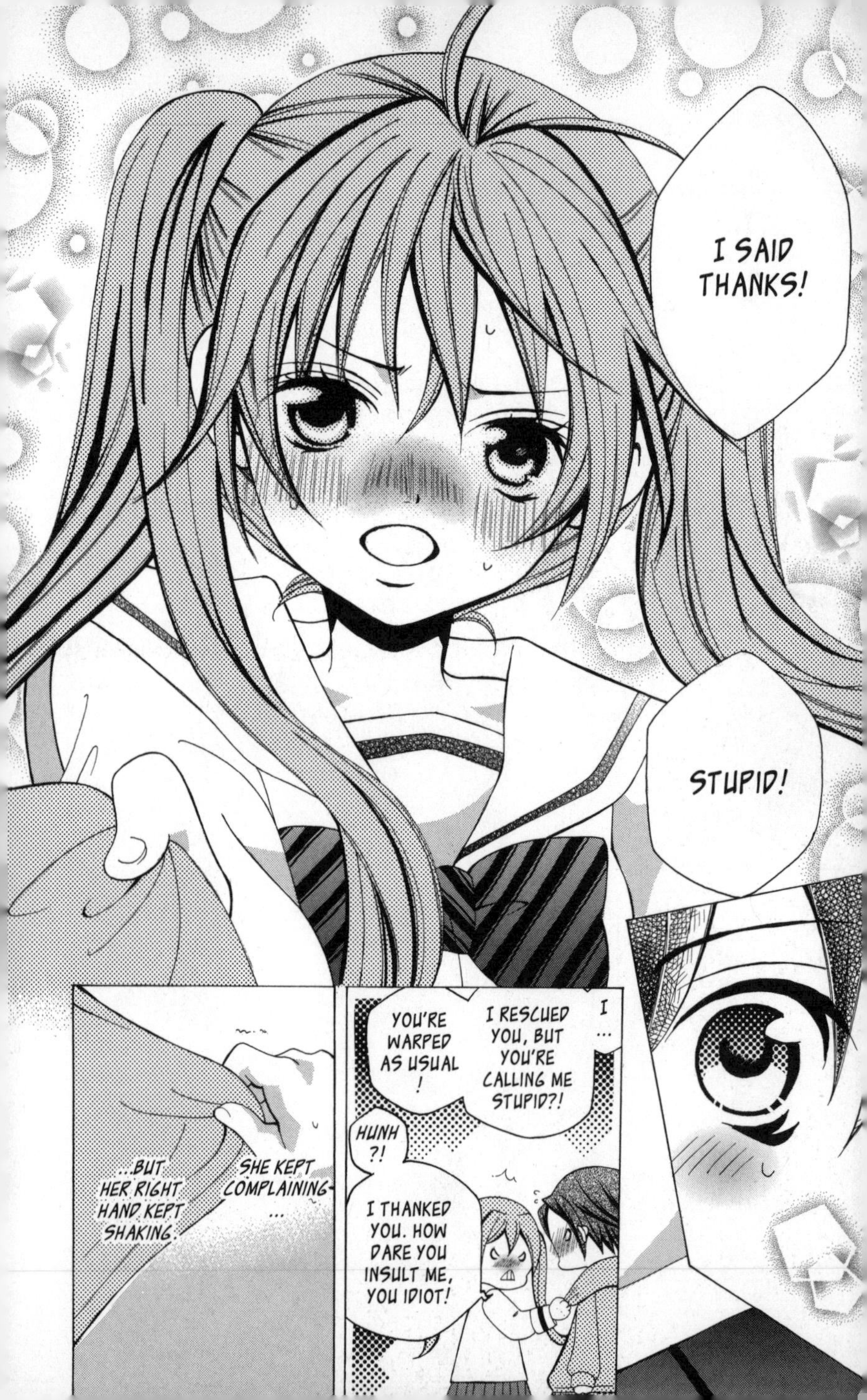
I SAID THANKS!
STUPID!
I ...
I RESCUED YOU, BUT YOU'RE CALLING ME STUPID?!
YOU'RE WARPED AS USUAL!
HUNH ?!
I THANKED YOU. HOW DARE YOU INSULT ME, YOU IDIOT!
SHE KEPT COMPLAINING ...
...BUT HER RIGHT HAND KEPT SHAKING.

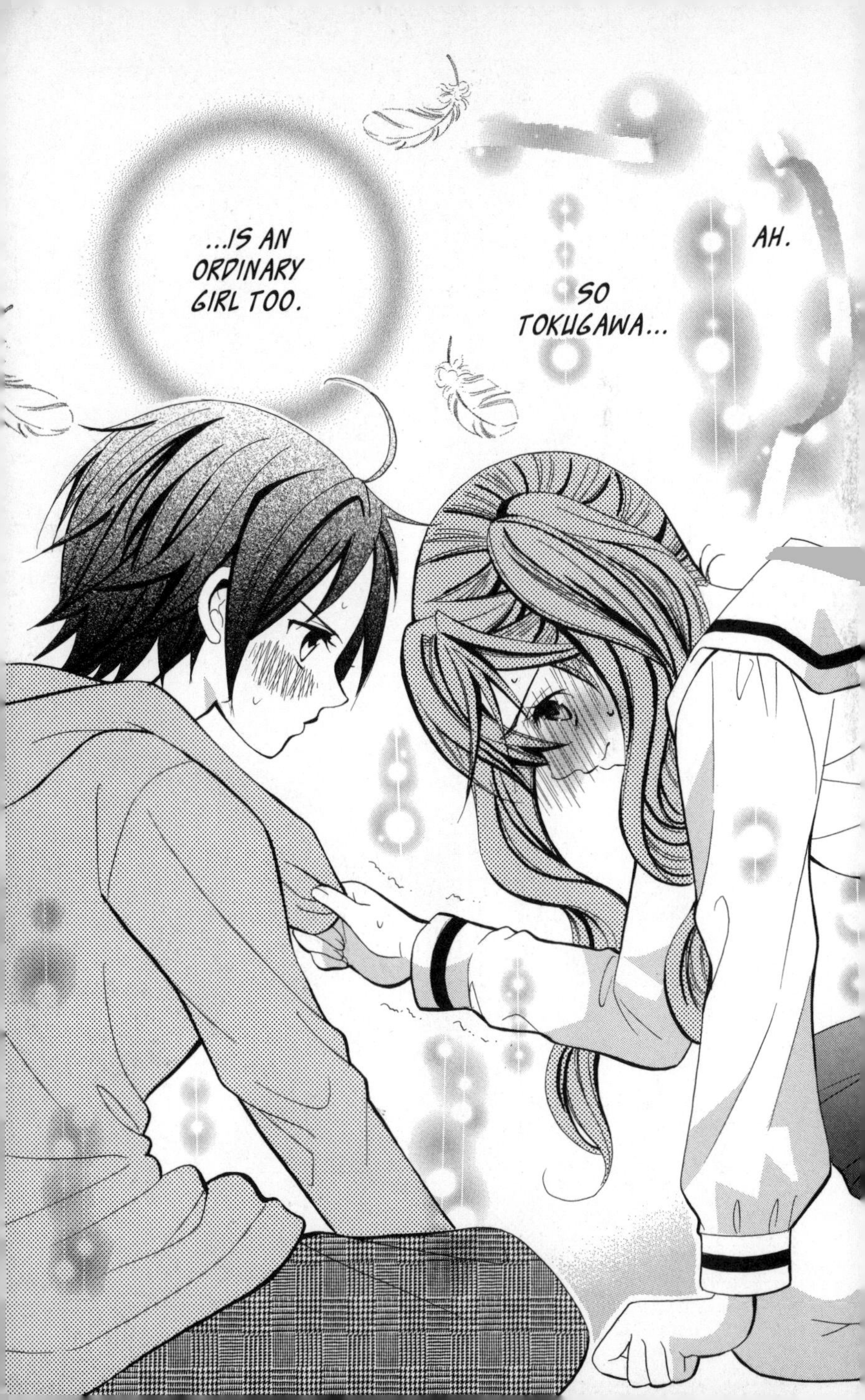
AH.
SO TOKUGAWA...
...IS AN ORDINARY GIRL TOO.

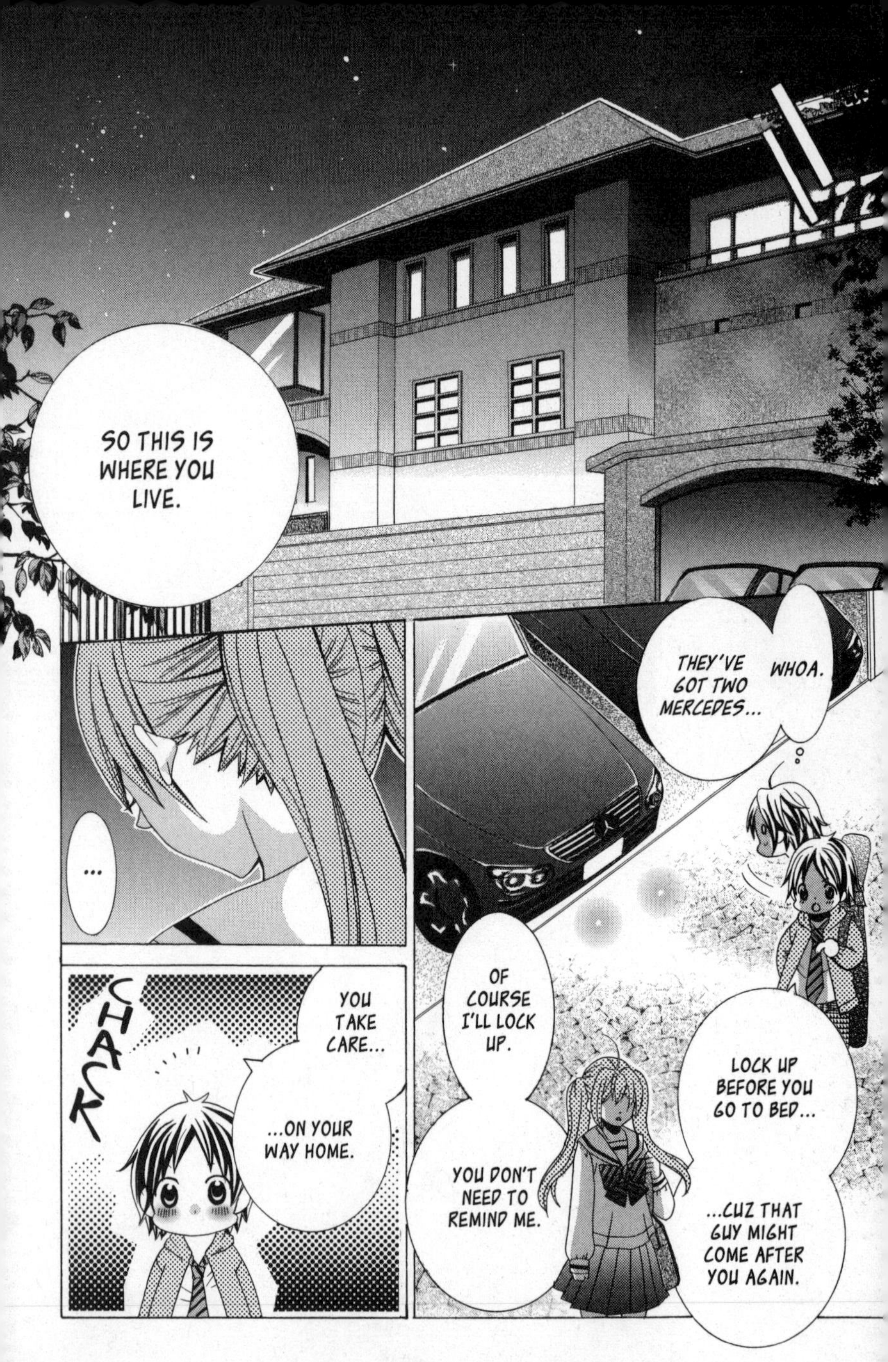
SO THIS IS WHERE YOU LIVE.
WHOA. THEY'VE GOT TWO MERCEDES...
LOCK UP BEFORE YOU GO TO BED...
...CUZ THAT GUY MIGHT COME AFTER YOU AGAIN.
OF COURSE I'LL LOCK UP.
YOU DON'T NEED TO REMIND ME.
...
CHACK
YOU TAKE CARE...
...ON YOUR WAY HOME.

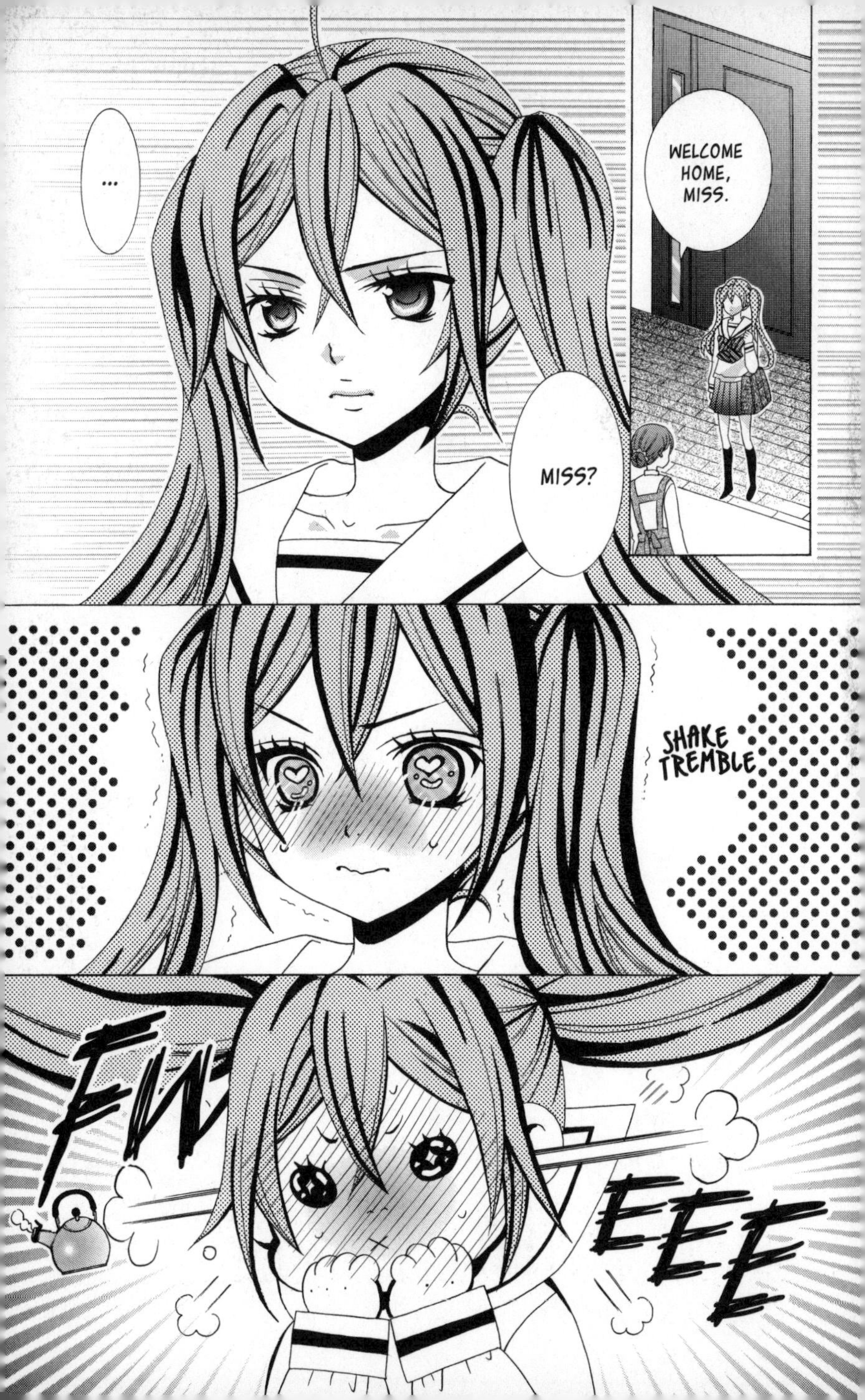
WELCOME HOME, MISS.
MISS?
...
SHAKE TREMBLE
FW
EEE

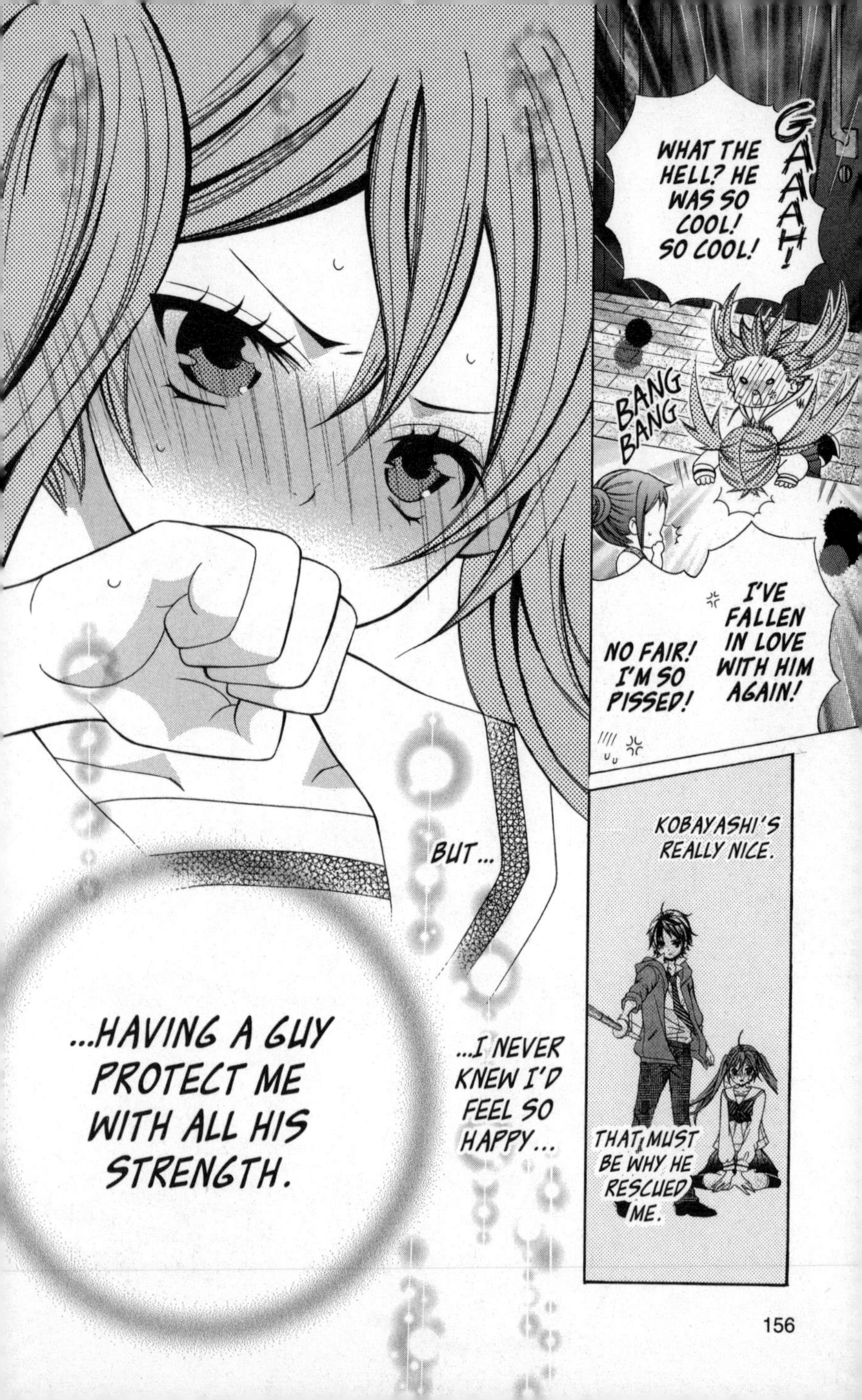
WHAT THE HELL? HE WAS SO COOL! SO COOL!
GAAAH!
BANG BANG
I'VE FALLEN IN LOVE WITH HIM AGAIN!
NO FAIR! I'M SO PISSED!
KOBAYASHI'S REALLY NICE.
THAT MUST BE WHY HE RESCUED ME.
BUT...
...I NEVER KNEW I'D FEEL SO HAPPY...
...HAVING A GUY PROTECT ME WITH ALL HIS STRENGTH.

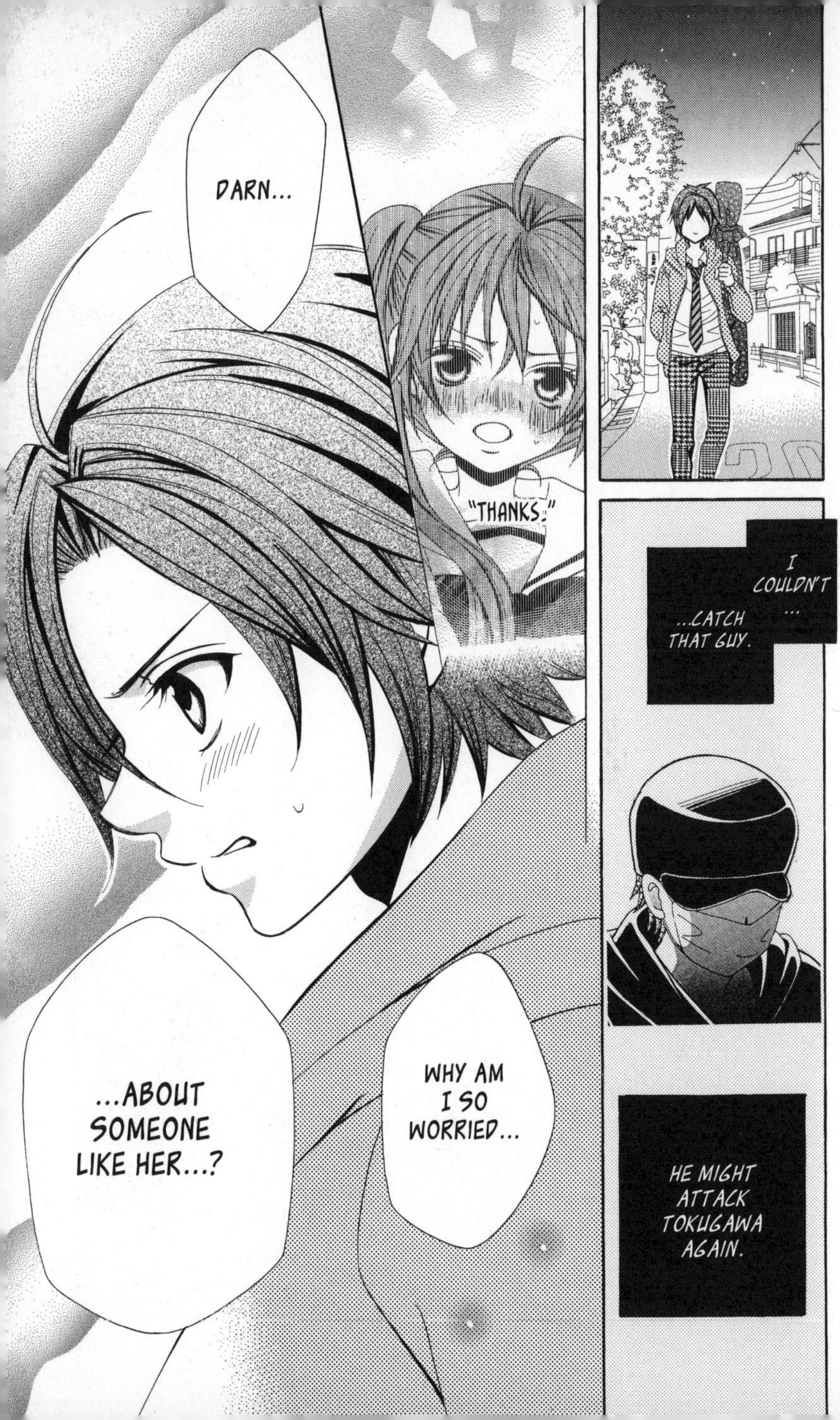

I COULDN'T ...
...CATCH THAT GUY.
HE MIGHT ATTACK TOKUGAWA AGAIN.
DARN...
"THANKS."
WHY AM I SO WORRIED...
...ABOUT SOMEONE LIKE HER...?

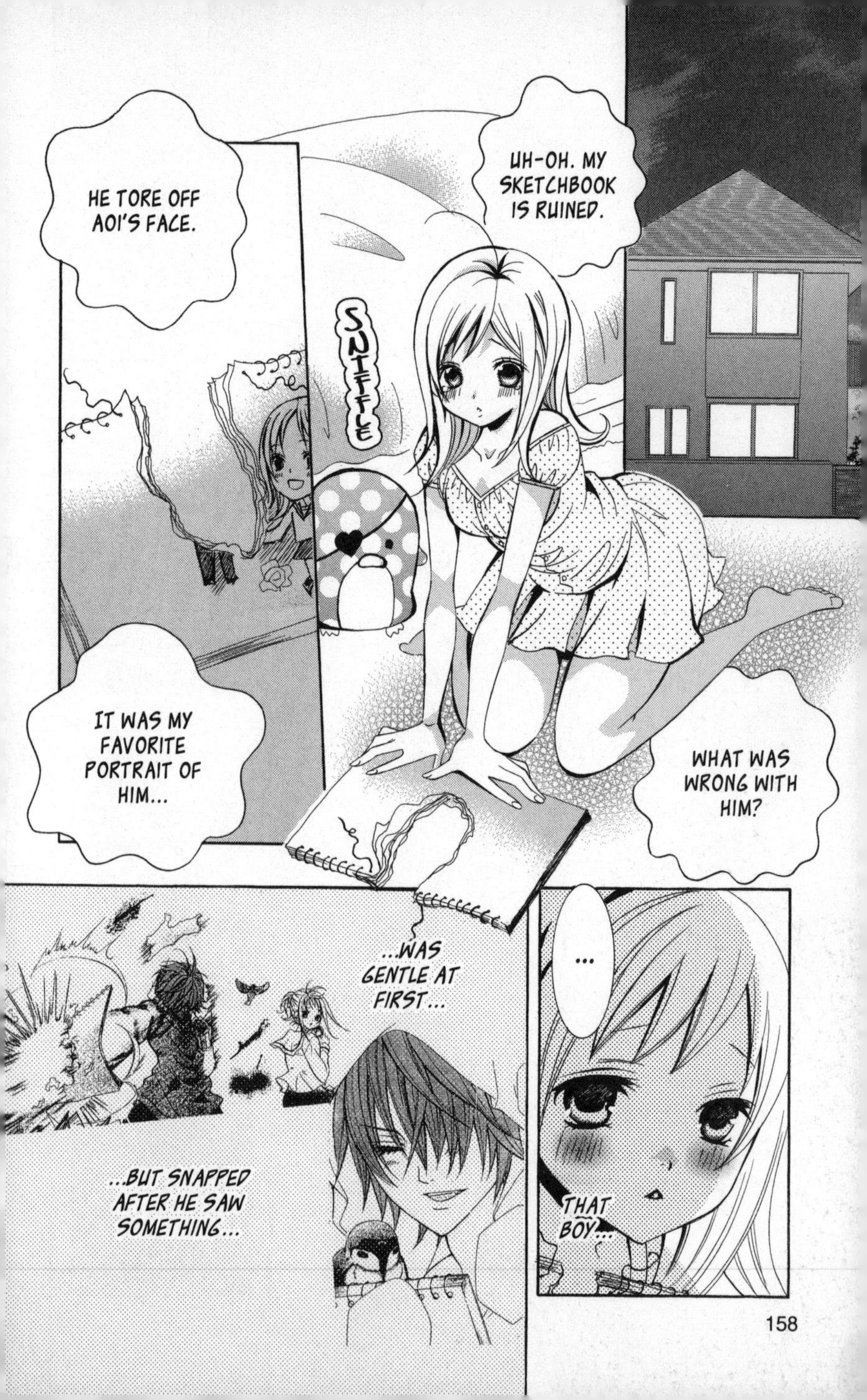
UH-OH. MY SKETCHBOOK IS RUINED.
SNIFFLE
HE TORE OFF AOI'S FACE.
IT WAS MY FAVORITE PORTRAIT OF HIM...
WHAT WAS WRONG WITH HIM?
...
THAT BOY...
...WAS GENTLE AT FIRST...
...BUT SNAPPED AFTER HE SAW SOMETHING...

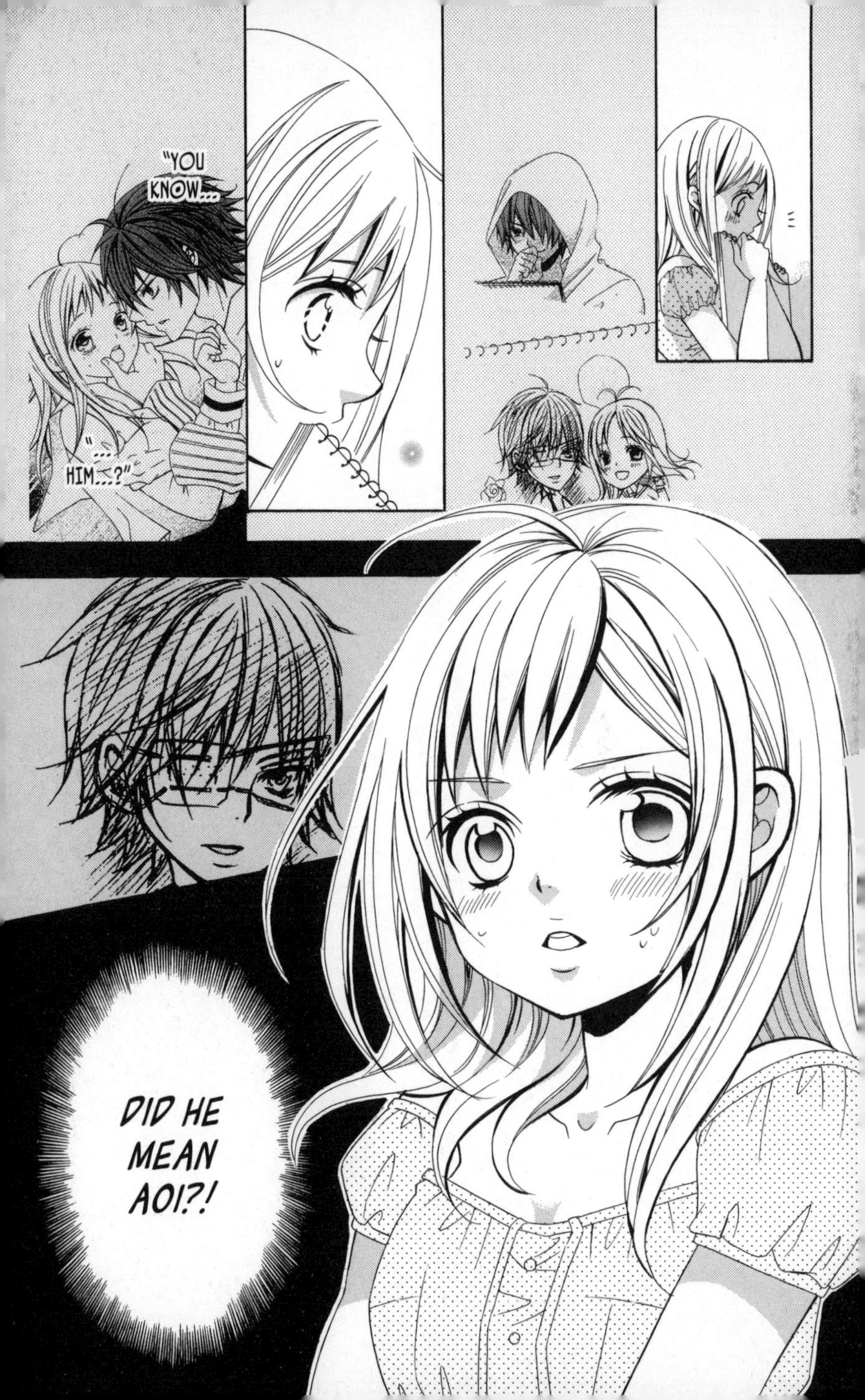
"YOU KNOW...
"... HIM...?"
DID HE MEAN AOI?!

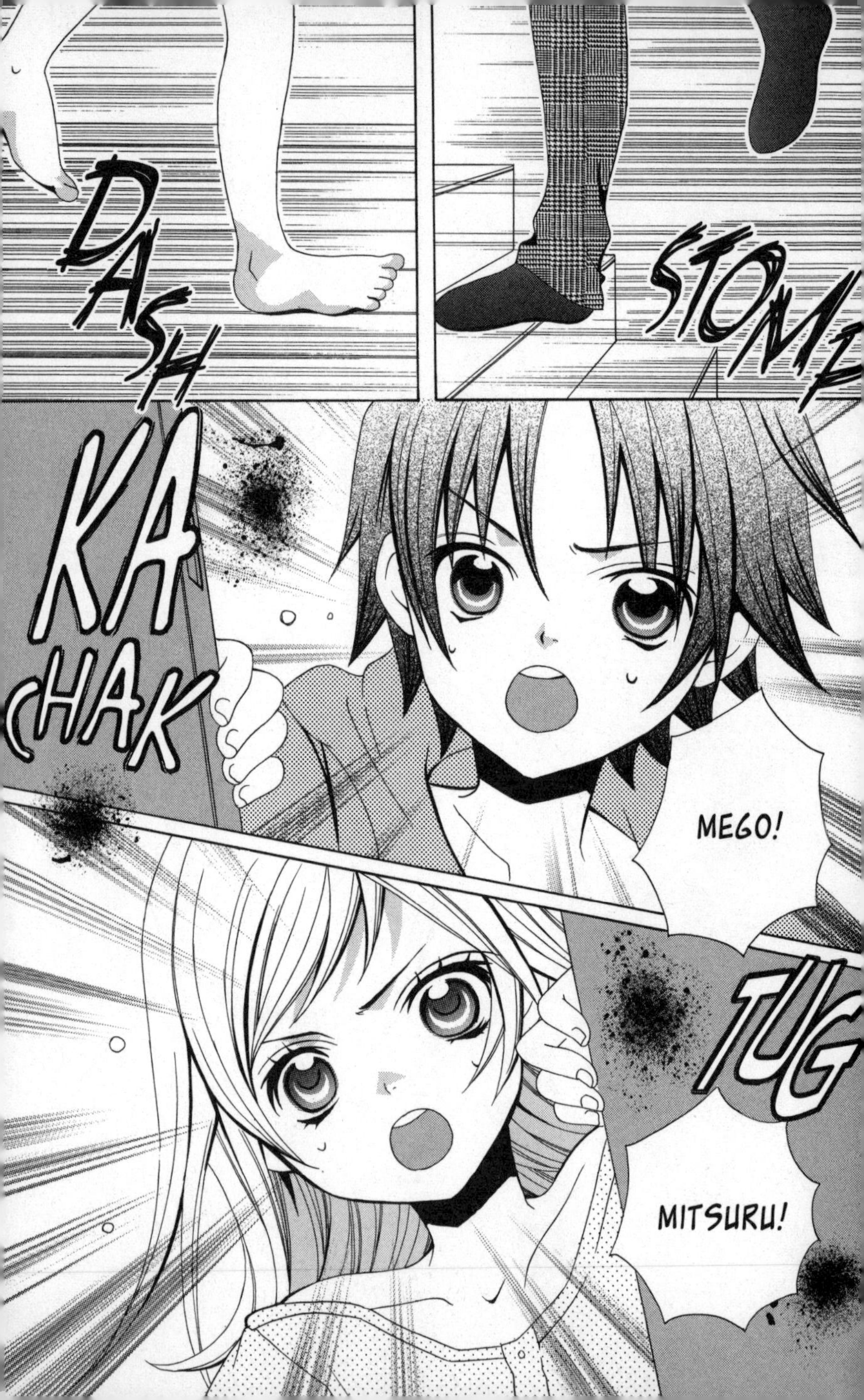
STOMP
DASH
KA CHAK
MEGO!
TUG
MITSURU!

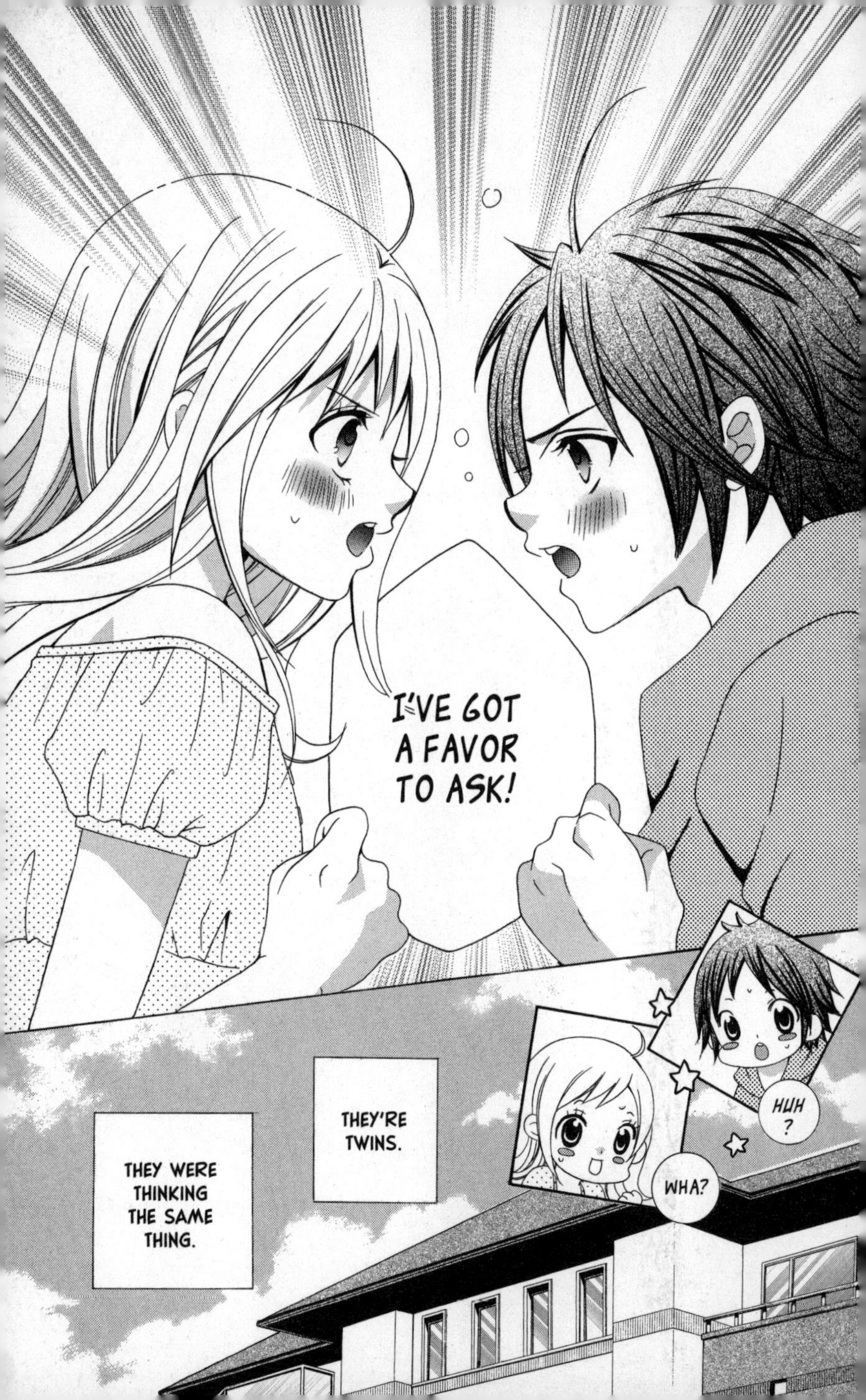
I'VE GOT A FAVOR TO ASK!
HUH ?
WHA?
THEY'RE TWINS.
THEY WERE THINKING THE SAME THING.

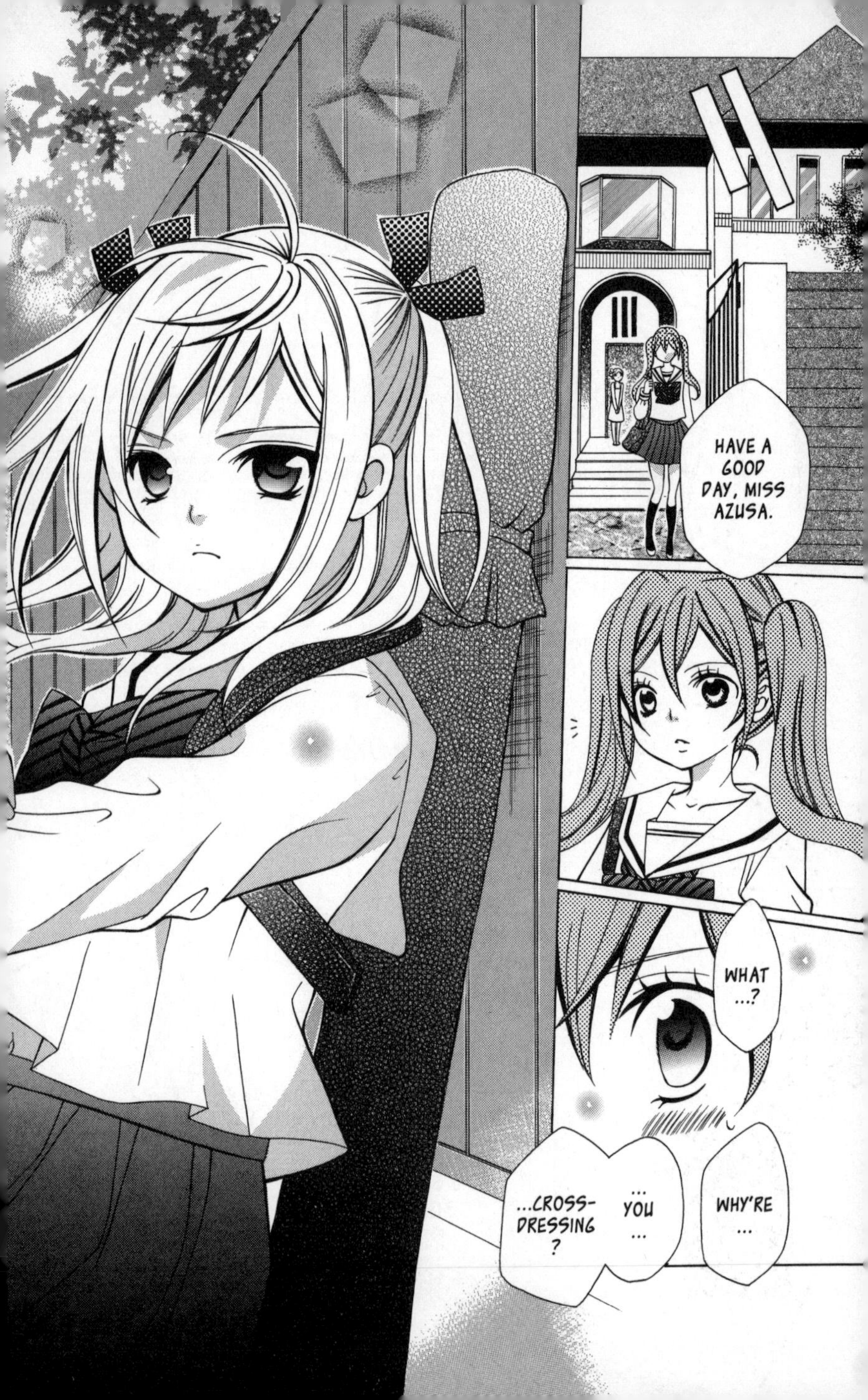
HAVE A GOOD DAY, MISS AZUSA.
WHAT ...?
WHY'RE ...
... YOU ...
...CROSS-DRESSING ?

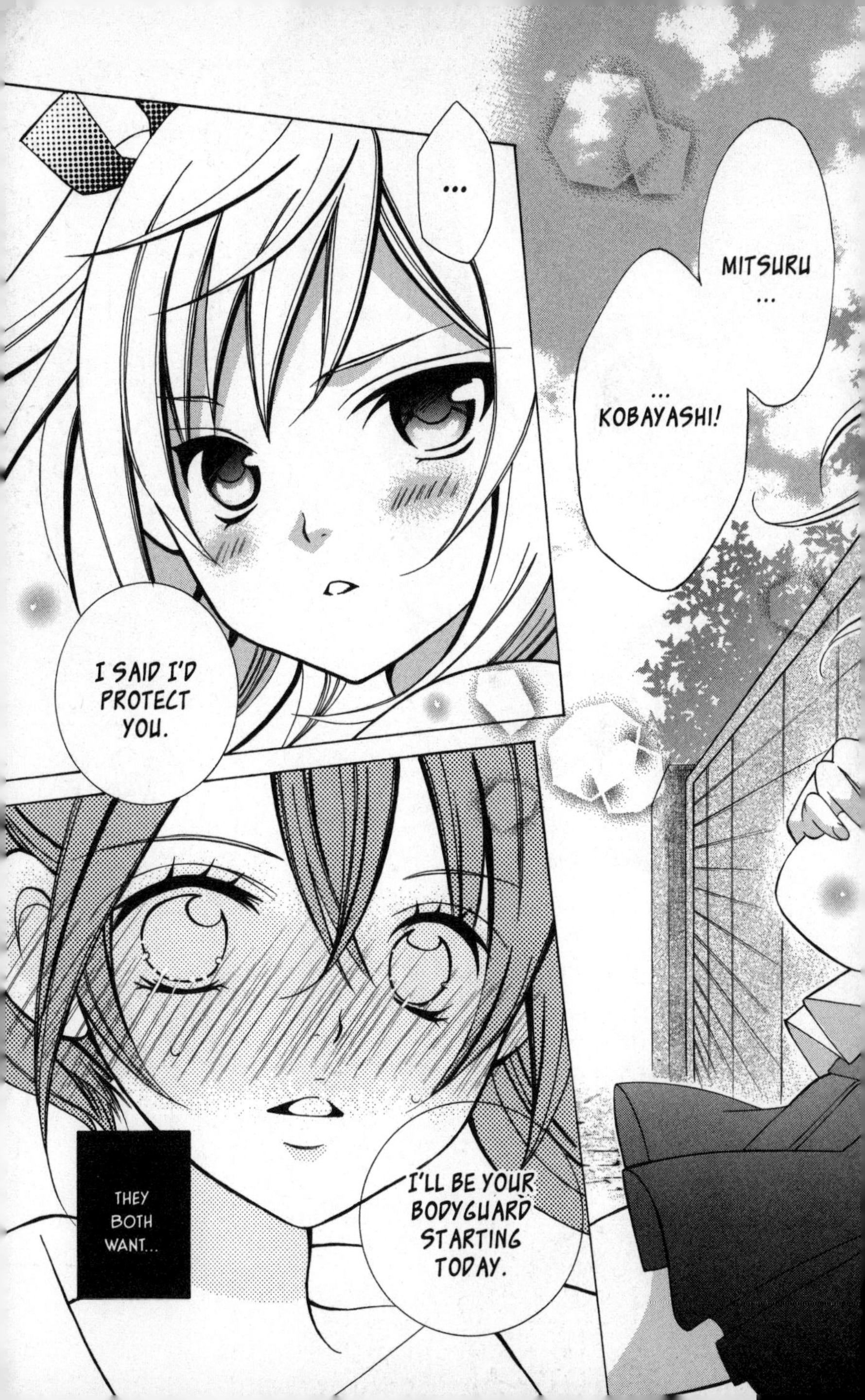
MITSURU ...
... KOBAYASHI!
...
I SAID I'D PROTECT YOU.
I'LL BE YOUR BODYGUARD STARTING TODAY.
THEY BOTH WANT...

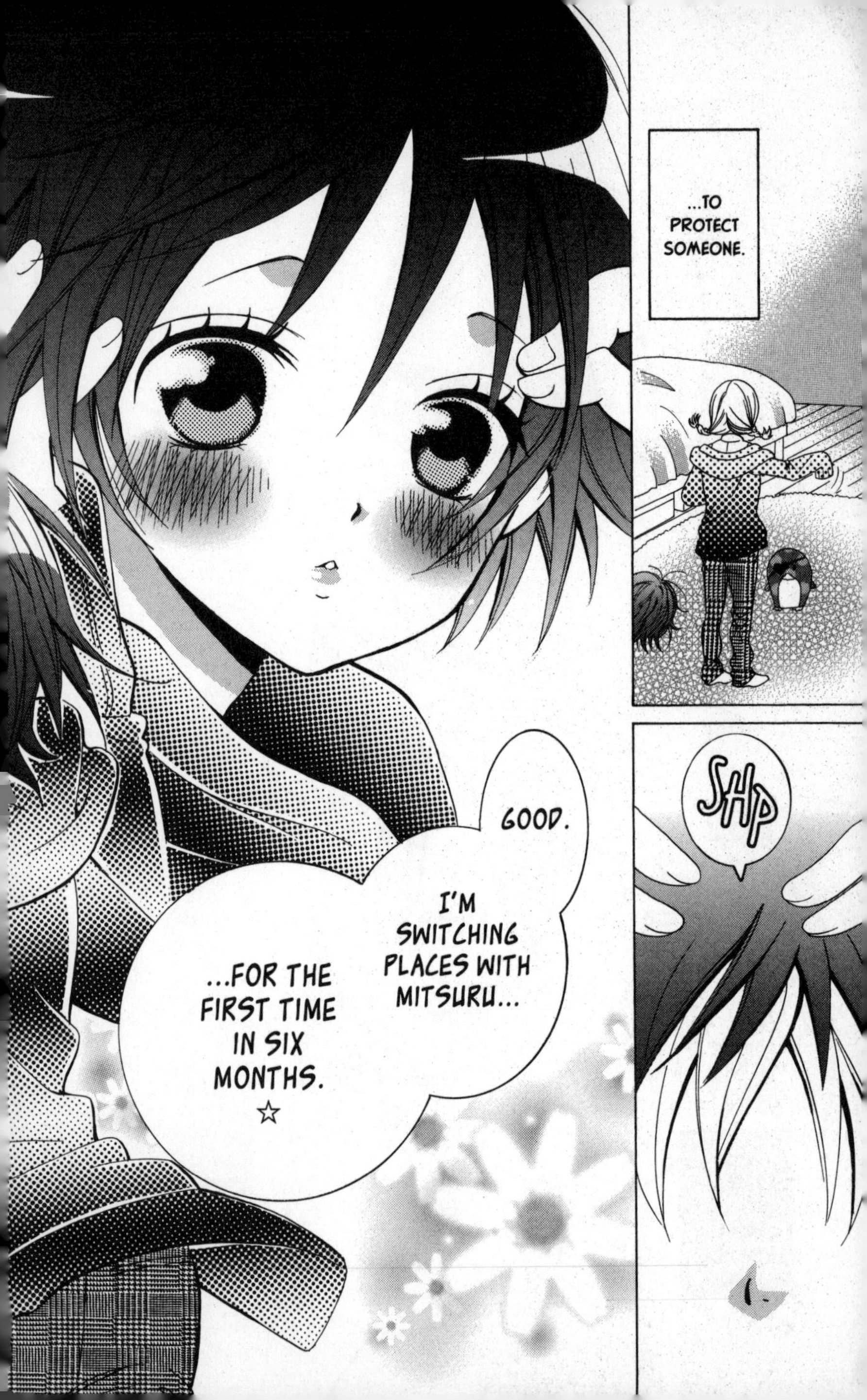
...TO PROTECT SOMEONE.
SHP
GOOD.
I'M SWITCHING PLACES WITH MITSURU...
...FOR THE FIRST TIME IN SIX MONTHS. ☆

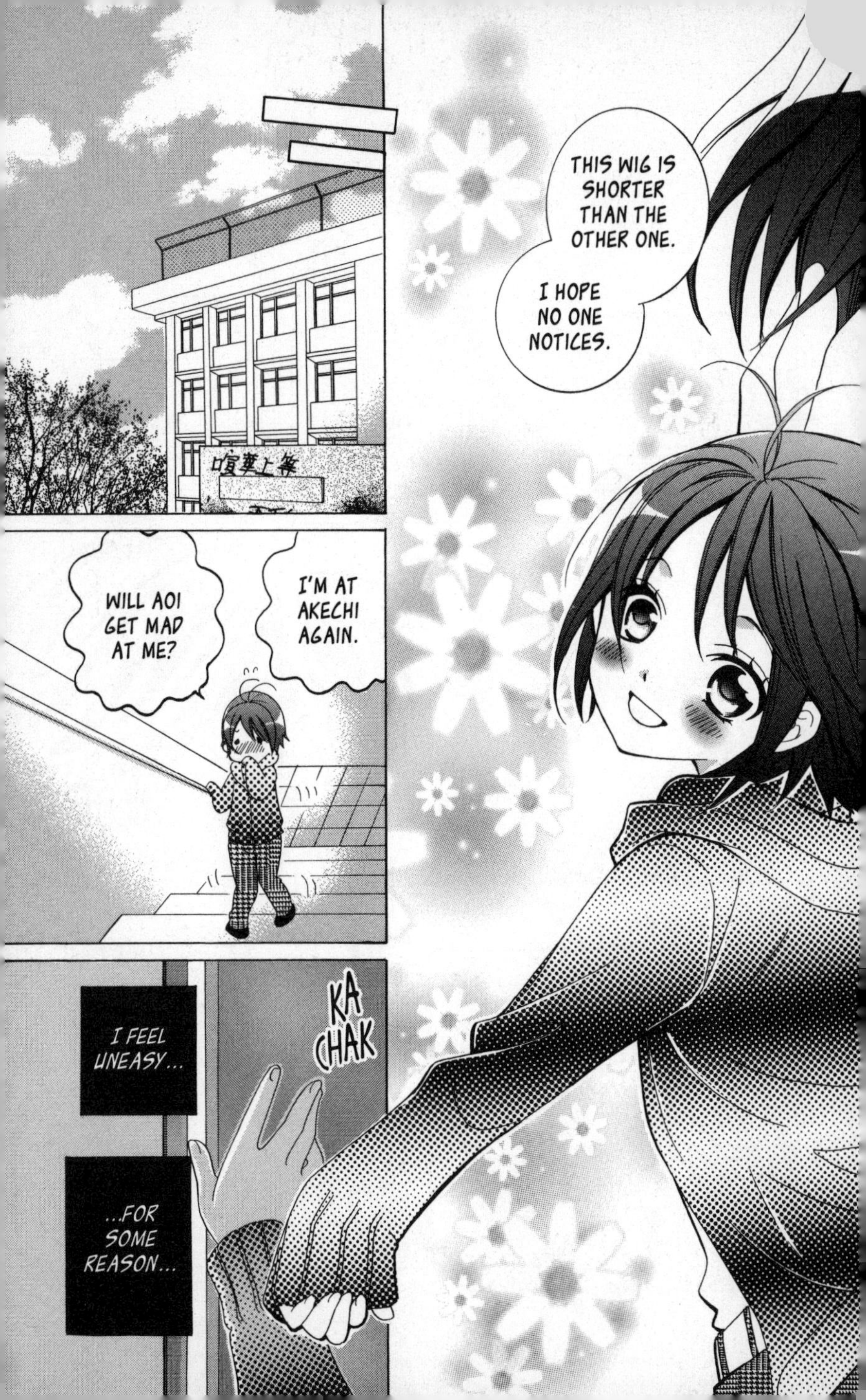
THIS WIG IS SHORTER THAN THE OTHER ONE.
I HOPE NO ONE NOTICES.
I'M AT AKECHI AGAIN.
WILL AOI GET MAD AT ME?
KA CHAK
I FEEL UNEASY...
...FOR SOME REASON...

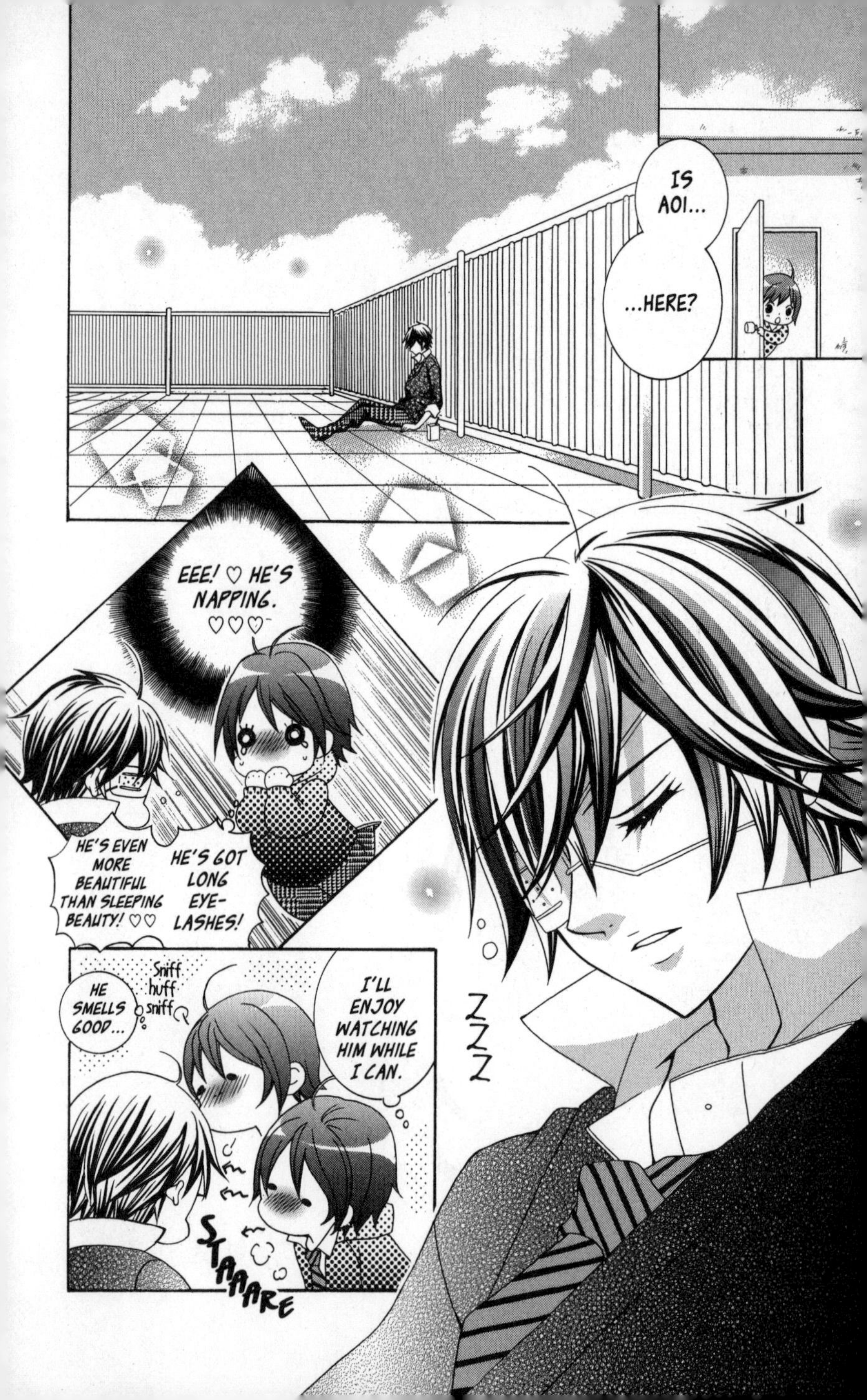
IS AOI...
...HERE?
ZZZ
EEE! ♡ HE'S NAPPING. ♡♡♡
HE'S GOT LONG EYE-LASHES!
HE'S EVEN MORE BEAUTIFUL THAN SLEEPING BEAUTY! ♡♡
I'LL ENJOY WATCHING HIM WHILE I CAN.
Sniff huff sniff
HE SMELLS GOOD...
STAAARE

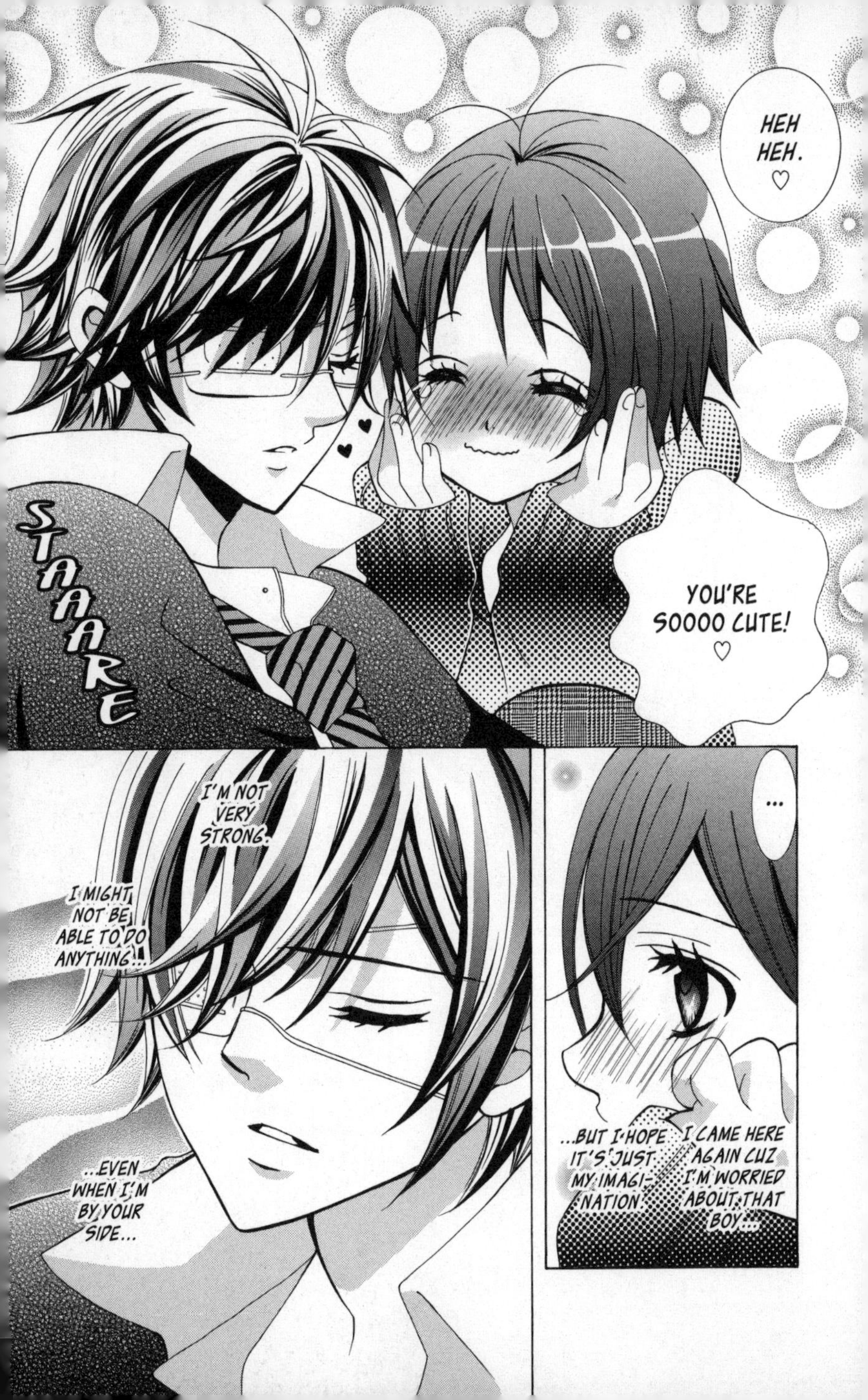
HEH HEH. ♡
YOU'RE SOOOO CUTE! ♡
STAAARE
...
I CAME HERE AGAIN CUZ I'M WORRIED ABOUT THAT BOY...
...BUT I HOPE IT'S JUST MY IMAGI-NATION.
I'M NOT VERY STRONG.
I MIGHT NOT BE ABLE TO DO ANYTHING...
...EVEN WHEN I'M BY YOUR SIDE...

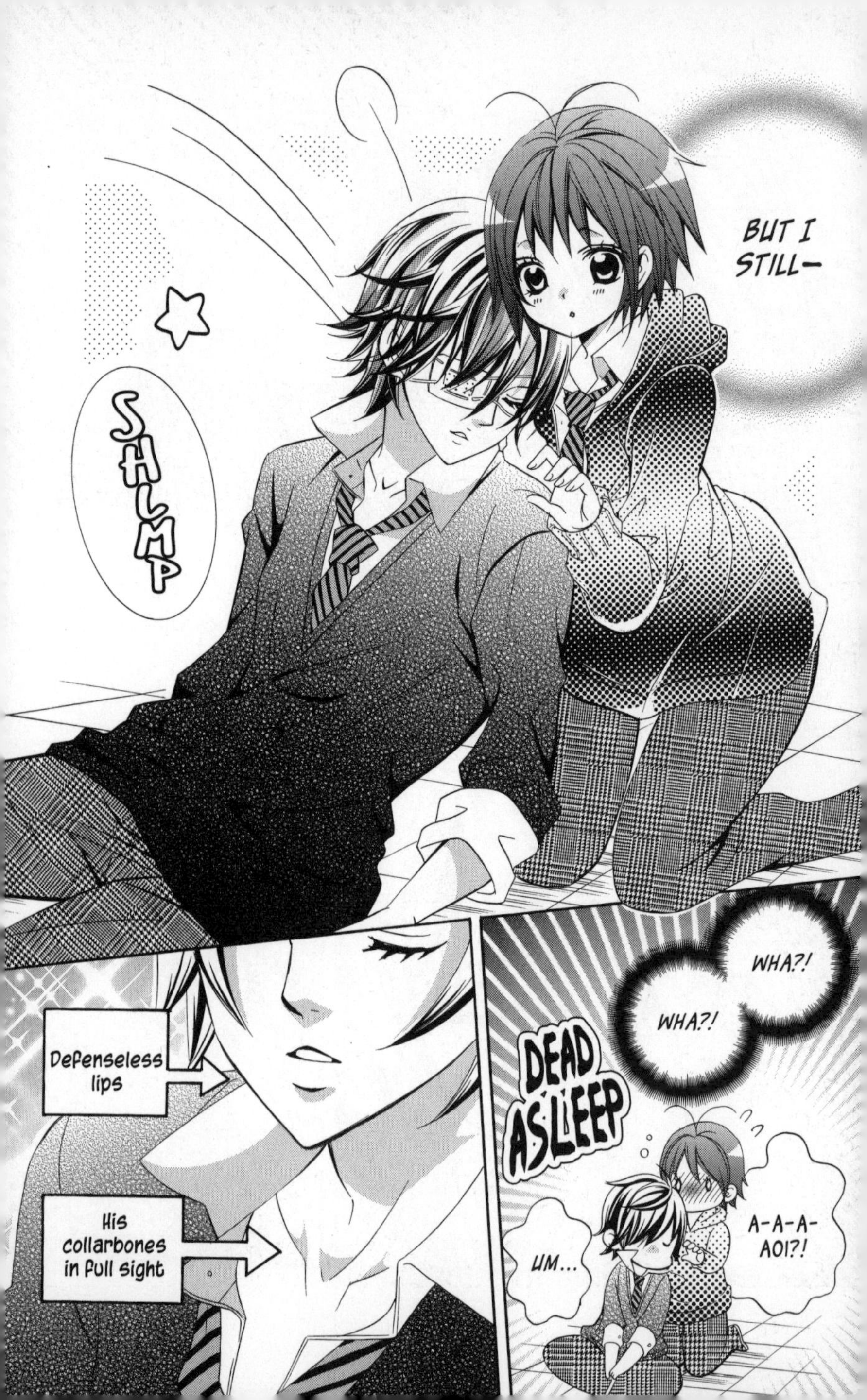
BUT I STILL—
SHLMP
WHA?!
WHA?!
DEAD ASLEEP
A-A-A-AOI?!
UM...
Defenseless lips
His collarbones in full sight

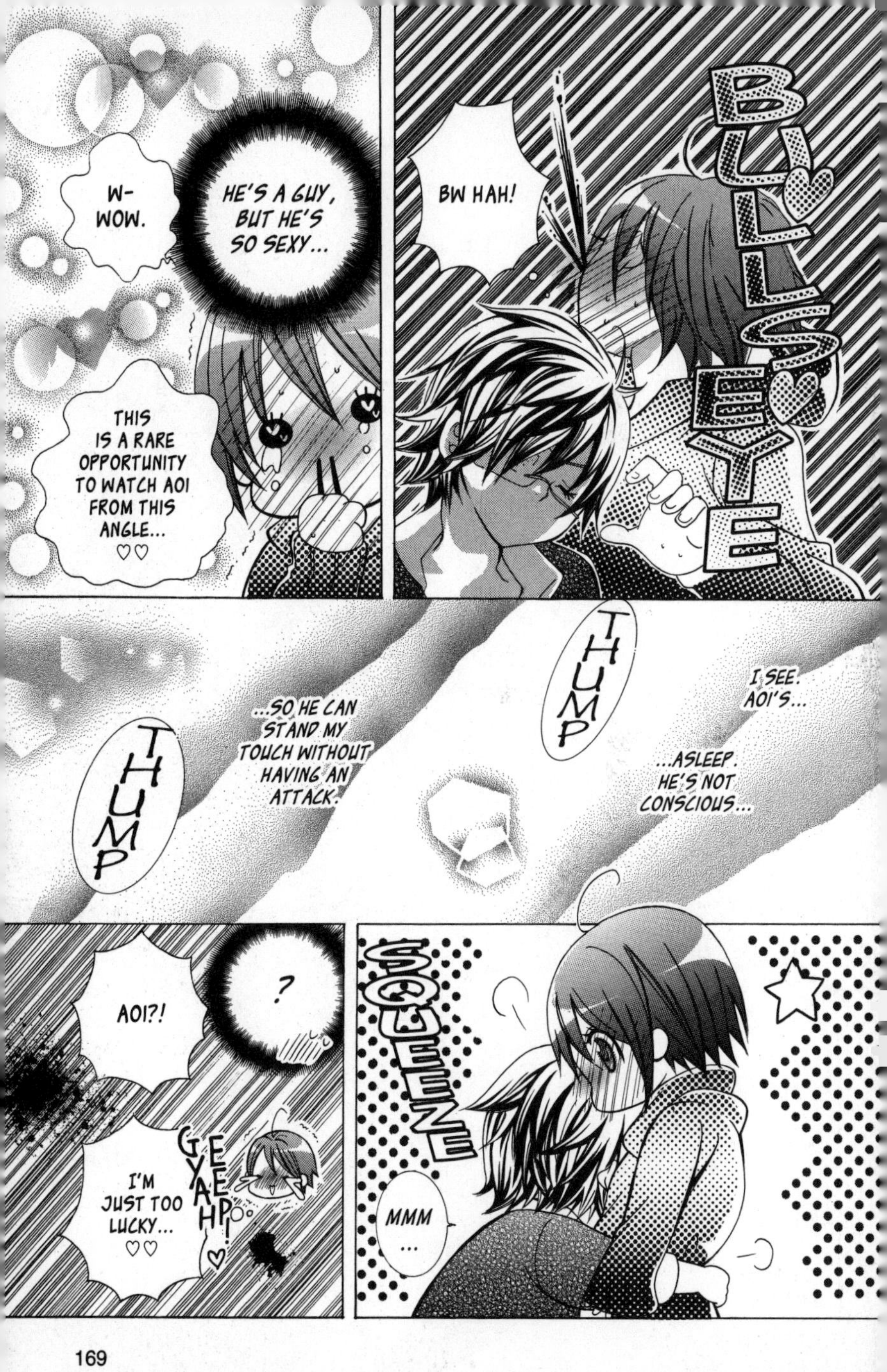
BULLSEYE
BW HAH!
HE'S A GUY, BUT HE'S SO SEXY...
W-WOW.
THIS IS A RARE OPPORTUNITY TO WATCH AOI FROM THIS ANGLE... ♡♡
THUMP
I SEE. AOI'S...
...ASLEEP. HE'S NOT CONSCIOUS...
...SO HE CAN STAND MY TOUCH WITHOUT HAVING AN ATTACK.
THUMP
SQUEEZE
MMM ...
?
AOI?!
GYAAH EEP!
I'M JUST TOO LUCKY... ♡♡

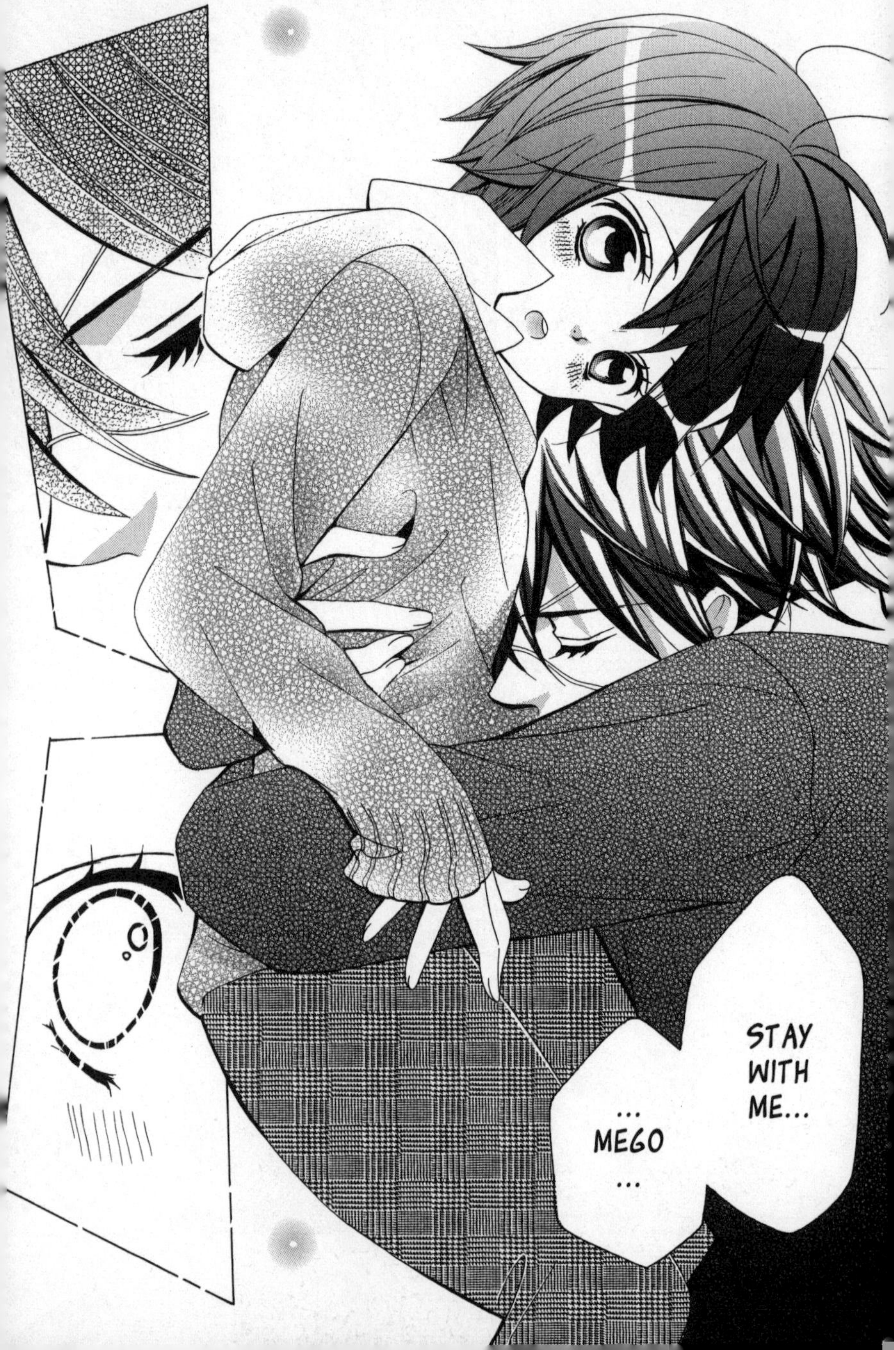
STAY WITH ME...
... MEGO ...

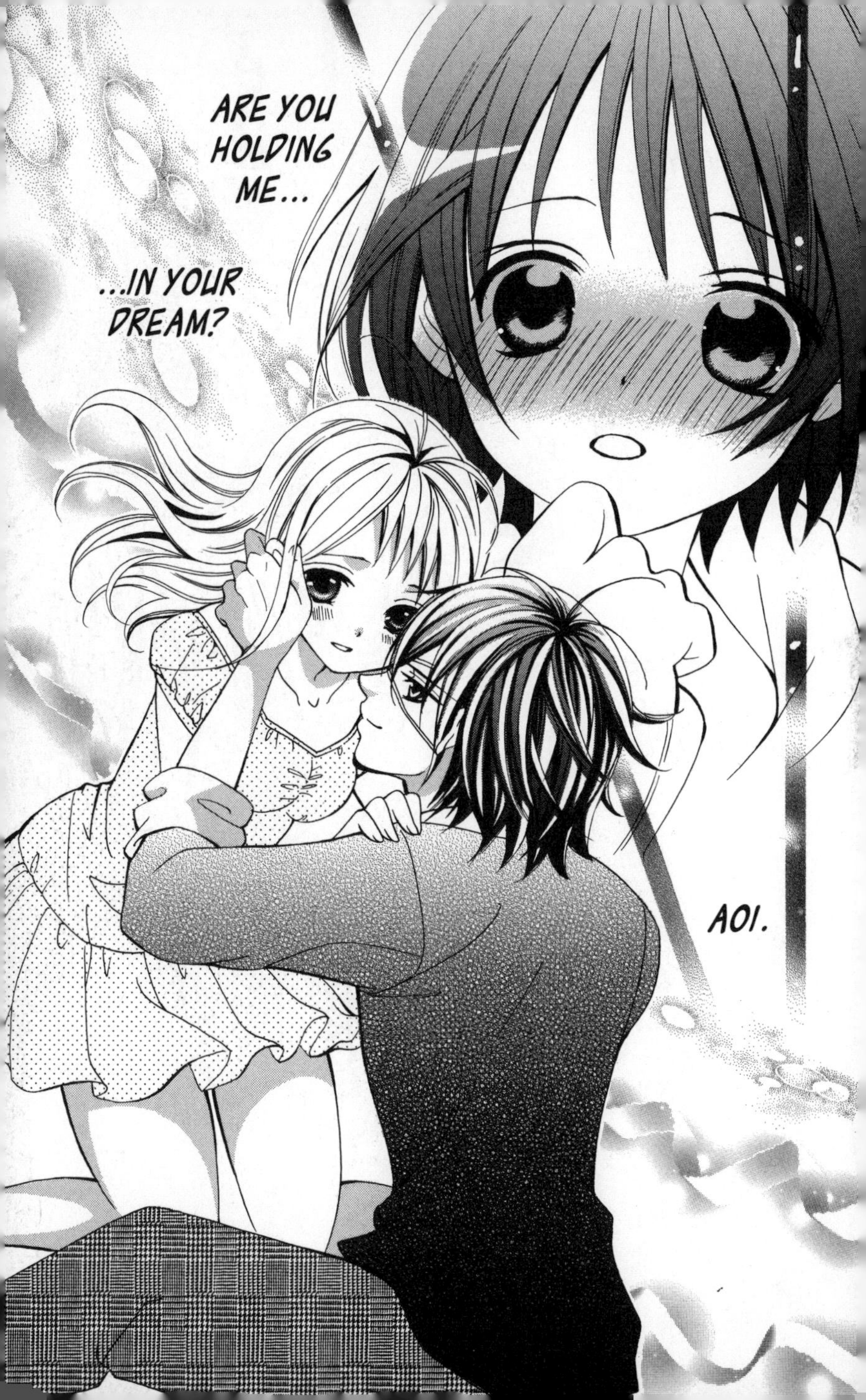
ARE YOU HOLDING ME...
...IN YOUR DREAM?
AOI.

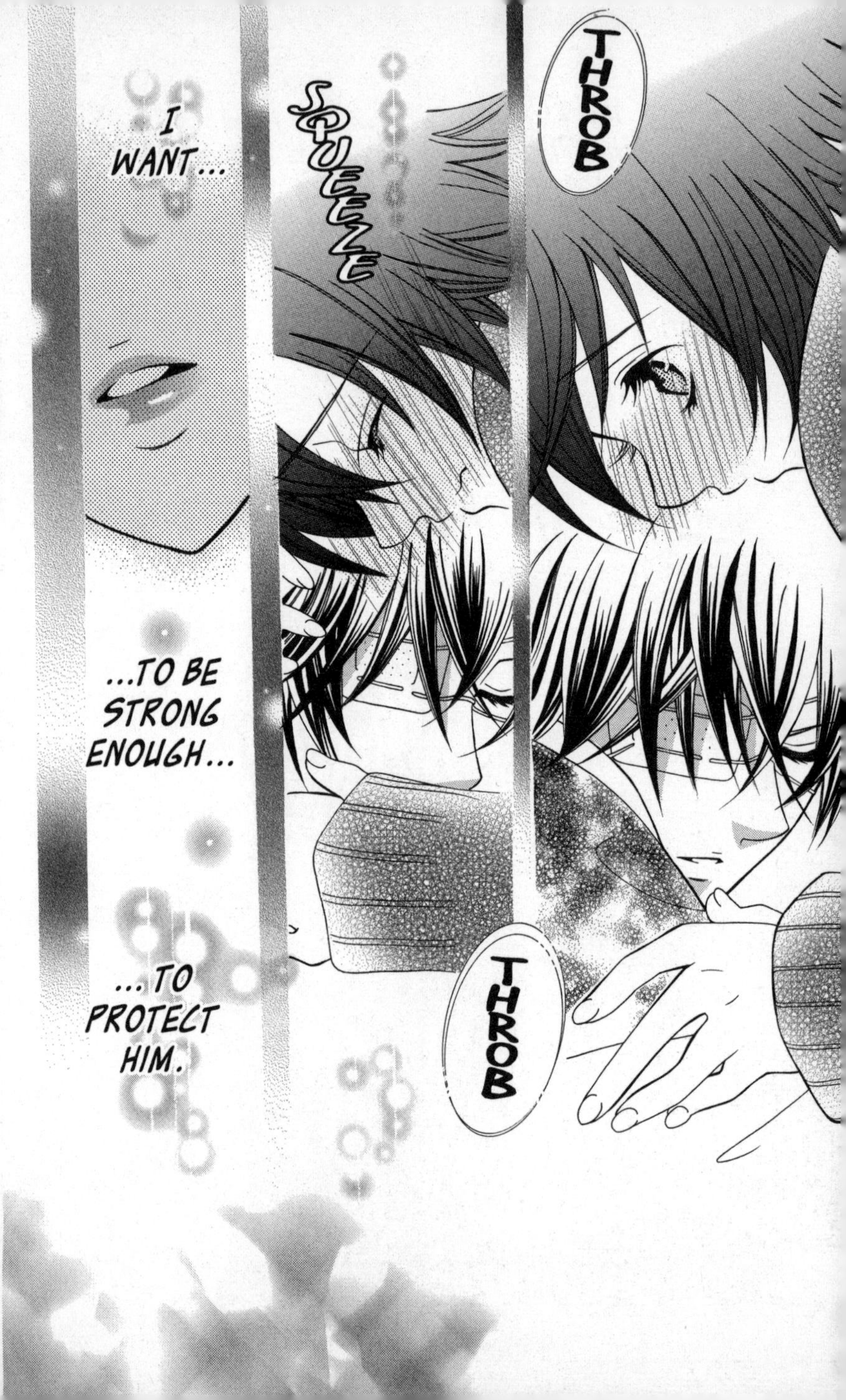
THROB
THROB
SQUEEZE
I WANT...
...TO BE STRONG ENOUGH...
...TO PROTECT HIM.

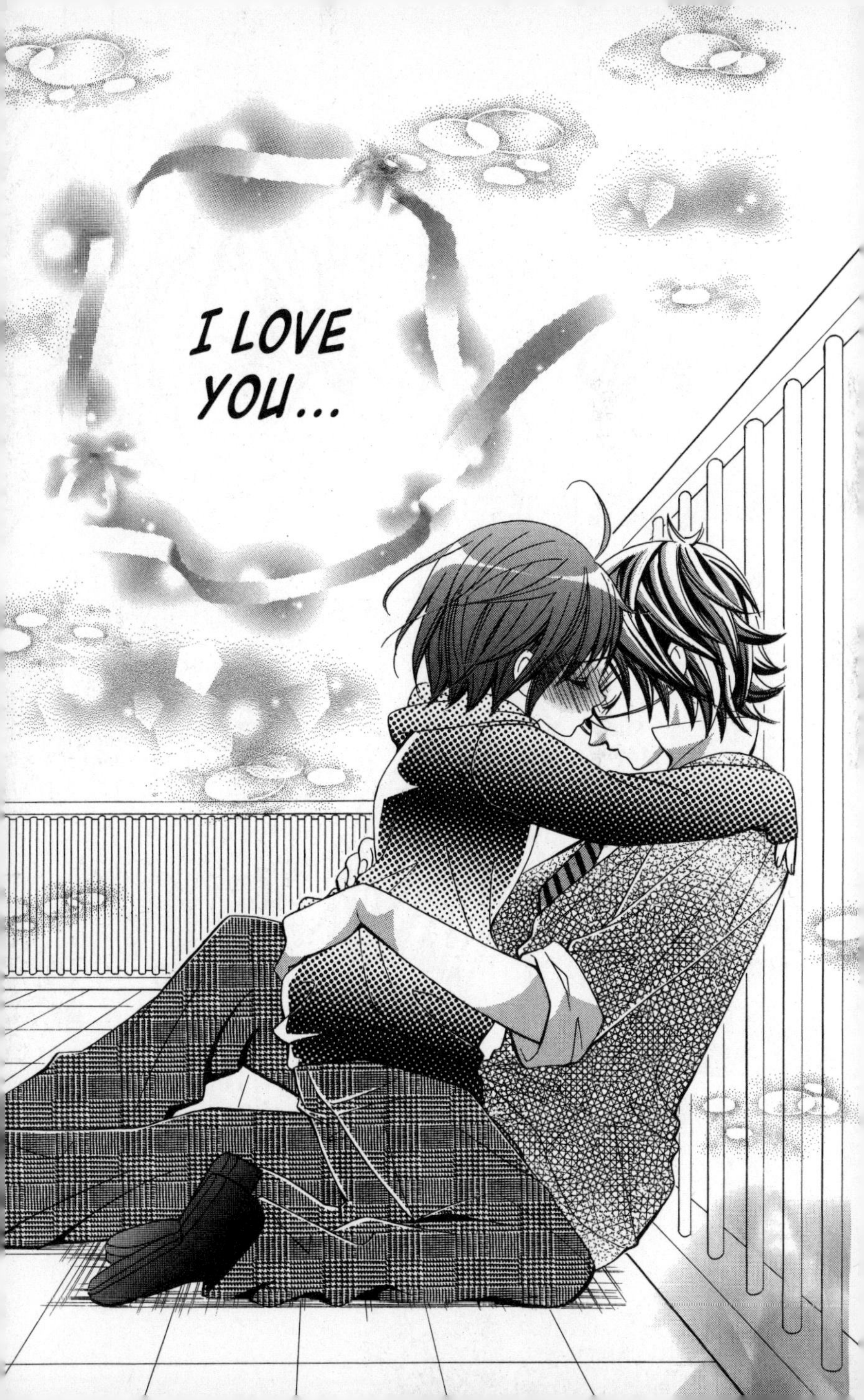
I LOVE YOU...

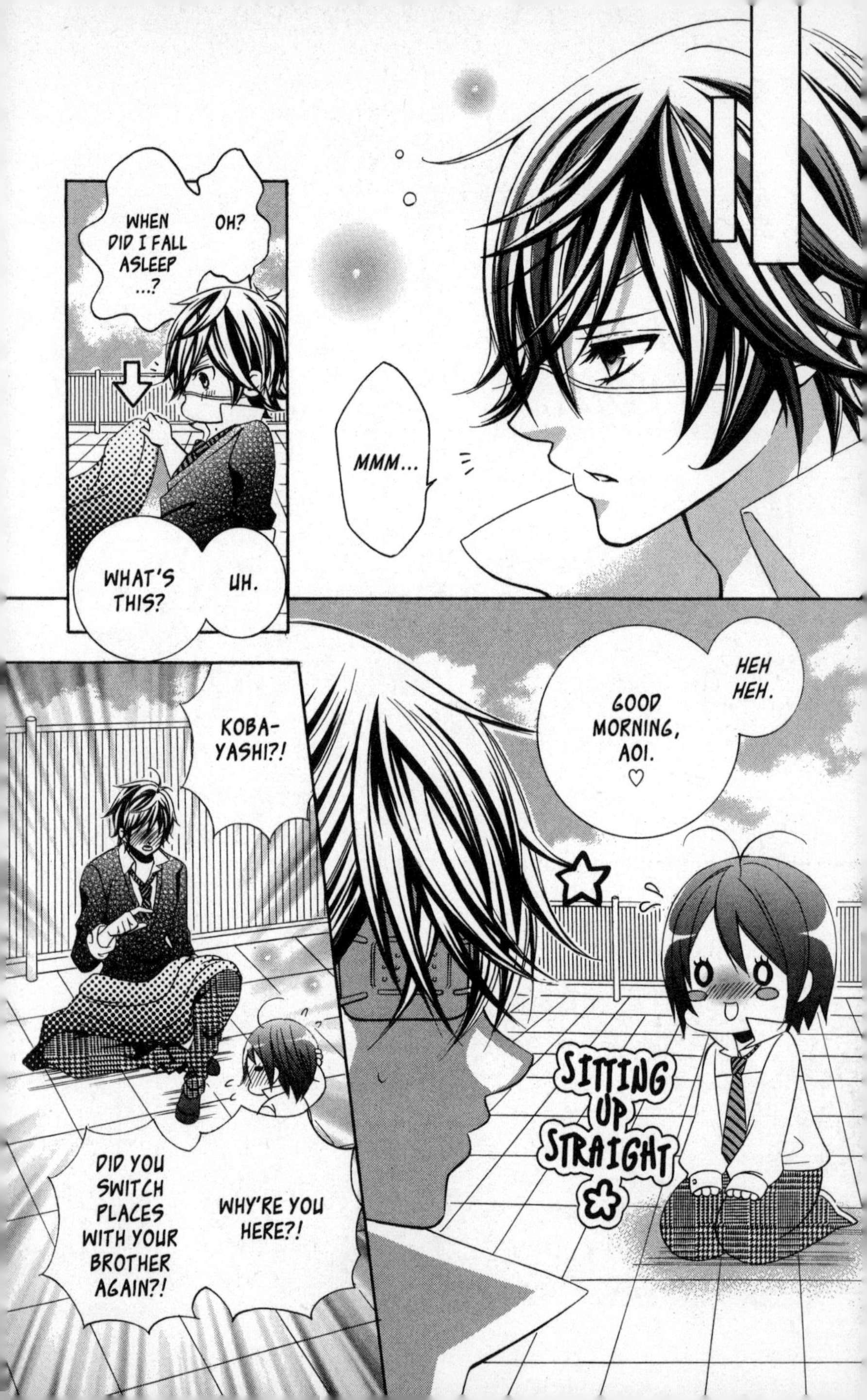
MMM...
OH?
WHEN DID I FALL ASLEEP ...?
UH.
WHAT'S THIS?
HEH HEH.
GOOD MORNING, AOI. ♡
SITTING UP STRAIGHT
KOBA-YASHI?!
WHY'RE YOU HERE?!
DID YOU SWITCH PLACES WITH YOUR BROTHER AGAIN?!

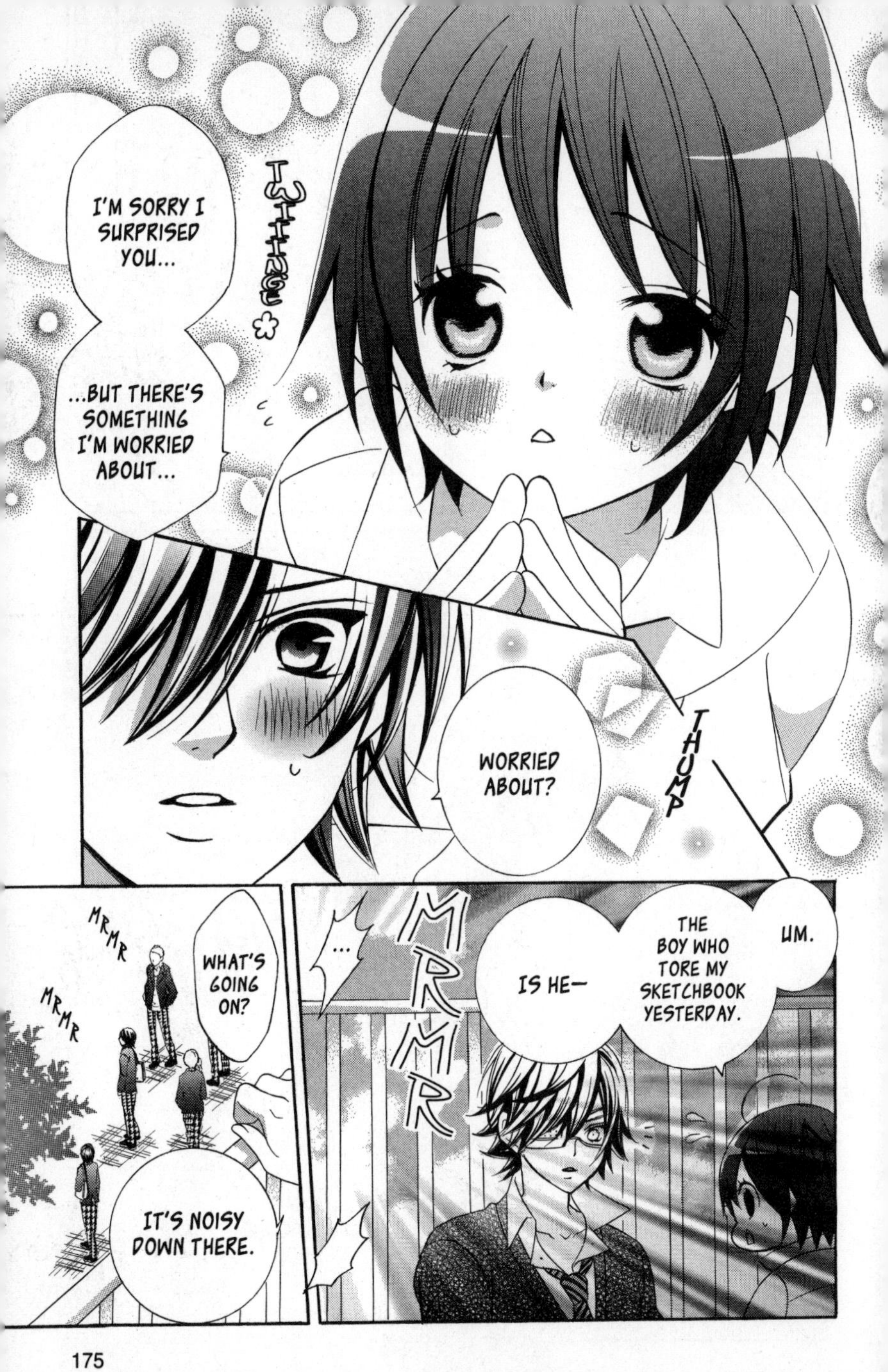
TWIIINGE
I'M SORRY I SURPRISED YOU...
...BUT THERE'S SOMETHING I'M WORRIED ABOUT...
WORRIED ABOUT?
THUMP
UM.
THE BOY WHO TORE MY SKETCHBOOK YESTERDAY.
IS HE—
MRMMR
...
MRMR
MRMR
WHAT'S GOING ON?
IT'S NOISY DOWN THERE.

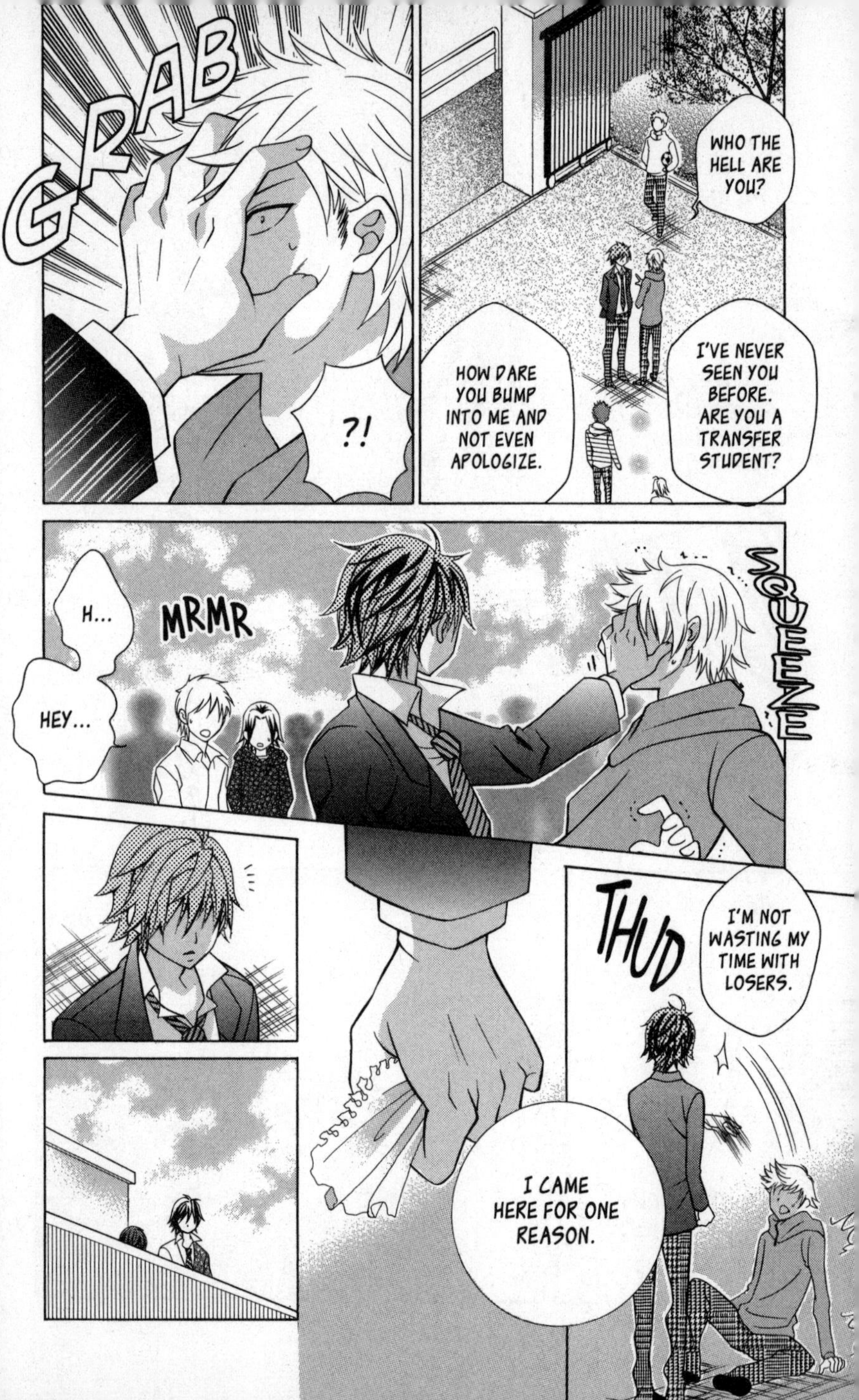
WHO THE HELL ARE YOU?
I'VE NEVER SEEN YOU BEFORE. ARE YOU A TRANSFER STUDENT?
HOW DARE YOU BUMP INTO ME AND NOT EVEN APOLOGIZE.
GRAB
?!
SQUEEZE
MRMR
H...
HEY...
THUD
I'M NOT WASTING MY TIME WITH LOSERS.
I CAME HERE FOR ONE REASON.

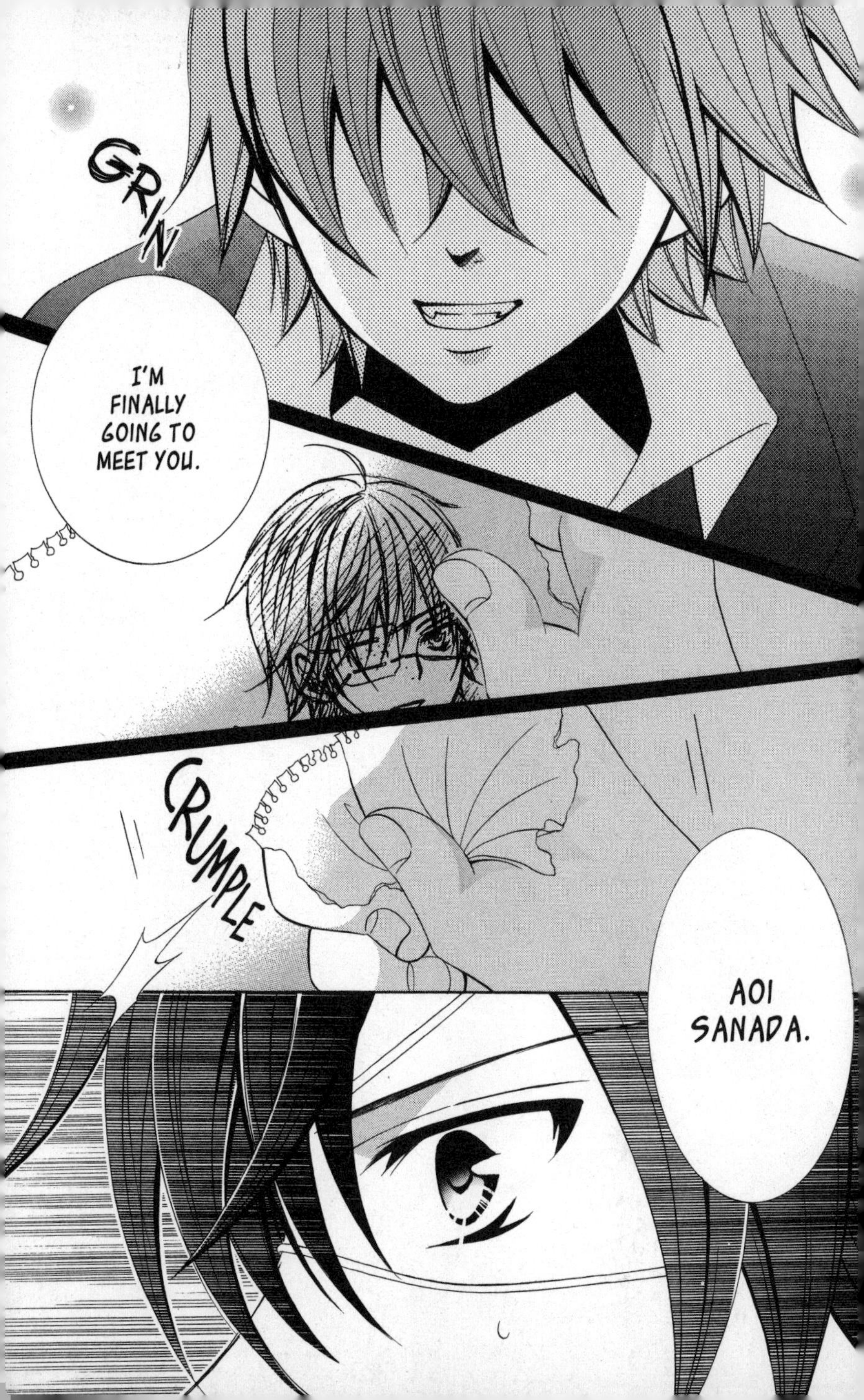
GRIN
I'M FINALLY GOING TO MEET YOU.
CRUMPLE
AOI SANADA.

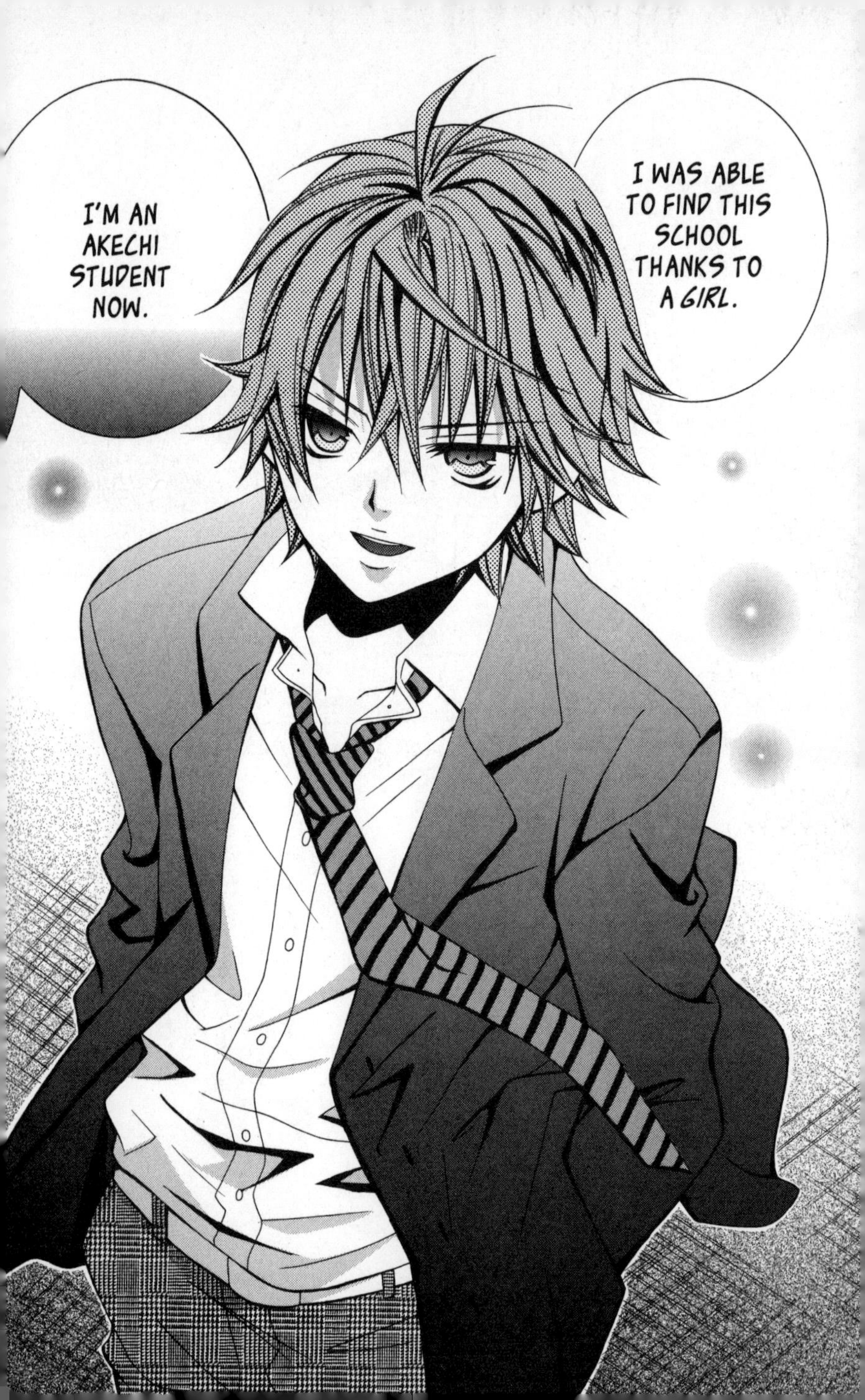
I WAS ABLE TO FIND THIS SCHOOL THANKS TO A GIRL.
I'M AN AKECHI STUDENT NOW.

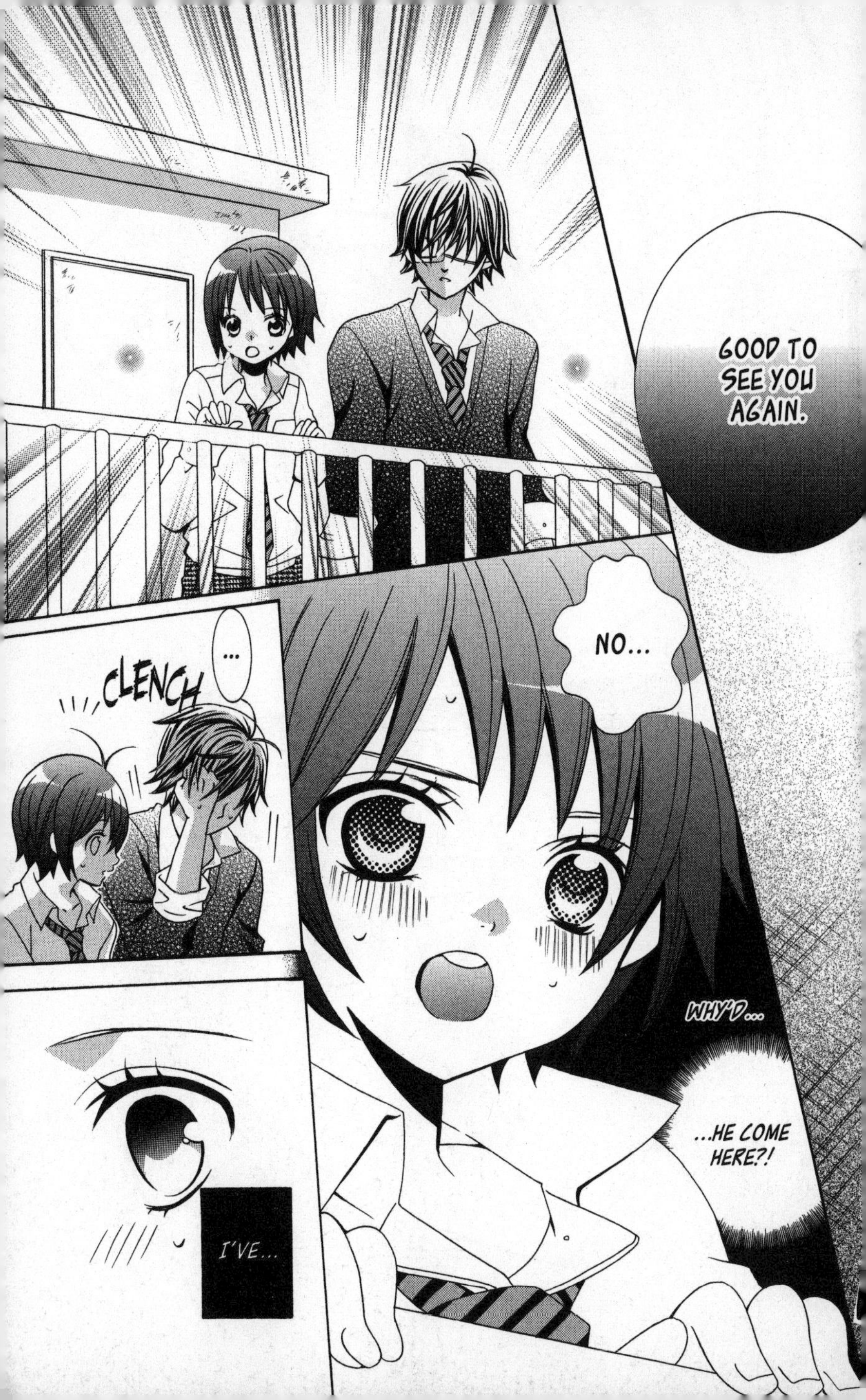
GOOD TO SEE YOU AGAIN.
NO...
WHY'D...
...HE COME HERE?!
...
CLENCH
I'VE...

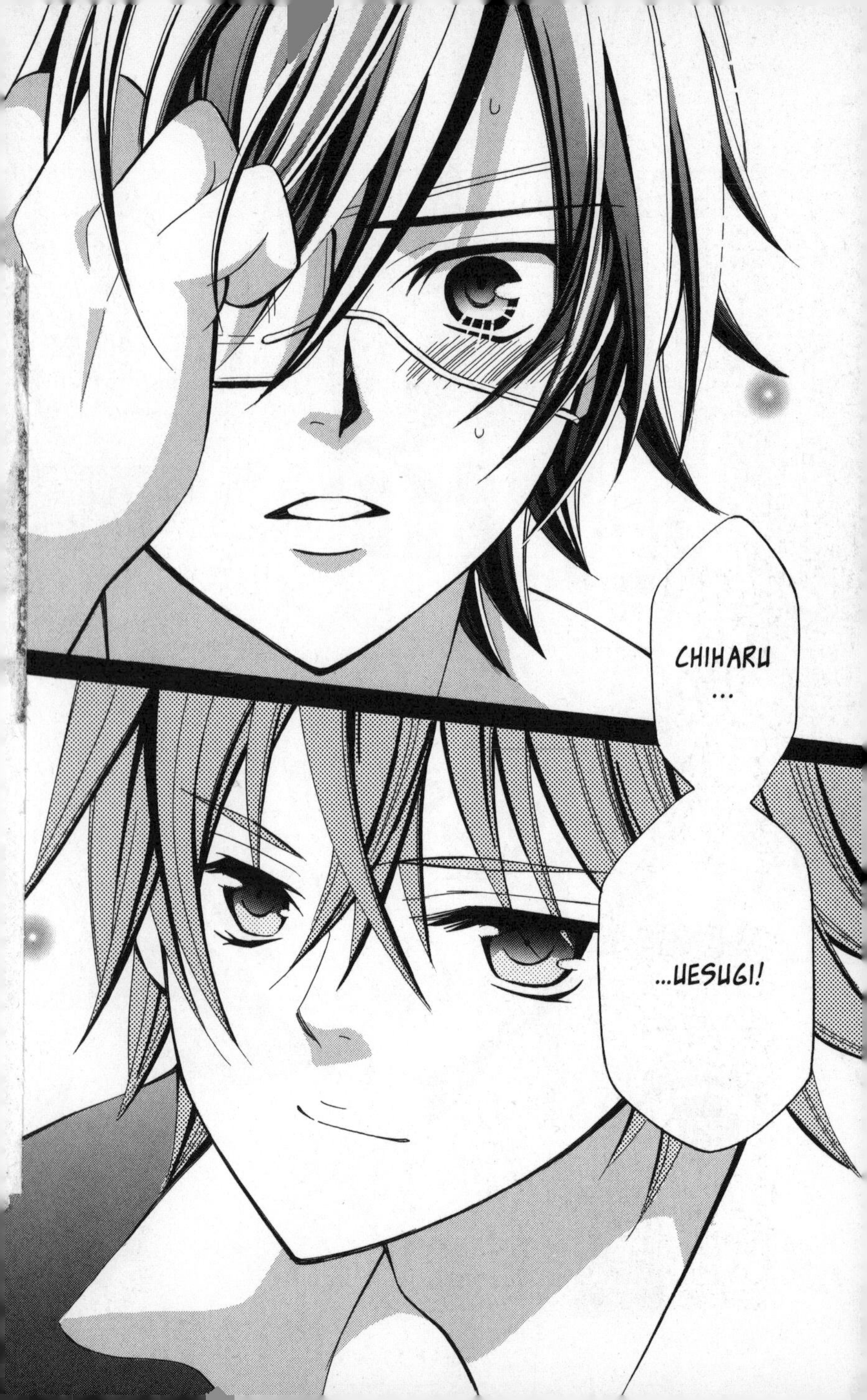
CHIHARU
...
...UESUGI!

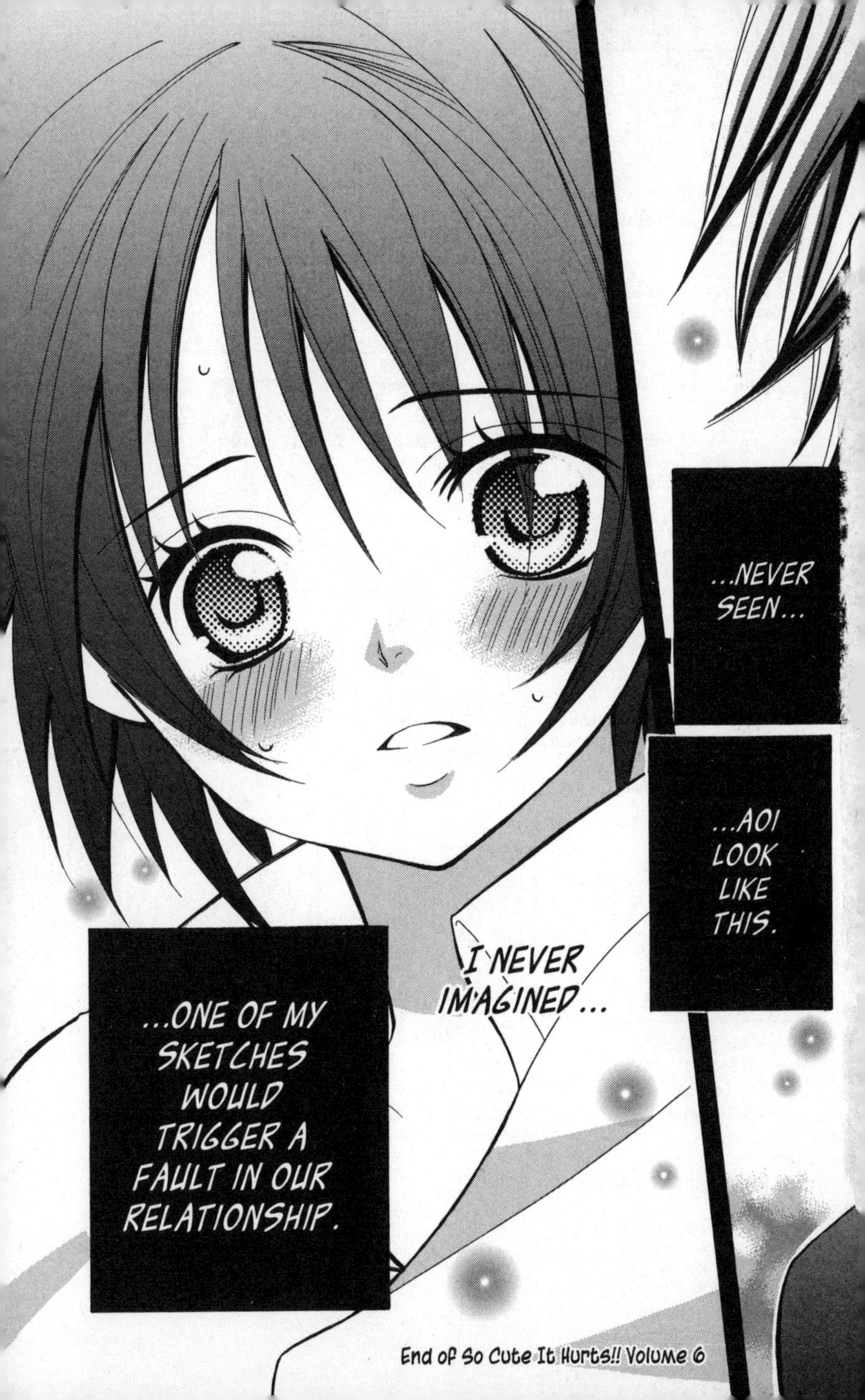
...NEVER SEEN...
...AOI LOOK LIKE THIS.
I NEVER IMAGINED...
...ONE OF MY SKETCHES WOULD TRIGGER A FAULT IN OUR RELATIONSHIP.
End of So Cute It Hurts!! Volume 6

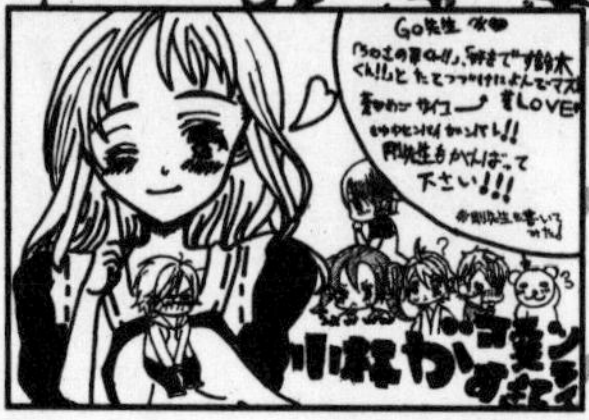

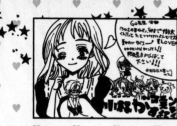

Editor: The tiny Aoi is cuuute! (>_<)

← Tomoka Igarashi (Fukui)

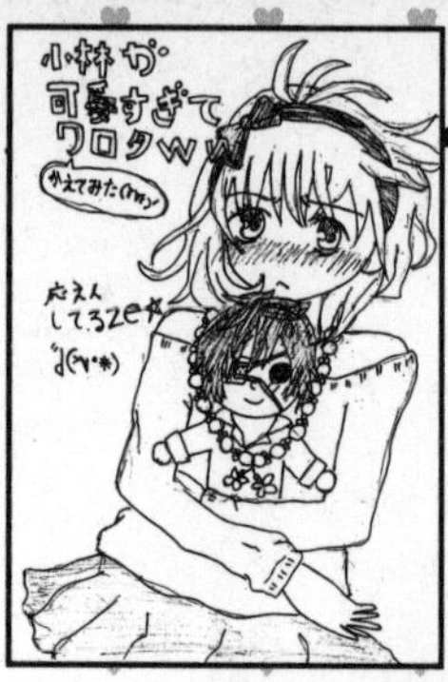
小林が可愛すぎてワロタwww

Editor: The Aoi plushie is so cute I couldn't help laughing—LOL LOL LOL!

Rio Hashida (Nagasaki) ←

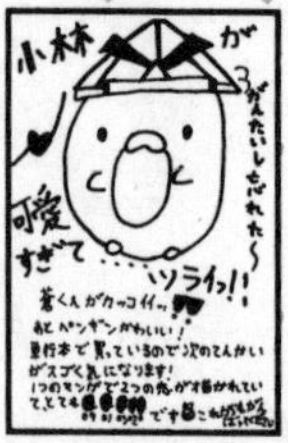

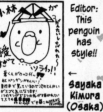

Editor: This penguin has style!!

← Sayaka Kimura (Osaka)

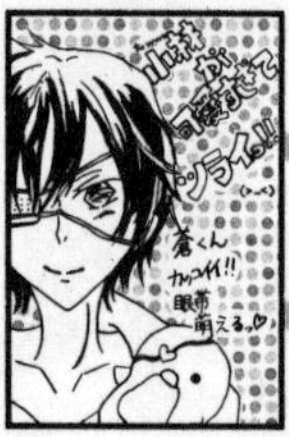

Editor: Gotta squee for the eye patch!!

← Mao Minami (Hyogo)

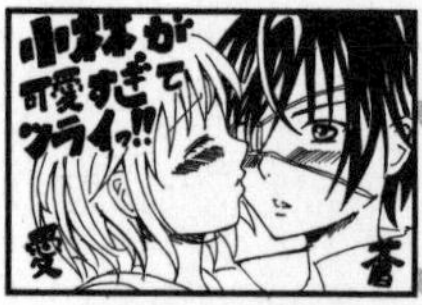
小林が可愛すぎてツライッ!!
愛
蒼

↑ Riho (Hyogo)

Editor: A k-k-k-k-kiss?!?!

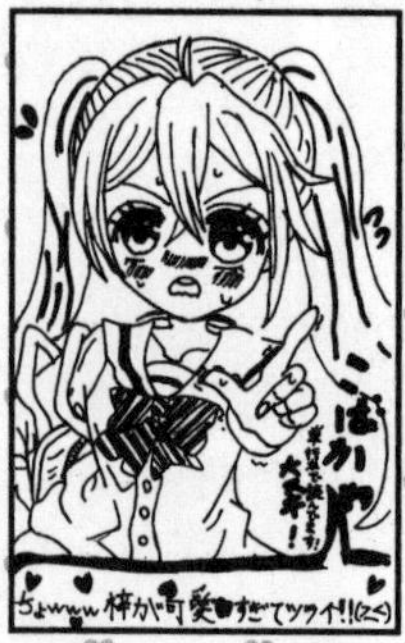

Editor: The tsundere is so cute it hurts!!

MARI desu ☆ (Osaka) ←

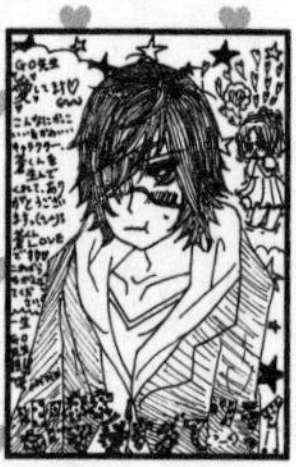

Editor: Fluttering hearts for the bashful Aoi. ♥

← I LOVE Aoi ♡

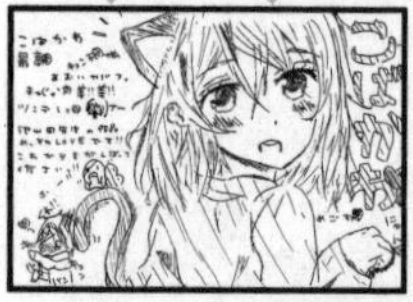

↑ Yamineko (Tokyo)

Editor: Yet another cat-ear! ♥ The tail's cute too!

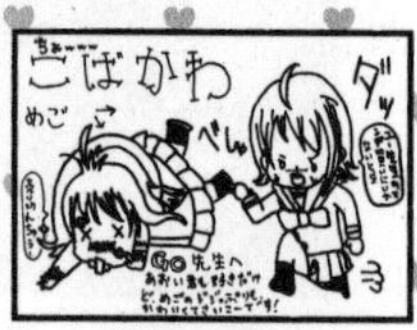
こばかわ

↑ Mako Yamada (Ishida)

Editor: Look at the klutzy Mego!

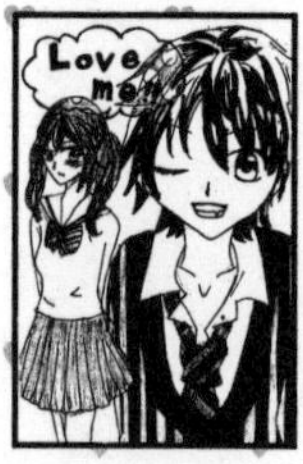
Love me

↑ Arurun (Hokkaido)

Editor: Will Mitsuru and Azusa become closer?

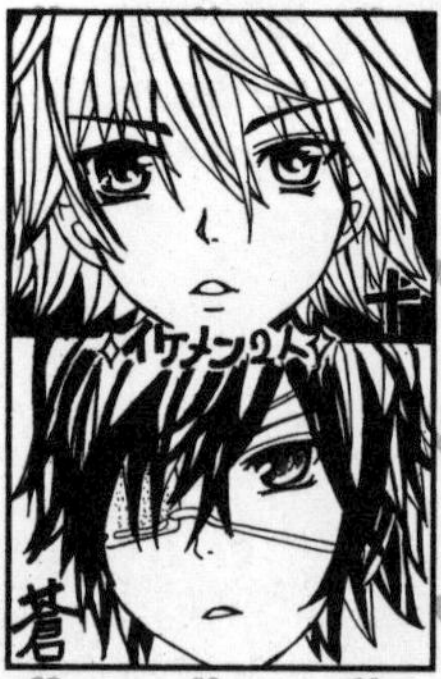
イケメン2人
蒼

Editor: Who do you prefer?

← Kari Kawauchi (Shiga)

Send your fan mail to:

Go Ikeyamada
C/o Shojo Beat
VIZ Media, LLC
P.O. Box 77010
San Francisco, CA
94107

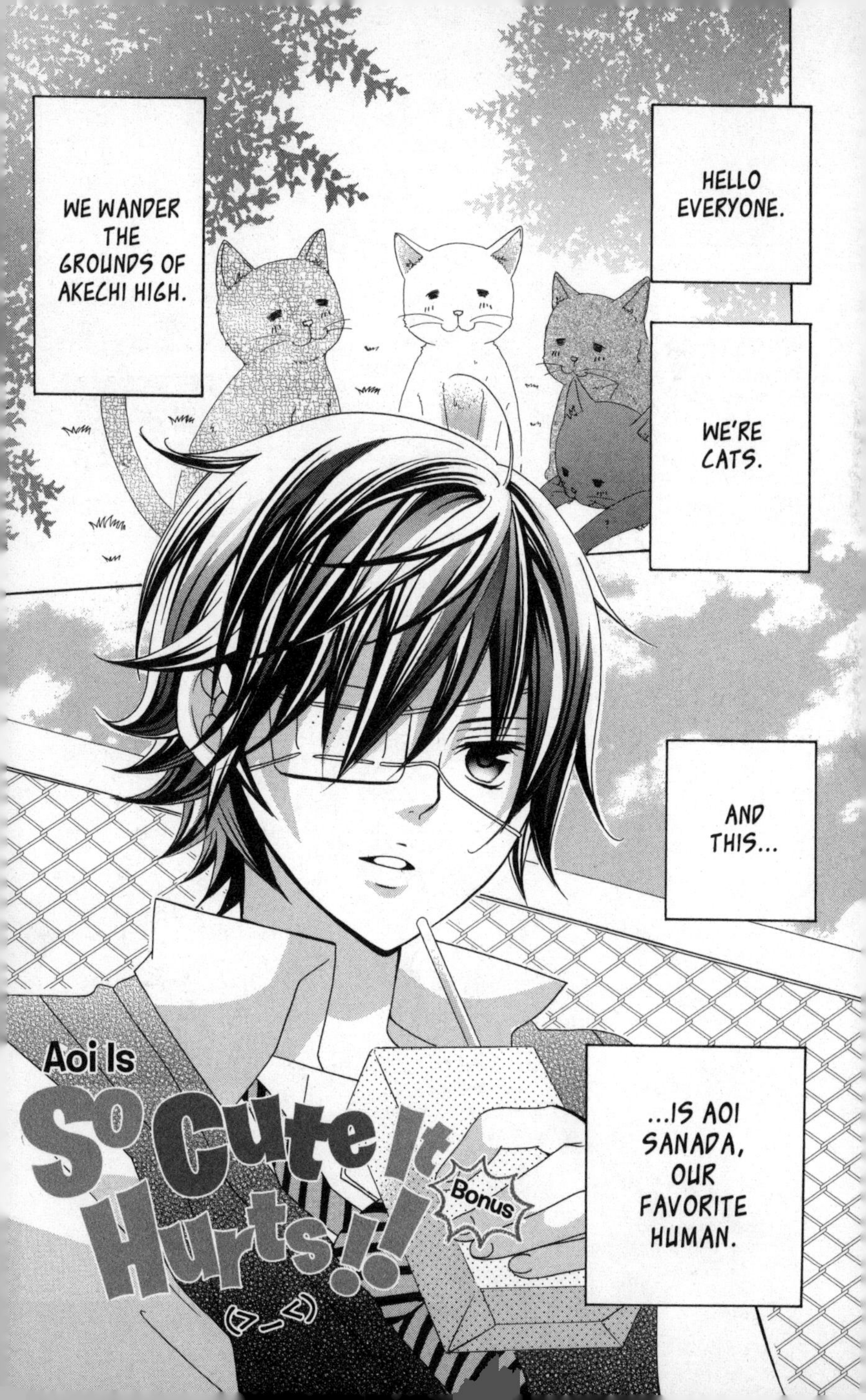
HELLO EVERYONE.
WE'RE CATS.
WE WANDER THE GROUNDS OF AKECHI HIGH.
AND THIS...
...IS AOI SANADA, OUR FAVORITE HUMAN.
Aoi Is So Cute It Hurts!!
Bonus

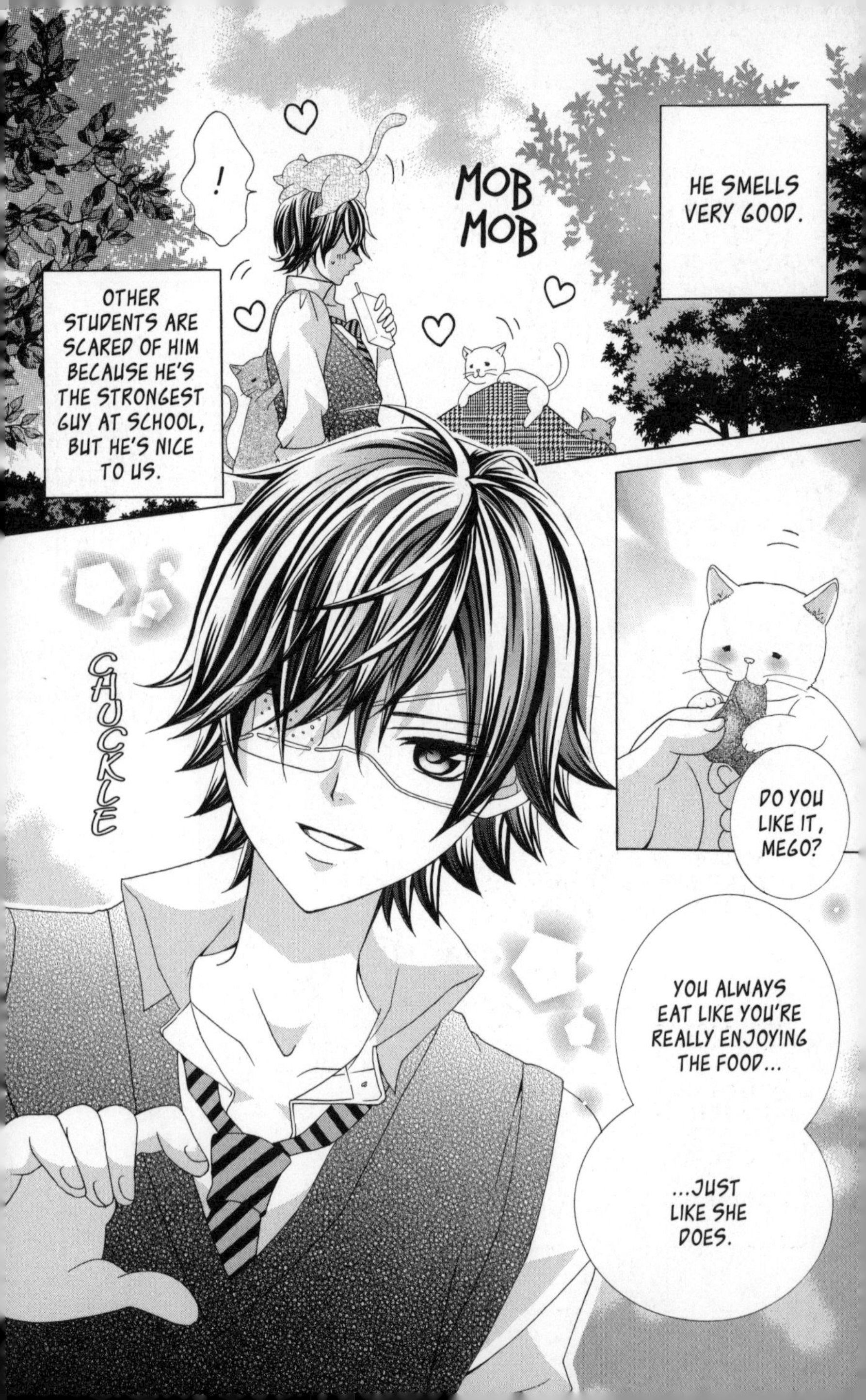
HE SMELLS VERY GOOD.
MOB MOB
!
OTHER STUDENTS ARE SCARED OF HIM BECAUSE HE'S THE STRONGEST GUY AT SCHOOL, BUT HE'S NICE TO US.
DO YOU LIKE IT, MEGO?
CHUCKLE
YOU ALWAYS EAT LIKE YOU'RE REALLY ENJOYING THE FOOD...
...JUST LIKE SHE DOES.

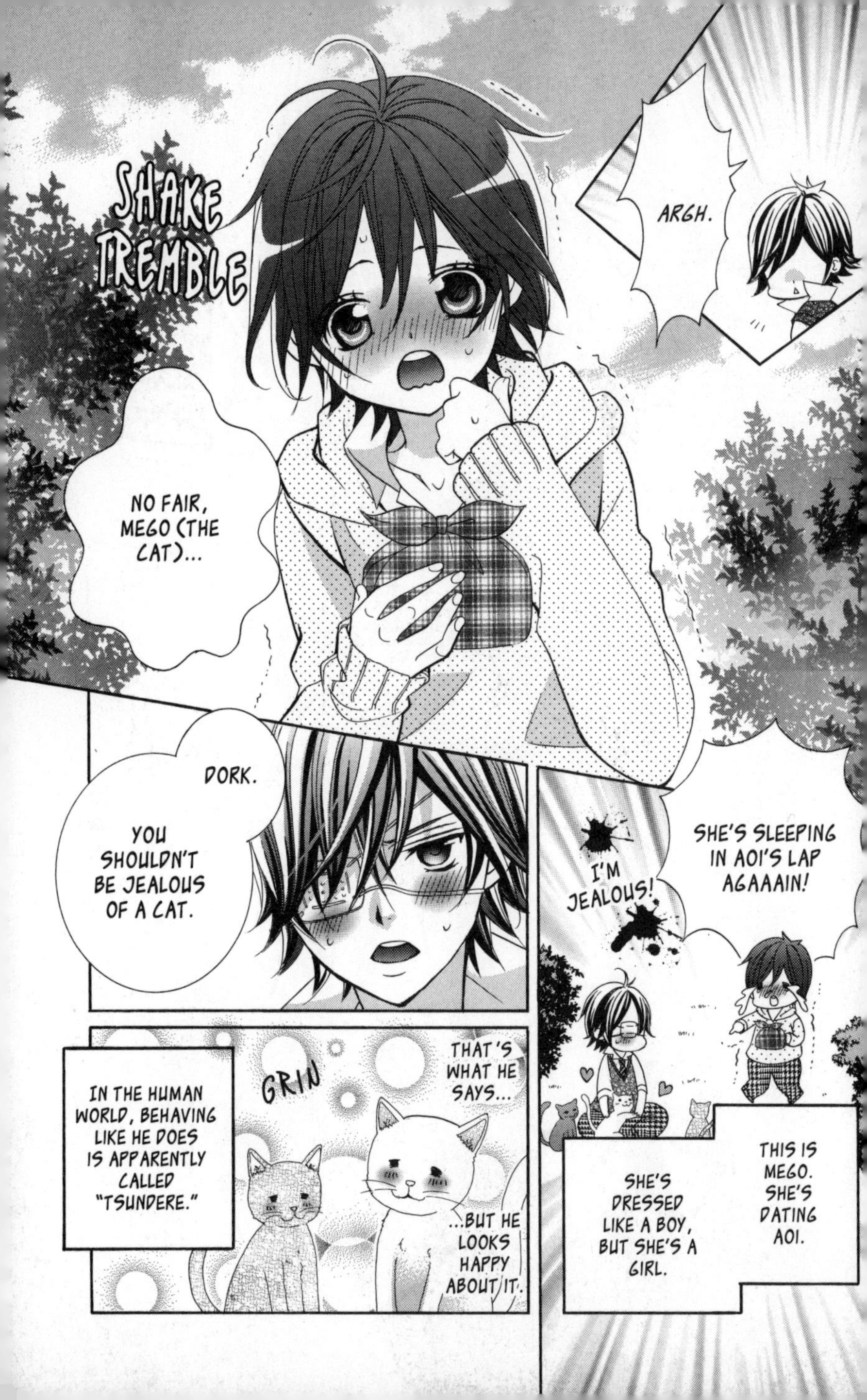
ARGH.
SHAKE TREMBLE
NO FAIR, MEGO (THE CAT)...
SHE'S SLEEPING IN AOI'S LAP AGAAAIN!
I'M JEALOUS!
THIS IS MEGO. SHE'S DATING AOI.
SHE'S DRESSED LIKE A BOY, BUT SHE'S A GIRL.
DORK.
YOU SHOULDN'T BE JEALOUS OF A CAT.
THAT'S WHAT HE SAYS...
GRIN
...BUT HE LOOKS HAPPY ABOUT IT.
IN THE HUMAN WORLD, BEHAVING LIKE HE DOES IS APPARENTLY CALLED "TSUNDERE."

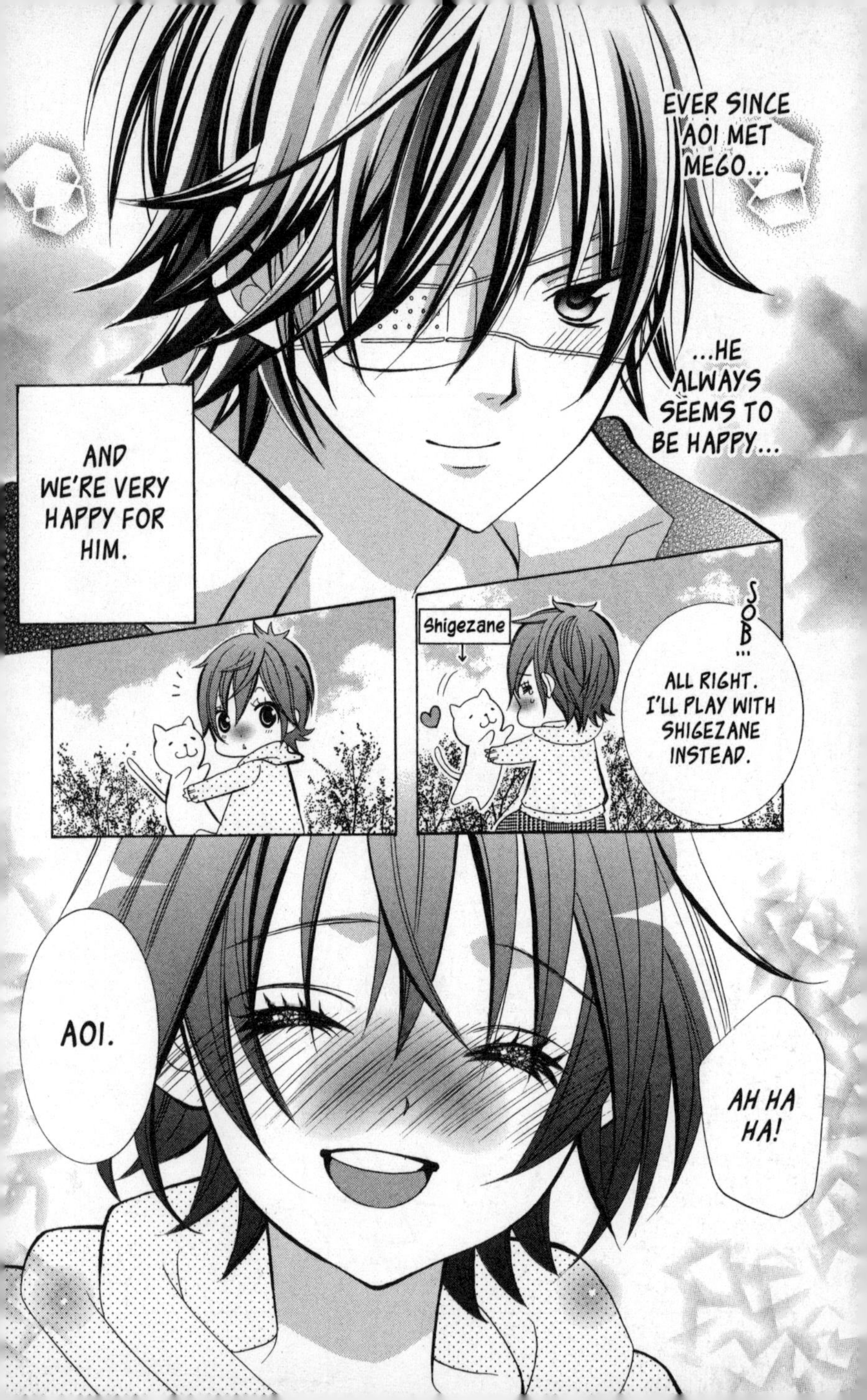
EVER SINCE AOI MET MEGO...
...HE ALWAYS SEEMS TO BE HAPPY...
AND WE'RE VERY HAPPY FOR HIM.
SOB...
ALL RIGHT. I'LL PLAY WITH SHIGEZANE INSTEAD.
Shigezane
AH HA HA!
AOI.

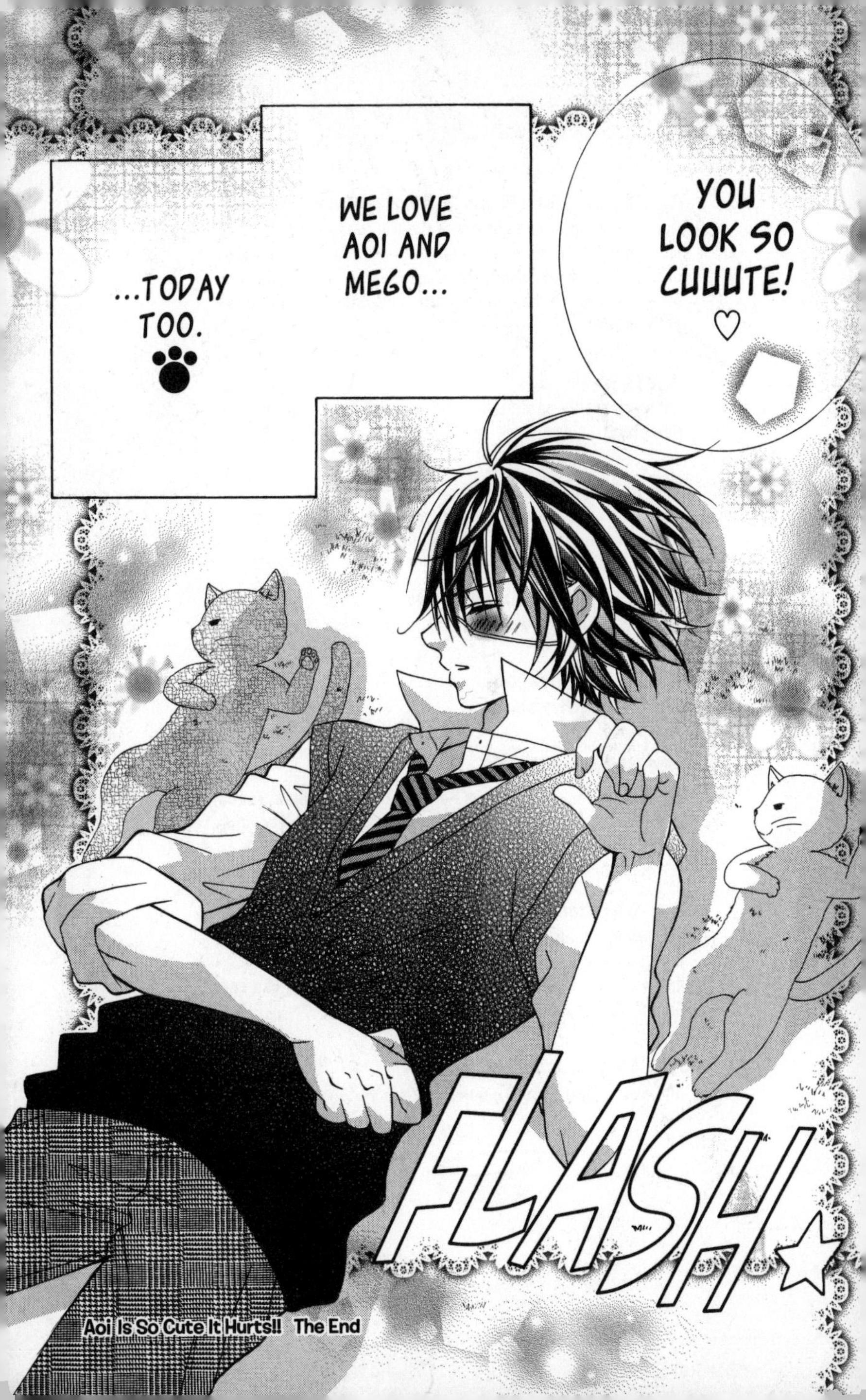
YOU LOOK SO CUUUTE! ♡
WE LOVE AOI AND MEGO...
...TODAY TOO.
FLASH☆
Aoi Is So Cute It Hurts!! The End

GLOSSARY

Page 12, panel 1: Lord Nobunaga, Ranmaru, Honno-ji Incident
Ranmaru Mori was an attendant to the feudal warlord Nobunaga Oda. The Honno-ji Incident refers to the rebellion of Mitsuhide Akechi, who attacked Honno-ji temple when his master Oda was staying there. Both Mori and Oda died at the temple.

Page 13, panel 1: Idols
Idols are media personalities with carefully crafted public personas.

Page 13, panel 2: Yaoi
Yaoi, also called Boys' Love, involves stories with male-male romances made for a largely female audience.

Page 61, panel 2: Self-Defense Force
The military forces of Japan.

Page 114, panel 2: Yakitori
Skewers of grilled chicken.

Page 180, panel 2: Uesugi
Chiharu's name comes from Kenshin Uesugi, another feudal warlord during the Sengoku era. He united Echigo Province, which is now present-day Niigata Prefecture.

Page 183, editor comments: Tsundere
Tsundere is a term that combines two Japanese words—*tsuntsun* (which means "unfriendly") and *deredere* (which means "lovestruck"). It is used to describe people who can be unfriendly one second but sweet the next.

Page 186, panel 2: Shigezane
Shigezane Date was the chief retainer of Lord Masamune Date.

AUTHOR BIO

The special edition of volume 6 in Japan comes with an anime DVD! ♪♪

The story is a new one you can only see on this DVD!! (^o^)

Super-gorgeous voice actors Mr. Daisuke Ono and Ms. Ayumi Fujimura play Aoi and Mego. Idol group palet sings the theme song! (//∇//)

I hope everyone watches it. It's a gorgeous and fun anime! ♪♪ (^o^)

Go Ikeyamada is a Gemini from Miyagi Prefecture whose hobbies include taking naps and watching movies. Her debut manga *Get Love!!* appeared in *Shojo Comic* in 2002, and her current work *So Cute It Hurts!!* (*Kobayashi ga Kawai Suguite Tsurai!!*) is being published by VIZ Media.

SO CUTE IT HURTS!!
Volume 6

Shojo Beat Edition

STORY AND ART BY
GO IKEYAMADA

English Translation & Adaptation/Tomo Kimura
Touch-Up Art & Lettering/Evan Waldinger
Design/Izumi Evers
Editor/Pancha Diaz

KOBAYASHI GA KAWAISUGITE TSURAI!! Vol.6
by Go IKEYAMADA
© 2012 Go IKEYAMADA
All rights reserved.
Original Japanese edition published by SHOGAKUKAN.
English translation rights in the United States of America, Canada,
United Kingdom and Ireland arranged with SHOGAKUKAN.

Printed in the U.S.A.

Published by VIZ Media, LLC
P.O. Box 77010
San Francisco, CA 94107

10 9 8 7 6 5 4 3 2 1
First printing, April 2016

www.viz.com   www.shojobeat.com

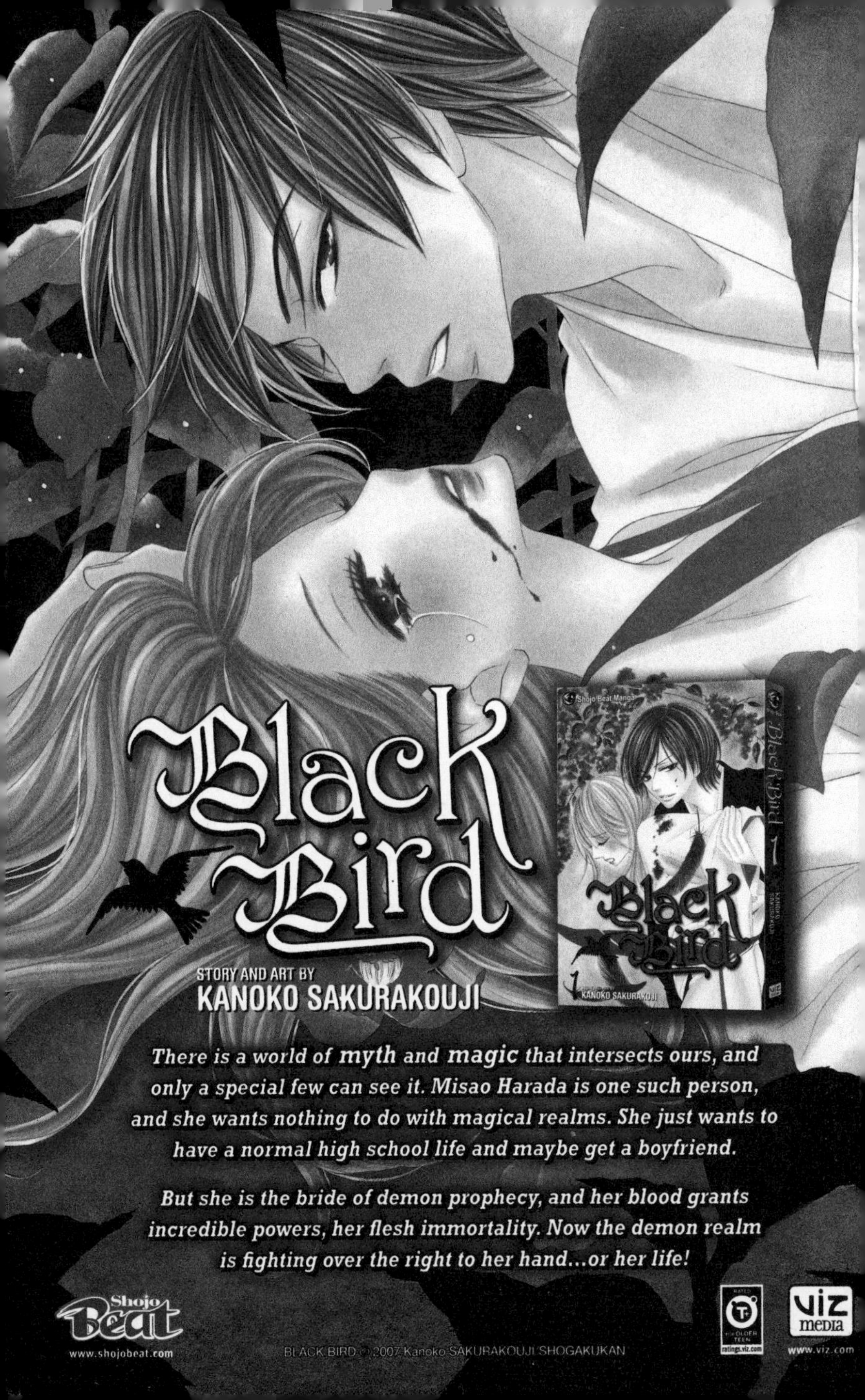
Black Bird
STORY AND ART BY
KANOKO SAKURAKOUJI
There is a world of myth and magic that intersects ours, and only a special few can see it. Misao Harada is one such person, and she wants nothing to do with magical realms. She just wants to have a normal high school life and maybe get a boyfriend.
But she is the bride of demon prophecy, and her blood grants incredible powers, her flesh immortality. Now the demon realm is fighting over the right to her hand…or her life!
Shojo Beat
www.shojobeat.com
BLACK BIRD © 2007 Kanoko SAKURAKOUJI/SHOGAKUKAN
OLDER TEEN
ratings.viz.com
viz media
www.viz.com

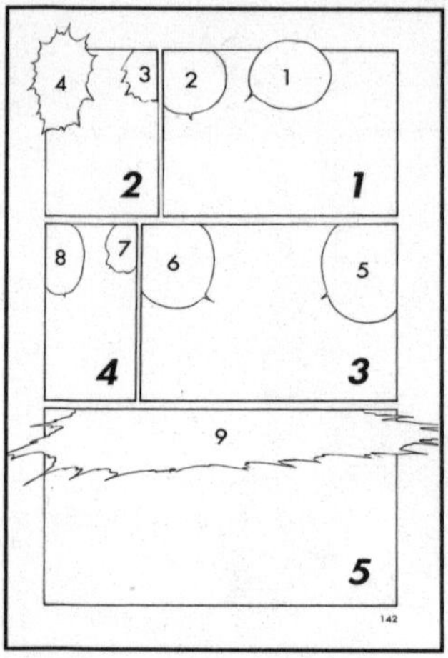
1
2
3
4
1
2
5
6
7
8
3
4
9
5
142

This is the last page.

In keeping with the original Japanese comic format, this book reads from right to left—so action, sound effects and word balloons are completely reversed. This preserves the orientation of the original artwork—plus, it's fun! Check out the diagram shown here to get the hang of things, and then turn to the other side of the book to get started!

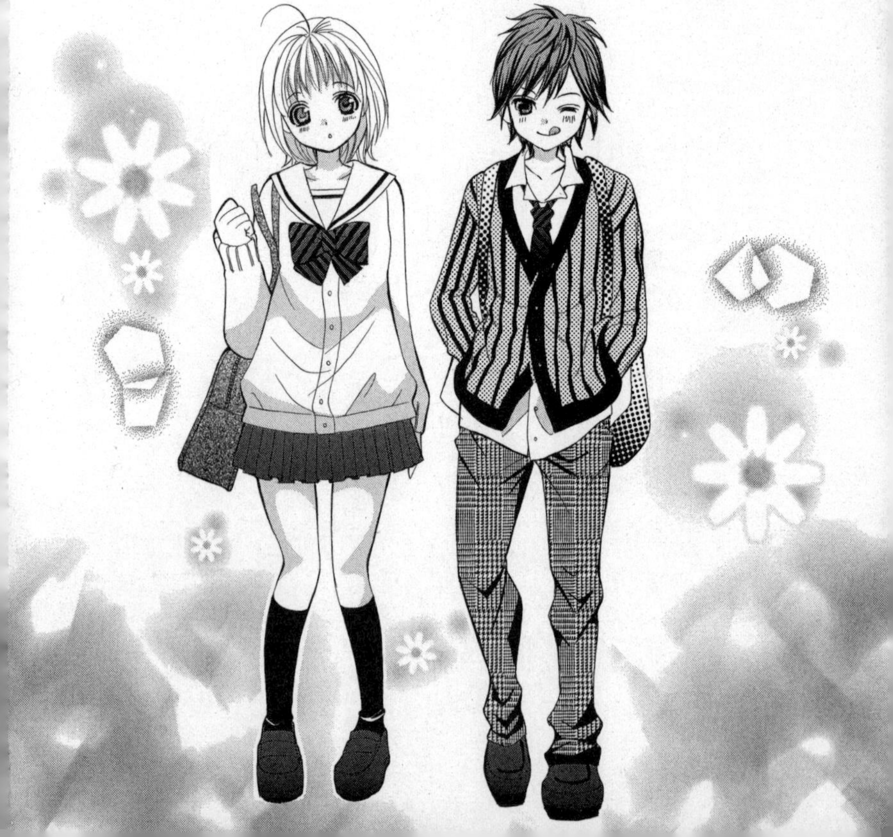